Balance in Small Groups

Balance in Small Groups

Howard F. Taylor
Syracuse University

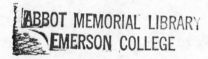

Sociological Concepts, Methods and Data Series
Mark Abrahamson, General Editor

VAN NOSTRAND REINHOLD COMPANY
New York   Cincinnati   Toronto   London   Melbourne

Van Nostrand Reinhold Company Regional Offices:
Cincinnati, New York, Chicago, Millbrae, Dallas

Van Nostrand Reinhold Company Foreign Offices:
London, Toronto, Melbourne

Published by Van Nostrand Reinhold Company
450 West 33rd Street, New York, N.Y. 10001

Published simultaneously in Canada by
D. Van Nostrand Company (Canada), Ltd.

15   14   13   12   11   10   9   8   7   6   5   4   3   2   1

This book is dedicated to my wife, Patricia, who must surely be commended for her ability to maintain structural balance in our own particular small group despite an occasionally absent and often preoccupied husband.

"Beauty is truth, truth beauty—that is all
Ye know on earth, and all ye need to know."

—Keats, **Ode on a Grecian Urn**

"Each man kills the thing he loves . . . ."

—Wilde, **The Ballad of Reading Gaol**

"People hate coughs, and Luden's coughdrops hate coughs;
that's why so many people like Luden's."

—T.V. Commercial

"O Romeo, Romeo? wherefore art thou Romeo?
. . . 'Tis but thy name that is my enemy.

—**Romeo and Juliet**, Act II, Scene 2

Preface

This book was developed in conjunction with research and teaching in the fields of small groups and social psychology, and will be of use to students, teachers and others in these areas.

It is intended to serve as a text for students unfamiliar with balance and social interaction, but also as a critical literature review for social scientists engaged in research and teaching in social psychology, and for persons currently contributing to the balance literature.

The underlying premise of this book is that most people, most of the time, whenever they are able, make attempts to perceive a pattern in randomness, to deduce order from apparent chaos, to see form in shapelessness. In particular, people will do this in regard to their social relations with other people. They attempt to bring about what we will call *balance* in their everyday interpersonal relations with others. The ways in which people attempt to achieve such balance in face-to-face social interaction are the explicit focus of this book.

The following pages are organized to proceed from the simple to the relatively complex. The first three chapters present and discuss the basic propositions of balance theory. The fourth through the seventh chapters review and evaluate research evidence pertaining to the theory of balance. Particular attention is paid to recent research findings and to results which refute portions of balance theory. The final chapter lists the currently unresolved issues in balance theory and research, briefly integrates the balance model with three other small-group models, and discusses hypotheses and problems for further research.

The study of small groups has been approached in the past from two roughly identifiable perspectives: the *inter*personal and the *intra*personal. The former perspective, which may be roughly described as a "sociological" approach, focuses on the ways in which people relate themselves to each other in groups, their likes and dislikes, aspects of their interaction, and so on. The second or "psychological" perspective is reflected in recent theories of "cognitive consistency," "balance," "dissonance," "congruity," and the like. These theories of intrapersonal process focus on the ways in which persons perceive things and then organize, arrange and relate these things in their own minds—in short, the ways in which persons deduce order from randomness. This book attempts to integrate these two developing areas of interest. Readers already familiar with the literature on cognitive consistency will recognize that this volume places greater emphasis on theory and research following a "balance" rather than a "dissonance" perspective.

My indebtedness extends to those who have, in specific and important ways, made this work possible: to Professors J. Zvi Namenwirth and Theodore M. Mills, for stimulating my early interest in small groups; to Professor Fritz Heider, for the benefit of a short and meaningful afternoon dialogue; and to my graduate students who, being relatively free from overspecialization, lent a fresh and critical eye to my work: Doug Davidson, Walter Davis, Eunice Sutton, Shaul Streifler, and particularly Charlotte Vaughan and Richard Houck. Professors Daisy M. Tagliacozzo and Richard Laskin, in ways that only the three of us understand, contributed to the completion of this volume. Gratitude is also extended to Professors Theodore M. Newcomb, William J. McGuire, Clinton DeSoto, Donn Byrne, James Davis, Allan Mazur, and Marcello Truzzi, for making important material of theirs available prior to publication. Professors Davis, Mazur and Truzzi receive particular thanks for their careful reading and very helpful criticism of various drafts and portions of the manuscript. To Mrs. Emma Waters, who typed the final draft, a note of gratitude is extended. A most special debt lies with my good friend and colleague, Mark Abrahamson, without whose encouragement and occasional hand-holding this book would not have been written.

Howard F. Taylor

Contents

Balance in Small Groups

1.

Introduction

It seems that man has always tried to discover some kind of *order* among things in the universe. He sees objects as possessing a relatedness, a pattern, a unity; he strives to see the whole and not only the parts. Seemingly random and unordered stimuli are received by the person and rearranged or altered in his own mind so that they "add up" or "go together"—in short, so that they make sense.

A principle of *perceptual consistency* regulates man's thoughts. He has a tendency to perceive the invariant, constant properties of clusters of objects. Thus, people will see a random scattering of dots on paper as a unified image or "gestalt." They will see a free-form inkblot as an interpretable configuration. They will perceive meaning and form in a highly abstract sculpture or painting. How else could one convince another that he is, in fact, able to "understand" the work?

It is the purpose of this book to acquaint the reader with the ways in which this principle of perceptual consistency can be applied to the small human group. The particular brand of consistency theory in which we will be primarily interested is called "balance theory." But before concerning ourselves with a detailed discussion of this theory, it will be necessary to accomplish two things: first, to define what is meant by the term "group," particularly the term "small group"; second, to examine briefly the postulates of what has come to be known as "system theory" in sociology and social psychology. The kinds of consistency theories with which we will concern ourselves can be seen as branches of system theory.

1 • 1 PROPERTIES OF GROUPS

A *group* is defined as a unit possessing the following five properties, *in toto:* (a) it consists of two or more people; (b) there is interaction or com-

1

munication between the people; (c) there are one or more symbolic objects present; (d) each person has some kind of relation or orientation toward other persons and toward one or more symbolic objects; and (e) what will be called "unit awareness."

Not only must there be two or more persons to constitute a group, but the persons must *interact* with each other. Interaction is defined as the occurrence of one or more acts of one person as a direct or indirect result of one or more acts by another person. An "act" represents any portion or bit of observable behavior, whether verbal or nonverbal, intended or unintended, simple or complex. Generally, though not always, interaction will involve *communication*— the conveyance of information from one person to another. Any act that has "content" and that conveys information, whether it be of a lower order (such as parts of words, grunts, or physical combat) or of a higher order (such as eloquent speeches, music, or paintings), is a communicative act.

In addition to having at least two persons and at least rudimentary interaction and communication between them, a group must contain *symbolic objects* that serve as points of focus or orientation for the persons. These symbolic objects may take various forms: cultural objects such as norms, roles, beliefs, and values, or noncultural objects such as topics of discussion, political issues, and acts of persons. These symbolic objects, particularly in the form of matters of overt or covert concern and interest on the part of the group members, constitute integral properties of group process.

A fourth characteristic of groups involves the *orientations* of persons toward other persons, on one hand, and of persons toward symbolic objects, on the other. Orientations of persons toward other persons take various forms. Examples of person-to-person orientations are: like-dislike, love-hate, positive or negative sentiment, high or low attraction, trust or distrust, respect or disrespect. Person-to-person orientations and person-to-object orientations should be kept analytically distinct. Assume that you are talking with someone about the topic, racial integration. Assume that you favor integration, that you have a favorable attitude toward this issue. This is a person-to-object orientation; the issue "integration" is the symbolic "object." The person to whom you are speaking may also be characterized by a person-to-object orientation: he may favor integration, or he may oppose it. As a matter of fact, whether or not he agrees with you in the object-orientation may well determine whether you like him or not; the object-orientation can determine the person-to-person orientation. Similarly, the latter type of orientation can determine the nature of the former type. The ways in which one kind of orientation can determine another are, to a very great degree, just what this book is about.

A fifth and final property of groups is "unit awareness." This means that the two or more persons involved consider themselves a distinct entity, a unit that has boundaries, an "us," a "we," a "membership." Fraternities exemplify this attribute best of all: clearly, the members of a fraternity maintain rigid boundaries between those who are in the fraternity and those who are not. The family is an example of another kind of group that has unequivocal criteria for membership. One can become a member of a family in only two ways—through a "blood relationship" or through marriage. In these instances, the distinction between "us" and "them" is very clear and rigid. But groups fall along a continuum defined by the degree of unit awareness. Some groups (like fraternities and families) make their boundaries rigid and unyielding, whereas other groups have more fluid boundaries. The members of a biology class, or the casual group formed by the people waiting at a bus stop, constitute two examples of groups with only a minimal degree of unit awareness.

In sum, a group is a unit that consists of two or more persons who interact or communicate, who have orientations toward one another and toward one or more symbolic objects, and who possess an awareness of a "we" or membership. The general type "group" having been thus defined, the sub-type "small group" can now be discussed.

A *small group* is a unit or collective that meets all the above criteria plus the following one: each person in the group must receive an impression or perception of *each other* person distinct enough so that he can, at any time, give some reaction or opinion, however minimal, to each of the others as an individual. This is the much-cited definition provided by the small-group sociologist Bales (1951, p. 33), and it is the one that will be used in this text. The point is that the group must be sufficiently small in size so that each person can recall one or more impressions or perceptions of every other person in the entire group. Hence, although a political convention meets the basic criteria for being a group, it does not meet the latter criterion; no delegate could recall one or more things about every other delegate who attended. For this reason, a political convention is a group, but not a small group. Thus, the criterion for distinguishing a small group from a "large" one is based upon the potential range of perception of persons, and not strictly upon a size criterion involving a limitation to the number of persons involved. In terms of actual numbers, however, a group is usually considered by sociologists to be "small" if it ranges from two up to about twenty persons (Hare, 1962, p. 10).

This text will deal mainly with small groups of two up to six or seven persons. In most cases, the number of persons involved will be only two or three. It would seem unnecessary to cite examples of small groups, but the following ones can nevertheless be given: families, fraternities, construction crews, play groups, bomber crews, bridge clubs, athletic teams, boards of directors, therapy groups, classroom groups, juries, discussion groups, seminars, gangs, and hunting parties. All are small groups, the kind of social unit with which this book is concerned.

In addition to possessing the six properties cited above, a small group may possess an additional set of properties—the properties of a "system." The following section describes the characteristics of systems.

1 • 2   PROPERTIES OF SYSTEMS

Small groups can be seen as systems. They possess the four principal characteristics of systems, viz.: (1) nonadditivity; (2) mutual interdependence of variables; (3) equilibrium; and (4) intervening processes or mechanisms. We will begin with a very general discussion of additivity versus nonadditivity, the first characteristic.

The philosopher of science Von Bertalanffy (1950; 1957) distinguishes two kinds of general theoretical perspectives in science. One of these perspectives involves the notion that the unit or entity (the "case") under study has various parts that are distinct, separate and unrelated to each other. What happens to any given part of the whole is regarded as having no effect upon other parts. This perspective is called the *independence* or *additive* model. The term "additive" suggests that the whole is simply a sum of the parts, and that *no relationships* exist among the parts.

The concept of independence or additivity can be illustrated first with a strictly mechanical example, and then with a biological example. Let us use the automobile as the mechanical example of an additive whole. The outer lighting components of the auto—the headlights, tail and parking lights, and battery—can all be seen as a complex that is, to a great degree, independent of the whole. The lights can work regardless of whether the engine is running or not, regardless of whether the car is moving or not and, in many cases, regardless of whether the ignition is on or off. In fact, one could *remove* the outer lighting complex from the auto altogether, and the lights, powered by the battery, would still work. The complex is independent of the other parts of the automobile.

The biological example of additivity or independence is illustrated by the reflex arc of the human central nervous complex. A message received by a sensor (for example, touching a hot stove with the fingers) is transmitted via nerves to the synapse in the spinal column, which causes an impulse to contract the muscle involved (the hand is jerked away from the stove). The reflex arc is a process unrelated to other parts of the central nervous complex; the impulse does not go directly to the brain.

It should be understood that the question of independence is a matter of degree. There can be a high degree of independence, or a relatively lower degree of independence. Thus, in the automobile example just cited, an "ideal type" illustration was given, simply to get across the notion of independence. The outer lighting complex is to a great *degree* independent of the rest of the automobile, but at the same time there is some relationship between the lighting complex and other parts of the auto—there is some *lack* of independence. The lights work from the battery, which is charged by the generator, which is in turn operated by the engine. Similarly, in the reflex arc example, the hand can be jerked from the hot stove as a result of an impulse not coming from the brain (in which case the reflex arc is an independent process), but biologists have recently speculated that the brain keeps the fluid in the spinal column charged electrochemically so as to "interact" with an impulse coming directly from a sensor. Thus, to some degree, the reflex arc may not be independent of the central nervous complex.

Implied in the foregoing paragraph is the idea that the parts of the whole are not independent of each other, but are *related*. The second perspective Von Bertalanffy identifies, the *system* or *nonadditive* perspective, involves the notion that the parts are not independent of each other. This means that what happens to one part of the whole or unit will have some effect upon other parts of the unit. The criterion of relatedness among parts is a major criterion—though not the only one—for distinguishing a system unit from an additive unit. The system model may apply to a variety of units of analysis: biological systems, such as the human body; physical systems, such as the atom; psychological systems, such as the personality; and, finally, sociological systems, such as the small group. Take as an example the solar system. The sun and the planets represent the "parts" of the whole, but in themselves do not constitute a system. The planets plus their interrelations to one another, and to the sun, do constitute a "system." These "interrelations" are of several kinds. One kind of interrelation is centripetal force, or the gravitational attraction of any two masses. Another is centrifugal force, or the outward force generated by the movement of the planet. By means of these forces or interrelations, the planets remain in orbit around the sun. These sets of interrelations, plus the planets themselves, constitute the solar *system* as such. In this way, a system is a "non-additive" whole; the whole may be said to be something greater than merely the sum of the parts.

Zelditch (1955) defines a system as a whole consisting of two or more parts related in such a way that a change in the state of one part will be followed by a change in the state of another part, which, in turn, results in a change in the state of the former part. The sociological concept of interaction clearly illustrates this principle: some action by person *A* results in some action by person *B*, which in turn results in a reaction by person *A*. A conversation between two persons constitutes the simplest possible system in this respect. Person *A* asks person *B* a question and person *B* gives an answer. Person *A* then responds to *B*'s answer, and so on. Interchanges of this sort represent the most common illustration of the system principle in everyday human interaction.

A more exact delineation of the properties of systems is offered by Hagen (1961). First, the "parts" or "elements" of the system are defined as the *variables* of the system. It is important to understand that if the system consists of, say, a group of two persons in conversation, then the variables of the system are selected *attributes or properties* of these two persons (or of their conversation)—not the persons themselves. The rate or rapidity at which a person speaks during a conversation is an example of an attribute or variable. If the rate at which one person speaks affects the rate at which the other speaks, *then to that extent the variables are related rather than independent.* Second, the variables are related to one another so that a change in one produces a change in another, which subsequently results in a change in the former. Hence, there is no immediate concern for the direction of causation between variables; they are viewed as related in a web of mutual interdependence. This means that regardless of which variable changes, other variables in a system will be affected; each change may "cause" the other. By contrast, in the independence or non-system (additive) model, changes in a given variable are not expected to produce changes in other variables.

Homans' (1950) "sentiment-interaction" hypothesis constitutes an example of the hypothesized mutual interdependence between variables as attributes of human groups: the more frequently people talk with each other, the more they will come to like each other. Conversely, the greater the amount of sentiment or liking between persons, the more often they will talk to each other.[1] *Hence, either variable (degree of sentiment or frequency of interaction) may be taken as the "causally prior" or "independent" variable, the other then becoming the "dependent" variable.*

It is important for the reader to distinguish the concept of nonadditivity (relatedness among variables) from the concept of mutual interdependence. If a change in X produces a change in Y, but change in Y does not produce change in X, then the variables are *related*—as opposed to being independent—but they are not related in a mutually interdependent way. Only if change in X produces change in Y and change in Y produces change in X can there be mutual interdependence. The former case is sometimes referred to under the heading of "asymmetric causation" (X causes Y but Y cannot cause X), whereas the latter case refers to "symmetric causation" (X and Y can cause each other). A system does not exist unless the attributes (variables) of the system are symmetrically related.

In sum, a system has been characterized so far in two ways: (1) it is a nonadditive whole, such that the variables are related rather than independent, but they are related in a particular way—through (2) mutual interdependence. The postulates of nonadditivity and mutual interdependence are integral characteristics of systems. A third property, *equilibrium,* must now be considered.

One must first distinguish stable equilibrium, on one hand, from "non-equilibrium" or an "unstable state," on the other. If stable equilibrium or *homeostasis* exists, then the values of the variables in the system tend to remain constant. After some disturbance changes the value of a variable, the variable is returned to its initial value through its relationship to some other variable (Hagen, 1961). Take as an example the relationship between epidermal skin temperature of the human body and perspiration rate. If a "disturbance" (say, a warm room) results in an increase in the temperature of the skin, then the perspiration rate is increased. This, in turn tends to reduce the skin temperature in the direction of its initial, or original, value. Note, incidentally, that both variables

1. For empirical tests of this hypothesis, the reader is referred to Riecken and Homans (1954), Guetzkow and Dill (1957), and Penny and Robertson (1962).

(skin temperature and perspiration rate) are related in mutual interdependence so that each may produce the other: an increase in skin temperature results in an increase in perspiration rate; an increase in perspiration rate produces a decrease in skin temperature; a decrease in skin temperature results in a decrease in perspiration rate. Both skin temperature and perspiration rate will then remain constant until some new disturbance is introduced.

In the case of nonequilibrium or *unstable states*, by contrast, a disturbance causes the variables to change farther from their initial values. It is possible that a disturbance can upset the stable equilibrium of a system, causing certain permanent changes in the values of the variables; this, in turn, can result in some renewed state of stable equilibrium. As an example, take the familiar sociological model of deviance and sanction, which involves both stable and unstable states. Assume that during a conversation in a group, one person says something "out of line," something that is defined as deviance from a group norm. At this point, some negative sanction or punishment is evoked (perhaps a raised eyebrow, or something more severe such as overt scolding or even banishment from the group). This results in some feeling of mortification or shame on the part of the person emitting the deviant act, thus rendering it unlikely for that person to again commit a similar infraction. Hence, the quality of the interaction is returned to its previous level. Conformity is assured, illustrating the principle of stable equilibrium. Now, suppose that some *innovation* is introduced into the group that necessitates a change in existing norms and sanctions. In such an instance, action that would have been previously regarded as deviance might now be regarded as conformity to a new norm or set of norms. To the extent that a new and stable equilibrium results in this way, the previous state was unstable.

Buckley (1967) points out that such an observation is essentially *ex post facto;* the new equilibrium developing after innovation allows us to label the prior state of equilibrium "unstable." The problem, then, is to identify *a priori* a system that is not a homeostatic one, but that is "growing" or "developing," thereby illustrating a "dynamic" rather than a stable equilibrium. Toward this end, Buckley advocates a rejection of the concepts of "stable" and "unstable" and substitutes the concepts of *morphostasis* and *morphogenesis*. Examples of morphostasis, or homeostatic equilibrium, would be the skin temperature–perspiration rate example given above, or the occurrence of *ritual* in groups or societies. Examples of morphogenesis ("growth"; "development"; "dynamic equilibrium") would be biological evolution, learning, or social change. To the degree that such morphogenetic processes can be predicted, the *ex post facto* problem is resolved.

A fourth property of systems involves the principle of an equilibrium-maintaining mechanism. A mechanism is to be conceptualized as an *intervening variable* or *process* that tends to maintain the state of equilibrium of a system. The simple thermostat is a mechanical illustration: the temperature in a room (the independent variable) affects the thermocouple in the thermostat itself (the intervening variable or mechanism), which in turn results in the furnace being turned on or off (the dependent variable). As a result, the room temperature tends to remain constant, illustrating the principle of homeostasis, and the interdependence between the "independent" and "dependent" variables.[2]

The work of Bales and associates illustrates how one kind of mechanism, psychological tension, serves to maintain a stable equilibrium in "task oriented" discussion groups (Bales, 1953; Bales and Strodtbeck, 1951; Psathas, 1960). Bales observes that at the outset of a discussion, persons concern themselves primarily with asking for and obtaining information, orienting themselves to the topic, defining the nature of the topic, and evaluating one another's comments. Such issues are referred to as "instrumental" issues. During these early phases of the discussion, however, other issues remain undiscussed. These include such things as the participants' feelings toward one another, their stresses and anxieties, their hostilities and antagonisms. These issues are referred to as "expressive." During the initial portion of the interchange, then, a certain pressure or tension toward expressive activity is built up, since such activity tends to gratify the emotional needs of the group members. These pressures do not become manifest until the latter portion of the discussion, when the group moves into expressive activity. During this latter phase of discussion, tension release behavior—joking, laughing, joshing, etc.—is evident. Bales' observation that tension *release* is excessively high during the later phases of the discussion suggests that certain pressures or tensions were high during the *initial* phases of the discussion, and that these tensions tend to "drain off" as the discussion progresses.

2. The concept of "feedback" is often discussed in conjunction with such intervening processes. *Feedback* can be defined as the "reverse" connection or relationship between the dependent and independent processes. Hence, in the above example of the thermostat, the temperature of the room (independent variable) affects the thermostat (intervening variable), which affects the furnace (dependent variable), and the furnace directly affects the room temperature. This last step is the "feedback loop," and may be illustrated as follows:

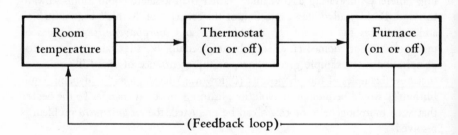

An example of feedback in the human personality would be learning and subsequent modification of behavior as a result of learning. In a group context, the "overthrow" of a leader might be the result of feedback—the receipt of negative or unfavorable information regarding the leader just prior to his overthrow. For an excellent and recent discussion of feedback processes, see Buckley (1967).

Once these tensions are released, the stage is set for the resolution of new instrumental issues, and the cycle of stable equilibrium is completed. The equilibrium-maintaining mechanism, or intervening variable, can be thought of as tension: the group began with instrumental activity; high tension during this phase resulted in a decrease in instrumental activity and an ensuing increase in expressive activity. This produced a drain-off or reduction in tension, thus preparing the group for renewed discussion of instrumental issues.

Other variables besides tension can constitute intervening mechanisms. The deviance-sanction paradigm, illustrated above, can be used to exemplify the role of negative sanction as a mechanism that tends to maintain a homeostatic state. During a group discussion, the "out-of-line" comment is negatively sanctioned, and interaction is returned to its prior quality. The mechanism is negative sanction.

The operation of negative sanction is also illustrated in Homans' (1950) analysis of "output regulation" in an industrial work group. If one man in the group tended to produce too much, he was defined as a "rate buster." He made the others "look bad" in the eyes of management, and he was consequently sanctioned or punished through ridicule and ostracism. On the other hand, if a group member produced too little, he was defined as a "chisler," and negative sanctions against him were still evoked. Note carefully that if "output" is taken as the dependent variable, it is kept at a constant level by the operation of the sanction mechanism (output can be neither too high nor too low), a clear illustration of homeostasis. One variable (output) is kept at a relatively steady value through its relationship to some other variable (the frequency of negative sanction).

1 • 3   SUMMARY

A group is defined as a social unit that consists of two or more persons who interact or communicate, who have orientations toward one another and toward one or more symbolic objects, and who possess an awareness of a "we" or membership. A small group is defined as a social unit possessing these attributes plus an additional one: each person in the group must receive an impression or perception of *each other* person distinct enough so that he can, at any given time, give some reaction or opinion, however minimal, to each of the others as an individual. Small groups can be seen as systems to the degree that they are characterized by the four principal properties of systems. These properties are:

1. Nonadditivity—a group is something more than merely the sum of the individuals in it.

2. Mutual interdependence—the variables of group process are related in a web of "symmetric causation" such that any given variable may be taken as

either independent or dependent, for in a system a change in any one variable produces change in other variables.

3. Equilibrium—the variables are related such that each tends to keep the other at a constant value (stable equilibrium), or such that the values of the variables are not constant, but increase or decrease over time in a predictable way (dynamic equilibrium). Homeostasis, or stable equilibrium, is a concept central to balance theory, the primary focus of this book. For this reason, conditions of unstable states, or of dynamic equilibrium, will not be treated further, although discussion of unstable states and dynamic equilibria usefully illustrates homeostasis.

4. Intervening mechanisms—if homeostatic equilibrium is present, then there will be an intervening variable or mechanism that serves to maintain a state of homeostasis.[3]

Several varieties of system theory have appeared in the sociological and social psychological literature. In the next chapter, a particular type of system theory, namely balance theory, will be reviewed. It will be shown that the four properties of systems described above apply to balance theory. Toward this end, the preceding discussion of the general characteristics of systems seems relevant and antecedant to a discussion of balance theory.

3. In a discussion of systems, the distinction is often made between "open" and "closed" systems. Hence, if something "external" to the system can cause changes in the values of system variables, then the system is "open." If not, then the system is "closed." I regard this distinction (even if seen as a continuum) as archaic and of limited theoretical use, since it is often difficult to determine empirically what is "external" and what is "internal" to a sociological system. At the outset, however, one must realize that all groups (even in the laboratory) are open systems; they are subject to the influence of "confounding" or "extraneous" variables or disturbances. The extent to which "confounding" variables affect the balance process in groups is given extensive treatment in this book, particularly in Chapter 5.

2..

Substantive Models of Balance

This chapter is devoted to a review of the theoretical literature on balance processes. It begins with a discursive, nontechnical treatment of the balance or consistency principle as it applies to everyday human experience. The varieties of balance theory are reviewed and contrasted, the concepts of "balance" and the "balance process" are defined, and the role of tension in the balance process is discussed. Balance theory is then compared to system theory, illustrating that balance theory is a subtype of the general theory of systems. It should be emphasized that for the most part, the present chapter discusses only the major theoretical works in the area of balance. The review of empirical studies and research findings is a task reserved for later chapters. A firm understanding of the varieties of balance theory, and of their similarities and differences, must precede detailed treatment of the empirical literature.

2 • 1   BALANCE AND EVERYDAY EXPERIENCE

The basic assumption underlying theories of balance is that people tend to organize their perceptions of things in consistent and comfortable ways. One need only recall his own casual observations of human experience to illustrate this principle. Christian Scientists do not generally enroll in medical schools; Jews are rarely active in neo-Nazi organizations; John Birch Society members are not likely to sympathize with pacifist philosophies. A highly prejudiced white person would not marry a Negro, nor could the cancer researcher easily justify his smoking two packages of cigarettes daily. From childhood, one learns that consistency is desirable—that "handsome is as handsome does," and that the "good" person is also "trustworthy," "helpful," "considerate," "kind," and so on. An inconsistent person—such as one who does not "practice what he preaches"—is likely to be labeled a "hypocrite." In school one is taught, inadvertently or otherwise, that "Beauty is truth, truth beauty—that is all ye know on earth, and all ye need to

11

know" (Keats, *Ode on a Grecian Urn*). If that which is true is also ugly, then we find it difficult to understand.

Such observations might serve to illustrate human preference for cognitive consistency. Things that are inconsistent are "odd" or "out of the ordinary." Consequently, when faced with an inconsistency of some sort, people will attempt to eradicate or at least reduce it. We will often go to great lengths to reduce inconsistencies. Stories about the relationship between cancer and smoking have appeared in newspapers and magazines, and on T.V. and radio. In one survey conducted in Minneapolis, it was found that non-smokers found no difficulty in believing these reports. But what about the heavy smokers? Only 7 percent of the heavy smokers believed that smoking caused cancer, whereas 29 percent of the non-smokers believed the reports (Festinger, 1957, p. 155; Feather, 1963). It is cognitively inconsistent to believe one way and behave another; heavy smokers find it easier to disbelieve such information. This disbelief coupled with heavy smoking (or belief and discontinued smoking) reduces the inconsistency created by the research results appearing in the mass media.

Other illustrations of attempts to reduce inconsistency or imbalance appear in everyday life. A man and wife are interested in purchasing an automobile, but they disagree on the make or color of the car. There exists, then, a certain pressure toward attaining agreement, as disagreement is inconsistent with marriage. The husband and wife will modify their feelings and attempt to arrive at a compromise. If, on the other hand, the man were to discuss his preferences with someone he did not love, then he would be less prone to seek compromise.

Before the United Nations, the Premier of Russia makes sweeping proposals for world disarmament. This is incongruous with the American public's conception of the Russian Premier. A distrustful, ignoble man does not make honest, noble proposals. The press attempts to reduce this incongruence by editorializing about the deceptive nature of his proposals, holding that his program actually represents a carefully planned move in the Cold War rather than a sincere overture toward peace.

Assume that we are favorably disposed toward the Vice President of the United States. Let us further assume that in Uruguay, he is greeted with flowers and smiles, but in Paraguay a mob of students boo him and have to be dispersed with tear gas. Having little information and generally neutral attitudes toward these obscure countries, we find ourselves favorably disposed toward the former and rather hostile toward the latter. Subsequent news that Uruguay lives under a harsh dictatorship, and that Paraguay has a democratic form of government much like our own, is hard to assimilate. We would rather believe the reverse. We attempt to maintain balance among our attitudes toward the countries and our beliefs about them, often at the expense of reality.[1]

Such casual observations constitute discursive illustrations of the consistency principle. Not until recently, however, have there appeared in the psycho-

---

1. Some of the examples given here were taken from Osgood (1960).

logical and sociological literature any systematic and detailed attempts to construct unified and precise theories about the ways in which people deal with inconsistencies. It is the purpose of this chapter to review these theories: Heider's model of "balance," Newcomb's theory of "systems of orientation," Festinger's "dissonance" principle, and the Osgood-Tannenbaum formulation on "attitude congruity." Each of these formulations is to be subsumed under the general heading of what has been referred to as "theories of consistency" (Zajonc, 1960), the "principle of consistency" (Brown, 1965), "theories of cognitive consistency" (Feldman, 1966; Abelson et al., 1968), and the theory of "cognitive balance" (Jordan, 1966a). This text refers to these four varieties collectively as *balance theory*, due to their historical connection with Heider's early writings regarding the principle of balance in interpersonal perception. Detailing the meaningful similarities and differences among the four models is the task of the following section.

2 • 2   VARIETIES OF BALANCE THEORY

Perhaps the earliest writings on the balance principle can be attributed to the great philosophers. Spinoza implies that agreement between two persons is a precondition for their liking each other: "We can easily show . . . that causes of hatred depend solely upon differences, and not on the agreement between men's natures" (Heider, 1958, p. 197). An early psychologist, Franke, tells us that ". . . there is nothing in human character that contradicts itself. If a person . . . seems to be incongruous with himself that is only an indication of the inadequacy and superficiality of our previous observations" (Franke, 1931, p. 45).

This latter hypothesis—if it may indeed be called an hypothesis—is, of course, extreme. Clearly, there are many instances in daily life where contradictions, inconsistencies and imbalances are tolerable and even pleasurable. Party jokes, which often involve gross inconsistencies indeed, are not only tolerated but induce pleasure. People go to a magician to experience inconsistency, and it is a pleasurable experience. Conditions under which the balance principle does *not* apply are discussed systematically in later chapters. It is the purpose of this chapter to specify the conditions under which it does apply.

In the following review of the theoretical literature, the reader should understand the terminology to be applied by the present author. The *objects* of a particular theory are defined as either persons, or as non-person entities that can be perceived by persons. The relations between persons, or between persons and non-person objects, are the *variables* of the particular theory. The objects plus the relations between them together comprise the *theoretical unit*. Take as an example the following: Two people discussing some common topic. The two persons and the topic are the three objects. The way in which each person is orientated toward or related to the other (such as liking or disliking the other), and the way in which each is oriented toward the topic (such as favoring or disfavoring it), are the variables. The objects plus their relations constitute the theoretical unit.

2 • 2a Heider's Model of Balance

The earliest systematic formulation of a theory of balance is generally attributed to the psychologist, Heider (1944; 1946; 1958). Drawing upon the work of Lewin (1936; 1939; 1951) and the assumptions of Gestalt psychology, Heider proposed that a person perceives the objects in his environment as forming a unified whole. Things must "go together" or "add up." Through the principle of *perceptual consistency,* people tend to perceive the invariant, constant properties of objects. Thus, individuals will see a relatively unstructured and ambiguous "abstract" painting as revealing an interpretable configuration, or a free-form inkblot as a familiar image. In forming such unified perceptions, the person becomes what Heider calls a "naive psychologist"—he attempts to fit things together in his own mind so that they make sense.

Heider's theory focuses mainly upon interpersonal perception and behavior. Hence, it is applicable to what we previously defined as the small group. The theory contains three *objects* (Heider calls them "entities"): a focal person, designated as P, another person, O, and a non-person object, X. Either of the two persons may be designated as P, the other then becoming O. The focal person is simply the one upon whom theoretical interest is momentarily being focused. The object X may be any number of things, from a physical object such as an automobile or home, to a symbolic object such as a topic of discussion, a political issue, or an idea. Relations between the focal person and the other are called "sentiment relations." Sentiment involves liking and feeling—generally, an emotional or affective relation. Relations between either person and X are called "unit relations." These involve favorable or unfavorable attitudes toward the object, ownership–nonownership of the object, association–nonassociation with it, proximity (near–far), kinship (related–not related), and "causality" (responsible–not responsible), as examples. Heider does allow for the possibility of unit relations existing between persons, although research in balance usually interprets a unit relation as a relation between a person and a non-person object. Generally, sentiment relations (between persons) and unit relations (between persons and non-person objects) are two types of *variables* in Heider's theory. The objects plus their relations constitute the *theoretical unit.*

Heider dichotomizes sentiment into "like," or positive sentiment, and "dislike," or negative sentiment. Broadly speaking, a person can like or dislike the other. The orientation or relation of each person to X may also be positive or negative. Examples of positive unit relations are "P owns or is associated with X"; "P is responsible for X"; "P is in favor of X." Negative unit relations involve disapproval or disfavor.[2] Hence, three separate variables are involved:

2. The distinction between *negative* (−) and *absent* (0) relations is discussed in following chapters.

the focal person's orientation toward the other, his orientation toward X, and the focal person's perception of the other's orientation toward X. Note that each variable is some orientation made by the focal person himself; each is seen from the "viewpoint" of the focal person. The variables are part of his *cognitive structure*. If each of these three variables is dichotomized into positive and negative, then eight "configurations," or patterns of variables, result. These eight configurations are diagrammed in Figure 1, where each variable is given a positive (+) or negative (−) sign. The directions of the arrows signify the direction of the focal person's orientation. In the case of the arrow going from O to X, the arrow is intended to represent the focal person's perception of the other's orientation toward X.

In Figure 1, if the focal person's orientation toward X is of the same sign as the other's perceived orientation toward X, then their orientations are "similar." If the orientations of the focal person and the other are of opposite signs, then their orientations are "dissimilar." Conditions of positive sentiment (liking) and similarity, or negative sentiment (dislike) and dissimilarity, are defined as *balanced*. Conditions of positive sentiment and dissimilarity, or negative sentiment and similarity, are *unbalanced*. The concept of balance–unbalance can be simplified by representing it in the following taxonomy:

		Orientations of P and O toward X are:	
		Similar in sign	Dissimilar in sign
P's sentiment toward *O* is:	Positive	Balance	Unbalance
	Negative	Unbalance	Balance

A short method of identifying which of the eight configurations in Figure 1 are balanced and which are unbalanced was introduced by Cartwright and Harary (1956). Note that there are three signs in each of the eight configurations. If the algebraic product of these signs is positive, then the configuration is balanced. If the product is negative, then the configuration is unbalanced. For example, assume a condition where the focal person likes the other, favors X, but perceives the other as disfavoring X. The algebraic product of these three signs, taken in any order, is negative: $(+)(+)(−) = (−)$. The configuration of relations is therefore unbalanced.

FIGURE 1   EIGHT CONFIGURATIONS OF BALANCE AND UNBALANCE*

Configurations	Description

Balanced Configurations

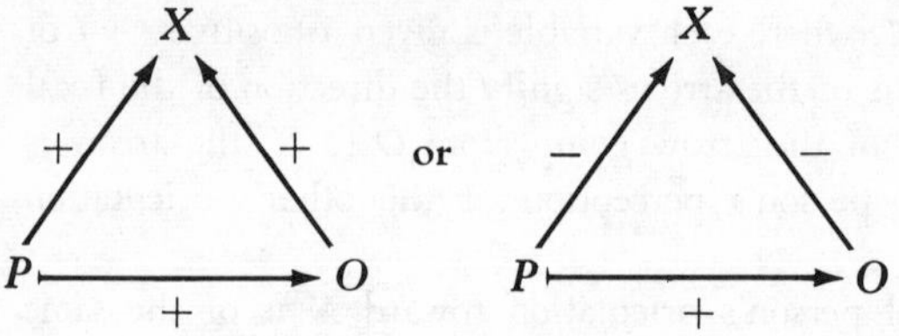

P likes O; P and O have similar orientations toward X

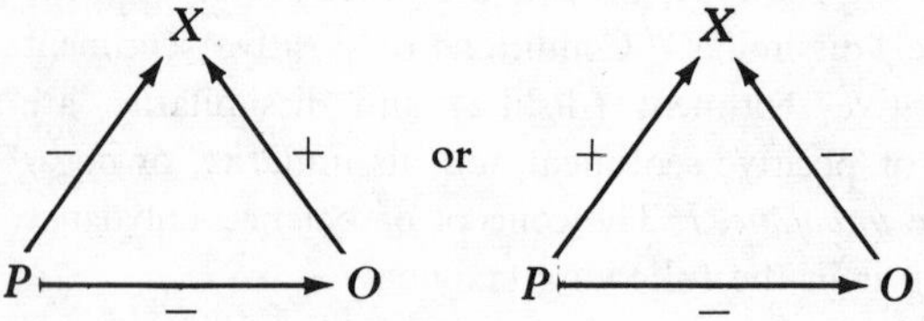

P dislikes O; P and O have dissimilar orientations toward X

Unbalanced Configurations

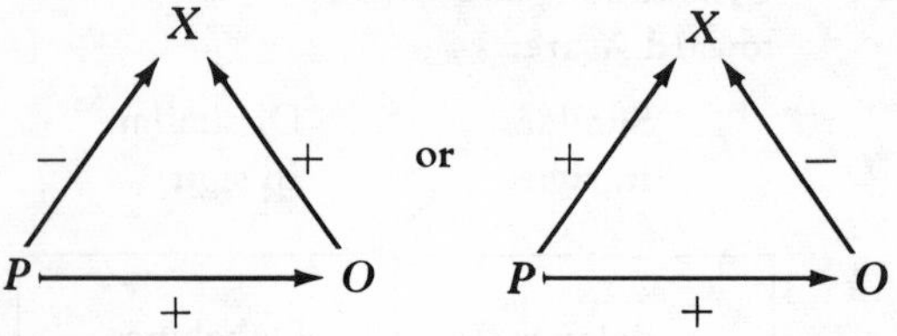

P likes O; P and O have dissimilar orientations toward X

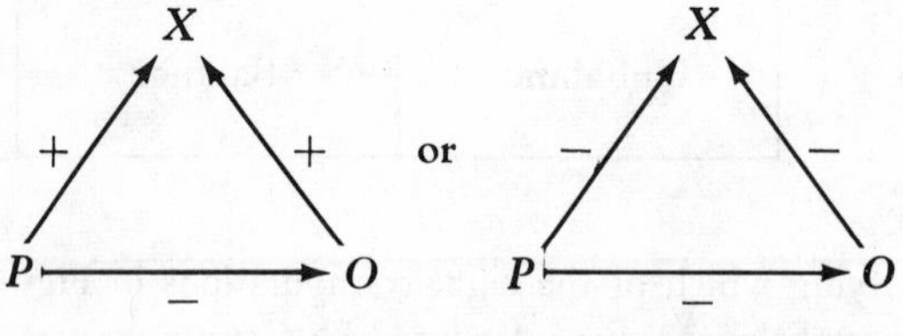

P dislikes O; P and O have similar orientations toward X

* This figure is adapted from Heider (1958, pp. 174–217), and Zajonc (1960, p. 283). Jordan (1963) asserts that the unbalanced configuration with three negative signs was introduced into the literature by him in 1953 (Jordan, 1953), but the configuration represents a direct extension of Heider's formulation.

Note carefully that no distinction is being made here with respect to the *strength* of a relation, but only with respect to *sign*. One might wish to distinguish between a "strong positive" relation and a "weak positive" relation, or among three positive relations that are "very strong," "moderately strong," and "slightly strong." Heider, however, does not make distinctions in terms of strength, but only in terms of sign. Other theorists to be reviewed shortly—particularly the Newcomb and Osgood-Tannenbaum models—have considered the matter of strength. Hence, in order to identify the kind of balance that Heider is talking about, it will be useful to say that if the algebraic product of the signs in a configuration is positive, the configuration is *sign-balanced*. If the product is negative, it is *sign-unbalanced*.

The central hypothesis in Heider's theory is that people prefer balance to unbalance. Situations of unbalance are inconsistent, odd and confusing to the person. In an unbalanced situation, the various relations or orientations do not "fit together" or "add up." Such conditions are characterized by a *force* or *tension* toward the attainment of balance. Heider predicts that "if a balanced state does not exist, then forces toward this state will arise" (Heider, 1958, p. 201). In attempting to define "force," Heider equates the concept with the concept of psychological stress and with the notion of "unpleasantness" or "discomfort."

This force or tension constitutes a pressure toward change, from unbalance to balance. The hypothesis is simple: given any unbalanced condition, the focal person will undergo tension or discomfort. This will cause him to *change* one or more orientations in the direction of balance. By contrast, given any balanced condition, the focal person undergoes less tension. Hence, no changes in orientations are expected. To illustrate this hypothesis, suppose that you (*P*) and a friend (*O*) begin a discussion on a political candidate (*X*). You are against his candidacy, and you are of the initial impression that your friend shares this view. This represents a balanced cognitive configuration. Now assume that during the discussion, your friend tells you that he is really in favor of the candidate. The configuration is now unbalanced; a pressure toward the re-establishment of balance results. According to the hypothesis, you have at least three alternatives, each representing a change in orientation toward balance: (a) you can modify your own attitude toward the candidate, and become more favorably disposed toward him; (b) you can find yourself liking your friend less; or (c) you can modify your perception of your friend's opinion of the candidate—for example, convince yourself that he isn't really in favor of the candidate.

These three changes represent examples of the central predictions from Heider's model. Clearly, other alternatives are available. You may decrease the importance of the issue (*X*) and convince yourself that "the whole thing doesn't really matter much, anyway." You may attempt to persuade your friend to change his views by arguing with him. Or, you may think that your friend is certainly entitled to his own opinions, and that he undoubtedly has opinions toward *other* issues that are similar to your own views on those issues. Although these latter alternatives, plus additional ones, are given some treatment by the balance theorists, they do not represent the core predictions from the balance model and are treated later in this chapter.

There are certain notations that will be used throughout this book, and it is worthwhile for the reader to familiarize himself with them now. The expression $+PO$ means that "P likes O"; the expression $-PO$ means that "P dislikes O." Note that the "P" is given first and the "O" is given second, so that if we wish to signify that O *likes* P, we write: $+OP$. If P likes O but O dislikes P, it is written as: $+PO$, $-OP$. The expression $+PX$ means that "P favors X," and $-PX$ means that "P disfavors X." If O favors X (or if P perceives that O favors X), we write: $+OX$; if O disfavors X, it is expressed as $-OX$.

To illustrate both this notational scheme and Heider's hypothesis that people prefer balance to unbalance, it is interesting to examine the way in which the sponsor of a TV program might try to induce you to buy his product. A very straightforward example is the commercial, "People hate coughs, and Luden's coughdrops hate coughs; that's why so many people like Luden's." An analysis of this simple appeal shows that the advertiser might be applying something approximating a balance principle. If we "personify" Luden's as O, "people" becomes the symbol P, and "coughs" becomes X, then the configuration formed by people hating coughs ($-PX$), Luden's hating coughs ($-OX$) and people liking Luden's ($+PO$) is balanced.

Another example from advertising involves the well known man in the Hathaway shirt. The obviously aristocratic gentleman with the eyepatch is favored by us ($+PO$), and the man clearly likes Hathaway shirts ($+OX$), since he is wearing one. Hence (so the advertiser hopes), there is a force that will compel you to like Hathaway shirts ($+PX$), since anything else (such as $-PX$) represents unbalance, an unpleasant and uncomfortable psychological state. The principle of "snob-appeal" is present (that is why you like and admire the Hathaway man) but so is the principle of balance. Of course, if you really wanted to pull a fast one on the advertiser, you would forget about the shirt and go buy yourself an eyepatch! (Whereupon you would still be exhibiting a preference for balance rather than unbalance: You favor the man ($+PO$) who likes eyepatches ($+OX$), which you then might buy ($+PX$).)

The hypothesis that people prefer or change toward balance need not be confined to the social *dyad*—any group consisting of exactly two persons. The POX unit is a dyad. Heider's formulations can be extended to the three-person unit, or *triad*.[3] In this case, the three objects are three persons (P, O, and Q), and the variables become: the focal person's (P's) sentiment toward the other (O) and toward a second other (Q), plus the focal person's perception of the senti-

3. In articles on balance, the POX unit is often referred to as a "triad"—a unit consisting of three objects. If this is done, both the POX and POQ units are called "triads." To distinguish the two in this text, the two-person (POX) unit is called a dyad, and the three-person (POQ) unit is called a triad.

ment relation between each of the other persons. Hence, all three variables are part of the focal person's cognitive structure. In an instance where the focal person likes two others who are perceived as disliking each other, the triad is unstable (unbalanced), and a variable will change in the direction of increased balance. Decreasing the liking for one other (O or Q, but not both) would represent a change toward greater stability or balance.

The sociological theorist Homans presents a strikingly similar hypothesis:

> If the relationship between [persons] A and B is of a particular kind, and the relationship between B and C is close and warm, the relationship between A and C will tend to resemble the relationship between A and B (Homans, 1950, p. 255).

Hence, Homans is predicting that a relationship between two persons will tend to be in balance with the relationships between each of these persons and a third person. The enemy of a friend is one's own enemy; the friend of a friend is one's own friend; the friend of one's enemy is one's own enemy. Note that this proposition applies to variables that are not necessarily part of the focal person's own cognitive structure. Although A's sentiment toward B and C is part of A's cognitive structure, B's sentiment toward C (or C's sentiment toward B) is not. Thus, Homans' hypothesis extends the principle of balance to include variables that are not part of the focal person's cognitive structure. This distinction between the "cognitive" and "collective" structures is taken up in detail in the next section of this chapter.

Heider's model can also be generalized to *four objects*—three persons and one X, or four persons. Furthermore, it is clear that any given *pair* of objects can be characterized by two or more orientations—a person can like or dislike another and have some simultaneous perception of the other's liking for him. In such instances, the matter of determining whether or not the unit is balanced, and ascertaining which changes will result in balance, is quite complicated. Recent mathematical formulations of Heider's model have approached this issue directly, and are dealt with in the next chapter.

In sum, Heider's hypothesis is: Under given conditions of balance, the focal person experiences little tension, and is therefore not likely to change an orientation. By contrast, under conditions of unbalance, the focal person will undergo relatively more tension and thus change an orientation in the direction of less tension or balance. Furthermore, changes toward balance result in a reduction in the focal person's tension. This entire process may be referred to as the "balance process," and is diagrammed in Figure 2.

Heider therefore proposes that the *POX* unit is a *system* characterized by stable equilibrium. The variables—the orientations—are interdependent, since under given conditions of balance, a change toward unbalance in any of the three variables will result in a change toward balance in *either* of the other two

FIGURE 2   THE BALANCE PROCESS

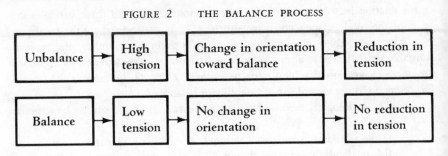

variables. This interdependence property of the *POX* unit is illustrated above in the example of you and your friend discussing a political candidate. If, before the discussion, you think that both you and your friend disfavor the candidate, but your friend tells you that he actually favors him, then the predicted change in either your sentiment toward him or your attitude toward the candidate illustrates the principle of interdependence among the orientations. Any change in an orientation toward balance is expected to reduce your tension or discomfort. This hypothesized "return" to a balanced state illustrates the principle of *homeostasis* or stable equilibrium. The equilibrium-maintaining mechanism is the magnitude of your (the focal person's) tension.

2 • 2b   *Newcomb's Model of Systems of Orientation*

Heavily influenced by Heider's earlier writings on the balance principle, the social psychologist Newcomb later developed and extended the theory to render it more applicable to group situations involving interaction and communication (Newcomb, 1953; 1956; 1959; 1960; 1961; 1963). The theories of Heider and Newcomb are similar in five respects. First, the objects that comprise Newcomb's basic theoretical unit are a focal person (called person *A*), another person (*B*) and a non-person object, *X*. In Newcomb's formulations, the object *X* is generally an issue or topic of potential or actual discussion between *A* and *B*, whereas for Heider, *X* may be any symbolic or physical object. The second similarity to Heider's theory is that two types of variables characterize Newcomb's unit. The orientation of one person toward the other is one of high or low *attraction*. The concept of attraction is defined by other concepts such as liking, admiration, respect, and trust (Newcomb, 1960). Hence, liking is only one type of attraction. (Recall that Heider defined "sentiment" and "liking" as synonymous.) The orientation of the focal person toward *X* is defined as an *attitude*, ranging from favorable to unfavorable. The focal person's perception of the other's orientation toward *X* is a *perceived attitude*. The orientation "attraction" is to be thought of as distinct from the orientation "attitude." Whereas attraction refers to an affective, emotional, person-to-person orientation, attitude refers to an evaluative, instrumental, person-to-X orientation.

The third similarity between the two theories is that Newcomb's concept of "symmetry" is analogous to Heider's concept of balance. Conditions under which the focal person is attracted toward the other and perceives that he and the other have similar attitudes toward X, or where attraction is low and there is perceived dissimilarity, are defined as "symmetric" or balanced. Conditions of high attraction and perceived dissimilarity, or low attraction and similarity, are asymmetric or unbalanced.

A fourth similarity is that Heider and Newcomb propose a force toward the attainment of balance. Where Heider uses the concepts of "force," "pressure" and "tension," Newcomb uses the concept of "strain." Strain comes into operation under conditions of unbalance, thereby producing changes in attraction, attitude or perceived attitude in the direction of balance or less strain. This unbalance-strain-change process is illustrated in the following proposition from Newcomb: Given a condition of unbalance, then the "... effects of strain are those of system change: strain tends to result in strain-reducing changes in one or more orientations or perceived orientations of others. *Thus system stability varies inversely with intensity of strain*" (Newcomb, 1961, p. 14, italics added). The hypothesized relationships between symmetry, strain, change and strain reduction are the same as Heider's postulated relationships between balance, tension, change and tension reduction. This common proposition, the balance process, was diagrammed in Figure 2.

Note from the above quote by Newcomb the fifth similarity between the two theorists: both treat the group as a system tending toward stable equilibrium. Just as Heider proposes that a change toward unbalance in an orientation will produce a balance-maintaining change in one or more other orientations, Newcomb holds that the orientations are "dynamically interdependent" and that "the totality of these orientations is therefore regarded as having system properties, in a sense that a change in any one of them [toward unbalance] induces change in one or more of the others" (Newcomb, 1959, p. 392). Newcomb, however, is more explicit than Heider in attributing degree of stability to magnitude of strain or tension. Whereas Heider briefly alludes to this mechanism, strain plays a major role in Newcomb's formulations.

Despite these similarities between the two theorists, there are five crucial differences in their respective formulations. The first difference is that while Heider expresses relations in terms of sign only, Newcomb considers the sign *and strength* of the attraction, attitude and perceived attitude relations. This results in Newcomb's focus on the degree of difference or *discrepancy* between the PX and perceived OX attitudes. Generally, *"agreement" is defined as similarity-dissimilarity in the signs of the PX and OX relations, such that agree-*

ment exists if the PX and OX relations are of the same sign, and disagreement exists if the PX and OX relations are of opposite sign. On the other hand, "discrepancy" refers to the algebraic difference in the strengths of the PX and OX relations.

Let us say that we wish to quantify the strength *and* the sign of a relation in terms of what is called a "Likert Scale," as follows:

$+3$ = a strong positive relation
$+2$ = a moderate positive relation
$+1$ = a weak positive relation
0 = a neutral relation
-1 = a weak negative relation
-2 = a moderate negative relation
-3 = a strong negative relation

Thus, it is possible for P and O to "agree" on X, yet be discrepant in their orientations toward X. For example, if P strongly favored X ($+3$ PX) but perceived that O weakly favored X ($+1$ OX), then there is agreement (similarity in sign) but a discrepancy of two scale values. If P moderately disfavored X (-2 PX) and perceived that O strongly favored X ($+3$ OX), then there is both disagreement (the signs are opposite) and a discrepancy of *five* scale values.

The distinction between discrepancy (made by Newcomb) and agreement (Heider) leads to a second difference between the two theorists. Each theorist defines "stability" in a different way. For Heider, if there is *sign-balance*, the structure is hypothesized to be stable and not likely to change. Hence, according to Heider, the following structure of three relations is stable, since it is sign-balanced and contains "agreement": $+1$ PX, $+3$ OX, and $+3$ PO. But according to Newcomb, this very same structure is *unstable* ("asymmetric"), due to the discrepancy in the PX and OX relations—a discrepancy of two scale values. The fact that P likes O strongly ($+3$ PO) is not in balance with the fact that the PX and OX relations are discrepant, even though they are of the same sign. The important point being made here is that while Heider would predict "no change" in this structure, Newcomb considers it unstable, and one or more of the three relations is likely to change. A change from $+1$ PX in the *positive direction* (i.e., toward $+3$ PX), or a change in $+3$ OX in the *negative direction* (i.e., toward $+1$ OX), represent two of the hypothesized changes. Thus, as an example, the following two structures would be considered stable according to Newcomb (and also Heider): (a) $+1$ PX, $+1$ OX, $+3$ PO or (b) $+3$ PX, $+3$ OX, $+3$ PO.

It should be pointed out that in the writings of Newcomb, the term "symmetry" actually carries three different meanings. (1) Symmetry can refer to the overall character of the structure, namely, whether it is stable ("symmetric") or unstable ("asymmetric"). It is for this reason that Newcomb's first meaning of symmetry is analogous to Heider's concept of "balance." (2) Symmetry can refer to the two relations formed when considering only two persons: P's attraction toward O, and P's *perception* of O's attraction toward P. If P likes O and P also perceives that O likes him $(+PO, +OP)$, then we say that "the PO relation is symmetric." Symmetry also exists if P dislikes O and perceives that O dislikes him $(-PO, -OP)$. *Asymmetry* exists if the PO and OP relations are of opposite sign $(+PO, -OP;$ or $-PO, +OP)$. This second meaning of the concept of symmetry is that typically used by small-group theorists and researchers in areas besides balance theory. (3) The term *lateral symmetry* (Newcomb, 1968) refers to the similarity *in sign* with respect to the PX and OX relations. The concept of lateral symmetry is identical to the concept of agreement, if one is considering the PX and OX relations (as opposed to other pairs of relations): $+PX$ and $+OX$, and $-PX$ and $-OX$ both represent lateral symmetry; $+PX$ and $-OX$, and $-PX$ and $+OX$ represent lateral asymmetry. The term *lateral symmetry* can also refer to the similarity-dissimilarity in signs of the PX and PO relations compared, or to the similarity-dissimilarity in signs of the PO and OX relations compared. Thus, in a structure of three relations, there are three separate paired comparisons of lateral symmetry that one can make. More will be said about lateral symmetry, and also about the second meaning of symmetry, in later chapters.

A third difference between the two theorists concerns Newcomb's recent "three-category" balance scheme (Price, Harburg and Newcomb, 1966; Newcomb, 1968). Recall from Figure 1 that Heider's scheme can be broken down into four basic categories: like-agree (balance), dislike-disagree (balance), like-disagree (unbalance) and dislike-agree (unbalance). Newcomb has questioned the empirical accuracy of this breakdown, finding through a re-analysis of data gathered in several studies that a major distinction in terms of stability and tension can be made between the like-agree and like-disagree conditions, but that less of a distinction can be made between the dislike-disagree and dislike-agree conditions. Namely, the distinction between dislike-disagree and dislike-agree seems to have no psychological meaning to people, nor does it empirically predict change or tension. On the other hand, the distinction between like-agree versus like-disagree tends to result in large differences: (a) there seems to be a psychological distinction between them; (b) change is more likely to occur in the latter (like-disagree) than in the former (like-agree), suggesting that the former is more stable; and (c) tension tends to be much lower in the like-agree condition than in the like-disagree condition. Newcomb therefore argues that any condition involving dislike (dislike-agree or dislike-disagree) should be called *nonbalanced* and relatively stable. The like-agree condition is *balanced* (very stable), and the like-disagree condition is *unbalanced* (unstable). This represents a substantial contradiction of Heider, who regards the dislike-agree condition as unstable (unbalanced) and the dislike-disagree condition as quite stable (balanced). A complete discussion of Newcomb's three-category scheme, and the problems connected with it, is found in Chapter 7.

The fourth difference between the Heider and Newcomb formulations involves the number of variables contained in the theoretical unit. The reader will recall Heider's delineation of three variables: the focal person's liking for the other, orientation toward X, and perception of the other's orientation toward X. Newcomb includes these variables in what he calls the *individual system* of orientation. A fourth variable is added, however: the focal person's *perception* of the other's attraction toward him, which is also a part of the individual system. In the above example of the discussion between you and your friend about the political candidate, there would be at least four variables to consider as part of your cognitive structure or individual system: your attitude toward the candidate, the degree of attraction toward your friend, your perception of your friend's attitude toward the candidate, and your perception of your friend's degree of attraction toward you. Under a condition of unbalance (such as your friend's speaking out in favor of a candidate you disfavor), a decrease in the extent to which you thought your friend liked you would be a predicted change toward balance.

Important to Newcomb's model is his specification of the difference between the individual system and the *collective system*. In addition to including the four individual system variables, the collective system includes attributes of the *other's* cognitive structure: his actual attitude toward X and his actual degree of attraction toward the focal person. This distinction is crucial, since (a) the focal person's perception of the other's attitude need not be the same as the other's actual attitude, and (b) the focal person's perception of the other's attraction toward him need not be the same as the other's actual attraction toward him.

Although Newcomb does not clearly develop his formulations to cover all logical types of variables, an extension of his model can be attempted here. The individual system consists of four variables: the focal person's attitude, perception of the other's attitude, attraction toward the other, and perception of the other's attraction toward him. All four variables represent what Newcomb calls a "co-orientation"—meaning that the focal person simultaneously makes all four orientations. Clearly, the other can also co-orient himself to the focal person and to X. In instances (a) where both the focal person and the other are oriented toward the same X, and (b) where each is oriented toward the other, a collective system exists. Hence, Newcomb's "collective system" can be defined simply as the combination of two or more individual systems.

Figure 3 diagrams the distinction between the individual and collective systems, considering two persons and one X. Solid arrows indicate objective orientations made by the focal person or the other, whereas dotted arrows signify *perceived* or subjective orientations. The direction of the arrow denotes the direction of the objective and perceived orientations. In Figure 3A, four variables are diagrammed as part of the focal person's individual system. Figures 3B and C combine the two individual systems into one collective system. From this diagram, it is seen that the minimal collective system consists of eight distinct variables.

The fifth and final major difference between the models of Heider and

FIGURE 3   INDIVIDUAL AND COLLECTIVE SYSTEMS

A. *The Individual System*

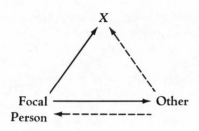

B. *The Collective System**

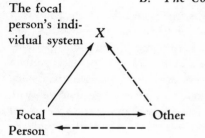

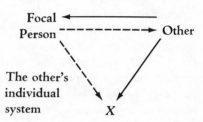

C. *The Collective System†*

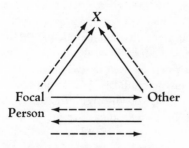

* The two individual systems are diagrammed separately here for purposes of clarity. They should be seen as superimposed over each other, as in Figure 3C.

† The two individual systems are superimposed over each other, thus giving a collective system consisting of eight separate variables.

Newcomb lies in the latter's treatment of the role of communication or interaction. Remembering that in Newcomb's terminology, A is the focal person and
B is the other,

> . . . . A observes that an attractive B differs from him on an important issue
> and seeks symmetry by trying to persuade B to his own point of view; or A
> seeks to reassure himself that B does not disagree with him; or A gives
> information to B about X or asks B for information about X. From all these
> acts we may infer the perception of asymmetry and the direction of com-
> munication toward symmetry. Selected observations concerning symmetry as
> a consequence of communication are equally plentiful; there is, in fact, no
> social phenomenon which can be more commonly observed than the tendency
> for freely communicating persons to resemble one another in orientation
> toward objects of common concern" (Newcomb, 1953, p. 398).

Close examination of these predictions reveals two distinct components of
communication in the group: *receiving* and *sending* information about X. The
first component, where the focal person receives information from the other
about X, is important as it tends to result in greater *accuracy* of the focal person's
perception of the other's attitude. To the extent that the focal person's perception
of the other's attitude prior to communication is inaccurate, communication with
the other results in greater accuracy of perception. Referring to the earlier
example of your discussing the political candidate with a friend: If you initially
felt that he disfavored the candidate, but you reversed this perception when he
told you that he favored him, then under the condition that your friend was being
truthful, greater accuracy of your perception would be achieved. Your initial perception that your friend's attitude was of negative sign is changed in the direction
of a positive sign. Generally, the first component of communication, then, is the
conveyance of the sign of the other's attitude toward X.

The second component of communication is the complement of the first:
sending information from the focal person to the other about X. The implications
of both components can best be seen by example. Prior to the discussion with
your friend, you disfavor the candidate, but do not know your friend's attitude.
During discussion with him, you discover that he favors the candidate—illustrating the first component—and the situation is unbalanced (asymmetric).
Referring only to your friend's attitude and your perception of it, two alternative
changes toward balance are available to you. The first, a "communicative alternative," illustrates the second component: you can attempt to change your friend's
attitude by arguing with him, by giving him new information about the candidate,
or by evaluating and criticizing his prior information. Any resulting objective
change in his attitude toward disfavoring the candidate represents the hypothesized change toward balance. The second alternative, an *"autistic"* alternative,
would be illustrated by your perceiving your friend as *disfavoring* the candidate
prior to communicating with him about it. Or, despite communication where he

indicates favoring the candidate, you convince yourself that he is incompetent to evaluate the issue, or that the issue is of little importance, or that your friend is not being truthful and did not really mean what he said, or you simply deny that he indeed said he favored the candidate. Any such autistic perceptions represent attempts on your part to reduce the tension created by unbalance.

By the way of summary, the core hypothesis common to both Heider and Newcomb is that under given conditions of unbalance, the focal person experiences high tension or strain. This will cause him to change one or more variables in the direction of balance, and a reduction in his tension will result. By contrast, under conditions of balance, there is no tension toward change, and hence the variables are expected to retain their initial values (not change). This sequence of events represents the balance process. Both theorists hypothesize a system in stable (homeostatic) equilibrium, as—given balance—any variable change toward unbalance will increase tension and bring about changes in other variables toward renewed balance. This hypothesis predicts that the variables are interdependent and that the directions of change in each are regulated by the tension mechanism.

The central differences between the Heider and Newcomb models are:

1. Heider considers only the signs of relations, whereas Newcomb considers both the signs and the strengths of relations.

2. This leads to conflicting definitions of balance, such that a given configuration or structure can be sign-balanced (stable, not likely to change) according to Heider, but at the same time be "asymmetric" (and hence unstable, likely to change) according to Newcomb.

3. Newcomb has recently hypothesized that any configuration containing dislike is "non-balanced," and is *more stable* than the like-disagree condition, and *less stable* than the like-agree condition. This is a clear difference with Heider, who predicts that configurations containing dislike can be either stable or unstable, depending upon whether there is agreement or disagreement.

4. Newcomb distinguishes between an "individual" versus a "collective" system, whereas Heider makes no such distinction.

5. The process of communication plays a major role in Newcomb's theory, whereas the importance of communication in the balance process is largely ignored by Heider.

2 • 2c   Festinger's Model of Cognitive Dissonance

○   Whereas the theories of Heider and Newcomb explicitly focus upon a theoretical unit consisting of two or more persons and one or more X's, Festinger's well known theory of cognitive dissonance applies to "cognitive elements." A "cognitive element" is "any knowledge, opinion, or belief about the environment, about oneself, or about one's behavior" (Festinger, 1957, p. 3). The possible relations between elements are defined by Festinger in a general manner:

pairs of elements exist in consonant, irrelevant or dissonant relations. Two elements are *consonant* (cf. "balanced") if, considering the two alone, "one element follows from the other," and *irrelevant* if they have nothing to do with each other, or if they are not connected or associated in the mind of the individual. Two elements are *dissonant* (cf. "unbalanced") if "the obverse of one element would follow from the other" (Festinger, 1957, p. 3). An example of what Festinger would call "post-decision" dissonance would be purchasing a used automobile and then questioning the wisdom of the purchase because of minor defects in the car. In this instance, one "element" (the fact that the auto was purchased) is dissonant with another "element" (perception of the auto's defects). Consonance would exist if the auto had no perceivable defects or objectionable qualities, or, if defective, it were not purchased.

A major assumption in Festinger's theory is that dissonance has motivational characteristics, namely, that dissonance is a *drive state,* like the psychological drives of hunger, thirst, or sex, and that the existence of dissonance will motivate the individual to reduce it, that is, gratify the drive (Brehm and Cohen, 1962, pp. 223–231; Feldman, 1966, passim). Festinger differs from both Heider and Newcomb in this respect; neither theorist postulates that unbalance represents a drive state. Although occasional references to the "drive-like character" of asymmetry may be found in the writings of Newcomb (e.g., Newcomb, 1960, p. 108), the concept of drive is not central to his model. Heider similarly makes no assumptions about drive states, but locates the idea of balance–unbalance in the "stimulus field." The "field" consists of objects in the person's environment and the perceived relations between these objects. The objects and their relations constitute either a "good" *Gestalt* (balance) or a "bad" *Gestalt* (unbalance). The locus of balance–unbalance is thus "external" to the personality—in the stimulus field—and one need not refer to the "internal" or motivational domain when discussing Heider's theory. The balance–unbalance of objects in the external field, on the one hand, and the internal tension aroused by unbalance, on the other, are two attributes that remain conceptually distinct.

The core prediction of Festinger's theory is similar to the central hypothesis of Heider and Newcomb: under conditions of dissonance, the individual will attempt to reduce the dissonance and achieve consonance by changing a cognition in the direction of consonance. Take the example cited above. A person purchases a used auto that has minor defects (chipped paint, rust, etc.). His objection to these shortcomings is dissonant with the fact that he has just purchased the auto; he is therefore motivated to reduce the dissonance. The most typical means of doing so would be to de-emphasize the objectionable qualities of the auto—to convince himself, few example, that the chipped paint does not affect the auto's performance.

An additional and interesting example of dissonance arousal and reduction under "forced compliance" occurred in an experiment by Brehm (1959). In an experimental condition, eighth-grade children were induced to eat a disliked vegetable by the offer of a small reward. They were told that their parents would be informed of which vegetable they had eaten, thus implying that they would be expected to eat more of this vegetable at home. Children under a control condition had to eat a disliked vegetable, but were told nothing. Children in both conditions rated their fondness for the vegetable both before and after the experiment. The children who were led to expect that they would be eating more of the vegetable at home showed a significantly greater increase in their fondness for the vegetable than did the children in the control condition. The investigator thus inferred that the dissonance created by the expectation of eating a disliked vegetable at home was reduced by increasing the fondness rating of the vegetable.

The hypothesis of dissonance reduction can be applied not only to strictly mental processes, as in the above examples, but also to group interaction. The group is often seen as a *source* of dissonance arousal. Aronson and Mills' (1959) experiment on college women is an illustration. In one experimental condition, a "severe initiation" condition, the girls were asked to read embarrassing sexual material aloud before a male experimenter. The girls were told that this initiation was necessary before they could be permitted to join a group discussion on sex. In a contrast condition, a "mild initiation" condition, girls had only to read bland material. In both conditions, the girls were invited afterwards to participate with the group in a very dull, uninteresting discussion. The investigators found that the women in the severe condition rated the discussion as "interesting," whereas the women in the mild condition rated the discussion as relatively dull. The investigators speculated that in the case of the severe initiation condition, the idea of reading highly suggestive material was dissonant with the fact that the actual discussion following was dull and unsuggestive. This led the investigators to infer that the high rating of the group afterwards constituted an attempt at dissonance reduction.

This latter study illustrates one of several alternatives for reducing dissonance: changing one's own attitudes or opinions in the direction of consonance. In a group context, however, at least two additional alternatives are available: (1) The person can seek out others who share his opinions—hence gaining the "social support" of these others; or (2) he can attempt to persuade others who disagree with him to change their views. Both represent alternatives to changing one's own views.

In a classic study of a "doomsday cult" in the early fifties by Festinger and associates (Festinger et al., 1956), these two alternatives were dramatically illustrated. The study involved the observation of a group of people who firmly believed that the world was coming to an end. The investigators were interested in how these people would react when their prophecy failed to be confirmed (as, since we are all still here today, it was not). The intense belief in the inevitability of the end of the world would be dissonant with the cognition that it had not occurred.

On the night of the expected occurrence, most of the believers gathered at a member's home where they awaited a flying saucer that was to rescue them at midnight. Several members, however, were instructed to wait in their own homes. The flying saucer, apparently, was to make various "stops" in much the same manner as a bus or train. Much to the surprise and dismay of the group, midnight came and passed, without the appearance of the flying saucer. Their reactions to this failure were of two general types. The first was the seeking of social support. After a short period of utter disbelief that their prediction had not been validated, they became convinced that the earth had not been destroyed precisely because. of their belief and their faith. The group was able to accept and believe this explanation since they could support one another and convince each other that it was a valid explanation. It is important to note that this "consensual validation" tended to reduce the dissonance created by the failure; almost none of the group members actually *changed* their initial belief, illustrating that social support is an alternative to cognitive change. The importance of such support in reducing dissonance is shown in the contrast provided by members of the cult who were instructed to wait alone in their own homes for the end of the world. These members did not maintain their initial beliefs. Without the continuous support of their fellow cultists, they renounced their belief in the movement despite their heavy commitment to it.

The group's second reaction was to undertake a campaign to recruit new members into the movement. Prior to the disconfirmation of the prophecy, attempts to proselyte were nil. Contact with the nonbelieving public was avoided. But after the disconfirmation, their behavior changed drastically. On four successive days afterward, they called press conferences, gave lengthy interviews, posed for pictures, and generally actively pursued the task of recruiting new followers.

These latter behaviors—seeking social support and proselyting—constitute alternatives to changing one's beliefs or attitudes. It should be pointed out that these alternative means of dissonance reduction, as specified by Festinger, are analogous to predictions derivable from earlier formulations by Heider and Newcomb. The first, seeking "social support," can be more rigorously defined as communicating with liked others who share one's views. Such situations clearly constitute preference for balanced states. The second alternative, proselyting, is analogous to Newcomb's "communicative" alternative for achieving balance: attempting to change the view of the other by offering him information about X (the predicted event), or by evaluating his previous information, or by debating with him.

There are several areas in which Festinger's formulations, by comparison with the Heider-Newcomb formulation, seem deficient. The first concern derives from the high level of abstraction of Festinger's theory. Magnitude of dissonance is a general theoretical construct assumed to exist in the mind of the individual. Consequently, there is no way to directly and objectively measure degree of dissonance. Its existence is inferred or deduced from some measurable, presumably dependent, phenomenon. For example, in the Aronson and Mills experiment on college women, subjects under the "severe" initiation condition rated the discussion as more interesting than those under the "mild" condition. This dependent observation led the investigators to infer the existence of dissonance as a result of reading highly suggestive material before a male experimenter and then listening to a bland, dull discussion afterwards. Dissonance is only inferred (and not measured) in such instances because the dissonance concept is so abstract. By contrast, the Heider-Newcomb concept of balance is less abstract. It refers to specifically delineated variables—attraction and attitude, for example. Balance-unbalance is then defined in terms of these measurable variables. In short, the distance between the "real world" and the Heider-Newcomb concept of balance-unbalance seems less than the distance between the real world and Festinger's concept of consonance-dissonance.

There is a second shortcoming in Festinger's model. Since the term "cognitive element" is so broadly defined, it is difficult to pinpoint the specific types of "elements" to which the theory addresses itself; consequently, one cannot identify elements to which the theory does *not* apply. Does the model pertain to all thoughts, cognitions, perceptions? The nature and quality of the elements is unclear; the *variables* of the theory remain unspecified. What is needed is a taxonomy of variables, a scheme that would allow one to identify the types of elements to which the theory is applicable. In contrast to Festinger, Heider and Newcomb clearly specify the variables in their models. Similar comparisons between Heider, Newcomb and Festinger have been made by Brown (1965, pp. 594–595) and Pepitone (1966, pp. 261–262).

A third weakness in Festinger's theory is evident. The generality and high abstraction of the theory make it difficult to determine whether or not two elements are in fact dissonant, consonant, or irrelevant with respect to each other—if, indeed, one can identify the "elements" in the first place. The *conditions* of dissonance, consonance, or irrelevance are unspecified. The reader of the dissonance literature is found asking himself, "Now in this example (or study), exactly what is dissonant with what?" Specifically, what does Festinger mean by the "obverse" of a given element, such that the "obverse" is "dissonant" with the given element? To date, this sticky problem in Festinger's model has not been adequately resolved (Pepitone, 1966, pp. 265–266), although it is clearly of central importance to the theory. Heider and Newcomb, unlike Festinger, spell out precisely which combinations of variables are hypothesized to be unbalanced (cf. dissonant) and which combinations are hypothesized to be balanced (cf. consonant).

A fourth and often-cited weakness of the Festinger model is that one need not refer to the dissonance principle at all in order to explain the results obtained in a study of dissonance (Chapanis and Chapanis, 1964; Brown, 1965; Pepitone, 1966). There are usually several alternative explanations for the findings obtained. One writer (Jordan, 1963) has maintained that almost any dissonance experiment can be explained without reference to the principle of dissonance. Consider as an example the Aronson-Mills (1959) study, cited earlier. It was found that girls under the "severe initiation" condition—those who had to read aloud lewd sexual passages—rated an ensuing discussion as "interesting." In contrast, those who read only bland, uncharged material rated the discussion as relatively "dull." It was hypothesized that in the case of the former condition, reading suggestive material was "dissonant" with the following dull, unsuggestive discussion, and the subsequent rating of "interesting" represented an attempt at dissonance reduction.

There are at least three other explanations for these findings, neither of which refer to the dissonance principle. (1) The subjects under the "severe" condition might have actually perceived that the discussion was sexual in nature. Even though no one talked of sex in an outright way, the subjects may have felt that they "*really* knew what was going on," that the discussion carried a "double meaning," and that sex was in fact being discussed but in a devious manner. The type of initiation condition could have *sensitized* the subjects to perceive such latent meanings in the discussion. Such perceptions could certainly account for the rating of "interesting." (2) The subjects may have felt greatly relieved, finding that an anticipated vulgar and tasteless discussion was actually quite mild. This feeling of relief could have resulted in the high rating of the discussion. (3) The subjects might have actually enjoyed the *initiation* very much, and expressed their enjoyment of it by the only means made available to them—by rating the *discussion* highly.

The reader should understand that this latter criticism regarding alternative explanations can also be leveled at the Heider and Newcomb models. For example, Heider predicts that conditions of like-agree and dislike-disagree (both are sign-balanced) arouse less tension in the focal person than conditions of like-disagree and dislike-agree (both are sign-unbalanced). Hence, the concept of balance–unbalance is used to account for differences in tension. Basically, balance–unbalance can be seen as the *combination* or *interaction* of liking and agreement. But several researchers, among them Taylor (1968), Rodriques (1967), Price et al. (1966), and Jordan (1953), have found that the variable like-dislike alone accounts for tension differences at least as well as—if not better than—the variable balance–unbalance. Namely, dislike arouses greater tension than liking (and this is certainly not surprising), regardless of whether there is agreement or disagreement. The effects of like-dislike upon tension are independent of the effects of balance–unbalance. Zajonc's (1968) re-analysis of several studies shows that the variable agree-disagree also affects tension independently. These findings, plus additional ones relevant to the question of alternative explanations, are given a complete treatment in later chapters of this book.

Although the alternative explanation weakness is not peculiar to Festinger, a review of the literature does reveal that it is a greater liability in the Festinger model than in the Heider or Newcomb models. The criticism is more often cited in conjunction with Festinger-inspired studies and experiments than in conjunction with studies employing the Heider or Newcomb models. However, this may well be due, at least in part, to the fact that studies employing a dissonance (Festinger) framework tend to outnumber studies employing a balance (Heider) or symmetry (Newcomb) model.

Although these defaults in Festinger's formulations reveal a certain lack of precision, they in no way detract from the potential *utility* of the theory. It is precisely the high degree of abstraction of the theory that permits a wide range of applications. The Heider and Newcomb formulations, because of their narrower scope, are applicable to a narrower range of empirical phenomena. The clearest evidence of this is the greater body of empirical research stimulated by Festinger's formulations, particularly in the area of decision-making and its consequences. It appears that the amount of research clearly following a Heider or Newcomb perspective is somewhat less, by comparison (McGuire, 1966; Brown, 1965; Chapanis and Chapanis, 1964).

2 • 2d   The Osgood-Tannenbaum Model of Attitude Congruity

Both the Heider and Newcomb varieties of balance theory are theories that employ what we shall call an *interpersonal perspective*. This is because the objects contained in the theoretical unit always consist of two or more persons. Another variety of the general theory employs a *cognitive perspective*—the theoretical unit typically (though not necessarily) consist of only one person and two or more non-person objects. The Festinger model utilizes this perspective (the "objects" can be non-person cognitive "elements"), although the Festinger variety *can* apply to groups of persons, as we saw in the previous section. The fourth variety of balance theory to be considered, one that employs a cognitive perspective, is the Osgood-Tannenbaum theory of attitudinal "congruity" (Osgood and Tannenbaum, 1955; Osgood et al., 1957; Osgood, 1960; Tannenbaum, 1967).

The Osgood-Tannenbaum model is similar to Festinger's in that a state of incongruence or unbalance is regarded as a drive state. The model is similar to Heider's and to Newcomb's in its degree of precision. The variables that are congruent or incongruent are identified, and the objects of the theory are specified. The *objects* are: a focal person (P), a source of information, communication, or assertion (designated as S—not necessarily another person), and the subject or "concept" (C) of the assertion. The *variables* are: (a) the focal person's attitude (favorable or unfavorable) toward the source (S) of information—the *source attitude;* (b) the focal person's attitude toward the concept (C), or *concept attitude;* (c) the sign (positive or negative) of the source's *assertion* about the concept. An example of incongruence would be as follows: The person (P)

is in favor of a source of information (S)—such as a newspaper—and the source makes a positive assertion about something (C) that the person disfavors. By substituting Heider's POX for Osgood and Tannenbaum's PSC, respectively, it can be seen that the eight configurations presented earlier in Figure 1 are created. Generally, the Osgood-Tannenbaum theory applies to the attitudes of a single person toward two non-person objects. Hence, their theory is "cognitive" rather than strictly interpersonal.

As do all balance theorists, Osgood and Tannenbaum predict that conditions of incongruence are unstable and are therefore likely to change, whereas conditions of congruence are not. Given incongruence, the person will modify both the source attitude and the concept attitude. An example involving mass media and current events will illustrate this combined change. Assume that your favorite newspaper $(+PS)$ criticizes the President of the United States $(-SC)$ whom you voted for and favor $(+PC)$. This is an incongruent cognitive structure. To reduce this incongruence, the Osgood-Tannenbaum model predicts that both the source attitude (the PS relation) and the concept attitude (the PC relation) will change away from each other. One will change in the negative direction, and one will change in the positive direction; one will become "less positive" (a change in the negative direction), and one will become "more positive" (a change in the positive direction). Hence, (a) a change in the $+PS$ attitude in the positive direction plus a change in the $+PC$ attitude in the negative direction both represent the predicted changes toward congruence, since the assertion (the SC relation) is negative; or (b) a change in $+PS$ toward the negative and a change in $+PC$ toward the positive also represent the predicted changes toward congruence. Note, however, that to make these predictions (a and b), one must assume that the SC assertion does not change.[4]

Like Newcomb, and unlike Heider, Osgood and Tannenbaum consider the strengths of relations. Each relation is expressed as varying on a continuum from $+3$ (strong positive) down through zero to -3 (strong negative). Yet, the Osgood-Tannenbaum model gives differing predictions than the Newcomb (and also the Heider) model. This is best illustrated by a discussion of the various structures diagrammed in Figure 4. This is an important figure, since it clearly illustrates the differing predictions of the Heider, Newcomb and Osgood-Tannenbaum models, as applied to an interpersonal POX unit. In short, it shows some of the inconsistencies among the consistency theorists themselves!

Examine Figure 4A. This condition is sign-unbalanced according to the Heider formulation; it is a like-disagree condition, and the algebraic product of the three signs is negative. It is therefore hypothesized to be unstable, and one or more of the three relations will change in the direction of balance. Newcomb's model also considers this an unstable (asymmetric) condition, due to the obvious discrepancy in the PX and OX relations and the high (i.e., positive) attraction

4. The matter of assuming a constant assertion is discussed in more detail in Chapter 5.

FIGURE 4   A COMPARISON OF THE HEIDER, NEWCOMB, AND
OSGOOD-TANNENBAUM MODELS

A.

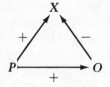

Sign-unbalanced (*unstable*), according to Heider;
asymmetric (*unstable*), according to Newcomb;
incongruent (*unstable*), according to
    Osgood-Tannenbaum.

B.

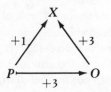

Sign-balanced (*stable*), according to Heider;
asymmetric (*unstable*), according to Newcomb;
incongruent (*unstable*), according to
    Osgood-Tannenbaum.

C.

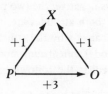

Sign-balanced (*stable*), according to Heider;
symmetric (*stable*), according to Newcomb;
incongruent (*unstable*), according to
    Osgood-Tannenbaum.

D.

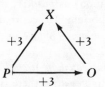

Sign-balanced (*stable*), according to Heider;
symmetric (*stable*), according to Newcomb;
congruent (*stable*), according to
    Osgood-Tannenbaum.

of P to O. If O is treated as analogous to the "source" (S) in the Osgood-Tannenbaum model, and the X-object is treated as analogous to the "concept" (C), then the structure is unstable (incongruent), since the two positive attitude-objects are linked by a negative assertion (the OX relation). Clearly, all three models agree that the structure exemplified in Figure 4A is unstable, likely to change, and characterized by high tension.

Now proceed to Figure 4B, where the strengths of relations are given. Here, Heider would consider it sign-balanced and stable (it is a like-agree condition, and the product of the signs is positive), but Newcomb and Osgood-Tannenbaum would consider it unstable. Heider's model predicts "no change" here, whereas the Newcomb and Osgood-Tannenbaum models predict change in one or more of the three relations. The Newcomb model considers the structure to be unstable, due to the *discrepancy* in the strengths of the two positive PX and OX relations coupled with high attraction of P to O (+3 PO). It is unstable according to the Osgood-Tannenbaum formulation, since, although the OX relation is positive, there is still a discrepancy in the PX and PO relations.

Let us next examine Figure 4C. It is sign-balanced (stable) according to Heider, and stable according to Newcomb, since there is *no discrepancy* in the PX and OX relations. According to Newcomb, no discrepancy coupled with high attraction (the +3 PO relation) is completely stable. But the structure is *still* unstable according to the Osgood-Tannenbaum model. Why?

To answer this question, two points must be made. (1) The X-object is to be treated as analogous to the concept (C) in the Osgood-Tannenbaum model, and the O-object is to be regarded as analogous to the source (S). (2) The Osgood model posits a principle of *maximal simplicity* in the structure of attitudes: if the source attitude and concept attitude are both positive *but of differing strengths,* then if the assertion is positive (regardless of its strength), they will tend to "regress" toward each other. (If the assertion is negative, the two positive attitudes will change away from each other.) Only if both attitudes are initially equal in strength is "maximal simplicity" attained. That is why the structure in Figure 4C would be considered unstable by the Osgood-Tannenbaum model.

Generally, the Osgood-Tannenbaum model predicts the following:

1. If the two attitudes (the PX and PO relations) *are of the same strengths and signs,* and if the assertion (the OX relation) is *positive,* then the structure is maximally congruent, stable, and in equilibrium. Hence, if the OX relation is positive and *both* the PX and PO relations are +3, +2 or +1, or even −1, or −2, or −3, then the structure is stable.

2. If the two attitudes *are of opposite sign but equal in strength* (e.g., +3 and −3, or +2 and −2, etc.), and the assertion is *negative,* there is still a state of maximum stability or equilibrium (congruence).

3. Note that both conditions 1 and 2 require the two attitudes to be of equal strength—this is the principle of maximal simplicity. No other conditions (conditions not cited in "1" and "2" above) are maximally congruent. Any other condition will be unstable, and the *degree of instability* will depend upon the magnitude of difference in the strengths of the two attitudes. Since the structure in Figure 4C contains PX and PO relations of unequal strengths—even though the signs are the same and the OX relation is positive—it is hypothesized to be unstable.

We arrive now at Figure 4D. Osgood and Tannenbaum would now say that the criterion of maximal simplicity has been satisfied. The structure fits condition 1 above, and is therefore stable. Clearly, both Heider and Newcomb would agree, since it is sign-balanced (Heider), and there is no PX/OX discrepancy coupled with high attraction (Newcomb).

It should be pointed out that while Newcomb's model is quite explicit in allowing the perceived OX relation to vary in strength and sign, the vast majority of studies conducted under the Osgood-Tannenbaum model express the SC assertion (the analog of the OX relation) only in terms of sign. Only the source and concept attitudes are expressed in terms of strength and sign. Thus, the comparisons drawn in Figure 4B through D, which express the perceived OX relation in terms of strength and sign, represent an extension of the Osgood-Tannenbaum model for purposes of comparing it to the Heider and Newcomb models. *Osgood and Tannenbaum's omission of the strength of the assertion is, in fact, a weakness in their model.*

There are still further differences between the Osgood-Tannenbaum and Heider or Newcomb models. The Osgood-Tannenbaum model provides two *corollaries* to the general theory. The first corollary is called the "correction for incredulity." Assume that your favorite newspaper $(+PS)$ makes a negative assertion or statement $(-SC)$ about the President of the United States, whom you like $(+PC)$—a condition that, fortunately, is considered unstable by all three models. But let's say that you did not believe that the newspaper made the negative statement, that you were incredulous about the SC assertion. Under conditions of incredulity, the predicted changes in the PC and PS attitudes are less likely to occur. Thus, only under the condition that P believes the assertion are the predicted changes expected to take place.

A second corollary of the theory, the "polarity corollary," states that both the *likelihood and magnitude* of change in a relation is a function of its strength or *polarity*, such that weak relations are more likely to change than strong relations, and the degree or magnitude of change in a weak relation will be greater than the degree or magnitude of change in a strong one. Take the following incongruent structure as an example: $+1$ PX, $+3$ PO, and $+OX$ (expressed in sign only). Assuming that the OX relation stays the same (which is not always the case), then the weaker PX relation is more likely to change than the relatively stronger PO relation. Furthermore, if in fact both relations do change, the degree of shift or change in the weaker PX relation is expected to be greater than the degree of shift in the relatively stronger PO relation. From this polarity corollary, Osgood has suggested a mathematical formula for predicting magnitude of change in a relation. The formula has been heavily criticized and modified, however, and a complete treatment of the polarity corollary will have to await thorough discussion in Chapter 5. The polarity corollary (and formula) is considered a major component of the Osgood-Tannenbaum model, and we will have to dismiss it for the moment in order to do it justice later.[5]

5. A third corollary involves an "assertion constant" principle, which states that the concept attitude is more likely to change than the source attitude, since a greater "constant pressure" or "constant force" acts on the concept rather than on the source. The assertion constant and research relevant to it are discussed in Chapter 5.

2 • 2e   *The Rosenberg-Abelson Modifications*

Additional modifications or corollaries to the general theory are provided in Rosenberg and Abelson's formulation on attitude organization (Rosenberg and Abelson, 1960; cf. Abelson and Rosenberg, 1958). Putting aside the matter of strengths of relations, and considering signs only, take the interpersonal *POX* structure where *P* likes *O* (+*PO*) and disfavors *X* (−*PX*), and the other favors *X* (+*OX*). Under this unbalanced (and asymmetric and incongruent) condition, several *molar processes* or changes are expected to take place. In contrast to Heider and Newcomb, who are unclear on this matter, Rosenberg and Abelson point out that there are three distinct changes possible, representing changes in one, two, or three variables simultaneously:

1. *One-variable changes.* The focal person can change his attitude toward *X* in the positive direction; or he can decrease his liking for the other; or he can perceive the other as disfavoring *X*, despite communication from the other to the contrary. Each of these changes taken separately represents a change in the direction of balance. The first of these is diagrammed in Figure 5A.

2. *Two-variable changes.* It is possible that two *simultaneous* changes can restore balance. For example, the focal person can decrease his liking for the other and *intensify* his negative attitude toward *X*. These changes are represented in Figure 5B. The circle around the negative sign indicates a change in the same direction of the original attitude, i.e., the attitude retains its negative sign but increases in intensity.

3. *Three-variable changes.* Under the assumption that variables will change in the direction opposite their initial sign, it is still possible for all three variables to change simultaneously toward balance. Figure 5C illustrates these changes. The focal person simultaneously becomes favorable toward *X,* decreases his liking for the other, and perceives the other as disfavoring *X*.

Given these three molar alternatives, one must now ask: Which is most likely to occur? In attempting to answer this question, Rosenberg and Abelson introduce a principle of *least cost*. Balance will be restored through the path requiring least effort—the fewest number of sign changes possible. The idea of least cost is derived from Hilgard's (1948) principle of "least action" or "least effort," which states that people tend to achieve goals through a minimum expenditure of energy. Generally, "the order of preference for paths toward restoring an unbalanced structure to balance will correspond to an ordering of the paths according to the number of sign changes required, from the least to the most" (Rosenberg and Abelson, 1960, p. 128). Hence, using the examples illustrated in Figure 5, the most likely change would be that involving only one variable change (Figure 5A).

An additional contribution of Rosenberg and Abelson has been to differentiate between the above molar processes, on one hand, and certain *micro-*

FIGURE 5 EXAMPLES OF ALTERNATIVE MOLAR CHANGES TOWARD BALANCE

A. *A One-Variable Change toward Balance*

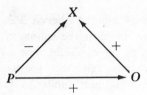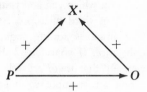

B. *A Simultaneous Two-Variable Change toward Balance*

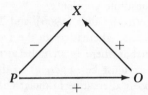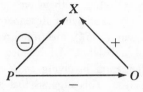

C. *A Simultaneous Three-Variable Change toward Balance*

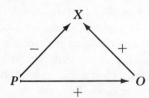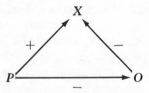

processes, on the other. Whereas molar processes refer to changes in either the sign or intensity of a variable, microprocesses refer to cognitive changes that do not directly involve manipulations of sign or intensity. Microprocesses are not necessarily substitutes for molar changes, but can occur prior to them. An example of one microprocess is *denial.* Under the condition that a liked other makes a positive statement about something which the focal person disfavors, the focal person may convince himself that the other "did not really mean what he said." If a friend of yours speaks out in favor of a political candidate whom you disfavor, you are likely to entertain the possibility that your friend was "joking" with you or "testing" you, particularly if you were of the prior opinion that he had strong feelings against the candidate.

A second microprocess—*differentiation* or *segregation*—can also take place. Differentiation occurs when the person dissociates or segregates a single cognition into two or more parts. In the instance where your friend speaks favorably about the candidate, you might say that "my friend does have a number of peculiar enthusiasms; this accounts for his favoring the candidate." Or you might tell yourself that he favors certain aspects of the candidate and not others; or convince yourself that there are other, perhaps more important, issues on which you and your friend agree.

A third microprocess identified by Rosenberg and Abelson is *bolstering*. This involves adding cognitions that tend to minimize the tension created by unbalance. If your friend disagreed with you on the candidate, then convincing yourself that there are other friends of yours who agree with you would constitute an example of bolstering. This process is quite similar to Festinger's "seeking social support" as a means of reducing dissonance. It is also similar to the Heider-Newcomb principle that people tend to seek out and interact with others whose combination with symbolic objects forms balanced states, and to avoid others with whom interaction would constitute unbalance.

Following Rosenberg and Abelson, both McGuire (1966) and Tannenbaum (1967) identify three more "microprocess" alternatives to the resolution of unbalance. All balance theorists agree that if there is an unbalanced configuration involving an X-object, the X-object must be *important* to the focal person. This suggests that a fourth microprocess alternative to molar changes is *decreasing the importance* of the X-object. Finding that you and your friend disagree on the political candidate, you might elect to decrease the importance of the whole matter rather than change your liking for your friend, your attitude toward the candidate, or your perception of your friend's attitude.

A fifth alternative would be for the focal person to change his perception of the nature of the X-object as opposed to changing his attitude (or his perception of the other's attitude) toward it. Let us say that you disfavor the political candidate simply because you dislike all politicians in general. But after communicating with your friend (who favors the candidate), you are convinced that the candidate is not, in fact, a run-of-the-mill politician. You assign a different *cognitive status* to the X-object. As a result, you may change your attitude toward him in the favorable direction, but only after you are convinced that he is "not a politician after all." In this instance, a microprocess (changing the cognitive status of the object) occurs *prior* to a molar (attitudinal) change.

A sixth and "last resort" alternative is to "grin and bear" the unbalance. You might simply think, *"C'est la vie,"* "That's the way the cookie crumbles," "That's the way it is." Interestingly, this may be the most common empirical alternative to the resolution of unbalances in everyday life, although there is surprisingly no precise research evidence to this effect. It is peculiar that the balance theorists themselves ignore this alternative. Scientists are well known for simply regarding inconsistencies (cf. "unbalances") between and within experiments or between and within theories as a fact of life. Undeniably, a certain amount of inconsistency in any scientific theory can even be regarded as desirable. It keeps things interesting; it enables books like this one to be written. Apparently the "consistency" theorists themselves rather like inconsistencies (see

Figure 4)! Or, perhaps the consistency theorists do not intend their theories to apply to themselves.

For many black Americans, subjected to the gross and nearly unmanageable inconsistencies, contradictions and unbalances of ghetto life ("You tell us there is 'opportunity' for all to attain wealth—you tell us of the 'Constitution' and the 'Bill of Rights'—yet the social structure denies us the educational and occupational means to attain wealth."), the *c'est la vie* alternative is frequently the only one available.

2 • 3   THE TENSION CONCEPT

Integral to any discussion of the balance process is the concept of tension. The balance theorists, particularly Heider and Newcomb, treat psychological tension in one form or another as the variable that intervenes between unbalance, on one hand, and change toward balance, on the other. The role of tension as an intervening variable or "mechanism" was discussed earlier in connection with Figure 2. The expected changes toward balance will not take place, however, unless the following condition holds: the focal person must perceive or be aware of unbalance in order to undergo high tension. An example will clarify this point. Assume that the focal person likes the other and favors X, and the other actually disfavors X. The dyad is therefore *objectively* unbalanced. If, however, the focal person perceives the other as favoring X, then the dyad is *subjectively* balanced. This condition, corresponding to Newcomb's "autistic" balance, is illustrated in Figure 6. Here, the focal person's perception of the other person's attitude is inaccurate. Under similar conditions of objective unbalance but subjective balance, the focal person is not expected to undergo high tension and hence will not take steps to restore balance. Note that if the other correctly informs the focal person of his attitude, then the configuration is both subjectively and objectively unbalanced, and the predicted changes toward balance will occur. Through communication with the other, the focal person discovers the other's attitude toward X. In this respect, *communication allows the tension mechanism to operate in the balance process.*

Tension has been defined in various ways by the balance theorists. Newcomb (1960, p. 108) predicts that changes in attitude or attraction tend to remove the "stress" created by unbalance, and that "psychological strain" is associated with unbalance. Heider (1958, p. 201) uses the term "stress" in the same context, treating balance as a state where there is no "stress toward change." Perhaps one of the more useful conceptualizations of the intervening variable involves the notion of *pressure* toward change. Cartwright and Harary (1956, p. 105), in evaluating the theoretical position of Heider, predict that, given a condition of perceived unbalance, "pressures will arise to change [some variable] toward a state of balance." Festinger (1957), passim) uses the term

FIGURE 6   OBJECTIVE UNBALANCE BUT SUBJECTIVE BALANCE

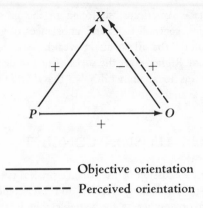

——————— Objective orientation

— — — — — Perceived orientation

"pressure" in a similar manner, and frequent references to pressure are made by Osgood and associates (Osgood, 1960).

An additional conceptualization of the intervening variable involves the notion of discomfort. Newcomb (1961), Zajonc (1960) and Davis (1963) predict that "psychological discomfort" is present under conditions of perceived unbalance. Hence, tension may be defined as the degree of discomfort experienced by the individual. This definition seems preferable to the former one, where tension is defined as a pressure toward change. Although it may be helpful to think of tension as a pressure toward change, to define tension in this way would actually constitute a proposition or hypothesis, not a definition. *Defining tension as a pressure toward change implies that changing an orientation or relation is the only means available to the person for reducing unbalance.* As previously indicated, changes in orientations ("variables") are not the only means for achieving balance.

Balance theory can be seen as a theory of tension management. The general model predicts that since unbalance produces high tension in the focal person, tension can be reduced by a change in the direction of balance. This tension-reduction is the final stage in the balance process illustrated in Figure 2. It does not follow, however, that a balance-maintaining change will bring about a decrease in tension *if the cause of high tension is something other than unbalance.* Thus, balance theory may be seen as a *specific* theory of tension management: tension is reduced by a change toward balance under the condition that unbalance has been the cause of high tension. Other theories of tension management can be regarded as more *general* ones—theories that posit certain processes that bring about a tension decrease, regardless of the original cause of high tension. In personality theory, Freud's mechanisms of ego defense may be seen not only as ways in which people maintain personality stability, but also as mechanisms of tension management. Repression is an example. A person will repress some unpleasant experience rather than undergo tension aroused by that experience. Freud's theory or ego defense is general since it predicts that any experience—if tension-arousing—is dealt with through a mechanism of defense such as repression.

Other general theories of tension management pertain to tension reduction in groups. Parsons' "external" defense mechanisms, such as dependency, can be seen as means for reducing tension aroused in interpersonal situations. For example, a person who is insecure in his social relations with others might become excessively dependent upon another, thereby reducing the tension aroused by the insecurity.[6] The Bales "phase hypothesis" (Bales, 1953; Bales and Stodtbeck, 1951; Psathas, 1960) focuses upon activity as a means of reducing tension during group interaction. Typically, members of discussion or "task-oriented" groups begin by orienting themselves toward the topic, defining the topic, and evaluating one another's comments. During these earlier phases of the discussion, however, certain latent or "expressive" issues remain undiscussed. These include such things as the participants' feelings, anxieties, hostilities. Since these issues are undiscussed during the initial phases, a pressure toward expressive activity tends to build up; expressive activity is emotionally gratifying for the group members. Hence, during the latter phases, the group moves into expressive activity as a means of reducing the psychological tensions aroused by the earlier task-oriented discussion.

It is undoubtedly clear to the reader by now that an assumption underlying all varieties of balance theory is that people will always want to reduce tension. It is posited that if high tension is produced by unbalance, then changes toward balance will occur and reduce the tension, *since* low tension is more desirable than high tension. But what if a high or moderate state of tension is desirable? It then seems reasonable to speculate about a preference for *un*balance rather than balance as a means of maintaining a high-tension state. Although such conditions are given more complete treatment in the fifth and eighth chapters, one tongue-in-cheek example can be cited here. As any red-blooded boy knows, a mother will typically prefer a certain amount of tension in a situation involving her son (let's call the son P), herself (O), and a girl (X) whom the son brings home for the mother to meet. The high tension "keeps things interesting." Clearly, the mother-son relation is typically positive ($+PO$), as is the boy-girl relation ($+PX$). But just as naturally, the mother suspects the girl of deceiving and stealing her nice boy. She says: "You're going to get her pregnant and you're still in college!" Hence the OX relation is negative ($-OX$), representing unbalance and obviously high tension. After suf-

6. See Parsons and Shils (1951, p. 255) for a listing of "external" or interpersonal defense mechanisms. Freud's mechanisms of ego defense are referred to by Parsons as "internal," or personality, mechanisms.

ficient criticism from the mother, the son finally decides not to date the girl anymore, thus changing the $+PX$ relation to $-PX$ and balancing the structure. (Note that he is certainly less likely to change the mother-son relation to negative.) But to keep things interesting, the mother says something like, "What's the matter with you—can't you make up your mind?" This represents a change toward $+OX$. The mother (O) does not appear to dislike the girl after all, again putting the system into unbalance and high tension. Now the son thinks that the mother liked the girl all along, so it is all right to date her and bring her home—a change back to $+PX$ and balance. But then the mother's suspicions are renewed; she is now thoroughly convinced that the girl is out to corrupt her son. She says, "I thought you decided not to date that girl anymore," a change toward $-OX$, and we are right back where we started: an unbalanced high-tension structure containing the relations $+PX$, $+PO$ and $-OX$. Maybe that's just the way mothers are.[7]

2 • 4 BALANCE THEORY AND SYSTEM THEORY

The general concept of system was discussed in Chapter 1. Theories embodying this concept can be divided into two broad classes: sociological or social-psychological theories that employ the system concept, on one hand, and "other" theories employing the concept, on the other (theories of physical, biological, mechanical or astronomical systems, as examples). Theories of sociological or social-psychological systems may be further subdivided. Included would be the traditional "mechanistic" models of Pareto, the "organic" theories of Spencer and Ward, and the "ecological process" models of Small, Park and Burgess.[8] The Parsonian variety of system theory, employing the concepts of homeostasis and system self-maintenance, would constitute another subdivision or variety of general system theory (Parsons and Shils, 1951; Parsons, 1951; Parsons et al., 1953). The Bales "phase hypothesis," discussed in Chapter 1 and cited immediately above, which treats the instrumental and expressive dimensions of interaction as interdependent and subject to homeostatic regulation through the operation of a tension mechanism, would also be included. Clearest of all system models is Homans', which hypothesizes a mutual interdependence among four dimensions of group life: activity, interaction, sentiment, and norms (Homans, 1950).

Balance theory constitutes one of these subtypes of social-psychological system theory. The theory is "sociological" in that it deals with units consisting typically of two or more persons, their orientations toward each other, their orientations toward symbolic objects, and—especially for Newcomb—their com-

---

7. This example was borrowed, with much paraphrasing, from Mazur (1967).
8. For an excellent and recent review and critique of system theory and its sociological varieties, see Buckley (1967).

munication. The theory is "psychological" inasmuch as balance–unbalance must be perceived by the individual in order for the "balance process" to take place, and inasmuch as the balance-maintaining mechanism is intrapersonal rather than interpersonal, in the form of tension, stress, strain, discomfort, or drive. The different *varieties* of balance theory treated in this chapter represent different (but clearly related) subclasses of the class, balance theory. These varieties belong to the same class since they all treat their respective units of analysis as systems tending toward stable equilibrium.

The similarities between system theory and balance theory can be clearly seen if they are listed *seriatim*. First, proponents of system theory hold that the unit of analysis is greater than the sum of the parts of that unit; the unit is "nonadditive" since the parts are related to each other in some way. Balance theory (particularly the Heider and Newcomb varieties) specify two kinds of "parts": persons (at least one focal person and at least one other) and non-person objects ("X's"). These parts are related through interpersonal or sentiment orientations, such as liking, and unit orientations, such as attitudes. These orientations or relations constitute *properties* or *variables* of persons. Balance–unbalance, as a variable, is a *property of the system unit* rather than of the persons. Second, general system theory proposes mutual interdependence between variables: variation in one variable produces variation in another, which in turn results in variation in the former. Balance theory clearly embodies this idea. Unbalance among the variables liking and attitude produces high tension, which leads to changes in the same variables toward balance with a subsequent reduction in tension. This hypothesis illustrates the third similarity between system theory and balance theory. The variables are related in stable or homeostatic equilibrium, where a "disturbance" (a cause of unbalance) results in a tendency for the variables to return to their "initial," or pre-disturbance, value (a return to balance). Finally, both system theory and balance theory employ the notion of a mechanism or intervening variable which tends to maintain a state of stable equilibrium. For Festinger and Osgood-Tannenbaum, this mechanism is the "drive" exerted on the individual by a state of dissonance or incongruity. For Heider and Newcomb, the mechanism is the degree of tension experienced by the focal person.

In many social-psychological and sociological theories, the question of stability versus change is often regarded as a perplexing one. It need not be. Visualize the following structure: $+PO$, $+PX$, $+OX$. This is a stable structure. Now assume that O tells P that he is against X, a *change* to $-OX$. This unbalances the structure; it is unstable; it is likely to change, according to the theory. Assume further that P balances the structure by changing his attitude toward X to $-PX$, thus giving a total structure of: $+PO$, $-PX$, $-OX$. We would now say that the structure has changed "back" to balance—a change to a "prior" state that by definition represents stable equilibrium or homeostasis. But why cannot one argue that the structure is now in a *different* state, i.e., that it has changed into something other than what it was initially? After all, the PX and OX relations are now negative, whereas they were initially positive. This would mean that the example just given does not involve homeostasis at all (a change "back" to a prior state), but a change to a "new" state altogether. If this is the case, you ask, then balance theory is not a homeostatic or "stability" theory at all, but a theory of change. Why the contradiction?

The answer is quite simple; there is no contradiction. Putting it broadly, the structure has changed in some respects (both the PX and OX relations changed from positive to negative) but not in others (it went from balance to unbalance back to balance). In order to put it more precisely, one must consider the *levels of abstraction* involved in the theory. Let us now define the use of different levels of abstraction in balance theory.

If concept A is defined by reference to concepts B and C, then we say that concept A is on a "higher level of abstraction" than concepts B and C. Example: "social class" (concept A) can be defined on the basis of occupational rank (concept B) and amount of education (concept C). The concept of "social class" is defined by less abstract or *lower-order* concepts such as occupation and education. The concepts of occupation and education are more directly measurable than the concept of class; they are closer to "reality." The concept of "personality" is an abstraction of a very high order; many needs, predispositions, drives, attitudes, etc., all combine to form what we call "personality." The concept of "culture," similarly, is a very high-order abstraction, defined by lower-order concepts such as norms, technology, and the like, which are themselves then definable in terms of still lower-order concepts. The biologist's taxonomy of "kingdoms" (plant versus animal) all the way down through phyla, classes, etc., to "genus" and "species," represents the clearest possible example of levels of abstraction. Any given concept is defined by those below it, by its subcategories.

Levels of abstraction can be illustrated with Heider's model. The concept of "like-dislike," involving the relation between P and O, is at the lowest level of abstraction. Clearly it is not a highly abstract notion, but it is sufficiently close to "reality"—we all have at least some idea of what Heider means by "like-dislike." Let us call this a *first-order abstraction*. Similarly, the PX relation (P's attitude toward X—favorable or unfavorable) is to be regarded as a first-order abstraction, as is the OX relation.

The concept agree-disagree, however, is at a higher level of abstraction; it is a *second-order abstraction*, since the concept "agreement" is defined on the basis of the signs of the PX and OX relations combined. P and O "agree" if the signs are similar, and "disagree" if the signs are dissimilar. Since agreement is defined in this way, by reference to two first-order abstractions, the concept of agreement becomes a second-order abstraction.

The concept of balance–unbalance is now plainly seen as a *third-order abstraction*. It can be defined on the basis of two lower-order concepts, the concept of liking and the concept of agreement. We saw earlier that conditions of like-agree and dislike-disagree were defined as balanced by Heider, and conditions of like-disagree and dislike-agree were defined as unbalanced. Balance–unbalance is defined through reference to one first-order abstraction (liking) and one second-order abstraction (agreement). (But note that balance–unbalance could also be defined on the basis of the *PO*, *PX* and *OX* relations taken separately—by the product of the signs of these relations. Since these three relations are all first-order abstractions, if defined in this way, then balance–unbalance would be a second-order abstraction rather than a third-order abstraction.)

Three levels of abstraction are diagrammed in Figure 7. What does this tell us about the question of stability versus change? Just this: *one can account for stability at one level of abstraction by describing the changes that occur at lower levels of abstraction.* Taking the above example, a change in a structure from +*PO*, +*PX*, +*OX* to +*PO*, −*PX*, −*OX* certainly represents a change in signs of the *PX* and *OX* relations (a change at the first level of abstraction), but *no change* at the second level—both situations represent "agreement." Furthermore, stability is located at the third level, in regard to the balance concept. Since the changes are toward balance, one can say that the structure changed "back to" balance. Should there be a progression from like-agree (balance) to like-disagree (unbalance) to dislike-disagree (balance), then changes have

FIGURE 7   LEVELS OF ABSTRACTION IN HEIDER'S THEORY

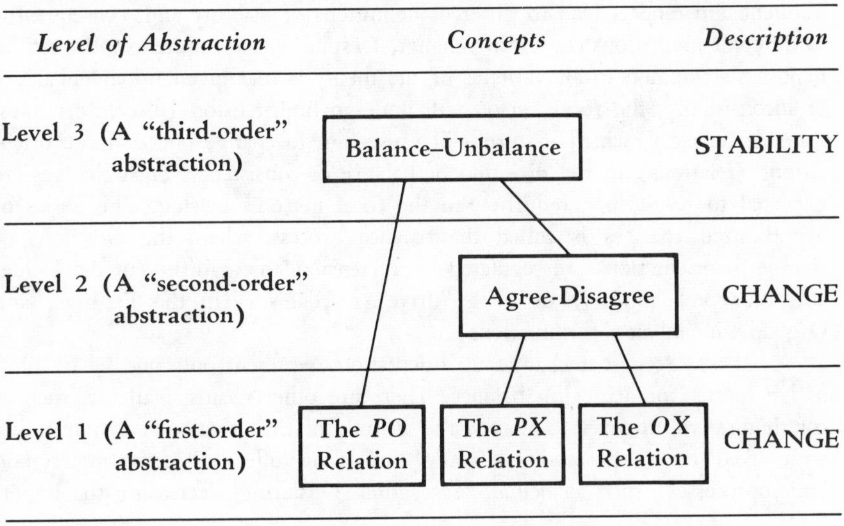

Level of Abstraction	Concepts	Description
Level 3 (A "third-order" abstraction)	Balance–Unbalance	STABILITY
Level 2 (A "second-order" abstraction)	Agree-Disagree	CHANGE
Level 1 (A "first-order" abstraction)	The *PO* Relation The *PX* Relation The *OX* Relation	CHANGE

occurred at *both* levels 1 and 2, but not at level 3. We have described changes at levels 1 and 2 in order to account for stability at level 3. If the progression is seen in this way, one need not become bogged down with such seeeming paradoxes as "The kind of system we are talking about changes, yet it does not change."

The question whether systems change to a "new" state (suggesting that some theory of change is preferred over a homeostatic or stable equilibrium theory), or whether they "return" to some prior state (suggesting the applicability of a homeostatic theory) can in many instances be resolved if the matter of levels of abstraction is taken into account. Changes at one level may simply reflect stabilities at another. Hence, to discuss balance theory by reference to both stability and change is not paradoxical or contradictory. Perhaps many such "perplexing" questions in sociological and psychological "grand theory" could be resolved if only the levels of abstraction involved were clearly delineated.[9]

2 • 5   SUMMARY

This chapter was devoted to a review of the theoretical literature on balance. After a discursive treatment of consistency or balance in everyday life, the principal varieties of the theory were outlined and contrasted, showing both their similarities and their differences: Heider's model of balance, Newcomb's theory of systems of orientation, Festinger's formulation on cognitive dissonance, the Osgood-Tannenbaum model of attitude congruity, and the modifications of Rosenberg and Abelson. It was shown that the Heider, Newcomb and Osgood-Tannenbaum models lead to different definitions of stability and, consequently, to different predictions concerning change. Despite certain differences, the central hypothesis common to all varieties of the theory is that given initial unbalance or inconsistency, the focal person will undergo high tension (discomfort, pressure, drive, etc.), which in turn will cause him to change one or more orientations (relations) in the direction of balance or consistency. Such changes are expected to result in a reduction in the focal person's tension. This series of hypothesized changes is called the balance process, where the directions of change in orientations are regulated by a "tension" mechanism (in the Heider and Newcomb models) or by a "drive" mechanism (in the Festinger and Osgood-Tannenbaum formulations).

It was seen that changes in orientations represent only one set of alternative means for achieving balance. There are other means available, such as communicative attempts to change the attitude of the other, or communicating with liked others possessing already similar attitudes, or activating certain "microprocesses" such as denial, segregation, bolstering, decreasing the impor-

9. The author is indebted to Charlotte Vaughan and Richard Houck for their suggestions regarding levels of abstraction in balance theory.

tance of the X-object, changing the "cognitive status" of an object, or simply bearing the unbalance. It was pointed out that such microprocesses can represent alternatives to changes in orientations, but they can also occur *prior* to changes in orientation.

Finally, the role of tension in the balance process was discussed, and it was noted that (a) the focal person must perceive unbalance (there must be subjective unbalance) in order for the tension mechanism to operate, and (b) changes in orientations or relations toward balance are expected to result in tension reduction only under the condition that unbalance was the cause of high tension. If the cause of high tension is something other than unbalance, then one or more changes toward balance are not expected to reduce tension. It was stated that balance theory presumes that people generally seek tension reduction, a condition that does not always hold true. Balance theory was contrasted with system theory, showing that balance theory is a sub-type of general homeostatic system theory, and the question of "stability" versus "change" was analyzed in terms of the levels of abstraction in Heider's model.

The foregoing chapter represents a treatment of the *substantive* models of balance. The following chapter presents, discusses and evaluates *formal* models. The task of that chapter will be to add precision and refinement to the original substantive formulations of the balance theorists. It will not be until Chapter 4 that we begin a complete examination of *research evidence* pertaining to the theory of balance.

3...

Formal Models of Balance

In Chapter 2, the principal substantive varieties of balance theory were reviewed and contrasted. This chapter focuses upon recent formal, or mathematical, treatments of the theory of balance. The purpose of formalization is to extend, clarify, refine, and redirect the original substantive theory. It is the purpose of this chapter to present these formal models in clear fashion, and to evaluate critically their overall contribution. The discussion in this chapter is to be regarded as introductory. In Chapter 6, a more complete discussion involving empirical issues is found.

3 • 1 GRAPH THEORY AND BALANCE THEORY

3 • 1a *Basic Concepts: Point, Line, Graph, and Cycle*

Heider's theory can be represented in part by diagramming his POX unit as a series of objects connected by lines having a positive or negative value. This suggests an intimate connection between Heider's model and the theory of graphs discovered by Euler in 1736 and developed by the German mathematician Koenig (1936). The connection was first made by Cartwright and Harary (1956), who translated the basic concepts of Heider's theory into those of graph theory.

Graph theory deals with a collection of points, *A, B, C*, etc., with *lines* connecting pairs of points. A set of two or more points, plus the lines connecting them, is called a *graph*. Either all, some or none of the points may be connected. Figure 1 illustrates the principal kinds of graphs. Figure 1A represents a *simple graph,* where certain pairs of points are connected by one line. Each line is taken as "symmetric," where the line *AB* is equivalent to the line *BA*, and no distinction is made with respect to direction. Figure 1B illustrates a *signed graph,* where each line receives a positive (+) or negative (−) value. The absence of a line (for example, no line appears between *A* and *C*) signifies

51

FIGURE 1   KINDS OF GRAPHS

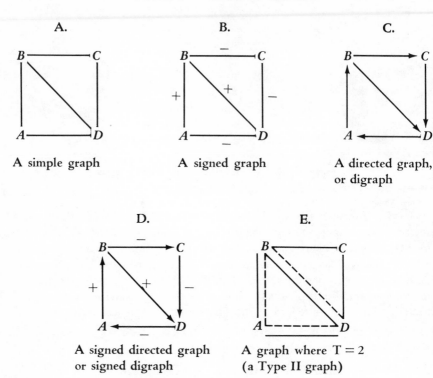

A.

A simple graph

B.

A signed graph

C.

A directed graph,
or digraph

D.

A signed directed graph
or signed digraph

E.

A graph where T = 2
(a Type II graph)

the absence of a relation between points. Figure 1C illustrates a *directed graph* or *digraph,* where the lines are asymmetric and indicate the direction of relation. Hence, the line going from A to B would be distinguished from a line going from B to A. In Figure 1D, representing a *signed digraph,* each directed line receives a positive or negative sign. Each line could, for example, represent the liking or disliking of one person for another. The AB line in Figure 1D connotes that person A likes person B, but the absence of a BA line might suggest "indifference" of B to A.

In Figure 1A through D, only a single type or class of line appears between two points. T, the number of types of lines, has a value of one. Such graphs are called "Type I" graphs. Now suppose that one wishes to consider two types of relations—for example, liking and attitude. In this instance, two types of lines will appear between points (Figure 1E), and $T = 2$ (a "Type II" graph). The graph drawn in Figure 1E connotes that one is *simultaneously considering two types* of relations between the pairs AB, BD and AD, but only one type of relation between the pairs *BC* and *CD*. It is important that the reader distinguish between the number of *types* of relation (the value of *T*) and the *sign* a particular relation may have. It is clear that one may have various combinations yielding very complex graphs, thus obtaining signed digraphs where $T = 2$, or graphs where $T = 3, 4, 5$ and so on.

The reader has at this stage no doubt noted the close correspondence between Heider's concepts of entity, relation and system, and the graph concepts of point, line and graph, respectively. These similarities are detailed in Table 1. In addition, Newcomb's concepts of object, orientation and system are presented. These concepts are juxtaposed with the concepts of object, variable and theoretical unit used previously in this text.

The first row of Table 1 shows the correspondence between Heider's "entity," Newcomb's "object" and the graph theory concept of point. Heider and Newcomb distinguish two classes of objects, person and non-person, whereas graph theory makes no such distinction. The notion of "variable" as used in this book corresponds to the concepts of relation (Heider), orientation (Newcomb) and line (graph theory). The differentiation of the positive, negative or neutral sign of a variable corresponds to Heider's "character" of a relation, Newcomb's "sign" or "quality" or orientation, and graph theory's concept of the sign of a line, where the absence of a line signifies no orientation or relation, or a variable of zero value. Treating relations between persons as one class of variable (sentiment, liking, attraction) and relations between persons and non-person objects as another class (unit relations, attitudes), it is seen that graph theory makes this distinction by assigning numerical values to

TABLE 1   A COMPARISON OF CONCEPTS OF HEIDER AND NEWCOMB TO CONCEPTS OF GRAPH THEORY

THIS BOOK	HEIDER	NEWCOMB	GRAPH THEORY
Object (person versus non-person)	Entity (person versus non-person)	Object (person versus non-person)	Point (no distinction is made between classes of points)
Variable	Relation	Orientation	Line
Sign of variable	Character of relation	Sign or quality of orientation	Sign of line
Type or class of variable	Type of relation (sentiment, unit relation)	Type of orientation (attraction, attitude)	Value of *T*
Theoretical unit	System	System	Graph

T, the number of types of lines in a graph. The theoretical unit for balance theory, a system consisting of objects and their relations, is analogous—but not identical—to the concept of graph. (The concept "graph" corresponds to the concept of "theoretical unit," "structure," or "configuration," but it does not correspond to the concept "system." Since graph theory presents no hypotheses about the interdependence between lines, a graph does not suggest a "system," but only an abstract unit consisting of points and lines. Whether or not the lines are "interdependent" (and form a system) is irrelevant. The postulate of interdependence is provided by the substantive theory, not the formal theory.)

Integral to graph theory, and by implication to balance theory, is the concept of *cycle*. Referring to Figure 1D, let each point represent a person and each line represent a liking or disliking. Clearly, there are several ways to analyze this graph. (a) One may consider only dyads, or pairs of persons plus the relations between them; (b) one may consider triadic units; (c) one may consider only certain relations and not others; and (d) one may consider the entire graph. With more than four points, the matter would be very complex. Graph theory explicates this problem in the following manner: A *path* is two or more lines connecting consecutive points in a graph. In Figure 1D, the lines AB and BD are a path from A to D. A *cycle* is any path that returns to the point of origin. Hence, in Figure 1D, the lines AB and BD plus the line DA are a cycle. The *length* of a cycle is defined by the number of lines in it. A two-line cycle, or more succinctly, a 2-cycle, would consist of two directed lines, for example, AB and BA (not represented in Figure 1). A 3-cycle contains three lines, a 4-cycle contains four lines, and so on. There are two three-line cycles in Figure 1D (AB, BD, DA; and BC, CD, BD) and one four-line cycle (AB, BC, CD, DA). The entire graph thus contains three cycles.

The distinction is sometimes made between a *cycle* and a *semicycle* (Cartwright and Harary, 1956, p. 713; Harary et al., 1965, p. 41). In Figure 1D, the lines AB, BD and DA form a cycle, but the lines BC, CD and BD form a semicycle. Thus, a cycle consists of lines forming a recursive or "circular" path, whereas a semicycle is a non-recursive path (note that *two* lines are directed toward point D in Figure 1D). This distinction is unnecessary for purposes of the present discussion. Only the term "cycle" will be used, and it is intended to refer to both strict cycles and strict semicycles.

Each cycle is a different "way" of looking at a graph. Thus, in asking whether or not the entire graph is "balanced," one may wish to determine *whether or not the separate cycles themselves* are balanced. The question of determining balance of a cycle or graph is taken up in a later section of this chapter. For the moment, however, the reader may deduce from the previous chapter that a cycle is balanced only if the algebraic product of its lines is positive. If the product is negative, the cycle is unbalanced. Thus, in Figure 1D, the cycle AB, BD, DA is unbalanced, since the product of its three lines is negative: $(+)(+)(-) = (-)$. It is easily seen that the cycle BC, CD, BD is balanced, and the only 4-cycle in the graph is unbalanced: $(+)(-)(-)(-) = (-)$. *Distinguishing different cycles in a graph is crucial. If one treats the graph as representing a four-person group, the group would be balanced in some respects, but not in others.*

3 • 1b   *Methods of Counting Cycles*

In the literature on formal models, there have appeared three distinct methods of counting the number of cycles in a graph. The first method, which will hereafter be referred to as "Method 1," is used by Cartwright and Harary (1956). Refer to Figure 2A. According to Method 1, this graph consists of one cycle; *AB, BC* and *CA.* Another method is posed by Berger et al. (1962); yet, these authors do not point out that their method differs from that used by Cartwright and Harary. By the Berger et al. method—"Method 2"—the graph in Figure 2A consists of not one but three cycles. Three cycles are present since *each point* starts and ends on a cycle: *AB, BC, CA; BC, CA, AB;* and *CA, AB, BC.* There is one cycle per point; the graph contains three points, hence three cycles. By Method 1, the graph in Figure 2B contains five cycles (four 3-cycles and one 4-cycle). But by Method 2, this same graph contains sixteen separate cycles: One 4-cycle and three 3-cycles are present for each of the four points. For example, point *A* is a member of three 3-cycles (*AB, BC, CA; AB, BD, DA;* and *AC, CD, DA*) and one 4-cycle. Method 2 of counting cycles is, however, logically redundant. This redundant property is discussed in the next section.

It is evident that as the number of points in a graph increases, the possible number of cycles in the graph increases much faster. Counting cycles by visual inspection would be very cumbersome indeed. For this reason, formulas have been developed for determining the number of lines possible for *n* number of points, the number of cycles possible per point, and the number of cycles possible in a graph of *n* points. These formulas are presented and illustrated in the appendix to this chapter.

A third method of counting cycles is proposed by Morrissette (1958). This method—"Method 3"—considers graphs where $T = 2$, or where two types of relations are simultaneously considered. The graph in Figure 2C illustrates two types of relations between each pair of points. Method 3 distinguishes between "pure" and "mixed" cycles. A pure cycle is one which contains only one type of line (all solid or all broken), whereas a mixed cycle contains two types of lines. For Figure 2C, Method 3 gives a total of nine mixed cycles: (a) three 2-cycles (one for each pair of points); (b) three 3-cycles consisting of one broken line and two solid lines; (c) three 3-cycles consisting of two broken lines and one solid line. The graph contains only two pure 3-cycles, and no pure 2-cycles. Hence, there are eleven cycles all together. The distinction between "pure" and "mixed" cycles rests upon the substantive theoretical assumption that people cognitively distinguish between classes of relations, and these dis-

FIGURE 2   DIFFERENT METHODS OF COUNTING CYCLES

A. A graph containing one cycle by Method 1, and three cycles by Method 2.

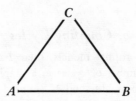

B. A graph containing five cycles by Method 1, and sixteen cycles by Method 2.

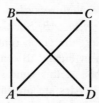

C. A graph containing nine "mixed" and two "pure" cycles, by Method 3. Method 1 gives eleven cycles, and Method 2 gives thirty cycles.

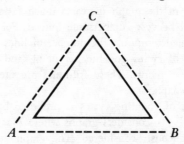

tinctions should be taken into account in formal analysis. Note, incidentally, that Method 1 also gives eleven cycles: three 2-cycles plus eight 3-cycles.[1] Methods 1 and 3 will always give the same total number of cycles; Method 3 simply distinguishes between pure and mixed cycles. If Method 2 is used, there are thirty separate cycles in the graph in Figure 2C (six 2-cycles and twenty-four 3-cycles).

1. There are three 2-cycles in the graph: *AB, BA; BC, CB;* and *AC, CA.* There are eight 3-cycles: one consisting of all solid lines; three consisting of one solid and two broken lines; three consisting of two solid and one broken line; and one consisting of all broken lines. Altogether, there are eleven cycles.

3 • 1c   Balance of a Graph

Of particular importance to the study of cognitive and group structures is the concept of balance of a cycle or graph. Consider first the balance of a given cycle. Cartwright and Harary's definition derives from Heider: a cycle is *balanced* if the algebraic product of its lines, taken in any order, is positive. A cycle is *unbalanced* if the product is negative (Cartwright and Harary, 1956, p. 714). Note the graph in Figure 3A. This graph contains three cycles, by Method 1; all are balanced, as the product of the signs of the lines in each cycle is positive. Generally, *a graph is completely balanced if and only if all of its cycles are balanced.* It is evident that Method 2 of counting cycles yields identical results. For example, all three of the 3-cycles containing points A, B and D have the same (positive) product, since the lines are common.

Note that the product of the lines in a cycle counted by Method 1 is always the same as the product by Method 2. This will always be the case. (For example, in Figure 3A: By Method 1, the points A, B, and D are members of one cycle, and the product of the three lines in this cycle is positive. By Method 2, there are three cycles containing the same points and the same lines. Hence, the products of the three cycles are all the same.) Thus, Method 2 is *redundant*—it gives the same product as Method 1, but uses each cycle (as determined by Method 1) more than once. Method 3 of counting cycles in Figure 3 is not applicable, since $T = 1$.

For the sake of clarity, from this stage on only Method 1 will be used to count cycles unless otherwise indicated. Actual research in balance does not use Method 2. The redundant property of Method 2 was not pointed out by its inventors (Berger et al., 1962).

Figure 3B illustrates a graph containing three cycles, only one of which is balanced. The ABDA cycle is unbalanced, as is the ABCDA cycle. Only the BCDB cycle is balanced. The entire graph is therefore unbalanced.

For cycles containing many lines, it would be cumbersome to multiply the signs of each line to obtain the product. The following "theorem" simplifies this procedure: *A cycle is balanced if it contains an even number of negative lines* (Harary et al., 1965, p. 341; Berger et al., p. 24). By this theorem, it is easily seen that the graph in Figure 3A is completely balanced: The ABCDA cycle contains two negative lines; the ABDA cycle contains no negative lines (zero is an even number); and the BCDB cycle contains two negative lines.

A second theorem, the *decomposition* or *structural* theorem, further simplifies the matter of determining whether or not a graph is balanced. This theorem states that *if a graph can be decomposed into two mutually exclusive subsets, and each positive line joins two points from the same subset and each negative line joins points from different subsets, then the graph is completely balanced* (Cartwright and Harary, 1956, p. 717; Berger et al., 1962, p. 34;

FIGURE 3   BALANCE OF A GRAPH

A. A completely balanced signed digraph.

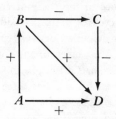

B. A signed digraph containing two unbalanced and one balanced cycle.

C. A signed digraph readily seen as balanced by the decomposition theorem.

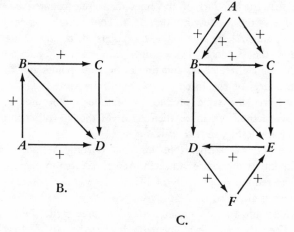

B.

C.

D. A signed graph seen as balanced by the decomposition theorem.

E. A vacuously balanced graph.

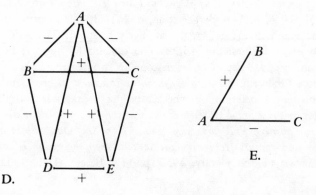

D.

E.

Harary et al., 1965, pp. 342–344). The graph in Figure 3C is not easily seen as balanced, if one wishes to count cycles. By the decomposition theorem, its balance can be easily determined. Note that there are two subsets, one containing points A, B and C, the other containing points D, E and F. Only positive lines appear within a subset, and only negative lines join subsets; the graph is therefore completely balanced. This can be verified by noting that any cycle in this graph containing any negative lines has an even number of negative lines (two or zero); hence, the graph is completely balanced by the "even number" theorem. The graph in Figure 3D is also balanced according to the decomposition theorem. One subset (points B and C plus the positive line joining them) is connected by only negative lines to the other subset (points A, D and E, all joined by positive lines).

An interesting substantive hypothesis can be derived from the decomposition theorem. Assume that each of the points in the graph represented in Figure 3C are persons, and that each line represents like or dislike. Clearly, the group is divided into two "cliques." Nevertheless, the entire network of relations is balanced. According to the balance hypothesis, the structure is stable and is therefore not subject to change, even though certain members dislike other members. Hence, the general empirical hypothesis suggested by the decomposition theorem is that if a group is decomposed into two cliques, where only liking appears among members within each clique and only dislike appears between members of different cliques, the group is stable (balanced) and no changes are expected to result. (This hypothesis is relevant to what Harary (1959) and Davis (1967) call "clustering" in a graph or structure—a very interesting topic to be taken up in Chapter 6.)

One of the major advantages of formalization has been to clarify ambiguities that were present in the original substantive models. One of these ambiguities concerns Heider's "unit relation." Heider simply dichotomized the unit relation into "present" (U) and "absent" (not-U), treating the U relation as positive and the not-U relation as implicitly negative. However, this conceptualization does not distinguish between the *complement* and the *opposite* of a relation. Logically, a U relation (e.g., ownership) would imply a positive relation, but "not-U" (non-ownership) would imply neutrality or absence (complement) of a relation rather than a negative (opposite) relation. This distinction has been supported by Cartwright and Harary's (1956) and Runkel's (1956) re-analysis of data gathered by Jordan (1953). In Jordan's experiment, subjects were presented with sixty-four situations representing different combinations of like–dislike relations, and U–not-U relations. The tension or "pleasantness" of each situation was rated by the subjects. On the average, balanced situations were rated as more pleasant than unbalanced situations, as predicted by Heider's hypothesis on the relationship between balance and tension discussed in the previous chapter. Cartwright-Harary and Runkel noted, however, that when situations containing not-U relations were eliminated, the predicted relationship between balance of the situation and mean pleasantness rating was increased.

Furthermore, the mean pleasantness ratings of situations containing not-U relations were about neutral.

These interpretations led Cartwright and Harary to adopt the convention that a graph is *vacuously balanced* if it contains no cycles. Figure 3E is a vacuously balanced graph. Note also that one may use the term *vacuous "cycle"* if a cycle *would* be formed by the presence of one or more lines. Hence, Figure 3E is a vacuous "cycle." So is the ABCA "cycle" in Figure 3A. Thus, a vacuously balanced "cycle" (i.e., a vacuous "cycle") is to be distinguished from a strictly balanced or a strictly unbalanced cycle. The reader must take care in noting that in the computation of indices of *degree* of balance of an entire graph (covered in the following section), vacuous "cycles" are *not* considered to be "balanced." Vacuous "cycles" are *ignored* in the computation of indices of degree of balance.

3 • 1d   *Degree of Balance of a Graph*

In the foregoing section, it was stated that a graph is *completely* balanced only if all of its cycles are balanced. It is possible, however, that a graph can be characterized by its *degree* of balance, or the ratio of positive cycles to total number of cycles. Remembering that the sign of a cycle is the sign of the product of its lines, Cartwright and Harary (1956) present a simple formula for the degree of balance of a graph or structure, $b(G)$:

$$b(G) = \frac{+c(G)}{c(G)}$$

where

$+c(G)$ = the number of positive cycles in the graph;

$c(G)$ = the total number of cycles in the graph.

This index ranges from 0 (complete unbalance) to 1 (complete balance).[2] The following illustration, a play, represents an interesting application of this formula; refer to Figure 4.

SCENE 1:   Hero discovers that his friend Buddy likes the villian Blackheart whom he despises. As the scene ends, a stranger, Goodman, encounters Blackheart and instantly dislikes him.

INTERPRETATION: The graph formed by these relations has a degree of balance of zero, hence making the play interesting, but uncomfortable and unpleasant to the audience.

2. The ratio of positive to total cycles will be unity, if vacuous "cycles" are not counted:

$$\frac{+c(G)}{c(G)} + \frac{-c(G)}{c(G)} = 1.$$

Noting this, Flament (1963, p. 99) suggests a formula for *degree of unbalance* of a graph: Degree of unbalance $= 1 - b(G)$.

FIGURE 4   AN ILLUSTRATION OF THE CARTWRIGHT-HARARY DEGREE OF
BALANCE FORMULA*

SCENE 1:

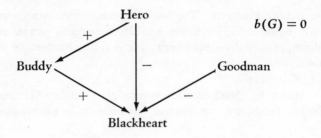

$$b(G) = 0$$

SCENE 2:

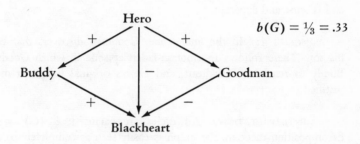

$$b(G) = \tfrac{1}{3} = .33$$

SCENE 3:

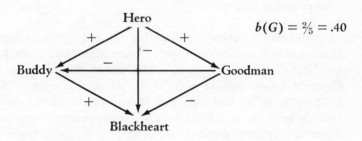

$$b(G) = \tfrac{2}{5} = .40$$

SCENE 4:

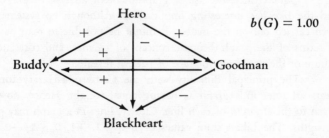

$$b(G) = 1.00$$

* Adapted from Harary et al. (1965), pp. 348–349.

SCENE 2: Hero meets Goodman and finds him to be most likable. Hero tries, without success, to change Buddy's liking for Blackheart.

INTERPRETATION: The graph contains three cycles, one of which is positive; hence, $b(G) = \frac{1}{3}$ or .33. The audience is pleased that Hero likes Goodman (who dislikes Blackheart) but is still uncomfortable about the whole situation.

SCENE 3: Much interaction takes place between Goodman and Buddy. As the scene ends, it is apparent that Goodman cannot tolerate Buddy.

INTERPRETATION: Two of the graph's five cycles are positive, and $b(G) = \frac{2}{5} = .40$. The audience feels that the play has reached a preclimax, and is tense and expectant.

SCENE 4: In the final scene, Goodman discovers that Buddy is really his son. There follows an emotion-laden episode in which Goodman convinces Buddy to renounce Blackheart, and Hero's original judgment of Blackheart is justified.

INTERPRETATION: All cycles are balanced; $b(G) = 1.00$. By the decomposition theorem, the graph is easily seen as completely balanced. Balance was achieved by changing two relations in the direction of balance. The audience is happy and in high spirits.

Recently, Stanton (1967) has applied graph-theoretic analysis to Shakespeare's *A Midsummer Night's Dream*. After plotting who-loves-whom and who-hates-whom for each act, it is seen that in Act I, $b(G) = .50$. In Act II, degree of balance falls to $b(G) = .33$, and it rises again in Act III back to $b(G) = .50$. In the final acts (Acts IV and V), degree of balance attains unity (perfect balance), and $b(G) = 1.00$. Similar analyses done in terms of the degree of balance of graphs representing plays at various stages have been carried out by Harary (1963; 1966).

Quite clearly, the use of graph-theoretic analysis of plays, novels, movies and the like has interesting implications. Although no systematic research has been carried out on the matter, it might be possible to map out plot sequences in terms of the graph-theoretic concept of balance, and correlate the success or failure of the opus with the type of pattern revealed!

The principal difficulty with the Cartwright-Harary formula is that it treats all lines in a graph as having equal weight. Hence, no consideration is given to the *strength* of each line. Clearly, lines in a graph may possess differing strengths. The Likert scale values of +3, +2, +1, 0, −1, −2, and −3, commonly used in research, would be ignored by the Cartwright-Harary formula. Harary and Norman (Cartwright and Harary, 1956) introduce the concept of graph strength, σ, but without elaboration. Morrissette (1958) introduced a formula which expresses the balance of a graph as a function of the strengths of the lines of its cycles. Let σ be the strength of a cycle, which is defined as the algebraic product of the strengths of its lines. Hence, a 3-cycle containing the lines $+2$, -3 and -1 would have a positive product of the strength: $+6$. Let each cycle be designated as $Z_1, Z_2, \ldots, Z_r$, where $r =$ the number of cycles in the graph. Thus σZ is the strength of a given cycle, and let $p\sigma Z$ represent the strength of a positive cycle. The Morrissette formula of balance becomes:

$$b(G) = \frac{\displaystyle\sum_{k=1}^{r} p\sigma Z_k}{\displaystyle\sum_{k=1}^{r} \left| \sigma Z_k \right|}$$

which is read as follows: the degree of balance of graph G is the sum of the strengths of all positive cycles divided by the absolute sum (ignoring signs) of the strengths of all cycles in the graph.

To exemplify this formula, and to contrast it with the Cartwright-Harary formula, consult Figure 5. Each line in the graph is represented by a scale value or strength: $+3$, $+2$, etc. The Morrissette formula demands that one first obtain the strengths of the positive cycles. Only the $BCDB$ cycle is positive; its strength is $(+2)(-3)(-1)$ or $+6$, thus giving the numerator in the formula. If the graph were larger and contained more positive cycles, their products would be

FIGURE 5   A SIGNED DIGRAPH SHOWING LINES OF DIFFERING STRENGTHS

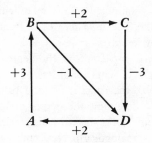

$b(G)$ (Morrissette formula) $= .125$

$b(G)$ (Cartwright-Harary formula) $= .33$

summed to obtain the numerator. The denominator is obtained by summing the absolute strengths of all three cycles. The overall degree of balance is

$$b(G) = \frac{(+2)(-3)(-1)}{|[(+3)(-1)(+2)] + [(+2)(-3)(-1)] + [(+3)(+2)(-3)(+2)]|}$$

$$= \frac{+6}{48} = .125$$

Note that the Cartwright-Harary formula gives $b(G) = ⅓$ or .33 as the degree of balance for this graph. This is greater than the degree of balance as determined by the Morrissette formula.

Whether or not the Morrissette formula is better than the Cartwright-Harary formula is subject to debate. The question of which index best orders empirical data is complicated by the fact that other indices of balance have been introduced, among them: (a) Morrissette's $\gamma(G)$ index (Morrissette et al., 1966), which incorporates vacuous "cycles" (note that both of the indices just presented ignore the number of vacuous "cycles" in the graph); (b) a "line index" of balance, developed by Harary (1959) and Rosenberg and Abelson (1960) which is discussed below; and (c) an index developed by Phillips (1967) based on a factor-analysis of the matrix corresponding to a particular graph. The question of which among all these indices is generally best for research in groups is a complex one. For this reason, a detailed treatment and comparison of indices of balance will have to await presentation in Chapter 6, where various empirical issues which we have yet to encounter, and which are relevant to the problem of indices of balance, are considered.

Further modifications of the degree of balance formula, an overall or "total" index of balance, have been introduced by Harary (Harary, 1955–56). These modifications involve the concepts of local balance and n-balance. *Local balance* is the degree of balance considering only cycles passing through a given point. Thus, the degree of local balance at point A in Figure 5 would consider only the $ABDA$ and $ABCDA$ cycles. The degree of balance considering only these cycles could then be computed by means of either the Cartwright-Harary or the Morrissette formula. The *n-balance* of a graph is the degree of balance considering only cycles of length n or less. Combining both concepts, one may ascertain the degree of *local n-balance,* or the degree of balance at a particular point considering only cycles of length n or less.

For complex graphs, the concept of local balance has great utility. One may wish, for example, to determine the degree of balance in a group structure as seen from the "viewpoint" of some particular member. Broadly speaking, the concept of local balance is analogous to Newcomb's *individual system* of orientation, which contains only variables which are part of the focal person's cognitive structure. The "total" index of balance, $b(G)$, is analogous to Newcomb's substantive concept of the *collective system,* a structure consisting of all objective and perceived variables.

3 • 1e   *Means of Achieving Balance: Some Hypotheses*

The Rosenberg-Abelson *least cost hypothesis,* discussed in the previous chapter, states that given unbalance, the individual will attempt to achieve balance through the fewest possible sign changes. A precise statement of this hypothesis is made possible through Harary's (1959) concepts of the negation, deletion and alteration of lines in a graph. A *negation-minimal* set of lines is the smallest number of lines in a graph whose negation results in complete balance. "Negation" means changing the sign of a line to the opposite sign. According to the negation-minimal criterion, it is possible to suggest a *line index,* λ, the fewest number of lines whose negation results in balance. Note that the graph in Figure 5 has a line index of 1. Negating the *AB* line *or* the *DA* line results in complete balance. Only if it is necessary to negate a minimum of two lines simultaneously will $\lambda = 2$. Although the negation of lines *BD* and *CD* would also result in balance, these two simultaneous negations or changes are not the minimum necessary negations.

A *deletion-minimal* set of lines is the smallest number of lines whose *removal* results in balance. In Figure 5, the removal of either the *AB* line or the *DA* line results in balance, and $\lambda = 1$ by the deletion-minimal criterion. Note that the negation of the same two lines also resulted in balance. Interestingly, it is always true that *for any given graph, the lines in a negation-minimal set are the same as the lines in a deletion-minimal set, and vice versa* (Harary et al., 1965, p. 350).

A third criterion, the *alteration minimal* criterion, combines the concepts of negation and deletion. An alteration-minimal set of lines is obtained when the negation of one or more lines and the simultaneous deletion of one or more lines results in balance. By this criterion, λ is always $\geqq 2$.

The above principles permit a precise restatement of the Rosenberg-Abelson least cost hypothesis. If the lines of a graph are allowed to represent either sentiment attitudinal relations, then *the group thus represented constitutes a negation-minimal, deletion-minimal or alteration-minimal set of relations.* Hence, if one asks, "In a given group, *which* relations will change toward balance?" the hypothesis predicts changes in relations which are a negation-, deletion- or alteration-minimal set. Relations which are not part of such a set are not subject to change. Remembering that the lines in any negation-minimal set are the same as those in a deletion-minimal set, this hypothesis can be stated in terms of only the negation (or deletion) and alteration criteria alone. It is interesting to note that if restated in this way, the Rosenberg-Abelson hypothesis predicts that balance in a group is achieved by *either* (a) changing the signs of (negating) the minimum number of relations, *or* (b) simply changing the values of these *same* relations toward zero (deleting).

We have seen that negation, deletion and alteration constitute hypothesized means available to group members for achieving balance. These means pertain to affective or attitudinal relations (lines in a graph). It is conceivable that the deletion criterion can also apply to persons, or points in a graph. Toward this end, Harary (1959) introduces a *point index*—the smallest number of points whose deletion results in balance. The graph in Figure 6, representing a five-person group, has a point index of one, for the deletion of either *A*, *B* or *E* results in balance. Note that neither of the other points, *C* and *D*, has this property.

Letting each line in Figure 6 represent a mutual liking or disliking, an important hypothesis emerges: Even though *D* is the least-liked member of the group, he is not "expendable" in that his expulsion or deletion does not result in balance. Yet, the best-liked member, person *B*, *is* expendable by the point-deletion criterion! Generally, one may hypothesize that it is not only the liking or disliking of a member which determines his potential expulsion, but whether or not his expulsion will result in balance. If the point index of a group structure is zero, then expulsion is not likely to occur. If the point index is equal to or greater than one, then expulsion of one or more members is likely to occur. One may predict, them, that likelihood of expulsion is a function of the degree of balance of the structure rather than of the extent to which a particular member is liked or disliked.

This hypothesis would seem to apply to the oft noticed occurrence of "scapegoating" in groups. A puzzling question, raised in the past by small group researchers, is "which person in a group is most likely to become a scapegoat?" Perhaps the answer lies in the extent of balance of the group structure rather than in certain peculiarities or personality attributes of the individual. Under the assumption that scapegoating is the symbolic expulsion of a group member, then

FIGURE 6   A GRAPH ILLUSTRATING A LEAST-LIKED PERSON, D, WHO IS
NOT "EXPENDABLE"

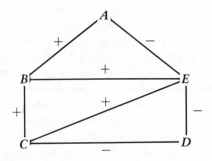

the above hypothesis has merit: The member most likely to become a scapegoat is that member whose deletion will result in a balanced structure.

3 • 2   EVALUATION OF FORMALIZATIONS: STRONG POINTS

In what way does graph theory improve upon the original substantive formulations of the balance theorists? This question is addressed in the present section. The ways in which formal treatment extends, refines, clarifies and redirects the substantive varieties of balance theory are discussed. In the section following this one, the "weak points" of the formalizations are presented. Both sections together constitute an evaluation and critique of formal models of balance.

3 • 2a   *Generality*

One of the more obvious strong points of formalization is that it allows one to generalize beyond the original statements of the balance theorists. Graph theory allows for the extension of the basic *POX* unit to more than three objects and more than one type of relation between objects. The formulations of the balance theorists are not easily conceptualized for units consisting of more than two persons and more than one *X*. The graph concept of cycle greatly aids this conceptualization; each cycle represents a different way of analyzing a complex structure. The cycle concept allows one to systematically examine possible combinations of relations in a unit.

Formalization provides some answers to such pragmatic questions as, how many relations are possible in a structure of *n* points? What are the number of cycles possible for each point, and the number of cycles possible in the entire structure? How many structures or graphs are created if each relation is allowed to have two or more signs? The appendix to this chapter presents and illustrates formulas for answering these questions. Prior to the development of applications of graph theory to balance theory, answering such pragmatic questions was difficult for researchers and students of the balance process. For example, Jordan (1953) recommends a cross-tabulation technique for figuring out the number of "states" or "configurations" for a given number of points and signs. But this technique is cumbersome for graphs consisting of several objects (points) and three or more signs. Refer to the appendix at the end of this chapter for an alternative technique.

3 • 2b   *Refinement*

Of considerable aid in the study of balance of structures are the "theorems" of graph theory. It was shown that a cycle is balanced if the product of its lines is positive—which is equivalent to saying that it has an even number of negative lines. The structural or decomposition theorem permits one to identify quickly whether or not a graph is balanced by visually partitioning it into two mutually exclusive subsets. These "short cuts" add precision to the substantive formulations of the balance theorists.

The Cartwright-Harary and Morrissette formulas for obtaining the degree of balance of a structure add further refinement to the balance model. Prior to the development and explication of these formulas, determining the balance or unbalance of a complex structure was cumbersome. Harary's concepts of local and n-balance further increase this precision. Ascertaining the degree of balance of an individual system, in Newcomb's sense, is made possible through the conceptualization of local balance; balance of a collective system can be assessed by means of some index of balance of the total structure.

3 • 2c   Clarification

The original balance theorists were faced with certain ambiguities. For example, Heider dichotomized the unit relation into "U" and "not-U"—presumably representing relations *analogous* to "like" and "dislike," respectively. Cartwright and Harary, however, point out that if a *POX* unit is formed containing, say, a U relation between *P* and *X*, a "like" relation between *P* and *O* and a not-U relation between *O* and *X*, then the system created does not seem to be clearly unbalanced, as Heider originally stated. There is no "relation," as such, between *O* and *X*, and a "system" does not therefore exist. This ambiguity led Cartwright and Harary to adopt the convention that a cycle is "vacuously" balanced if it contains at least one absent (not-U) relation. Hence, the distinction was made between a relation (positive-U), its complement (not-U) and its opposite (negative-U). Given this clarification, it is evident that a structure consisting of the relations $P \xrightarrow{+} X$, $P \xrightarrow{+} O$, and $O \xrightarrow{0} X$ is neither balanced nor unbalanced. It is thus identified as vacuously balanced, thereby being distinguished from a strictly balanced or strictly unbalanced structure.

3 • 2d   Redirection

Graph theory permits a redirection of theoretical interest; it provides new hypotheses not originally conceptualized by the balance theorists. Harary's line index, λ, serves as a basis for new predictions. This index allows one to identify the smallest number of relations in a group structure that are most likely to be negated, deleted or altered in order to maximize balance. Prior to this "least cost" formulation, the balance theorists had no way of predicting which relations in a unit of many relations would change; they simply stated that given unbalance, relations would change in the direction of balance. The Harary formulation identifies not only the minimum balance-maximizing changes, but it also identifies the particular relations that are most likely to change.

Harary's point index—the smallest number of points in a graph whose deletion results in balance—provides additional hypotheses. Suppose one wishes to predict whether or not a group is likely to expell one of its members. If the balance principle is applied, then one would expect that groups with balanced structures would not expell members and that groups with unbalanced structures would. How many members would be expelled? According to the Harary index, the fewest whose expulsion results in balance. Assuming that scapegoating is symbolic expulsion, then the likelihood of occurrence of scapegoating can be treated as a function of the structure's point index. The introduction or "initiation" of persons into a group might also be explained on the basis of the point index: The group will not initiate anyone whose introduction would decrease the degree of balance of its structure. If the balance principle indeed regulates the process of initiation, expulsion and scapegoating of group members, then the Harary index would seem to have important implications for research. To date, however, there has been no empirical investigation of this hypothesis.[3]

3 • 2e Asymmetric Interpersonal Relations

One of the most troublesome issues facing the balance theorists was the matter of asymmetric relations. A relation, such as A's liking for B, is symmetric if it is of the same sign as B's liking for A; it is asymmetric otherwise. Asymmetric *interpersonal* relations were not adequately handled by Heider or by Newcomb. Heider seems to side-step the issue by hypothesizing that, over time, relations tend to become symmetric, thus eliminating the necessity of working the problem of asymmetric relations into his model (Heider, 1958, p. 205). Newcomb appears to avoid the issue altogether, as nowhere in his writings is there a systematic discussion of expected changes in relations if one or more interpersonal (PO) relations are asymmetric.

Figure 7 represents a three-person group containing asymmetric relations (liking) between A and B, and between A and C. The graph theory concept of cycle permits a precise analysis of this structure. By Method 1 of counting cycles, there are four 3-cycles, two of which are balanced, and two 2-cycles, each of which is unbalanced. (Note that an "asymmetric relation" can be simply defined as an unbalanced 2-cycle.) Two of the total of six cycles are balanced, and $b(G) = \frac{2}{6} = .33$, by the Cartwright-Harary formula. Complete balance can be achieved by changing the sign of two relations: B's liking for A and A's liking

---

3. In Chapter 8, a number of hypotheses for future research are systematically presented and discussed.

FIGURE 7   A SIGNED DIGRAPH ILLUSTRATING ASYMMETRIC
INTERPERSONAL RELATIONS

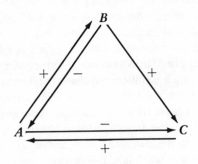

for C (change both to positive); or A's liking for B and C's liking for A (change both to negative).

3 • 3   EVALUATION OF FORMALIZATIONS: WEAK POINTS

Although in certain respects graph theory improves upon the substantive statements of the balance theorists, there are nevertheless omissions and ambiguities in the formalizations. Six weaknesses are treated here: (1) the problem of discrepancies between cycles in a given structure; (2) the role of tension in the balance process; (3) the use of indices of balance to describe changes over time; (4) the problem of ambivalent relations; (5) the problem of cycle length; and (6) the matter of multiplying the signs and/or strengths of the lines in a cycle. Let us take each point *seriatim*.

3 • 3a   *Discrepancies Between Cycles or Subsets of Cycles*

The question of whether or not a structure is balanced, and the matter of determining the degree of balance of a structure, derives from the question of whether or not the cycles in a structure are balanced. But what if certain cycles or subsets of cycles markedly differ in their respective degrees of balance? Does it then make sense to lump all cycles together into a degree of balance index? The concepts of local balance, n-balance and local n-balance do not adequately solve the problem, as these concepts do not allow for the definition of some clear index of cycle discrepancy.

Of what theoretical significance is the analysis of discrepancies between cycles or subsets of cycles? Newcomb's distinction between the individual and collective systems offers certain leads. The individual system consists of four variables: The focal person's attitude toward X and liking for the other (both are "objective" variables), and the focal person's perception of the other's attitude and liking for himself (both variables are "subjective"). The collective system consists of these variables as attributes of two or more persons.

It now seems important to ask: What if the degree of balance characterizing the focal person's individual system differs from the degree of balance characterizing a collective system of which he is part? Or, what if the degree of balance of the cluster of objective variables, taken as one subset, differs from the degree of balance of the cluster of subjective variables, taken as another subset? May not such discrepancies be sources of psychological tension for one or more persons, thus causing them to change one or more variables in an attempt to reduce this tension? Note that the extent of balance among one subset of variables per se is one source of tension; the *extent of discrepancy between two or more subsets* is a second, independent potential source of tension and change.

Given the distinction between degree of balance of a subset of variables, on one hand, and the extent of discrepancy between the degrees of balance of two or more subsets, on the other, it seems necessary to consider an index of this discrepancy. Let $b(G)_1$ represent the degree of balance of one subset of variables (such as the focal person's individual system), and let $b(G)_2$ represent the degree of balance in another subset (such as the collective system). The degree of discrepancy index, D, may be defined simply as:

$$D = b(G)_1 - b(G)_2,$$

or the difference between the degrees of balance of two subsets.

If more than two subsets are considered, the variance of their respective degrees of balance might be used as an index of discrepancy:

$$D^2 = \frac{\sum\limits_{i=1}^{K} [b(G)_i - \overline{b(G)}]^2}{K}$$

where

$b(G)_i$ = the degree of balance of a particular subset, i;

$\overline{b(G)}$ = the arithmetic mean (average) of the degrees of balance of all subsets considered;

K = the number of subsets considered.

The discrepancy index is defined generally, and is easily interpreted: The greater the index, the greater the discrepancy. The quantities $b(G)_1$, $b(G)_2$, ... $b(G)_K$, can represent the degrees of local balance at two or more points in a structure, or the degrees of balance of two or more mutually exclusive or non-mutually exclusive subsets of cycles, or even the degrees of balance of separate cycles. The greatest utility of this index would appear to lie in the analysis of subsets in large structures as defined by Newcomb's distinction between the individual and collective systems. At least four comparisons would be possible and theoretically meaningful: the discrepancy between (1) the focal person's individual system and the collective system; (2) the other's individual system and the collective system; (3) two or more individual systems; and (4) the balance among all subjective variables and the balance among all objective variables. Each type of discrepancy is a potential independent source of tension in either the focal person and one or more others. Hence, not only can the degree of balance of a structure be used to explain variations in tension, but the degree of discrepancy between two subsets can also serve as a potential explanation for variations in tension.

3 • 3b   *The Role of Tension*

The above mention of tension brings to mind a second shortcoming of the formalizations: The role of tension in the balance process is completely ignored. Nowhere in the graph theory literature is tension integrated into the formalization of balance theory. Is tension a simple linear function of degree of balance, or is the expected relationship nonlinear? The formal literature seems to imply that tension decreases in linear fashion as degree of balance increases, suggesting simple linear regression equation of the following form:

$$T = A + (-B) \, [b(G)],$$

where

$$T = \text{magnitude of tension};$$
$$b(G) = \text{degree of balance; and}$$
$$A, B = \text{regression constants.}[4]$$

However, no equation of this form is explicitly treated in the formal literature.

There is quite a bit of empirical evidence, to be reviewed later, suggesting that tension is not a simple linear function of degree of balance (Jordan, 1953; Price et al., 1965; Price et al., 1966; Jordan, 1966a; Jordan, 1966b). It would seem to be the province of formalization (certainly of quantification) to suggest formulas defining an expected nonlinear relationship between balance and tension. Given the integral role of tension in the balance process, such formulas are needed.

---

4. The formula is simply a restatement of the formula for linear regression expressing Y as a function of X, such that $Y = A + B(X)$. If the slope is negative (as hypothesized), then the equation becomes $Y = A + (-B)X$, or simply $Y = A - B(X)$. Hence, if $X = $ degree of balance, $b(G)$, and $Y = $ magnitude of tension, T, then the equation becomes $T = A + (-B) \, [b(G)]$, or $T = A - B \, [b(G)]$.

3 • 3c   Changes in Degree of Balance

Of critical importance in the study of the balance process is the assessment of directions of change in structures through time. Hence, one may wish to ascertain the degree of balance of a structure at Time 1 and again at Time 2, noting whether or not the change has been in the direction of greater balance, as predicted by the balance hypothesis. The Morrissette and Cartwright-Harary formulas, if computed for a given structure at two points in time, can give grossly different results.

Figure 8 illustrates a structure at two points in time. Each line represents a degree of liking or a degree of disliking. Before applying the Morrissette and Cartwright-Harary formulas to this structure, examine the substantive changes that have occurred from Time 1 to Time 2: At Time 1, the structure contains two unbalanced cycles and one balanced cycle; the entire structure is therefore not completely balanced. Note that A's liking for C and A's liking for B change from -2 to -1; i.e., A tends to dislike B and C less. Therefore, both relations have changed *in the positive direction*. Since B's liking for C and B's liking for A are positive and remain unchanged, one can argue that the overall changes represented are changes *in the direction of increased balance*. The changes occurring in the structure have been in such a direction as to make all relations positive; the composite changes have therefore been in the direction of balance rather than unbalance.

Do the Morrissette or Cartwright-Harary formulas correctly reflect these changes? Analysis of the structure at Time 1 and Time 2 illustrates that they do not. Note from the computations in Figure 8 that the Morrissette formula gives $b(G)$ at Time 1 as .60, whereas $b(G)$ at Time 2 is .43. This suggests that the overall change has been from a higher degree of balance to a lesser degree of balance—a change in the direction of unbalance rather than balance. This is the direct opposite of the interpretation given above. The Cartwright-Harary formula lends no additional insights: For both Times 1 and 2, $b(G) = \frac{1}{3} = .33$, thereby completely masking the changes that have occurred.

In sum, whereas the substantive changes represented in Figure 8 appear to be in the direction of balance, the Morrissette formula expresses the changes as being in the direction of unbalance, and the Cartwright-Harary formula expresses no changes at all. The ambiguity in the Morrissette formula arises when one multiplies the strengths of lines in order to obtain the strength and sign of a cycle. This multiplication procedure seems artifactual; it distorts the actual changes that have taken place in a structure. Therefore, an accurate empirical test of the balance hypothesis—that structures tend to change toward balance over time—is not possible.

To date, no clear solution to this sticky problem of different ways to ascertain the direction of change in a structure has appeared in the literature. Some recent attempts have been made, however. Phillips (1967) constructs an

FIGURE 8   A STRUCTURE AT TWO POINTS IN TIME

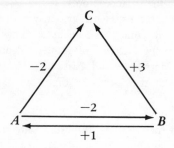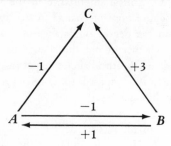

TIME 1   TIME 2

	Algebraic Product	Absolute Product
TIME 1		
One 3-line cycle: $(-2)(-2)(+3) =$	+12	12
One 3-line cycle: $(-2)(+1)(+3) =$	− 6	6
One 2-line cycle: $(-2)(+1) \quad =$	− 2	2
	Sum of strengths of positive cycles $= +12$	Absolute sum of cycle strengths $= 20$

$b(G)$ at Time 1 $= 12/20 = .60$

	Algebraic Product	Absolute Product
TIME 2		
One 3-cycle: $(-1)(-1)(+3) =$	+3	3
One 3-cycle: $(-1)(+1)(+3) =$	−3	3
One 2-cycle: $(-1)(+1) \quad =$	−1	1
	Sum of strengths of positive cycles $= +3$	Absolute sum of cycle strengths $= 7$

$b(G)$ at Time 2 $= 3/7 = .43$

index of balance on the basis of a factor-analysis of the adjacency matrix of a graph. The largest eigenvalue (cf. "factor") of the matrix, λ_1, is taken as a measure of degree of balance, and changes over time in λ_1 are taken as measuring changes in balance over time. Abelson (1967, p. 17) advocates a strikingly similar index, stating that the degree of balance of a structure is reflected by "the proportion of the total sum of squares explained by the first [largest] factor" extracted from the matrix of a graph, which is analogous to using the largest eigenvalue. However, the Phillips and Abelson procedures would seem to measure what is called "clustering" in a graph (Harary, 1959, Davis, 1967) rather than degree of balance. This whole matter is complex, and is taken up in some detail in Chapter 6.

It should be made clear to the reader that while many empirical studies have quite successfully measured the directions of change in a *given relation* in a graph or structure, no theoretical or empirical work has come up with a suitable procedure for measuring changes in a structure consisting of a number of relations *taken together*. Thus, an index capable of reflecting changes in degree of balance of either a cycle, subsets of cycles (such as "local" cycles), or a total structure has yet to be developed.

3 • 3d *Ambivalent Relations*

An ambivalent relation exists if, say, the focal person (P) favors some aspects of X but disfavors others, or if he "strongly" favors some aspects but "weakly" favors others. Or he may like certain traits in O and dislike others. How can one handle ambivalent relations in the theory of balance? Neither the substantive *nor* the formal theorists provide any leads.

One solution would be to treat the object of ambivalence as not one, but two objects. One would then adopt the convention that the two objects are themselves positively associated (since they are actually aspects of the same object), and ambivalence would then, by definition, become "unbalance." This makes sense substantively, because "ambivalence" certainly connotes "inconsistency," "unbalance," "dissonance," etc. For example, taking an X-object and splitting it into two "aspects" $(X$ and $X')$, then if P favored one aspect $(+PX)$ and disfavored another $(-PX')$, and if the relation between the two aspects is assumed to be positive (i.e., $+XX')$, then the cycle so obtained is sign-unbalanced. Such a cycle could then be included in any given total structure—containing one O, for example. This would give four objects $(P, O, X$ and $X')$, and one would record both P's and O's attitudes toward both X and X' separately. The structure would contain at least six lines (and five cycles, by Method 1), and the balance–unbalance of the total structure could be ascertained.

An additional, and possibly preferable, method of handling ambivalent relations considers the *strengths* of relations. The object of ambivalence would be treated as only one object, and one could get the "net result" of a relation.

For example, if P likes O in some respects with a strength of $+3$ but in other respects with a strength of $+1$, the "net result" (the difference) is $+2$. One would then record the PO relation as positive with a strength of $+2$ (i.e., as $+2$ PO). Generally, if the two relations of ambivalence are of the *same sign,* the net result is the difference between the two values; if they are of *opposite* sign, the net result is the algebraic sum of the two values. This latter case is illustrated if P like O in some ways with a strength of $+3$ but dislikes him in other ways with a strength of -2, then the net result (the algebraic sum) is $+1$. In short, P likes O more than he dislikes him. If one relation is $+3$ and the other -3, then they cancel each other, and the net result would be zero. This "net result" procedure would seem to be preferable to getting the average of the relations, which is essentially what is involved in typical Likert scaling procedures, where a person's responses on several scales are averaged together to get one index score. Whereas the averaging procedure tends to mask differences in scale responses, the net result procedure would emphasize them. One obvious disadvantage of the net result procedure is that it is not easily generalized to more than two relations of ambivalence.

3 • 3e   The Problem of Cycle Length

A very major and somewhat upsetting problem with formalization is the matter of considering the *length* of cycles in a total structure. The length of a cycle is the number of lines (relations) in it. It might make sense to talk about the balance–unbalance of a three-line cycle involving P, O and X. But what about a four-line cycle containing P, O, Q and X (three persons and one X), or persons A, B, C and D? And what about a cycle containing five, six, or seven or more lines? Is such a long cycle likely to form a structure of *interdependent* (*system-like*) *relations,* or is the interdependence quality likely to decrease as the length of the cycle containing the relations increases? Does the notion of balance–unbalance of a long cycle carry any meaning?

There is some recent evidence (Zajonc and Burnstein, 1965b) that a person's ability to learn and recall a structure depends upon the length of the cycles contained within the structure. The longer the cycle, the harder it is to learn and "absorb." This suggests that the longer the cycle, the less likely its relations are to form an interdependent structure—a necessary condition for the system-like hypotheses of balance theory to be empirically accurate. This suggests further that the balance–unbalance (the sign) of a long cycle will have less effect upon the focal person's tension than the balance–unbalance of a short cycle, and that the focal person's preference for balancing a long cycle will be less than his preference for balancing a short cycle.

Generally, one can speculate that the effects of a particular cycle upon P will decrease as its length increases. Consequently, is it not true that indices of degree of balance should be weighted according to the length of the cycles contained in the total structure? Indices currently in use weight all cycles in a structure equally, regardless of their length. The most striking implication arising from the consideration of cycle length involves the utility of graph-theoretic formalization itself: One is less likely to need formalization to describe small structures containing short cycles. Graph theory is advantageous for describing longer cycles. But if long cycles are outside the "perceptual range" of focal persons, if the relations contained in such long cycles are not interdependent, and if the balance–unbalance of long cycles is not likely to affect the focal person's tension, then what good is formalization?

Surprisingly, almost no systematic research has been carried out on the effects of cycle length. In addition, there has been no discussion in the formal literature of procedures for weighting indices of balance according to the lengths of cycles in a total structure. (One procedure would be to divide the product of the lines in a cycle (if strengths of lines are considered) by the number of lines in a cycle. This would make the product for that cycle smaller, as the number of lines increased.) Clearly, there is room for thought and research here. This issue is treated again in Chapter 6, where some specific hypotheses on the effects of cycle length are presented. The problem is a critical one, because the empirical utility of formalization seems to rest, to a great degree, on a solution to this issue.

3 • 3f   "To Multiply or Not To Multiply"

The logic underlying many indices of balance (such as the Cartwright-Harary and Morrissette indices) is that the balance–unbalance of a particular cycle, and consequently the effect of that cycle upon the focal person, can be ascertained by multiplying either the signs or the strengths (or both) of the lines contained in the cycle. McGuire (1966) points out that this procedure ignores other possible procedures, such as *adding* the various strengths but obtaining the sign of the cycle through multiplying the signs of the lines in it, or even by adding up the signs themselves. Do two negative relations imply a positive (balanced) structure—as would be obtained through multiplication—or do two negative relations mean a "greater negative," thus implying unbalance?

The question of "to multiply or not to multiply" becomes more important when one realizes that no less than *six* separate procedures have been used by various researchers in the past to measure the overall affects of the balance–unbalance of a structure upon P. While these procedures are given detailed treatment in Chapters 5 and 6, a brief listing here is worthwhile. The overall impact of inconsistency or unbalance upon the focal person has been variously ascertained by: (1) *multiplying* the signs and/or strengths of relations, a procedure derived from Heider's theory and used by Cartwright and Harary (1956) and Morrissette (1958); (2) *adding* the strengths of relations in a structure (Triandis and Fishbein, 1963; Fishbein and Hunter, 1964); (3) obtaining the discrepancy or *algebraic difference* between the strengths of relations, a procedure which is derivable from Newcomb's model (Price et al., 1965; Feather, 1966, 1967a, 1967b); (4) obtaining the *average* of the strengths of relations, a procedure derivable from the Osgood-Tannenbaum model, according to Triandis and Fishbein (1963) and Fishbein and Hunter (1964); (5) finding the strength of one or more *interpersonal relations* (as opposed to attitudinal or unit relations) in a structure, and basing the overall impact of balance–unbalance on such relations (Feather, 1966, 1967a, 1967b); and (6) basing an index of balance on the *relation of maximum strength* in a structure (proposed by Cartwright, cited in Price et al., 1965). This six-fold controversy still rages in the literature, and no clear solutions seem readily available.

3 • 4   SUMMARY

It has been the purpose of this chapter to present an introductory discussion of formal graph-theoretic models of balance. The concepts of point, line, graph and cycle were discussed, and the concepts of graph theory were compared to concepts appearing in the theories of Heider and Newcomb. Three alternative methods of counting cycles were illustrated, followed by a presentation of the ways in which one determines whether or not a graph is completely balanced (such as the "even-number" theorem and the decomposition theorem). Two indices of *degree* of balance were cited and contrasted.

Formal models of balance were critically evaluated, showing both their strong and weak points. Among the advantages of formalization are: (a) extending the original substantive theory beyond situations originally conceptualized by the substantive theorists; (b) refining the substantive theory by developing "short cuts" or theorems as means of dealing with complex structures: (c) clarification of ambiguities; (d) redirecting the original theory and suggesting new hypotheses; and (e) providing a technique for the treatment of asymmetric interpersonal relations.

Certain weak points of formalization become evident upon their review. Among the weaknesses are: (a) the issue of discrepancies between cycles or subsets of cycles is not adequately treated; (b) the role of tension in the balance process is ignored; (c) changes in structures over time are not accurately reflected by indices of balance currently in use; (d) the question of ambivalent relations is not handled by formalization (or by the original substantive theory); (e) cycles of differing lengths in a structure are given equal weight in indices of balance, whereas there is some evidence that the effects of a cycle upon P decrease as the length of the particular cycle increases; and (f) there is a standing controversy revolving around whether or not one should multiply the signs and/or strengths of the lines in a cycle or structure in order to ascertain degree of balance.

The two following chapters (Chapters 4 and 5) undertake a review of research evidence which tests the hypotheses of balance theory. Chapter 6 returns to the matter of formal models, and empirical issues which we will encounter in Chapters 4 and 5 can be taken into account at that time.

Appendix on Formal Models:
Some Useful Formulas

This appendix presents and illustrates formulas for obtaining (a) the total number of lines possible in a graph of n points; (b) the total number of local cycles possible for a given point in a graph of n points; (c) the total number of cycles possible in a graph; and (d) the number of "configurations" or signed graphs. Parts of the following material are adapted from Berger et al. (1962), who present some formulas without detailed elaboration. Some modifications and extensions are introduced here. The formulas apply to only Type I graphs (where $T = 1$ type of line). The formulas for determining cycles assume that there are no "vacuous cycles"; i.e., that each pair of points is connected by one directed or nondirected line.

1. *Determining the number of lines possible in a graph of n points.*

   a. Let n be the number of points in graph G. If each pair of points is connected by one line, then there are

$$\binom{n}{2}$$

lines in G.*

   b. *Examples:* The expression $\binom{n}{2}$ is read as

$$\frac{(n)\,(n-1)}{2!} \text{ or as } \frac{(n)\,(n-1)}{(2)\,(1)}.$$

Hence if G contains 5 points,

$$\binom{n}{2} = \frac{(5)\,(4)}{(2)\,(1)} = \frac{20}{2} = 10 \text{ lines possible in } G.$$

A graph of 6 points contains 15 possible lines, and a graph of 7 points contains

* The general expression $\binom{n}{r}$, sometimes written as ^nC_r, is to be read as

$$\frac{n(n-1)(n-2)\ldots(n-r+1)}{r!}$$

If $n = 7$ and $r = 5$, then

$$\binom{n}{r} = \binom{7}{5} = \frac{(7)\,(7-1)\,(7-2)\,(7-3)\,(7-4)}{(5)\,(4)\,(3)\,(2)\,(1)} = \frac{(7)\,(6)\,\cancel{(5)\,(4)\,(3)}}{\cancel{(5)\,(4)\,(3)}\,(2)\,(1)} = \frac{42}{2} = 21.$$

Note that the same number of terms appear in both the numerator and denominator, and that all like terms cancel.

21 possible lines. If n is small, the formula can be easily verified by drawing the respective graphs.

Readers familiar with matrix operations will recognize that

$$\binom{n}{2} = (n^2 - n)/2 = n(n - 1)/2,$$

the number of cells in half of a square matrix of n rows and columns minus the diagonal. Thus, if $n = 5$, then the resulting 5-by-5 matrix contains 5^2 or 25 cells. To consider each pair of points once, and exclude the diagonal, gives 10 cells. For a detailed treatment of the relationships between graph theory and matrix operations, see Harary et al. (1965).

2. *Determining the total number of* local *cycles possible for each point.*

   a. In a graph of n points,

   $\binom{n-1}{n-1}$ gives the total number of n-line cycles possible for each point;

   $\binom{n-1}{n-2}$ gives the total number of $(n-1)$-line cycles possible for each point;

   $\binom{n-1}{n-3}$ gives the total number of $(n-2)$-line cycles possible for each point;

   $\vdots$

   $\binom{n-1}{2}$ gives the total number of 3-line cycles possible for each point. (Where $T = 1$, a 3-line cycle is the smallest possible cycle.)

   b. *Examples:* If G contains 4 points, the total possible n-line cycles or 4-line cycles per point is

$$\binom{n-1}{n-1} = \binom{3}{3} = \frac{(3)(2)(1)}{(3)(2)(1)} = 1 \quad \text{4-line cycle for each point.}$$

The number of $(n-1)$-line or 3-line cycles possible is

$$\binom{n-1}{n-2} = \binom{3}{2} = \frac{(3)(2)}{(2)(1)} = 3 \quad \text{3-line cycles for each point.}$$

A graph of 5 points contains

$$\binom{n-1}{n-1} = \binom{4}{4} \frac{(4)(3)(2)(1)}{(4)(3)(2)(1)} = 1 \quad \text{5-line cycle for each point.}$$

$$\binom{n-1}{n-2} = \binom{4}{3} \frac{(4)(3)(2)}{(3)(2)(1)} = 4 \quad \text{4-line cycles for each point.}$$

$$\binom{n-1}{n-3} = \binom{4}{2} \frac{(4)(3)}{(2)(1)} = 6 \quad \text{3-line cycles for each point.}$$

Hence, the number of local cycles (of any length) possible for a *given point* in this graph is $1 + 4 + 6 = 11$ cycles.

Generally, the number of local cycles (of all lengths) in any graph that pass through a given point is

$$\binom{n-1}{n-1} + \binom{n-1}{n-2} + \binom{n-1}{n-3} + \cdots\cdots + \binom{n-1}{2}$$

Note that this procedure gives the number of local cycles possible for each point, and that the procedure is not redundant.

3. *Determining the total number of cycles possible in a graph.*

a. The total number of cycles possible in a graph of n points is simply the number of cycles per point times the number of points, or

$$n\left[\binom{n-1}{n-1} + \binom{n-1}{n-2} + \binom{n-1}{n-3} + \cdots\cdots + \binom{n-1}{2}\right]$$

Note that this procedure *is* redundant.

b. *Example:* In a graph of 5 points, there are 11 cycles possible for each given point (see the above example). Thus, there are (5)(11) = 55 cycles possible in a graph of 5 points.

4. *Determining the number of configurations (signed graphs).*

a. A "configuration" or "state" is a pattern of lines which have a positive or negative sign. Recall that in Figure 1, Chapter 2, with Heider's three points, P, O and X, where each pair is joined by a positive or negative line, there were eight possible configurations. C, the number of configurations, is defined as follows:

$$C = S^{\binom{n}{2}}$$

where

S = the number of signs that each line may have; and
n = the number of points in the graph.

b. *Examples:* In a graph of only 2 points, where the single line joining them may be positive or negative, there are

$$C = S^{\binom{n}{2}} = 2^{\binom{2}{2}} = 2^1 = 2 \text{ configurations.}$$

In a graph of three points, where each line joining any pair of points may have a positive or negative sign, there are

$$C = S^{\binom{n}{2}} = 2^{\binom{3}{2}} = 2^3 = 8 \text{ configurations (cf. Chapter 2, Figure 1).}$$

Note that this formula actually gives the number of signed graphs possible for n points and S signs. The formula is applicable even if a line is positive, negative, or neutral (absent). With three points, where each line is positive, negative or neutral, there are

$$\binom{3}{2}$$

3 or 27 separate signed graphs.

For a graph containing a small number of points, this formula can be easily verified using a cross-classification. With three points, A, B and C, and two signs $(+, -)$ possible for each line, a cross-classification yields eight cells, each cell representing a particular combination of signs:

The AB line is: +   −

The BC line is: + | − | + | −

The AC line is: + [table cells]
                        −

4....

Molar Processes

Chapter 2 of this book was intended as an introductory review of the substantive varieties of balance theory. Chapter 3 presented an introductory discussion of graph-theoretic formalizations of the theory. Both of these chapters focused primarily upon the theoretical literature; discussion of research findings was postponed until now. The task of the present chapter, and Chapters 5, 6 and 7, will be to present a detailed treatment of the empirical literature on balance. An outline of the strategy to be employed in our review of research findings is presented below. Whereas the present chapter will focus primarily upon studies which test deductions from one or more of the four "general propositions" of balance theory, Chapter 5 will review literature which yields "conditional" propositions or relationships—findings which modify, limit or refine the general propositions.

4 • 1   THE STRATEGY OF THE REVIEW

In any review of empirical studies, concrete observations and research evidence, the logic of scientific inquiry demands the close scrutiny of results in the light of, and as they have bearing upon, propostions or hypotheses. Two main kinds of propositions concern us here: general propositions and conditional propositions.

A *general proposition* or hypothesis is a statement of the expected relationship between two variables. The statement "Y (the dependent variable) is a function of X (the independent variable)," or more specifically, "Y is an inverse (or direct) function of X," is a general proposition. An example would be: "Under given conditions of unbalance, the focal person will change some orientation in the direction of balance. Under given conditions of balance, no change is expected." This is a general proposition which predicts a relationship between balance–unbalance (the independent variable) and change in orientation (the dependent variable).

Once a general proposition is stated, one or more *deductions* may be obtained from it. Loosely defined, a deduction is any specific derivation or inference from a general proposition. The deduction uses the general proposition as its "source" or "foundation." In most cases, a deduction is intended to apply to some concrete situation; it states the general proposition in a form which renders it testable in a specific empirical context. In this way, a deduction from a general proposition becomes a *working hypothesis* or *research hypothesis*. For example, from the general proposition stated in the preceding paragraph, the following deduction, a working hypothesis, can be made: "If a laboratory subject (P) likes the experimenter (O) but disagrees with him on an important political issue (X)—an unbalanced condition—then the subject will alter or change one or more of the following three variables in the direction of balance: his attitude toward the issue, his perception of the experimenter's attitude, or his liking for the experimenter. If, in contrast, he both likes and agrees with the experimenter, then no changes in these three variables are likely to occur." Such a prediction is a "deduction" since it applies to a specific empirical situation (in this instance, a laboratory experiment rather than a "freely formed" group), a specific person (the subject rather than the experimenter), and to specific variables (balance–unbalance, attitude, perceived attitude, and liking). The general proposition states the predictions broadly, and the deduction specifies and explicates them. The empirical studies to be reviewed in this chapter can be seen as tests of one or more deductions from the general propositions of balance theory.[1]

Whereas a general proposition predicts a relationship "between X and Y," a *conditional proposition* asserts that the relationship between X and Y will depend upon the value of some third variable, Z. "Tension (Y) is a function of balance–unbalance (X), such that more tension is produced by unbalance than by balance," is a general proposition. This prediction can be *modified* by the introduction of a third variable: "The relationship between tension (Y) and balance–unbalance (X) depends upon the importance of the issue (Z)." This prediction is clarified and made more precise if one says: "More tension is produced by unbalance than by balance if the issue is important. If the issue is unimportant, then conditions of balance and unbalance will not differ in tension." Such a conditional proposition is of the form, "Y is related to X only if Z; if not-Z, Y is not related to X."

This is a "strong" form of conditional proposition. Weaker forms are possible. For example: "Y is inversely related to X for *both* Z and not-Z, but the *degree* or *magnitude* of the relationship is higher if Z as opposed to not-Z." This is a relatively "weak" or moderate form of conditional relationship. Using the balance–tension example, one might want to predict that the correlation or

---

1. The technique of using general propositions as sources for deductions which are then evaluated against empirical evidence is employed by Homans (1961) in his review of small group studies pertaining to his "exchange theory."

degree of association between balance and tension is inverse regardless of the importance of the issue, but that the correlation is higher in magnitude if the issue is important than if it is unimportant. Hence, should one be using some measure of correlation or association, one would examine its magnitude—the "variance explained"—within the separate categories of the conditional variable, Z/not-Z. Other examples of "strong" and "weak" conditional propositions will be encountered throughout this and particularly the next chapter. *This text will devote considerable time to the discussion of research findings which lead to the statement of conditional propositions or relationships—relationships which modify, either in a strong way or in a relatively weak (but yet important) way, the general propositions of balance theory.*

4 • 1a The Structure of the Theory: The Propositions of Balance Preference, Balance Tendency, Tension, and Tension Reduction

There are four general propositions under which the literature on balance will be evaluated and examined. They will be referred to as the hypotheses (propositions) of Balance Preference, Balance Tendency, Tension, and Tension Reduction. These four hypotheses are intended to represent, collectively, the postulated balance process discussed in Chapter 2. Quite a few deductions are attainable from each. The present section will give each of the four general propositions in sequence, stating them in a clear way, and examining a few illustrative deductions from each. A general proposition will be abbreviated as "*GP*." This is to distinguish it from the conditional propositions ("*CP*") to be discussed later.

The balance process postulated in Chapter 2 encompasses not a single proposition, but a number of related propositions. Let us begin to break down "the balance process" into its component parts, these parts being the general propositions of the theory. The first one is the Balance Preference hypothesis:

GP 1 *(Balance Preference): At any given time, the focal person will prefer balance to unbalance.*

This represents a most general statement of one of the fundamental predictions of balance theory. Under it are subsumed an extensive variety of predictions (deductions) under varying conditions, settings, situations, and types of variables. A large number of deductions are tested in the literature. Some examples: (a) The focal person's (*P*'s) liking for the other (*O*) is a function of whether or not the focal person perceives that he and *O* are similar in their orientations to an issue, *X*. Liking is produced by perceived similarity ("agreement"), whereas less liking (or even dislike) is produced by perceived dissimilarity ("disagreement"). This prediction can be turned around, treating perceived similarity as the dependent variable, thus yielding another deduction: (b) If the focal person likes the other, he will tend to perceive the other as similar to himself in orientation toward X. If he dislikes the other, he will be less likely to perceive that he and the other are similar in orientation toward X. An additional deduction will be examined in this chapter: (c) If the person likes the other, he will tend to perceive that he and the other are similar with respect to X even if the other is in fact dissimilar to some degree. Thus, there may be a tendency for *perceived* similarity to be in excess of *objective* similarity (if P likes O)—a prediction discussed in the second chapter in connection with Newcomb's "autistic" balance. A fourth deduction is: (d) The focal person will *learn* a balanced structure faster and with fewer "errors" than he will learn an unbalanced structure. What is being predicted here is that at any given time, the focal person finds balance "easier" to perceive and absorb than unbalance; unbalance is a troublesome, uncomfortable state, to be generally avoided and "blocked out" whenever possible. Other deductions from the Balance Preference hypothesis are possible, but these few constitute clear illustrations.

Take another look at the Balance Preference hypothesis. It says: At any *given time,* balance will be preferred to unbalance. In this prediction, time is a constant. What if one *varies* time and is interested in predicting how structures will move or change from a given time (T 1) to some near or distant future time (T 2)? A second general proposition under which the empirical literature will be examined involves predictions about *changes* in orientations or relations. The prediction will be called the Balance Tendency hypothesis. To be accurately tested, at least two measures ("before" and "after"; "initial" and "final") of attitude, liking, etc., would have to be taken.

> GP 2   *(Balance Tendency): Given unbalance at time 1, the focal person will change an objective orientation or relation (such as attitude or liking), or a perceived orientation or relation (such as the perception of the other's attitude or liking) in the direction of balance; such changes take place subsequent to time 1. In contrast, given balance at time 1, no changes in orientations are likely to occur.*

This hypothesis has bearing on the matter of stability and change. A balanced structure of orientations is hypothesized to be more stable—less likely to change—than an unbalanced structure. As with the Balance Preference hypothesis, various deductions can be obtained. One set of deductions might concern changes in interpersonal orientations: sentiment, liking, attraction, and so on. Another set of deductions concern changes in attitudinal orientations—attitudes and perceived attitudes. (Whether or not attitudinal and interpersonal orientations are equally likely to change is an important question to be examined in the next chapter.)

It is necessary at this time to introduce a second meaning of the term "deduction." The first meaning has already been cited: A deduction from a *single* general proposition is a working hypothesis or research hypothesis; it predicts that the relationship stated in the general proposition will be applicable to some specific empirical situation. The first meaning of the term deduction is utilized by Homans (1961) in a review of small group studies. We will call this first meaning of the term deduction the "Homans meaning." A wholly different type of deduction, however, involves *two or more* general propositions as the source of the deduction. The second type of deduction is illustrated by the following syllogism:

(a) Proposition: A is directly related to B.

(b) Proposition: B is inversely related to C.

(c) Deduction: A is inversely related to C.

The deduction—the *conclusion* to the syllogism—follows logically, because if B increases as A increases, and C *decreases* as B increases, then it follows that C decreases as A increases—C is inversely related to A. This second meaning of deduction, involving two (or more) general propositions as premises and the deduction as the conclusion, was developed in sociology by Zetterberg (1954) and later refined by Costner and Leik (1964). We will refer to this second interpretation of deduction as the Zetterberg or "axiomatic" meaning: Given two general propositions, a third proposition (deduction) follows necessarily— it is "axiomatic."

Note that the Balance Tendency hypothesis (GP 2) is actually a deduction of this second type. It was reasoned in Chapter 2 that: (a) unbalance produces high tension, and (b) high tension produces change toward balance. It therefore follows that (c) unbalance produces change toward balance. This is just what the Balance Tendency hypothesis predicts. It is important to note, however, that while a given deduction follows *logically* from two general propositions, it is not necessarily true that the deduction will hold up *empirically*. We simply *predict* and *expect* that unbalance produces changes in orientations toward balance. Whether or not this actually happens is what we want to test. Furthermore, as Costner and Leik (1964) have shown, even if the relationship "A is directly related to B" is empirically upheld, and a relationship "B is inversely related to C" is also empirically upheld, the logical inference that A is inversely related to C will not always be validated empirically. This is why all three such propositions must be subjected to empirical test—and it is one reason why we are in the process of stating the general propositions of balance theory separately.

There are two additional general propositions subsumed under the postulated balance process. As above, one proposition holds time constant, whereas the other demands the examination of changes over time. The next proposition, taking tension as the dependent variable, time constant, is:

GP 3 *(Tension): At any given time, the focal person's tension will be higher under conditions of unbalance (at that time) than under conditions of balance.*

It will be recalled that tension is one posited "mechanism" or intervening variable in the balance process. Unbalance at a particular time produces relatively high tension; a state of unbalance is psychologically uncomfortable and unpleasant. This high tension state will—according to the theory—result in cognitive changes on the part of the focal person in the direction of balance. When this happens, a reduction in the magnitude of the focal person's tension is expected to result. Hence, a fourth proposition, predicting that tension is reduced as a function of changes in the direction of balance, can be stated. In this instance, one is interested in changes in tension through time rather than in the magnitude of tension at a "given time," as in GP 3.

GP 4 *(Tension Reduction): Under the condition that the focal person has changed an objective or perceived orientation in the direction of balance, then a decrease or reduction in his tension will take place. Under the condition that the focal person has made little or no change in orientation, then there will be no relative reduction in his tension.*

This proposition warrants close scrutiny. Note that in it, change/not-change is the independent variable, and tension reduction/non-reduction is the dependent variable. Change toward balance results in a reduction in tension. But this proposition can also be stated with balance–unbalance as the independent variable. In so doing, the second (axiomatic) meaning of deduction is employed: Initial unbalance results in high initial tension; high initial tension results in change in orientation; and change in orientation results in tension reduction. Therefore:

GP 4a *(Tension Reduction): Under conditions of unbalance at time 1, the focal person's tension will be reduced subsequent to time 1. Under conditions of balance at time 1, no relative reduction in tension will take place.*

Both GP 4 and GP 4a are different forms of the Tension Reduction hypothesis, since they treat tension reduction/nonreduction as the dependent variable. The only difference is that GP 4 takes change as the independent variable, whereas GP 4a takes balance–unbalance as the independent variable.

At the risk of being hyperformal (if we haven't been so already!) it should be pointed out that there are logically seven separate propositions embedded in the postulated balance process. The first four are taken as "given," the last three representing "axiomatic" deductions from the given ones. In simplified form, they are:

1. The focal person will prefer balance to unbalance (GP 1).
2. Unbalance results in high tension (GP 3).
3. High tension results in change toward balance.
4. Change toward balance results in a reduction in tension (GP 4).

These four predictions summarize the balance process, but imperfectly, since three more predictions can be deduced from the first four:

5. (Deduced from statements 2 and 3): Unbalance results in change toward balance (GP 2).
6. (Deduced from statements 3 and 4): High tension results in a reduction in tension.
7. (Deduced from statements 2, 3 and 4 together): Unbalance results in a reduction in tension (GP 4a).

Predictions 1, 2, 4, 5 and 7 have already been stated as general propositions. Statements 3 and 6 must remain unstated as "propositions" for two reasons. First, it was pointed out in the second chapter that prediction 3 is not a testable proposition *by itself,* since high tension will (so it is predicted) result in change toward balance *only if* the cause of high tension was unbalance. If the cause of high tension is something *other than* unbalance, then prediction 3 is not testable. Second, by itself, prediction 6 is not testable. To say that "high tension results in tension reduction" is meaningless, unless considered within the framework of the other statements.

The four general propositions just discussed are intended to serve as guides for our review of the empirical literature. First of all, they represent concise statements of the core predictions of balance theory. Second, they represent categories into which the rather large mass of research findings may be classified. Thus, our review of the empirical literature can proceed in a clear and systematic fashion. The specific working hypotheses from most studies can be treated as deductions (in the Homans sense) from one or more of the general propositions. Third, once the general propositions of the theory are concisely stated, it is possible to locate research findings which clearly modify, if not completely refute, a general proposition.

4 • 1b *Conditional Propositions*

A conditional proposition or relationship, for our purposes, will be defined as any proposition or relationship which modifies, refines, broadens, extends, cancels, or completely reverses the predictions of one or more of the general propositions. It is the purpose of this chapter to examine the literature having bearing on the general propositions. Consequently, this chapter will present a framework which can then be modified and restructured by the review of conditional propositions and relationships in Chapter 5.

The literature yields at least three broad sources or "origins" of conditional propositions. They are: (1) a proposition, hypothesis or principle which is itself not deducible from one or more of the general propositions of balance theory; (2) parameter variables; and (3) nonparameter variables. A description of these three sources of conditional propositions follows.

Any proposition which is not deducible from a general proposition of balance theory is a potential modification of one or more of the four general balance propositions, and therefore implies a conditional proposition. The Rosenberg-Abelson "least cost" hypothesis, introduced in Chapters 2 and 3, is an example. The postulation of least cost or least effort is not deducible from balance theory, yet it can be applied to the problem of balance maintenance, hence modifying one of the general propositions (in this case, the Balance Tendency hypothesis). The logic is as follows: First of all, a general *principle* is stated: "People prefer the line of minimum resistance or minimum effort to a line of greater-than-minimum resistance or effort." This psychological principle—and it is a "principle" in the truest sense—is not deducible from balance theory. It is a very broad prediction, having applicability to a number of areas in social psychology, sociology, economics, and in other disciplines. If it is applied to the problem of balance, it modifies the Balance Tendency hypothesis (GP 2). The appropriate modification is: "Given unbalance, the focal person will change toward balance *in such a way as to minimize the number of changes.*" This proposition is a conditional one, since it modifies a general proposition.

Whereas this kind (the first kind) of conditional proposition uses a principle not deducible from balance theory as its source, a second type of conditional proposition uses a *variable* (rather than a principle per se) as its source. "The relationship between balance and tension depends upon the importance of the issue" is a conditional proposition employing the conditional variable "importance of the issue." The hypothesis is a conditional one because it modifies the Tension hypothesis (GP 3).

Now, a conditional variable itself may be of two classes. One class will be called parameter variables, the other non-parameter variables. A *parameter variable,* within the context of balance theory, is some attribute or characteristic of the structural unit under study. Clearly, the variables like-dislike and agree-disagree are parameter variables—they are used to define states of balance and unbalance. Attitude, perceived attitude, liking and perceived liking are all parameter variables. Importance of the issue is also a parameter variable—it is an attribute which the focal person assigns to the object X; it is therefore part of the structure of relations under study.

Parameter variables can be used as independent variables in their own right. Hence, they can result in the modification of a general proposition. For this reason, parameter variables are a second source of conditional propositions.

Some examples of how this comes about might be cited. In a study, one might find that balance–unbalance is related to tension, but that the parameter variable like-dislike is also independently related to tension. In other words, the variable balance–unbalance predicts tension, but regardless of whether there is balance or unbalance, like-dislike also predicts tension. In a two-way analysis of variance test, there would be two "main effects"—both balance and liking affect tension independently of each other. In addition, an "interaction effect" might be observed, in which case both variables acting together affect tension. In the instance of two main effects (and no interaction effect), the Tension hypothesis (GP 3) is still modified; the information is of interest, because one of the parameter variables affects tension independently of balance–unbalance. Should one obtain two main effects *and* an interaction effect, a modified statement of GP 3 (i.e., a conditional proposition) would still be in order.

Findings of this latter sort would give rise to "weak" conditional propositions. But what if one found that *only* liking was related to tension, and that balance–unbalance was not; namely, a main effect of liking, but no effect of balance–unbalance (and no interaction effect)? Such a finding would result in a strong modification, indeed a very strong one, of the Tension hypothesis. It is because of this latter possibility, or analogous possibilities, that the evaluation of the separate effects of parameter variables is particularly important in our review. In this way, parameter variables constitute the second source of conditional propositions.

The term "corollary" is sometimes used in the balance literature to apply to some modification of the theory. In this text, *corollary* will refer to any conditional proposition that uses either of the two following sources: principles or hypotheses that are not deducible from balance theory, or parameter variables. The word corollary is used to distinguish conditional propositions that use these first two sources from conditional propositions that use the third source, to be described directly.

So far, then, there are two sources of conditional propositions: principles, propositions or hypotheses not deducible from balance theory, and parameter variables. A third source of conditional propositions consists of one or more *nonparameter variables*. A nonparameter variable is any potentially confounding or conditional variable which is not, conceptually speaking, part of the structure of relations under study. At least two broad classes of nonparameter variables are found to affect the balance process and are therefore taken into account in our review: (1) Personality variables, such as self-evaluation, authoritarianism, intolerance for inconsistency, cognitive complexity, affiliation need, and others; and (2) social-structural variables, such as competition-cooperation, or socioeconomic status. Although the literature is very meager in considering this latter class of conditional variables in relation to balance dynamics (it is not particularly systematic or thorough in regard to the former class, either), a section of the next chapter is devoted to the results that are available. Perhaps because a vast bulk of the literature on balance is written by social psychologists trained as psychologists rather than by social psychologists trained as sociologists, the former class of conditional variables (personality or "predispositional" variables) is evoked with greater frequency than the latter class.

Let us summarize what has been said so far. A *general proposition* is a statement of one of the fundamental predictions of balance theory, and specifies the expected relationship between one independent variable (such as balance–unbalance) and one dependent variable (such as tension, change, or tension reduction). Four general propositions were introduced: The hypotheses of Balance Preference, Balance Tendency, Tension, and Tension Reduction. Two meanings of the term *deduction* are used in this book: A deduction can be either a statement of a general proposition which makes it applicable to some concrete situation, or a proposition which is logically deduced from two or more general propositions. The first (Homans) type of deduction is obtained from a *single* general proposition, whereas the second (axiomatic) type is obtained from *two or more* general propositions. A *conditional proposition* is a statement which modifies, either in a strong way or in a weak (yet important) way, one or more general propositions. Conditional propositions have three sources: (1) principles, propositions or hypotheses which are not themselves deducible from balance theory (i.e., from the general propositions); (2) parameter variables (liking, attitude, agreement, and so on); and (3) non-parameter variables (personality or "predispositional" variables, and social-structural variables). A *corollary* is a conditional proposition which comes from either one of the first two sources.

4 • 2 MOLAR PROCESSES: TESTS OF THE GENERAL PROPOSITIONS

The remainder of this chapter will be devoted to the review of studies which test deductions from the general propositions of balance theory. It is evident that a general proposition postulates what was referred to earlier as a *molar process*—a "basic" or "fundamental" interpersonal or cognitive balancing process which involves parameter variables. For the remainder of this book, a molar process will be taken to mean any process which is predicted by one of the general propositions. Molar processes are to be distinguished from microprocesses (such as denial, differentiation, etc.) which do not involve preferences or changes in regard to parameter variables. It should be pointed out that this chapter examines empirical literature having direct bearing upon one or more of the general propositions, but only tangential—if any—relevance for conditional propositions. Chapter 5 reviews studies which are relevant for *both* general and conditional propositions.

The molar process literature is divided into two classes of theoretical perspectives, the *interpersonal perspective,* following the theoretical formulations of Heider and Newcomb, where at least two persons are part of the structural unit of analysis, and the *cognitive perspective* following the formulations of Osgood and associates, where the mind or "cognitive structure" of only one person is considered. Only one person is part of the structural unit of analysis, and other objects in the structure are non-person objects (issues, countries, political candidates, etc.). In this text, the former perspective is given somewhat more attention than the latter, due to the focus upon group processes. However, a section of the following chapter, and part of the sixth chapter, are devoted exclusively to the Osgood model and research following the cognitive perspective.

Empirical literature following the interpersonal perspective is further subdivided according to the type of *design* employed in the study. Section 4.2a below will review studies of the *interpersonal-concrete* design: studies done on or more persons who are actually interacting or communicating. An additional section (section 4.2b) reviews studies of the *interpersonal-hypothetical* design: studies which, although they clearly employ the interpersonal (rather than the cognitive) perspective, focus upon only one person or subject who is asked to imagine or visualize that he is one kind of group or another, or if he is not asked to "be" a member of some hypothetical group, he is nevertheless asked to form perceptions and answer questions pertaining to groups of persons.

4 • 2a   *Interpersonal-Concrete Designs*

Studies utilizing the interpersonal-concrete design are characterized in two ways. First, they focus on the Heider or Newcomb variety of the theory. For the most part, the *POX* (dyadic) or *POQ* (triadic) units constitute the units of analysis in the study. At least two persons are involved. Second, studies using the interpersonal concrete design examine groups of persons who are actually interacting or communicating. (This is contrasted with the interpersonal-hypothetical design, where interest is in group processes, but where only one noninteracting subject is studied.) Interpersonal-concrete studies are subdivided according to whether a measure of tension is employed. The following section reviews studies which measure tension.

Tension Measured: Preference, Tendency and Tension

Early research by Festinger and Hutte (1954), a sociometric study, focused upon triadic networks in discussion groups. The *POQ* unit (the triad), rather than the *POX* unit (the dyad), was of central interest. An experimental manipulation was employed, as follows: In one condition, the focal person (P) was led to believe that two of his positive sociometric choices (his friends, O and Q) liked each other. This was the balanced, or "stable," condition. In a second condition, P was led to believe that his two positive choices (friends) *disliked* each other—representing an unbalanced (unstable) condition.

Two hypotheses were tested. The first predicted that in the unbalanced condition, the focal person would feel uncomfortable and uncertain about his "social relations in the group." Hence, the study represents a test of the Tension hypothesis (GP 3): Unbalance produces more tension (discomfort and uncertainty) than balance. It was found that in fact, group members who perceived that their two friends disliked each other felt more uncomfortable and uncertain than group members who perceived that their two friends liked each other. The results supported the Tension hypothesis.

The second hypothesis of the study illustrates an application of the Balance Tendency prediction (GP 2). It was expected that after P discovered that his two friends disliked each other (unbalance), he would want to alter or change either his choice of O as a friend, his choice of Q, or his *perception* of the O–Q choice. In contrast, a focal person discovering that his two friends liked each other (balance) would be less likely to desire any of these changes. A balanced triad was therefore expected to be more stable than an unbalanced one. The data markedly supported the hypothesis. Not only were persons under the unbalance induction more likely to actually change their O and Q choices, but they were more likely to alter their perceptions of how O and Q felt toward each other; they tended to perceive O and Q as having *increased* their liking for one another. Persons under the balance induction were less likely to make any of these three changes.

The most obvious criticism of this study is that all combinations of signs were not examined. The investigators might have studied conditions under which P disliked both O and Q (who in turn would be perceived as liking or disliking each other), and conditions under which P liked O but disliked Q (with both like and then dislike between O and Q)—a condition isomorphic to P liking Q and disliking O. Thus, six conditions could have been created. As the study stands, it is the OQ bond that is the independent variable of the study, not balance–unbalance. The fact that P liked both O and Q in both conditions used means that the PO and PQ bonds were constants, and therefore cannot be used as explanatory variables in the study. It can therefore be argued that a person's perception of dislike between *any* pair of others in the group (regardless of whether P likes or dislikes the members of that pair) is a source of tension and desire for change; *there is no need to use the balance principle in explaining the results.* Surprisingly, this kind of conceptual error is made rather often in the literature, even in some very recent empirical studies (e.g., Price et al., 1965) and theoretical articles (e.g., Newcomb, 1968), to be reviewed later.[2]

An additional shortcoming of the Festinger-Hutte study can be identified:

2. Newcomb's (1968) recent "three-category" balance formulation defines "balance" as like-agree and "unbalance" as like-disagree. All situations of dislike are defined as "nonbalanced." But if defined in this manner, the distinction between balance and unbalance is only a distinction in terms of agreement; agreement, not balance–unbalance, is the explanatory or independent variable. This problem is discussed later in this chapter and again in Chapter 7.

Only symmetric OQ relations were considered: O and Q were presented to P as both liking or disliking each other. Conditions under which the perceived OQ relation is asymmetric ($+OQ$ and $-QO$, or vice versa) were not considered. The question of perceived asymmetric relations between two others has received some recent attention, and will be taken up later.

The first error, failure to examine all sign combinations (and thus erroneously attribute results to the balance principle), was also made in a study by Burdick and Burnes (1958). In contrast to Festinger and Hutte, these investigators studied the dyad, or POX unit. They established two conditions: (1) The experimental subject (P) liked the experimenter (O) and agreed with him on a topic (X) of discussion (the balance condition); and (2) the subject liked the experimenter but was forced to disagree with him (the unbalance condition). Liking was validated by a post-experimental questionnaire. Manipulation of agreement was made possible by means of a pre-experimental measure of the subjects' attitude, and the experimenter simply agreed or disagreed with that attitude during the ensuing discussion with the subject.

The study tested a deduction from the Tension hypothesis (GP 3), predicting that more tension accompanies unbalance than balance. Tension was measured by Galvanic Skin Resistance (GSR) deflections on the subject, a greater deflection indicating higher tension. As predicted, GSR deflections were greater under the like-disagree than under the like-agree condition. It is noted, however, that since liking is a constant (only the "like" category of the like-dislike variable was used), and only agreement was varied, it is agreement, not balance–unbalance, that is the source for the differences in tension. Again, one need not refer to the balance principle to explain these results, but only to the variable agree-disagree.

This conceptual error was eliminated in a study of the POX unit by Sampson and Insko (1964). The study used an autokinetic apparatus, where the subject (P) made judgments about the apparent movement of light (X). The role of the other (O) was played by a trained assistant. In order to induce P's liking for O, the assistant had a congenial discussion with the subject prior to the experiment. To induce dislike before the experiment, the assistant heavily criticized the subject's political views, berated his ability to judge people, and generally made himself very obnoxious. The like-dislike induction was validated by a post-experimental questionnaire. To manipulate agreement (similarity of judgment in light of movement), the assistant simply announced his judgment after the subject has announced his, and made it similar or dissimilar depending upon the desired induction. Hence, four experimental conditions were created: like-similar and dislike-dissimilar (balance); and like-dissimilar and dislike-similar (unbalance).

It was found that under the like-dissimilar (unbalance) condition, the subject tended to shift his judgment of light movement toward that of the assistant. This is a change or shift toward balance, as predicted. If the subject disliked the assistant but was initially similar to him in judgment (unbalance), then the subject would shift his judgment *away* from that of the assistant— also a change in the direction of balance. Subjects under the two balance conditions were less likely to shift their judgments. The results of this study thus provide support for a deduction from the Balance Tendency hypothesis: shifts in judgments of X (light movement) are more likely to occur under initially unbalanced than under initially balanced conditions, and such shifts are in the direction of increased balance.

An additional set of findings is of interest. The subject was asked, after the experiment, to rate his feelings during the experiment on a "nervous-calm" scale. It was found that "nervous" ratings were significantly more likely to occur under unbalanced than under balanced conditions, thus lending support to the Tension hypothesis. Furthermore, the independent effects of like-dislike and similar-dissimilar were not significant, demonstrating that balance-unbalance (rather than just liking or similarity) was the explanatory variable. Namely, it is not liking alone or similarity alone that determines tension, but both variables in combination (i.e., balance-unbalance). It should be noted, in addition, that no independent effects of liking and similarity were found with respect to change in judgment of light movement. Hence, the results of this study provide convincing supportive evidence for both the Balance Tendency and the Tension hypotheses.

Three limitations to the Sampson-Insko study, though they are not extremely severe ones, are apparent. First, in order to induce P's liking or dislike for O, O verbally agreed or disagreed with P on issues (X's) not directly involved in the following experiment. But this procedure assumes *a priori* that one of the hypotheses of balance theory is true: that agreement results in liking, and disagreement results in dislike. In fact, this is what the Balance Preference hypothesis (GP 1) predicts, and the induction was validated by means of a post-experimental questionnaire. This procedure is questionable since (a) liking might have changed to some degree *during* the experiment—the period between the induction and the administration of the post-experimental questionnaire; and (b) one wonders how many subjects were not successfully induced to like or dislike the assistant, O. It is possible that a number of subjects felt neutral toward O, or even that in one or two cases, dislike was induced when liking was supposed to have been induced, or vice versa. *On the average,* those receiving the dislike induction disliked O, and those receiving the like induction liked O. But all cases were lumped together in order to test for the validity of the induction, and a few cases might have been incorrectly induced. Such a "misinduction" could have affected the results that were observed during the experiment. One is unable to evaluate the number of "misinduced" cases since the investigators do not present case-by-case data.

A second limitation is that the investigators measured "nervousness-calmness" (tension) only after the experiment. They could have easily measured it both before and after, thus obtaining a longitudinal measurement of tension. It would then have been possible to test a deduction from the Tension Reduction hypothesis (GP 4)—that tension starts high and decreases under initially unbalanced conditions, but that it starts low and exhibits less (if any) decrease under initially balanced conditions. One could then infer that, as shifts in judgment from unbalance to balance are made, tension or nervousness is reduced.

This single modification (an initial measurement of tension) would have permitted a test not only of the Balance Tendency and Tension hypotheses (which was done), but also a test of the Tension Reduction hypothesis. Interestingly, to the author's knowledge, only one study (Taylor, 1968) tests the prediction that tension is reduced as a function of changes arising from unbalance. The results of this study, which support the Tension Reduction hypothesis, are discussed in Chapter 7. Past studies employing a measurement of tension, whether they are of the interpersonal-concrete, interpersonal-hypothetical, or cognitive varieties, have measured tension only in cross-sectional fashion, at one point (usually "after") in an experiment or study, thus not permitting a test of the Tension Reduction hypothesis.

A third limitation of the Sampson-Insko study, one that has very important implications, is that the longitudinal measurement of liking was not employed. The investigators assumed that once either like or dislike was induced, it remained constant during the period in which the subject made his judgments of light movement. The conclusions of the study might have been considerably different if liking was measured both before and after this period. Note that if the subject initially liked the assistant but was dissimilar to him in judgment, a shift in the subject's judgment toward that of the assistant was interpreted as a shift toward balance. But what if the subject *decreased* his liking for the assistant during the period in which he made the judgments? Taking the changes in liking and judgment together, they represent composite shifts in a direction of agreement and dislike—*shifts in the direction of unbalance rather than balance.* Such a finding would be opposite to predictions under the Balance Tendency hypothesis. *In this respect, the study was not sensitive to changes which could disconfirm the Balance Tendency hypothesis; the investigators did not permit the potential isolation of negative findings.*

The fact that studies in balance are typically not sensitive to negative findings has been noted before (Rosenberg and Abelson, 1960; McGuire, 1966). Yet, it is a shortcoming which has been only very minimally rectified. What is needed is a study which not only is sensitive to negative or disconfirming findings, but in addition provides suitable explanations for negative results that might be obtained. A few studies have obtained disconfirming results and provide attractive alternative explanations (although they were not done in interpersonal-concrete situations), most notably a study by Zajonc and Sherman (1967), who found no effects of the independent variable balance–unbalance, and two studies on negative self-evaluation by Kind (1965) and by Deutsch and Solomon (1959), who found that the predictions of the Balance Preference hypothesis are completely reversed if *P* evaluates himself negatively rather than positively. These studies, plus others which lead to disconfirming results, will be reviewed later. But by and large, disconfirming studies are few and far between. It is safe to say that *empirical studies using the interpersonal-concrete design (both those that employ a measure of tension and those that do not) have failed to produce any disconfirming or negative results.*

Tension Not Measured: Sociometric Studies of Balance Preference and Tendency

Certain studies of the interpersonal-concrete design test only the Balance Preference or Balance Tendency hypotheses, since no measurement of tension is employed. Typically, these studies are sociometric ones, measuring both positive (liking) and negative (dislike) sociometric choices. The earliest published study in the area of balance and consistency is of this variety, a study of the triad-and-*X* (*POQX*) unit (a unit consisting of *three* persons plus one *X*) by Horowitz et al. (1951). The group studied was a psychology class, and the object *X* represented various current event issues. Taking any given person in the group as the focal person (*P*), his liking for *two* others (*O* and *Q*) was ascertained. In addition, *P*'s attitude toward given issues was measured, as was his perception of the attitudes that *O* and *Q* had toward the issue. It was found that if *P* liked *O* and *Q*, they were perceived as having attitudes toward the issues which were similar to those of the self (*P*). Hence, *O* and *Q* were perceived as being similar to each other in their respective attitudes. In contrast, if *P* disliked *O* and *Q*, *P* perceived that the attitudes of *O* and *Q* were different from his own. The study therefore tested the Balance Preference hypothesis on a four-object unit (three persons and one *X*).

This study was followed by other sociometric investigations of dyadic and triadic structures. Whereas some of these studies employed longitudinal measurement of choice (liking) patterns, and hence could test deductions from the Balance Tendency hypothesis, other studies employed cross-sectional measurement, therefore focusing on the predictions of Balance Preference. A cross-sectional study of college roommate choices by Broxton (1963) showed that women choose as roommates those whom they perceive as similar to themselves on personality traits rather than those who are perceived as dissimilar. Note that the object "*X*" in this *POX* unit is a personality trait rather than a topic or issue. King (1964), after identifying cliques or subgroups in a psychology class, found that within-clique similarity of attitudes toward issues was greater than between-clique similarity. Since in this study no limit was placed on the number of persons per clique, the results suggest the applicability of the Balance Preference hypothesis beyond only dyadic and triadic structures, as did the results of the early Horowitz et al. (1951) study.

A study by Kogan and Tagiuri (1958) of choice patterns among Naval enlisted men is significant because it explores the question of objective versus subjective balance preference. The investigators studied triadic (POQ) structures in five separate work teams on a ship. *Objective balance* existed if, say, P chose both O and Q, and O and Q also chose each other. *Subjective balance* existed if P chose both O and Q, and *thought* that O and Q chose each other, regardless of whether they did or not. It was found that in all five groups, the number of subjectively balanced structures exceeded the number of objectively balanced structures. This finding lends support to Newcomb's (1959; 1961; 1963) proposition that autistically (subjectively) balanced structures occur more frequently than objectively balanced ones, suggesting that people will frequently distort reality in exhibiting a preference for balanced states. Identical findings have been obtained by other investigators: Byrne and Blaylock (1963) and Levinger and Breedlove (1966) find that married couples overestimate the extent to which they actually agree on political and current event issues. Similarly, in a study of a college rooming house, Newcomb (1961) found that subjective agreement with a liked other often exceeds objective agreement, and that it is exceedingly rare for the reverse to be true—that objective agreement exceeds subjective agreement. The Broxton (1963) study, cited above, showed that subjective similarity on personality traits of chosen roommates tended to be greater than objective similarity on these traits.

Unlike the foregoing studies, other sociometric studies ascertained changes in either attitudes or choice patterns by means of longitudinal measurement. Deductions from the Balance Tendency hypothesis were therefore tested. Gerard (1954) employed only one initial measure of choice (liking), but measured attitude change longitudinally. A number of groups consisting of union members who discussed labor-management issues were studied. Six experimental conditions were created, three of which were the "high-attraction" type, and three of which were the "low-attraction" type. In each category of attraction, persons were combined so that they either agreed, mildly disagreed or strongly disagreed with the others in the group. It was found that persons in the high-attraction–strongly-disagree condition were most likely to change their opinions of labor-management issues in the direction of the opinion of an attractive other. Persons in the high-attraction–mildly-disagree condition were next most likely to change. Persons in the high-attraction–agree condition, or in the low-attraction–disagree condition (both conditions represent balance) were least likely to change their opinions. Persons in the low-attraction–agree (unbalanced) condition did *not* change their opinions, however. According to the Balance Tendency hypothesis, opinions should have changed *away* from the opinions of the others (i.e., toward disagreement), since initial attraction was low.

How can this latter finding be accounted for? Two explanations seem plausible. The first involves the changes that might have occurred in attraction. Given a low-attraction–agree condition, if no opinion change is observed, one might note whether or not attraction itself changed. An *increase* in attraction would represent the change predicted by the Balance Tendency hypothesis. But this is not ascertainable, since a second ("after" or "final") measure of attraction was not taken.

A second explanation compliments the first. It has been noted in recent research, to be reviewed later in detail, that persons exhibit a "*cognitive bias*" toward agreement rather than disagreement. Namely, people generally prefer agreement to disagreement; independently of a tendency toward balance, there is a tendency to shift toward agreeing rather than disagreeing with the other. Hence, if one already agrees with the other (even if the other is disliked), to disagree with him might seem even more distasteful and uncomfortable. For this reason, the cognitive bias of agreement—agreement for agreement's sake—might have been operating in the Gerard study, and might be the reason that the subjects did not change from agree to disagree.

A second cognitive bias, a "positivity" bias, would explain why liking could have changed in the positive direction: Independently of agreement, it may be that liking the other is a more pleasant state than disliking the other. Thus, in the low-attraction–agree condition, the most pleasurable form of balance (like-agree) can be attained by changing liking in the positive direction, and not changing agreement at all. Considering both cognitive biases together, it is clear that both agreement and positivity biases, plus the Balance Tendency principle, can all work in the same direction, and would explain why no opinion change occurred in the Gerard study for the low-attraction–agree condition. In this condition, agreement is maintained (thus satisfying the agreement bias), but liking is increased (satisfying the positivity bias), hence approximating a balanced structure (and satisfying the Balance Tendency hypothesis). It is unfortunate that attraction was not measured longitudinally in the Gerard study, for if it had been, the accuracy of this explanation could have been ascertained.

Failure to take longitudinal measures of *both* liking and attitudinal variables together, as we have just seen, often creates problems in the interpretation of results. This was the case not only in the Gerard study just cited, but also in the Sampson-Insko (1964) study treated earlier. This shortcoming was eliminated in Newcomb's (1961; 1963) much-cited study of thirty-four college transfer students, which used both triadic (POQ) and dyadic (POX) structures within this larger group as the units of analysis. Longitudinal measures were taken of liking, perceived liking, attitude and perceived attitude. It was found that both triadic and dyadic units tend to form and develop over time in a balanced way, lending support to the Balance Tendency hypothesis for triadic units containing only sentiment orientations, and for dyadic units containing sentiment and attitudinal orientations, both perceived and objective. An interesting finding was that during the early stages of their acquaintance, students tended to like those who were similar to themselves in demographic and cultural variables, such as age, department in the university, religion, urban-rural background, and proximity in the residence hall (cf. Friedman, 1966). During the inter-mediate stages of their acquaintance, however, these early friendship bonds tended to give way to other friendships which were formed on the basis of per-ceived similarity of certain issues, such as desegregation in schools, or premarital sex.

4 • 2b Interpersonal-Hypothetical Designs

Designs discussed in the former section involved two or more persons who were actually interacting or communicating with each other and discussing some issue. A number of other "molar process" studies, however, involve situations where a subject is told to imagine himself in a situation with some hypothetical other or others, or, if not requested to do this, he is nevertheless asked to form perceptions and answer questions about groups. Studies of this latter variety are called interpersonal-hypothetical. These studies are further sub-divided according to whether a measure of tension is employed. The first section below reviews studies that measure tension; the second section discusses studies that do not employ a tension measure.

Preference and Tension

A much-cited study by Jordan (1953) provided the basis for later studies in the interpersonal-hypothetical mold. It was the first published study to employ a measure of tension ("pleasantness"), thus providing a test for both the Balance Preference and Tension hypotheses. Sixty-four separate POX structures were presented to each of 288 subjects. Each structure represented a different combi-nation of sentiment relations (like-dislike) and unit relations (e.g., "O has a relationship with X"; "O has no relationship with X"). The structures were presented to the subjects by means of written sentences, such as "I like O; I like X; O likes X" (balance). Thus, the subject was required to imagine himself in a social situation involving himself (as P), one other, and some X. After the structures were presented to the subjects, each was asked to indicate how "pleas-ant" the situation would be to him if he were actually in it. He did so by means of placing a check mark on a line with the adjectives "pleasant" and "unpleas-ant" appearing at each end. The position of the subject's check mark was pre-sumed to indicate the relative magnitude of pleasantness or unpleasantness. Note that the measurement of pleasantness (tension) was cross-sectional.

A weak relationship between balance–unbalance of the structure and pleasantness rating was found. On the average, balanced structures were rated as more pleasant than unbalanced structures. The principal finding of interest, how-ever, was that independently of balance–unbalance of the structure, situations involving positive sentiment relations (liking) were generally rated as more pleasant than situations involving negative sentiment relations (dislike). As a matter of fact, the effect of sentiment seemed to be greater than the effect of balance–unbalance. A definite test of this finding was not possible in Jordan's study, however, since a two-way analysis of variance, or some comparable procedure, was not used; the *relative* amount of variance in pleasantness explained by sentiment versus balance was not ascertainable. Later research, to be reviewed in the next chapter, strongly confirmed this preliminary finding of independent effects of sentiment upon tension.

A re-analysis of Jordan's data undertaken by Runkel (1956) provided insight into Newcomb's postulate of the "systemness" of the *POX* unit. Runkel noted that the relationship between balance–unbalance and pleasantness in Jordan's study was a very weak and unimpressive one. Of thirty-two balanced structures, 66 percent (twenty-one) of them yielded "pleasant" ratings, the remainder (34 percent, or eleven) yielding "unpleasant" ratings. The fact that 34 percent of the *balanced* structures showed "unpleasant" ratings makes the relationship rather weak. Of thirty-two unbalanced structures, 47 percent (fifteen) were rated as "pleasant" and 53 percent (seventeen) were rated as "unpleasant." The relationship between balance and pleasantness was considerably improved, however, when structures containing null (absent) unit relations were eliminated. For example, the statement "*O* has no relationship with *X*" is a null unit relation. This left a total of only twenty-seven structures containing definitely positive or definitely negative relations. Of the ten remaining balanced structures, all (100 percent) indicated "pleasantness" rather than "unpleasantness." Of the seventeen remaining unbalanced structures, all (100 percent) indicated unpleasantness. This is a perfect statistical relationship.

One may question the advisability of eliminating the "no relation" structures from the study. Furthermore, one may question the legitimacy of using the number of structures as the *sample* (*N*) in the analysis, thus violating the statistical assumption of randomness and independence between cases. Nevertheless, the Runkel re-analysis of the Jordan data is important for two reasons. First, it lends some weight to the system-theoretic postulate that objects in a structure must have some relation to each other, whether positive or negative, in order for the tension mechanism to operate in the balance process. The results perfectly support the Tension hypothesis after the "no relation" structures are eliminated. In the discussion of system theory in Chapter 1, it was asserted that objects in a structure must *be related* to each other in some way. If they have "nothing to do" with one another—if *P* does not know *O*, or if *O* has nothing to do with *X*— then a system cannot be assumed. Second, the Runkel re-analysis indirectly supports the Cartwright-Harary (1956) distinction between the *complement* and the *opposite* of a relation. Given a positive (+) relation, the complement has a null (0) value, whereas the opposite has a negative (−) value. This issue was discussed in Chapter 3.

It is worthwhile to point out the influence that the Jordan (1953) study has had on more recent research and thought. First of all, an independent effect of a parameter variable (sentiment, or liking) was found. The study was the first to discover and codify such an independent effect, and it served as the basis for later studies of "cognitive biases" which are operative in the balance process. Second, the study raised the question of what Jordan calls the *relative potency* of sentiment as opposed to attitudinal (or unit) relations. The relative potency of a relation may be defined as the degree to which it affects tension to a greater extent than the other relation affects tension. For example, if the sentiment relation like-dislike tends to affect tension more than the attitudinal relation favorable-unfavorable, then the sentiment relation has greater relative potency. If the attitudinal relation favorable-unfavorable affects tension more than the relation like-dislike, then it is the attitudinal relation that has the greater relative potency. If one considers the *PX* and *OX* relations together, then one can evaluate the relative potency of sentiment versus *agreement*. Stating the issue succinctly, does the sign (positive versus negative) of an *interpersonal* relation have a greater effect upon tension—greater relative potency—than the sign of an *attitudinal* (or *unit*) relation? Jordan's (1953) evidence suggests that interpersonal relations are more potent. Namely, liking tends to predict tension, whereas the sign of a *PX* or *OX* relation (or the "agreement" between these two signs) does not predict tension as well.

A third point should be made regarding the Jordan study. Because the kind of interpersonal-hypothetical design that Jordan used is rather easy to implement and can be used on fewer subjects than would be required if actual groups were used, recent studies employing the hypothetical design are considerably more frequent than studies utilizing the concrete design. It takes a much smaller sample to have a *given* subject rate *several* structures (conditions) than it does to have *a number of subjects* under a *given* structure (condition). For the most part, the latter is demanded by experimental studies of the interpersonal-concrete variety. The recent trend toward favoring hypothetical designs is not necessarily a lamentable one, even if one tends to favor the concrete over the hypothetical design, since studies using each type of design tend to yield similar results, as we are beginning to discover. Nonetheless, researchers conducting studies of the hypothetical variety are often too eager to generalize their findings to real groups. Although the validity of such generalizations has not yet been directly approached in the literature, some recent results suggest that it is not a valid one (Aronson and Worchel, 1966). This recent evidence is discussed in a later section of this chapter.

Finally, the Jordan study, and its suggestive findings on relative potency and independent effects of sentiment, have led Jordan himself to write extensive critiques of theoretical discussions and studies of balance (Jordan, 1963; Jordan, 1966a; Jordan, 1966b). These critiques question the original Heider formulation of eight basic states of balance and unbalance, pointing out that the distinction between balance and unbalance in the case of dislike ($-PO$) is ambiguous and may have no psychological meaning in the focal person's cognitive structure.

That is, the distinction like-agree and like-disagree may be more meaningful than the distinction between dislike-disagree and dislike-agree. The former distinction is hypothesized to better account for differences in tension, suggesting that the former distinction is a psychologically more meaningful one. Newcomb's (1968) re-analysis of past studies tends to support this speculation. A complete discussion of this matter, along with a critique of Newcomb's own re-analysis, is taken up in detail in the seventh chapter.

The Byrne Studies of Balance Preference

The final section in our treatment of interpersonal-hypothetical design concerns studies which do not employ a measure of tension. A large number of studies of this variety have been published by Byrne and associates at the University of Texas. The totality of the Byrne research is oriented toward testing one deduction from the Balance Preference hypothesis: If the focal person perceives that he and the other are similar in orientation toward X, then the focal person will find O attractive. If there is perceived dissimilarity, then the focal person will find O relatively unattractive. The Byrne studies focus only on the prediction that attraction is a function of perceived similarity, rather than on the prediction that perceived similarity is a function of attraction. Cross-sectional (rather than longitudinal) measurement is always used, and the subject (P) is always asked to rate a hypothetical rather than a "real" other (O).

Byrne's theoretical argument, derived from Newcomb (1953; 1956; 1959; 1961), who in turn got it from Skinnerian psychology, runs like this: People value and want positive reinforcement, or reward, rather than negative reinforcement, or punishment. Furthermore, the greater the number of positive reinforcements, the greater will be the amount of perceived reward. If the focal person finds that the other has an attitude similar to his own, this is a rewarding experience. Since people tend to like those who reward them, it follows that the focal person will like another who is perceived as attitudinally similar. In addition, as the number of similar attitudes that the other has increases, then the degree to which the focal person likes the other is expected to increase concomitantly and in linear fashion. Thus, the *degree* or *magnitude* of P's attraction for O is hypothesized to be a linear function of the *amount* of reward from O (which can be defined as the number of X-objects upon which P and O agree).

Byrne's first study (Byrne, 1961), as in subsequent studies, measured the orientation of a subject (P) toward an hypothetical "stranger" (O) by means of six Likert-type scales intended to reflect P's attraction toward O ("personal feelings" and "desirability as a work partner"), and P's "evaluation" of O (in terms of intelligence, knowledge of current events, morality, and "adjustment"). The independent variable of the study, perceived attitudinal similarity (dichotomized into similar-dissimilar), was experimentally manipulated by leading the subject to believe that another subject had rated certain issues, such as racial integration and premarital sex, either similar or dissimilar to the way in which the subject himself had rated the same issues. Scores on each of the six "attraction" and "evaluation" scales significantly differed between the categories of similarity; similar strangers were consistently rated as more attractive and more positively valued than dissimilar strangers.

Additional research led Byrne and his associates to explore whether or not the relationship between similarity and attraction would hold up under controls for other variables. Is the similarity-attraction relationship independent of potentially confounding conditions? This question was first examined in a study by Byrne and Wong (1962), who found, interestingly, that the similarity-attraction relationship was independent of the *racial prejudice* of a white subject who rated a Negro "stranger." White subjects rated attitudinally similar Negroes as attractive, and attitudinally dissimilar Negroes as relatively unattractive, regardless of the prejudice of the white subject. In analysis of variance, only a main effect of similarity was found; there was no effect due to prejudice. (In a more recent study [Byrne and McGraw, 1964], however, a significant effect of prejudice was found: Low-prejudiced whites rated Negroes as more attractive than did high-prejudiced whites. The effects due to attitudinal similarity were far more pronounced, however.) The implications of this study for race relations in the United States are interesting, implying that similarity in attitudes toward important objects influences a white person's liking for a Negro to a greater degree than does the prejudice of the white person. One cannot doubt, however, that Byrne's measure of prejudice may have been inadequate, or that his results would have been different if the white subject had rated the Negro other as a real in-the-flesh stranger rather than as a hypothetical other.

It has often been hypothesized (e.g., Adorno et al., 1950) that the *authoritarianism* of a person is related to racial prejudice. Authoritarianism pertains to a person's desire to control and be controlled by authority figures, and high authoritarians are more likely to rigidify, stereotype and categorize than are persons who are low on authoritarianism. Since the tendency to categorize and stereotype has been found to be a component of prejudice (cf. Allport, 1954), and since Byrne and Wong (1962) found that prejudice of a white P did not affect P's rating of a Negro O, one can speculate that authoritarianism will likewise not affect P's rating of O—i.e., that the similarity-attraction relationship is independent of the authoritarianism of P. Recent studies by Byrne (1965) and Sheffield and Byrne (1967) show this to be the case. The subject rated an attitudinally similar hypothetical stranger as attractive, and an attitudinally dissimilar stranger as unattractive, regardless of his (the subject's) degree of authoritarianism. (Both the subject and the hypothetical stranger were white.) The attraction ratings were explained only on the basis of perceived similarity, and not by authoritarianism nor by the interaction of similarity and authoritarianism. The inference to be made is that the similarity-attraction relationship is independent of the degree of authoritarianism of P.

The similarity-attraction relationship was found to be independent of *perceived liking* in a study by Byrne and Rhamey (1965). (Perceived liking is the focal person's perception of the other's like or dislike for the self.) It was argued that the focal person's perception of the other's attraction toward the self, rather than the perceived attitudinal similarity of the other, could be the primary determinant of the focal person's attraction for the other. Or perhaps the focal person, after discovering that the other is attitudinally similar, infers that the other likes him, and as a result, rates the other as attractive. The investigators found, however, that the relationship between similarity and attraction remains significant even when perceived liking is held constant. In this study, however, a separate effect of the control variable (perceived liking) was found: The subject rated the (hypothetical) other as more attractive if he perceived that the other liked him than if he perceived the other as disliking him. In addition, perceived liking and similarity interacted significantly, in such a way that the highest attraction scores were found under the condition of perceived similarity and perceived liking. Hence, similarity affects attraction (the main effect of similarity), but perceived liking also affects attraction (the main effect of perceived liking), and both independent variables (similarity and perceived liking) interact upon attraction (yielding a significant interaction effect). Still, one must note that the similarity-attraction relationship is independent of perceived liking.

Additional studies by the Byrne team show the similarity-attraction relationship to be independent of other factors. Byrne, Clore and Griffitt (1967) find that the *proportion* of similar attitudes (the number of "X's" upon which P and O agree divided by the number of "X's" rated) is related to attraction even if the *average discrepancy* is held constant. (On a Likert scale, "discrepancy" would be the difference between P's and O's ratings of a *given X*.) Byrne (1961; 1962) finds the similarity-attraction relationship to be independent of the personality variable, *affiliation need*. Regardless of whether P wants to like others and to be liked (high affiliation need), or whether his desire to like another and to be liked is less (low affiliation need), similar others are rated as attractive and dissimilar others as unattractive. Byrne and Clore (1966), using three different "modes" of presenting the attitude responses of the hypothetical other to the subject (questionnaire form versus tape recorder versus movie), find the similarity-attraction relationship to be independent of the *mode of presentation*. Byrne and Griffitt (1966a) show that the proportion of similar attitudes is related to attraction regardless of the *age* of the focal person. Byrne, Griffitt and Golightly (1966) demonstrate that the focal person's attraction for the other is independent of the *perceived occupational status* (physicist versus electrician versus janitor) of the other. In an admirable attempt to explore the social psychology of people other than college sophomores (all previous studies by Byrne, and by literally all of the balance researchers and also researchers in other areas besides balance, use college sophomores as subjects), Byrne, Griffitt, Hudgins and Reeves (1968) explored the similarity-attraction relationship among three categories of medical patients (who were not in college!): schizophrenics, alcoholics and surgical patients. Similarity and attraction remained strongly related, regardless of patient category. Using P's and hypothetical O's of the opposite sex, Byrne, London and Reeves (1968) find that the similarity-attraction relationship still remains even if the *physical attractiveness* of the other is held constant. Attitudinally similar others of the opposite sex are rated as attractive, and dissimilar others as unattractive, regardless of the physical attractiveness of the other. (Physical attractiveness was determined by the research team themselves rather than by the subjects.) There was, quite *un*surprisingly, an independent effect of physical attractiveness itself: Physically attractive others were rated as more attractive than unattractive others (how's that for a discovery!). The point is that controlling for the physical attractiveness of O does not cancel out the well established relationship between perceived attitudinal similarity and attraction of P and O.

In sum, perceived similarity-dissimilarity has been shown by Byrne to affect attraction independently of the following variables: prejudice of the focal person, authoritarianism of the focal person, perceived liking, attitudinal discrepancy (scale-by-scale discrepancy), affiliation need, mode of presentation of the attitudinal responses of the other, age of the focal person, occupational status of the other, type of medical patient (focal person), and even the physical attractiveness of an opposite-sex other. The relationship also appears, at least to some degree, to be independent of the *importance* that P attaches to the attitude object, X (Byrne and Nelson, 1964; Byrne and Nelson, 1965)—results that contradict past speculation on the role of the importance of X—but this question is explored in greater detail in Chapter 5. One contribution of the Byrne group, then, has been to show the consistency and stability of the similarity-attraction relationship across the categories of these control variables.

A second contribution of the Byrne team has been to show that the relationship between the *proportion* of similar attitudes and attraction is a linear one, even when certain variables are held constant. The relationship is linear within the categories of (i.e., controlling for) perceived liking (Byrne and Rhamey, 1965), mode of presentation of the attitude information to the subject (Byrne and Clore, 1966), age of the focal person (Byrne and Griffitt, 1966a), type of medical patient (Byrne, Griffitt, Hudgins and Reeves, 1968), and physical attractiveness of an opposite-sex other (Byrne, London and Reeves, 1968). Regression analysis shows that in each of these studies the linear equation

$$Y = a + bX,$$

where Y = attraction score and X = proportion of similar attitudes, fits the data quite well, and no departures from linearity seem evident. These two sets of results—independence of the similarity-attraction relationship and linearity—have resulted in Byrne's reference to the similarity-attraction relationship as "the law of attraction" (Byrne and Nelson, 1965; Byrne and Clore, 1966; Byrne and Griffitt, 1966a).

To refer to the relationship between perceived similarity and attraction as a "law" seems premature. There are at least five reasons why. First and foremost, the "independent conditions" (control variables) under which Byrne and associates test the similarity-attraction relationship are, for the most part, trivial. *The Byrne research tends to ignore conditional variables that might completely reverse the similarity-attraction relationship or cancel it altogether.* The findings of at least two studies (Deutsch and Solomon, 1959; Kind, 1965) suggest that if one controls for self-evaluation (the focal person's liking and respect for himself), the similarity-attraction relationship is completely reversed. If P "cannot stand himself," why should he be attracted toward another who is attitudinally similar to the hated self? Hating the other might be more pleasurable. Another study (Lerner et al., 1967) found that the relationship between similarity and attraction depends heavily upon social-structural conditions in the group, such as whether P and O are cooperating or competing with each other. It was found that under conditions of cooperation between P and O, perceived similarity is *unrelated* to attraction. (The results of the Deutsch-Solomon, Kind, and Lerner et al. studies are reviewed in Chapter 5.) The fact is that Byrne does not consider such crucial variables in his own research. In addition, other nontrivial variables, both personality and social-structural, certainly need to be considered before a "law" can be identified.

Second, in order to adequately test the similarity-attraction relationship, both variables should be measured longitudinally (through time), instead of cross-sectionally (at one point in time), as Byrne and associates do. Should not one examine *changes* in attraction as a function of *changes* in perceived similarity? Although Newcomb's (1961) results show this to be the case, there is no evidence at all that the relationship is still *linear* if both variables are measured longitudinally.

A third shortcoming of the Byrne research is evident. Byrne's research treats attraction as the dependent variable. On no occasion is attraction manipulated and the resulting perception of similarity or dissimilarity analyzed. If done in this way, is the relationship still linear, or does it change form, depending upon which is the independent variable? It is a major postulate of balance theory that the similarity-attraction relationship is an *interdependent* one. This means that *either* similarity or attraction may be taken as the independent variable; each may affect the other, if one is experimentally manipulated and variation in the other is observed. Although other nonexperimental studies (e.g., Newcomb, 1961) suggest that the relationship is "two-way," such matters need to be explored further before any "laws" can be identified.

Fourth, there is the concrete versus hypothetical problem. Byrne's research utilizes the interpersonal-hypothetical design, and it is therefore questionable whether his linear relationship is generalizeable to real groups. Aronson and Worchel (1966) found that in a "real other" (interpersonal-concrete) situation, *there was no relationship—linear or otherwise—between similarity and attraction!* Only perceived liking—the subject's perception of the other's liking for him—predicted the subject's attraction for the other; the effects of similarity, and the interaction of similarity and perceived liking, was not statistically significant. Byrne and Griffitt (1966b) criticized this latter study, holding that the *range* of the similarity-dissimilarity variable used in the study was not great enough. Byrne and Griffitt replicated the study, using a real other, and found similarity to be related to attraction. But only grossly discrepant attitudinal responses were used to manipulate the similarity variable (seven out of seven similar attitudes versus zero out of seven). But is the similarity-attraction relationship a "law" if one must use such largely discrepant categories in a real-other (concrete) experiment in order to get the results that one wants? Probably not. Of critical interest, too, is the fact that the similarity-attraction relationship has not been thoroughly tested in a concrete situation while holding a number of potentially confounding variables constant. All of the studies done by Byrne and associates which used control variables were done in strictly hypothetical-other situations.

It should be noted here that the Aronson-Worchel (1966) data constitute a negative finding under the Balance Preference hypothesis, and the study was interpersonal-concrete. These results are damaging to the balance principle, but even more damaging to Byrne's assertion that the similarity-attraction relationship is a "law." The question of interpersonal-hypothetical versus interpersonal-concrete designs and the meaning of the Aronson-Worchel results are taken up again in this chapter.

Finally, in regard to the "law," there is the question of intervening variables. Does P infer that an attitudinally similar O also likes him, and in turn likes O (in which case perceived liking is the intervening variable)? Is P's discovery that O is similar rewarding in and of itself, regardless of whether P perceives that O likes him (in which case the degree to which P values this kind of reward is intervening)? Is tension operative in the similarity-attraction relationship in the same way that it appears to operate in the balance process as a whole? While there is some evidence that perceived liking intervenes (McWhirter and Jecker, 1967), it is inconclusive, by the investigators' own admission. At any rate, the question of intervening variables is a complex one, far too complex to be ignored by Byrne and associates. It must be explored further before any "law" can be identified.

In sum, Byrne's reference to the similarity-attraction relationship as a law is unwarranted because (a) crucial confounding variables (such as self-evaluation and cooperation-competition) have not been considered by Byrne and associates; (b) it has not been demonstrated that the similarity-attraction relationship is still linear if longitudinal measurement is employed; (c) the interdependence question has not been adequately resolved; (d) there is no evidence that the linear relationship (and its independence from various potentially confounding variables) is generalizable from the interpersonal-hypothetical design to real groups (at least one recent study [Aronson and Worchel, 1966] suggests that it is not); and (e) the problem of intervening variables (in addition to tension) is still largely unexplored.[3] Of all these criticisms cited, the first three, and certainly the first, are the most relevant when asking whether or not one should refer to the relationship as a "law." As a matter of fact, the major criterion for determining whether a relationship is a law rests upon whether or not it remains across a large number of potentially confounding conditions. It seems that Byrne and team have preselected many "conditions" which are trivial and which on an *a priori* basis could be judged as not critically relevant to the similarity-attraction relationship. Relevant, crucial and important confounding variables are largely ignored. Granted, the relationship between similarity and attraction is a reasonably impressive one and has been upheld by studies in addition to those done by Byrne and associates. The relationship is, at best, a "principle"; but it does not yet have the status of a law.

4 • 3   SELECTED ISSUES

The review of the molar process literature gives rise to certain issues which, to date, have not been adequately explored. Three such issues are discussed below: (1) differences between interpersonal-hypothetical and interpersonal-concrete designs; (2) the question of intervening variables; and (3) the problem of balance in dyadic (*POX*) structures as opposed to triadic (*POQ*) structures. It should be emphasized here that this section presents only an introductory statement on the matter of "unresolved issues" in balance research. A detailed listing of unsettled issues will have to await presentation in the last (eighth) chapter, for there is much to be considered in the fifth, sixth and seventh chapters. What follows is a discussion of only some of the issues that have been encountered so far.

4 • 3a   Hypothetical versus Concrete Designs

The bulk of research on the Balance Preference, Balance Tendency, and Tension hypotheses tends to yield congruent results when those studies are conducted using either interpersonal-concrete or interpersonal-hypothetical designs. Overall, the results under each type of design are similar. Yet, one cannot over-

---

3. For that matter, conclusive evidence that tension is intervening in the balance process is lacking. To demonstrate that tension intervenes between the perception of unbalance and a change toward balance, tension would have to be measured and held constant statistically. If the initially observed relationship between balance–unbalance (manipulated) and change (the dependent variable) decreased or become not significant when tension is held constant, then one could infer that tension intervenes. Surprisingly, to the author's knowledge, this procedure, or some procedure carried out for a similar purpose, has not yet been undertaken. Note that if similarity (rather than balance–unbalance) is the independent variable, and attraction (rather than change) is the dependent variable, it is not likely that tension intervenes: Discovering that *O* is attitudinally similar is certainly not likely to produce tension (and as a result, high attraction)! A discussion of the problem of intervening variables is taken up in the next section.

look the implicit tendency, if not the explicit purpose, of balance researchers to generalize their findings gathered from hypothetical designs to concrete situations—in short, to real groups. It is quite clear that the former is intended to *simulate* the latter; contrived designs involving abstract structures to be rated, and hypothetical "strangers" to be judged on the basis of attractiveness, are all intended as an approximation model of actual real-life, face-to-face interpersonal processes.

That there are important differences between concrete and hypothetical designs is self-evident. Yet, two differences pertinent to the balance process are worth mentioning. First, the role of communication in the balance process is an important consideration. If the subject is asked to 'identify" with one of the "persons" in the hypothetical structure he is asked to rate, or if he is given attitudinal information supposedly representing a "stranger" which he has never met, then communication between the subject (who is taking the part of— "playing the role" of—the focal person) and one or more others is not possible. In an interpersonal-concrete situation, communication between the focal person and one or more others can—and even if the study is done in a laboratory setting, usually does—take place. It follows that to the degree communication between P and O facilitates the balance process (as hypothesized by Newcomb (1953; 1959) and as discussed in Chapter 2), to that degree communication plays an integral role in the dynamics of groups studied under the concrete type of design. From this it is possible to hypothesize that balance maintainance, as a result of communication, is more likely to occur in concrete as opposed to hypothetical conditions. Yet, no study has sought to investigate this issue. This is largely because investigators favoring the hypothetical form of design are prone to ignore the role of communication in the balance process.

A second difference between the hypothetical and concrete designs is that under face-to-face (concrete) conditions, P can receive a very large range of stimuli from O. The mannerisms, traits and visible attributes of O are all quite apparent to P in such situations. In contrast, the hypothetical design presents P with only a very narrow range of information about the other person or persons in the supposed group. Hence, P must make whatever judgments he is asked to make on the basis of these limited bits of information. Most typical of the studies of this sort are those by Byrne and associates, where the subject is given very restricted amounts of attitudinal information about an hypothetical stranger and is asked to judge O's attractiveness. Clearly, if P saw O face-to-face, his judgment of O's attractiveness would be influenced by a greater range of stimuli. Results directly pertinent to this statement were obtained in the Aronson-Worchel (1966) study, which found that attitude similarity-dissimilarity was *not* related to the focal person's attraction toward the other; only perceived liking predicted attraction. The design was interpersonal-concrete; P saw O face-to-face, in the flesh. This study represented a negative finding under the Balance Preference hypothesis, and suggests that this hypothesis is not as applicable in concrete situations as it is in hypothetical, contrived situations. The important inference to be made here is that balance research tends to be biased toward testing hypoth-eses in situaions which lend themselves to supportive results. When one realizes that the majority of findings reviewed in this chapter (and to be reviewed in the coming chapters) are gotten from interpersonal-hypothetical designs, this suspi-cion carries even greater weight. The fact that studies of balance exhibit the unfortunate tendency to be insensitive to disconfirming results has been men-tioned before, and will be alluded to again where appropriate.

It is bad enough that small group studies involving actual interaction but in laboratory settings are often criticized for being "artificial" representations of real-life interpersonal processes. Investigations employing the interpersonal-concrete mold, some of which were done in laboratory-like settings (with the notable exceptions of the studies by Kogan and Tagiuri (1958), Newcomb (1961), Broxton (1963), Byrne and Blaylock (1963), and Levinger and Breed-love (1966), among others), are themselves contrived simulations of uncontrived interpersonal dynamics. But interpersonal-*hypothetical* designs can themselves be seen as approximations of interpersonal-*concrete* studies. They are models of other models which are in turn approximations of reality! The hypothetical design is intended to approximate balance processes in unstructured face-to-face settings. Generalizing from the hypothetical design to reality therefore involves not one but two very large sources of possible error: It is a big jump from the hypothetical to the concrete laboratory condition, and another big (perhaps big-ger) jump from the concrete laboratory condition to the uncontrived (the "nat-ural") condition. That there are two such stages to this generalization procedure is a fact largely ignored by researchers favoring interpersonal-hypothetical designs.

4 • 3b The Problem of Intervening Variables

It has been posited before in this text that tension constitutes an inter-vening variable in the balance process. P's perception of unbalance produces tension which in turn produces a change toward balance on the part of P. But the question of intervening variables is not a simple one. Two points in this regard are made here: (1) No convincing test for intervening variables has appeared in the literature; (2) there are certain conditions under which variables *other than* tension are likely to intervene.

Let us take up the first point. Methodologically speaking, in order to show that variable X produces change in variable Z, which in turn produces change in variable Y—in short, to demonstrate that Z intervenes in the X-Y relationship, the researcher must do the following: (1) He must show that in fact X is significantly related to Y; (2) he must show that X is related to Z; and (3) he must show that Z is related to Y. Furthermore, he should present evidence, if at all possible, that (4) X "occurs before" (or at the same time as) Z, and that Z "occurs before" (or at the same time as) Y, If, say, X occurs *after*

Z, then Z certainly cannot be the *intervening* variable. In short, *temporal priority* of X over Z and Z over Y should be established. One last test must be performed: The researcher must demonstrate that (5) the originally observed relationship between X and Y must either *decrease* in magnitude or *disappear* (become not significant, statistically), *when Z is held constant.* The logic here is that if variation in X produces variation in Z, which in turn produces variation in Y, then if one "stops" the variation in Z—if you hold Z constant by some procedure—then the original X-Y relationship will decrease or disappear. This latter kind of test, referred to as a test for an intervening variable, is a standard research procedure, and is outlined in most intermediate texts on research methodology.

Despite the rather wide acceptance of this kind of test for an intervening variable, in no instance has this procedure, *or any procedure performed for a similar purpose,* ever been applied by a balance researcher. What is needed is a study which explicitly tests for intervening variables. To be sure, the relationship between balance–unbalance (X, the independent variable) and tension (Z, the hypothesized intervening variable) has been extensively researched, as has the relationship between balance–unbalance and change (Y, the dependent variable). Yet, no study has seen fit to relate balance–unbalance to change while holding tension constant, to see if, in fact, one can make the inference that tension is one intervening variable in the relationship between balance–unbalance and sentiment or attitudinal change.

If the entire balance process is conceptualized in a way similar to that outlined in Chapter 2 (and hence as given by the four general propositions), there are actually *two* "intervening" variables: unbalance (X) produces high initial tension (Z_1), which produces change (Z_2), which produces tension reduction (Y). Hence, tension reduction becomes the dependent variable, and initial tension and change become the respective intervening variables. We note in passing that studies taking tension reduction as the dependent variable (and therefore providing a test for GP 4) are far too rare. What is needed is a study that would examine all four stages of the process (unbalance, tension, change, and tension reduction), and in addition apply an appropriate test for intervening effects of initial tension and change.

The second point to be discussed concerns the kinds of conditions under which tension is *not* likely to be the intervening variable. This raises the question of what other variables besides tension constitute mechanisms in the operation of the balance process. A crystal clear instance of tension not intervening is as follows: If the independent variable is perceived similarity and liking the dependent variable, it is absurd to posit tension as intervening. Does P's perception of attitudinal similarity between himself and O result in high tension (which in turn results in P's liking for O)? Certainly not. Clearly, in the similarity-attraction relationship, other factors beside tension must intervene. Past speculation suggests at least two intervening processes: (1) The amount of reward which similarity between P and O constitutes for P. Similarity is perceived by P as reward, and we like those who reward us. (2) P's perception of O's liking for P (perceived liking). P's discovery that O is attitudinally similar causes P to think that O likes him. As a result, P likes O, since we tend to like those who like us. In contrast, the perception of dissimilarity causes P to think that O does not like him, and as a result P does not like O.

It can be said with assurance that the empirical literature has given quite a bit of attention to the tension variable (as dependent, not as intervening), yet very little attention has been given to other possible intervening variables. Conditions under which tension does not intervene remain inadequately explored. That variables other than tension intervene when perceived similarity is the independent (and attraction or liking the dependent) variable seems very plausible, as cited in the preceding paragraph. But what if attraction is the independent variable, and perceived similarity the dependent one? Do the hypothesized mechanisms (reward and perceived liking) operate in the same way? Conceivably, given that P likes O, then P might assume that O also likes him, and as a result infers attitudinal similarity. In this case, perceived liking again intervenes. But does the fact that P likes O constitute a reward for P? In this instance, it would seem that only perceived liking and not the perception of reward becomes the intervening process. In sum, the question of intervening variables in addition to tension has yet to be investigated. Furthermore, adequate designs that test for intervening processes, whether they involve tension or some variable other than tension, have not appeared in the literature.

4 • 3c   Dyads versus Triads

Whereas some studies on balance focus on dyads, or structural units consisting of two persons and one X, others focus upon triads, or units consisting of three persons. In both cases, the unit under study contains three objects or "entities." In the language of the literature, the former is called the POX unit, the latter, the POQ unit. Generally, studies of each type of unit tend to yield similar results, suggesting that the balance dynamics of dyadic and triadic structures are for the most part similar. Yet, it remains highly questionable whether one can justifiably generalize his results from one to the other. In many cases, the balance researcher finds himself doing just that in his attempt to identify the similarities and common patterns in the operation of the balance process for both dyads and triads. Heider himself tended to ignore the differences and focus on the similarities, taking the POX and POQ units as largely isomorphic. Most empirical studies, whether of the concrete or hypothetical variety, have not been sensitive to the ways in which the balance process may differ in dyads and triads. A delineation of at least some of the differences seems necessary.

That there are differences between dyadic and triadic interpersonal structures is by no means a new discovery. Simmel predicted that triads tend to segregate into a dyad and isolate, and as a result, the isolate could "gain" by forming a *coalition* with either of the members of the dyad. This principle of *tertius gaudans* ("the third gains") is well known in small-group research.

The point is that triads are generally *less stable* than dyads; the chances that either attitudinal or sentiment relations will change are greater in the case of triads. Since balanced structures are hypothesized to be more stable than unbalanced ones, the question of the relative stability (in terms of balance–unbalance) of dyads and triads is relevant. The lack of empirical evidence on this issue has been noted recently by Jordan (1966a, p. 11):

> ...when all is said and done, a dyad is basically a stable social grouping. On the other hand, a triad is notoriously unstable...who can tell the additional complexities added when X is replaced by Q?

Some limited evidence suggesting that the POQ unit is less stable than the POX unit has been presented by Price, Harburg and Newcomb (1966). The study measured pleasantness (tension) as the dependent variable, and studied the triadic POQ structure. Eight structures, corresponding to Heider's "basic eight" structures discussed earlier in Chapter 2, were presented to the subjects for pleasantness ratings. Only the P-to-O, P-to-Q, and O-to-Q relations were given. Not given were the O-to-P, Q-to-P, and Q-to-O relations. Hence, no "two-way" relations (whether symmetric or asymmetric) were considered. The O and Q of each structure represented two actual acquaintances of P; hence, the design was interpersonal-concrete.

It was found that balanced structures with a $+PO$ relation were rated as pleasant, and unbalanced structures with the $+PO$ were rated as unpleasant. This is consistent with predictions under the Tension hypothesis. Problems arose, however, with the four structures containing $-PO$ relations. Generally, they were rated as unpleasant or neutral regardless of whether they were balanced or unbalanced. This is not in accord with the predictions of the Tension hypothesis. In order to explain these negative findings, the investigators took into account data gathered in another study. It was found that if P likes O ($+PO$), *98 percent* of the P's expected that O also liked them. Namely, there is a 98 percent chance that a person expects a positive interpersonal relation to be reciprocated. On the other hand, if P dislikes O ($-PO$), then *only 27 percent expected reciprocation* ($-OP$). Thus, while there is a 98 percent "chance" that positive interpersonal relations are expected to be reciprocated, there is only a 27 percent chance that negative interpersonal relations are expected to be reciprocated. In the case of $-PO$, the greatest proportion of the persons (47 percent) were unsure and uncertain about the OP relation, and the remainder (26 percent) actually expected $+OP$.

The important inference to be made is that a focal person is more *certain* in making a prediction about an "ungiven" or "unknown" OP relation if the *given PO* relation is positive. If it is negative, uncertainty is present. What can this tell us about the *Q*-to-*P* and the *Q*-to-*O* ("unknown") relations in the *POQ* unit if the *P*-to-*O*, *P*-to-*Q* and *O*-to-*Q* relations are given or known (which was the case in this study)? And what can it tell us about the question of dyads and triads?

One immediately realizes that in the *POX* (dyadic) structure, the non-person object *X* *cannot* have an orientation toward either *P* or *O*. In contrast, in the *POQ* (triadic) structure, since *Q* is a person, he *can* have orientations toward *P* and toward *O*. Hence, in the case of triadic structures, particularly where the *PO* relation is negative, the focal person is more unsure and uncertain about the sum total of the relations in the structure: He is unsure about the *Q*-to-*P* and the *Q*-to-*O* relations. Note that the higher unpleasantness ratings of the *POQ* structures containing −*PO* can be explained on the basis of greater *uncertainty* about these structures as contrasted with *POQ* structures containing +*PO*. But even if the *PO* bond is negative (−*PO*), one would expect the *POX* structure to be characterized by *less* uncertainty, since *X*-to-*P* and *X*-to-*O* relations are impossible. This means that *a focal person who is a member of a dyadic structure will be less uncertain about the sum total of the relations in that structure than he would as a member of a triadic structure.*

This latter statement is speculative, since no study (including the Price, Harburg and Newcomb study just cited) has systematically tested *POX* and *POQ* differences within one experiment. A second limitation to the speculation is as follows: A direct test of the relative *stability* of *POX* and *POQ* structures would necessitate the measurement of changes or desired changes in relations or perceived relations. The findings just cited suggest that *uncertainty* involving unknown or ungiven relations is greater for *POQ* than for *POX* structures (and, in addition, that uncertainty is greater in the case of −*PO*), but this is not synonymous with saying that the *POQ* structure is "less stable." Stability (the likelihood of change over time) and uncertainty (a variable akin to tension) are two variables which must remain conceptually distinct. Yet, if uncertainty (tension) is thought of as preceding the change process, then one can make the inference that the *POQ* structure is less stable than the *POX* structure.

Although small group researchers in areas beside balance have examined, at least to some degree, dyadic and triadic differences, the question of differences *in balance dynamics* remains largely unexplored. What is required, ideally, is an interpersonal-concrete design involving focal persons in dyadic and triadic situations, both balanced and unbalanced, which would employ a measurement of tension and the longitudinal measurement of change in orientations (or at least a single measurement of "preference for change"). The evidence so far suggests at least three hypotheses: (1) That tension in triadic structures will be higher than tension in dyadic ones, especially if only the *PO, PQ* and *OQ* relations are "given" for the triadic structures. This is expected because if only these three relations are given, there is a greater *number of unknown* relations present in the triadic structure, and these unknown relations constitute a source of uncertainty and tension. (2) That change in relations, or the focal person's preference for changing them, will be greater in triadic than in dyadic structures, suggesting that triads are more unstable (and therefore more susceptible to balance forces) than are dyads. This prediction at least in part follows from the former one, where it is hypothesized that greater tension characterizes triads than dyads. Note that we are predicting that *an unbalanced POQ structure (triad) is more likely to change than—is more unstable than—an unbalanced POX structure (dyad), even though both are unbalanced.* (3) The two conditions (balance–unbalance and dyad–triad) will interact upon change, such that change is most likely to occur in *triadic* structures which are *unbalanced* than under any of the other three conditions (unbalanced dyad, balanced triad, and balanced dyad). Generally, it is possible to predict that change is *least* likely to occur in the balanced dyad and in the balanced triad, next in the unbalanced dyad, and most likely to occur in the unbalanced triad. Remember that in each case, only three relations are given.

4 • 4 SUMMARY

It has been the intent of this chapter to review the "molar process" empirical literature—studies which test the fundamental predictions of balance theory. The chapter began with a description of the strategy to be employed in reviewing the literature. The "structure of the theory" was stated in terms of four general propositions, and the role of two types of deductions (the Homans and axiomatic types) was discussed. The four general propositions were: Balance Preference, Balance Tendency, Tension, and Tension Reduction. The use and importance of conditional propositions were discussed. Research findings were divided into two classes: Those employing an interpersonal-concrete design, involving two or more persons who are actually interacting or communicating, and those employing an interpersonal-hypothetical design, involving subjects' ratings of hypothetical structures or hypothetical "others." These two classes were further subdivided according to whether or not a measure of tension was employed. Finally, three unsettled issues were discussed: (1) The dangers involved in generalizing from interpersonal-hypothetical designs to real groups; (2) problems in testing for tension as the intervening variable, and other possible intervening variables beside tension; (3) differences in the balance dynamics of dyads versus triads.

It should be stressed that the present chapter was concerned with studies which tested deductions from one or more of the four general propositions, but which were not concerned directly with conditional propositions or relationships—findings which would result in the modification of some general proposition. It was noted that molar process studies are not generally sensitive to findings which might lead to the disconfirmation of a general proposition, and for this reason, these studies tend to yield supportive results. The task of the next chapter will be to examine findings which justify the statement of conditional propositions. Succinctly, whereas the present chapter presented studies which for the most part tended to confirm the general propositions (though this was not always the case; recall the studies by Aronson and Worchel [1966] and by Price, Harburg and Newcomb [1966]), the next chapter gives a systematic treatment of findings which modify, qualify, or completely reverse the predictions of the four general propositions of balance theory.

5 .....

Conditional Propositions

Studies reviewed in the previous chapter focused primarily upon relationships which were deducible from one or more of the four general propositions of balance theory. Other studies, particularly recent ones, have obtained results which in some way alter these general propositions. As defined earlier, a *conditional proposition or relationship* is any proposition or relationship which modifies, refines, broadens, extends, cancels, or completely reverses the predictions of at least one general proposition. A conditional proposition may be "strong," in which case it is a severe modification of a general proposition, or it may be "weak," in which case it does not severely change a general proposition, but nevertheless presents a modification which is important and of interest. There are at least three *sources* for conditional propositions:

1. Principles, propositions or hypotheses which are not themselves deducible from balance theory (i.e., from one or more of the general propositions). The least cost hypothesis is an example.

2. Parameter variables, or variables (orientations or relations) which are part of the structural unit under study. Liking, attitude, perceived liking, perceived attitude, agreement, and importance of the X-object are examples of the principal parameter variables.

3. Non-parameter variables. Personality or "predispositional" variables (such as self-evaluation or authoritarianism) and social-structural variables (such as whether P and O are competing or cooperating, or the socio-economic status of either P or O) are two kinds of non-parameter variables which effect the balance process in groups, and are given attention in this chapter.

A conditional proposition or relationship which uses either of the first two sources (principles or parameter variables) is called a *corollary* to the theory of balance. Any conditional proposition arising out of the third source will, for the sake of distinctions, be called simply a "conditional relationship" or "conditional proposition."

This chapter is divided into three major sections, the first of which concerns corollaries to the theory. Section 5.2 discusses the effects of personality variables on the balance process, and Section 5.3 concentrates on the effects of social-structural variables.

5 • 1   COROLLARIES TO THE THEORY

The present section is concerned with reviewing the empirical literature which gives rise to conditional propositions or relationships based on parameter variables. Section 5.1a discusses what will be defined as the problem of "cognitive bias." Section 5.1b deals with importance of X. Section 5.1c is concerned with the Osgood model, particularly with what has come to be known as the "polarity corollary" to the general theory.

5 • 1a   *Cognitive Bias*

A postulated *cognitive bias* is any tendency a person has to perceive a number of objects, and the relations among those objects, in a certain way. The preference for balance among objects is itself a type of cognitive bias: People prefer balance to unbalance—it is postulated that there is a cognitive bias toward balance rather than unbalance. "Positivity" is another type of bias. Generally, people prefer positive relations (such as liking the other) to negative relations (such as disliking the other). At least seven types of cognitive bias have been treated in the literature. They are: agreement, reciprocity (symmetry), positivity, preference for interpersonal (rather than attitudinal) change, least cost, completeness, and extremity. *Each bias can be seen as a tendency or force which exists in addition to—independent of—balance forces.* Each bias is briefly defined below; a detailed review of the literature will follow these definitions. The following list is not intended to be an exhaustive representation of the kinds of cognitive biases potentially operative, but it does represent a listing of the biases on which data are available.

1. *Agreement.* The postulated bias is that people prefer to agree with another rather than to disagree with another. Thus, there is a tendency for the focal person to bring his orientation toward X into agreement with his perception of the other's orientation; such a tendency may be independent of the focal person's liking for the other. Hence, a preference for or a tendency toward agreement may exist independently of a preference for or a tendency toward balance. Taking preference, change and tension as respective dependent variables, it is expected that: (a) agreement is preferred to disagreement; (b) there will be a tendency for persons to change, through time, toward agreement rather than disagreement; and (c) agreement results in less tension than disagreement.

2. *Reciprocity (symmetry).* The postulated bias is that people prefer

reciprocal (symmetric) interpersonal relations to non-reciprocal (asymmetric) ones. This means that if *P* likes *O*, he will expect *O* to like him; if he dislikes *O*, he will expect *O* to dislike him. In graph-theoretic terminology, any unbalanced 2-cycle will tend toward balance, and any balanced 2-cycle will tend to remain balanced. In terms of preference, change and tension: (a) the focal person will prefer reciprocal to non-reciprocal relations; (b) non-reciprocal relations will tend to become reciprocal through time, and reciprocal relations will tend to remain reciprocal; and (c) non-reciprocal relations are a source of greater tension than reciprocal relations.

3. *Positivity.* People are expected to prefer positive relations to negative relations, like to dislike, positive sentiment to negative sentiment, high attraction to low attraction, and even positive (favorable) attitudes to negative (unfavorable) attitudes. Such a preference or tendency can exist independently of a preference for or a tendency toward balance. (a) There is a preference for positive rather than negative relations, whether interpersonal or attitudinal; (b) relations will tend to become positive over time. This means that the focal person will tend to change a negative relation to a positive one, and keep a positive relation positive. Note that an important implication may be deduced from this prediction. If one asks the question, "Which relation, among a number of relations, is most likely to change," one would predict that a negative relation would be more likely to change than a positive relation. (c) Negative relations arouse greater tension than positive relations.

4. *Interpersonal change.* The fourth bias pertains more to the problem of change rather than to the problems of preference and tension, although the relevance of this bias to preference will be discussed below. The postulated effect is that if the focal person changes a relation, an interpersonal relation (*PO, PQ,* perceived *OP*, etc.) will be more likely to change than an attitudinal relation (*PX,* perceived *OX,* etc.). As with the positivity bias, the postulation of the interpersonal bias sheds some light on the question, "Among several relations, which is most likely to change?" If this bias is applicable (if one is considering a structural unit containing both interpersonal and attitudinal relations rather than, say, only interpersonal relations—as in the case of the *POQ* unit), then one would expect interpersonal relations to be more likely to change than attitudinal relations.

5. *Least cost.* As discussed in Chapter 2, the least cost principle postulates that people prefer the line of least or minimal effort to the line of greater-than-least effort. The least cost bias applies more to the problem of change than to the problems of preference or tension management.[1] It states that the focal person will achieve balance through the fewest possible sign (relation) changes. As with the positivity and interpersonal change biases, it predicts which among a

---

1. In regard to tension, it might be interesting to hypothesize that if the focal person must achieve balance through some means *other than* the least effortful means, then tension will be greater than if balance could be attained by the least effortful means.

number of relations is most likely to change. In substantive terms, the relation or relations most likely to change are those which represent the minimum changes necessary to achieve balance. In formal graph-theoretic terms, the relation or relations most likely to change are those which are members of a negation- or deletion-minimal set of relations.

6. *Completeness.* The postulated bias is that people prefer completely connected structures of relations over structures which have one or more "missing" relations. For example, if P has some relation to O and Q (whether positive or negative), there will be a tendency for P to perceive that O and Q are somehow related. In graph-theoretic terms, complete structures or cycles are preferred over *vacuous* structures or cycles.

7. *The "extremity effect."* If the focal person is communicating with another about some issue or topic, then either the focal person or the other can state his position on the issue in a "moderate" way, or he can state it in a more "extreme" way. It is postulated that people, in general, will have a preference for moderately worded communication over strongly worded communication. It is a bias against "extremism." The implication is that a moderate communication from the other to the focal person is more likely to induce attitude or sentiment change in the focal person than a strongly worded communication. Hence, given the unbalanced structure $+PO$, $+PX$ and $-OX$ (the communicated position of O), then P is more likely to change the PO and PX relations if the communication expressing $-OX$ is moderately worded than if it is extremely worded.[2]

Note that three of the above biases pertain to the matter of predicting which relations among a number of relations are most likely to change: the positivity, interpersonal change, and least cost biases. Considering all three together, the following implication is evident: The relation most likely to change is one which is negative rather than positive, interpersonal rather than attitudinal, and which constitutes the minimum change necessary to achieve balance. The postulation of these biases in recent studies lends insight into the problem of types of relations which are most likely to change—a problem untreated by the substantive balance theorists.

There are four points to be made before a review of the cognitive bias literature can be undertaken. First, it is clear that some of the biases pertain to effects which can be obtained "independent" of balance; they *do not* presume a preference for or a tendency toward balance. Other biases are intended to complement balance predictions; they *do presume* a preference for or a tendency toward balance. An example of the former type is positivity: One need not postulate a preference for or a tendency toward balance in order to postulate a preference for or a tendency toward positivity. A person can prefer positive

---

2. It is not clear why the confusing term *"extremity* of message" is used in the literature rather than the less confusing term *"extremeness* of message." The term "extremity" is retained only for the sake of continuity.

relations independently of balanced ones; or, putting it more strongly, a person may prefer positivity *instead of* balance. For example, a change from −PO, −PX, +OX (balance) to +PO, −PX, +OX (unbalance) represents a change which satisfies the positivity bias but violates the balance principle. Three other biases (besides positivity) likewise do not presume a preference for or a tendency toward balance: completeness (a person can prefer a complete yet unbalanced structure), extremity (a person can prefer moderately worded communication from O independently of balance), and agreement (P can change from dislike-disagree (balance) to dislike-agree (unbalance), representing a tendency toward agreement but a violation of the balance principle).

In contrast to the positivity, completeness, extremity and agreement biases, the least cost and interpersonal change biases *do presume* a tendency toward balance; they presume that the balance principle is necessarily a valid one. The former says: Given that there will be a tendency toward balance, balance will be achieved through the fewest possible changes. The latter, similarly, says: Given an unbalanced structure consisting of both attitudinal and interpersonal relations, there will be a change toward balance through the alteration of an interpersonal, rather than an attitudinal, relation. This distinction between the positivity, completeness, extremity and agreement biases, on the one hand, and the least cost and interpersonal change biases, on the other, is a meaningful one because *if a preference for or tendency toward balance is not observed in a particular study, the latter two biases are no longer applicable, whereas the former four biases are.* Hence, in such an instance, only the former biases may be employed to explain the findings; the latter ones cannot be used in this way. For this reason, the biases of positivity, completeness, extremity and agreement constitute potential alternatives to the balance principle, whereas the least cost and interpersonal change biases complement (but cannot replace) it.

The second general point to be made pertains to the bias not mentioned directly above: reciprocity (symmetry). Not only does this bias presume a preference for and a tendency toward balance, but it is deducible from the balance principle itself. Clearly, the reciprocity bias simply states that any two-line cycle (the PO and OP relations, for example) will tend to be balanced. This is an extension of (a deduction from) the balance principle.

In regard to the agreement bias, it can be argued that it, too, is deducible from the balance principle. If the PX and OX relations are of the same sign (agreement), this is the same as saying that the algebraic product of the signs is positive—a statement analogous (but clearly not identical) to Cartwright and Harary's (1956) formal definition of balance. Clearly, the agreement bias is deducible from a general "consistency" principle; "agreement" can be defined as a type of "consonance" (cf. Festinger), and "disagreement" as a type of "dissonance." But to the extent that P can prefer agreement *instead of* balance (for example, prefer dislike-agree to dislike-disagree), then to that extent, the agreement concept cannot be treated as deducible from the balance principle.

Note, incidentally, that the term "presumes" is not synonymous with the phrase "is deducible from." While the least cost principle *presumes* a tendency toward balance ("How will balance be achieved, given that it will be achieved?"), it is *not deducible from* the balance principle. It is deduced from a general psychological principle of least resistance or least effort. In contrast, the reciprocity bias, for example, is deducible from (is an extension of) the balance principle; one need not refer to some other principle in order to obtain it.

The third point concerns the issue of which cognitive biases are true modifications to the theory of balance and which are not. As pointed out above, the agreement bias, and certainly the reciprocity bias, can be treated as extensions of the balance principle; the remaining biases cannot. The implication is that if a bias is *not* simply an extension of the balance principle, it is a true modification or "corollary"; it goes beyond the balance principle in explanatory power. By comparison, biases which are mere extensions of balance add less insight; they do not go beyond the balance principle, and are not true modifications. The empirical literature on cognitive bias, by and large, tends to give all biases the same "weight" in the degree to which they represent modifications of the general balance propositions. This should be kept in mind during the following review. By this reasoning, the following biases are true modifications of the theory of balance, since they are not deducible from the balance principle itself: least cost, positivity, preference for interpersonal change, completeness, and extremity. (In addition, the further stipulation is added that the least cost and interpersonal change biases *presume* a balance preference or tendency; positivity, completeness and extremity do not.) The reciprocity and agreement biases, since they can be regarded as deducible from the balance principle (or, at least from a general consistency principle), are not really true modifications of the theory.

The fourth and final point concerns the methodological-statistical problem of the *relative extent* to which the balance principle and a postulated bias explain a given dependent variable (preference, change, or tension). In a particular study, one might find an effect of a bias *instead* of an effect of balance–unbalance. In the language of analysis of variance, this would be a "main effect" of the bias, no main effect of balance–unbalance, and no interaction effect. Such a finding would constitute a severe blow to the balance principle. It would be a "strong" finding. The direct opposite would be a main effect of balance–unbalance and no effect at all of the bias, with no interaction effect. This is a "weak" finding—the weakest possible, in this context. Other findings would fall somewhere between the two extremes: Two main effects and no interaction effect, in which case the balance effect and the bias effect complement each other; or, two main effects and an interaction effect—still a "complementary" finding. Obtaining only an interaction effect would be a relatively strong finding—neither balance–unbalance nor the bias explains the dependent variable, but only in combination do they affect it. It would be a "strong" finding because the hypothesized effect of balance–unbalance would not be obtained. Other possible types of findings will be discussed as they are encountered below in the treatment of the literature.

The literature on cognitive biases is divided into three categories: (1) studies which modify the Balance Preference (GP 1) or Balance Tendency (GP 2) hypothesis; (2) the literature on least cost (The least cost bias is considered separately because excellent data are available on the matter of *comparing* the relative effects of least cost against the other biases.); (3) studies which employ a measure of tension, and hence modify the tension hypothesis (GP 3) (as noted earlier, empirical studies testing deductions from the Tension Reduction hypothesis (GP 4) are lacking.).

The Effects of Cognitive Bias upon Preference and Tendency

An interesting set of recent experiments have utilized the number of errors in *learning* a structure as the dependent variable. DeSoto (1960) introduced the technique, which involves keeping a record of the number of errors made over repeated trials in learning a particular structure. DeSoto found, among other things, that structures containing asymmetric (+, −) relations were more difficult to learn than (revealed more errors than) structures containing symmetric (+, + or −, −) relations. Although the balance–unbalance of the entire structure was not measured in this study, the evidence provides support for a reciprocity bias. Similar conclusions were reached by Mosher (1967).

The dependent variable "errors made in learning" is to be interpreted as a measure of "preference." If one finds, for example, that balanced structures are easier to learn (are learned with fewer errors) than unbalanced structures, one can infer a "preference" for balanced structures. Thus, the learning experiments are classified as testing deductions from the Balance Preference hypothesis. Similarly, in testing for a positivity bias, if it is found that positive relations are learned easier than negative ones, then a "preference" for positivity can be inferred.

DeSoto's learning technique was first applied directly to the problem of balance by Zajonc and Burnstein (1965a). The independent variable was the balance–unbalance of the structure; three balanced and three unbalanced structures were presented to each subject. The objects in each structure were two persons (P and O) and an issue (X). Thus, the design was of the interpersonal-hypothetical variety. The dependent variable was the number of errors made in learning the structure over repeated trials. Surprisingly, it was found that the effect of balance–unbalance of the structure upon errors in learning was not significant. The effect of a positivity bias, however, was noted: Structures containing two negative relations (e.g., $-PO$, $+PX$, $-OX$) were harder to learn (showed more errors) than structures containing less than two negative relations.

Since the main effect of balance–unbalance was not significant, these findings constitute evidence against the balance principle. One important reservation to this conclusion must be noted, however. When a control for *importance of the issue* (X) given in the structure is considered, the following results were obtained: If the issue was an important one (integration), then balanced structures are significantly easier to learn than unbalanced ones. If the issue is relatively unimportant (*Newsweek*), then the balance or unbalance of the structure does not affect learning. This is one explanation of why the overall effect of balance was not significant. When importance of the issue is taken into account, a different picture emerges. Hence, the easiest structures to learn were those which contained only positive relations, which were balanced, and which concerned an important X-object. The study presents evidence in favor of a positivity bias—the effects of which can be interpreted as at least as prominent as the effects of balance.

The results of another study by Zajonc and Burnstein (1965b) are of interest. This investigation obtained evidence supporting the balance principle but which, in addition, found the positivity, reciprocity, and interpersonal biases to be operative. The dependent variable was errors made in learning a structure. Using an interpersonal-hypothetical design, six structures were presented to the subjects, two containing *negative reciprocity* between P and O (−PO, −OP), two containing *positive reciprocity* (+PO, +OP), and two containing *nonreciprocity* (−PO, +OP only; +PO, −OP was not considered). The relative number of positive and negative relations in each structure was recorded, in order to evaluate the effects of positivity. Also noted was whether a relation was interpersonal (PO, OP) or attitudinal (PX, OX), in order to isolate the effects of an interpersonal bias.

The major findings were as follows: (a) Balance–unbalance and positivity affected learning independently of each other. Balanced structures were easier to learn than unbalanced ones (regardless of positivity), and ease of learning increased as the number of positive relations in the structure increased (regardless of the degree of balance of the structure). The interaction of balance and positivity, however, was not significant. (b) Reciprocity had an effect upon learning, but only for balanced structures. Thus, the interaction of balance and reciprocity was significant; the easiest structures to learn were balanced ones containing reciprocal relations between P and O. (c) Reciprocity and positivity interacted, such that structures containing *positive reciprocity* (+PO, +OP) were easiest to learn. Overall, the easiest structure to learn was one which was balanced, had the greater number of positive relations (positivity bias), and which contained positive reciprocal relations between P and O (demonstrating both a positivity and reciprocity bias).

Note that the dependent variable above was the number of errors made in learning the entire structure. When the number of errors made in learning the *separate relations* in each structure was considered, the effect of an interpersonal bias was found: Interpersonal (PO and OP) relations were easier to learn than attitudinal (PX or OX) relations. Interestingly, there was evidence that the subject used interpersonal relations as "anchors" or "mnemonic aids" in attempting to learn a particular structure. They first concentrated on learning the interpersonal relations, and next on learning the attitudinal ones.

The striking inference here is that in everyday social contact, people establish perceptions of interpersonal relations first, then concern themselves with perceptions involving attitudes or perceived attitudes. Perceiving and "absorbing" an entire structure is a complex matter, and for this reason the person will look for "clues" or "hints" upon which he can then base further perceptions. The evidence, though very minimal and only suggestive, implies that these "clues" are provided by relations of sentiment, attraction, liking, etc., rather than by unit or attitudinal relations involving persons and X-objects.

Before moving further into the cognitive bias literature, it will be worthwhile to state our first set of conditional propositions. The first three pertain to the positivity, reciprocity and interpersonal biases, taking "preference" as the dependent variable. Thus, they modify the Balance Preference hypothesis. The abbreviation "CP" will be used in identifying all conditional propositions stated in this text.

CP 1   *(Positivity and Preference): Independently of the balance–unbalance of a structure, the greater the number of positive relations in the structure, the easier it is to learn. From this, one may infer a preference for positive over negative relations.*

CP 2   *(Reciprocity and Preference): Reciprocal interpersonal relations (whether both relations are positive or both are negative) are easier to learn than non-reciprocal interpersonal relations. From this, one may infer a preference for reciprocal over nonreciprocal interpersonal relations. In addition, relations of positive reciprocity, or reciprocal positive relations between two persons, are easier to learn than (are preferred over) relations of negative reciprocity, or reciprocal negative relations between two persons.*

While the first sentence in CP 2 may seem to be only a restatement of the Balance Preference hypothesis (since reciprocity is a type of balance), it should be kept in mind that P can always prefer a reciprocal PO bond *at the expense of* balance with respect to X. Thus, a structure containing the following relations contains reciprocity, yet is unbalanced: $+PO$, $+OP$, $+PX$, $-OX$. In this way, reciprocity can affect preference (learning) independently of balance, as CP 2 implies.

The next conditional proposition pertains to the interpersonal bias:

CP 3 *(Interpersonal Preference): Independently of the balance–unbalance of a structure, the signs (whether positive or negative) of interpersonal relations are easier to learn than the signs of attitudinal relations. From this one may infer a preference for perceiving interpersonal relations over attitudinal relations, and that interpersonal relations rather than attitudinal ones constitute clues to the focal person for establishing perceptions of attitudinal relations in a structure.*

A recent study by Burnstein (1967) provides evidence which modifies the Balance Tendency hypothesis, since *restructuring*—alterations or changes in initially given relations made by subjects—was the dependent variable. Burnstein's findings pertain to the positivity, reciprocity and interpersonal change biases as these biases have bearing on the problem of change (as opposed to the problem of preference just discussed). Using a design of the interpersonal-hypothetical variety, a number of *POX* structures were presented to the subjects, who were asked to indicate which relations would be likely to change over time, and in which direction (postive or negative) each would change. Initially balanced structures were far less likely to be altered than unbalanced ones, and desired changes (restructurings) most often ended in a balanced structure. In addition, (a) initially non-reciprocal relations between *P* and *O* were changed in the direction of reciprocity; (b) initially negative relations, whether interpersonal or attitudinal, were changed in the positive direction, whereas initially positive relations were less likely to be altered (and hence, interpersonal changes were in the direction of positive reciprocity between *P* and *O*); and (c) interpersonal relations were more frequently altered than attitudinal relations. These findings enable the statement of the first three conditional propositions in terms of Tendency (therefore modifying the Balance Tendency hypothesis, GP 2):

CP 4 *(Positivity and Change): Independently of the initial balance–unbalance of a structure, the focal person will tend to change a negative relation in the positive direction, and tend to keep a positive relation positive.*

CP 5 *(Reciprocity and Change): Independently of the initial balance–unbalance of a structure, the focal person will tend to change non-reciprocal interpersonal relations in the direction of reciprocity. Furthermore, such changes are in the direction of positive reciprocity rather than negative reciprocity.*

CP 6 *(Interpersonal Change): Altered (changed) relations are more likely to be interpersonal rather than attitudinal.*

The isolation of the positivity and interpersonal biases by recent studies has implications for Newcomb's original speculation on the effects of communication upon balance tendency. Recall that one of Newcomb's predictions was that given unbalance, P would communicate with O about X in an attempt to convince O of his point of view. But what if P and O already agree, yet the structure is unbalanced—for example, $-PO$, $+PX$, $+OX$? Clearly, communication directed toward convincing the other of one's own point of view is not necessary. Postulation of the positivity and interpersonal change biases would explain the predicted change in the PO relation from $-PO$ to $+PO$. Such a change would satisfy both the positivity and interpersonal change biases, and would explain why a change from $+PX$ to $-PX$ would *not* occur, even though this latter change is toward balance. Given these biases, under conditions of agreement but unbalance, one need not necessarily hypothesize a "direction of communication toward the attainment of balance," as Newcomb does.

The "extremity" bias, defined above and researched by Feather (1967a) and Feather and Jeffries (1967), also pertains to the matter of communication between P and O. These investigators find that the originator (O) of an extremely worded communication is rated as less likable and also as less credible than the originator of a moderately worded communication. Thus, the extremeness of the communication *from O to P* can affect P's liking for O.

CP 7 *(Extremity and Preference): If O communicates an extremely worded message to P, then P will rate O as less likable and also less credible than if the message is moderately worded.*

It seems possible to deduce from this conditional proposition (and from the evidence provided by Feather, and Feather and Jeffries) that extremity of the message from O to P will lessen the likelihood that P will *increase* his liking for O. To the degree that an increase in liking would result in a tendency toward balance, to that degree extremity of the message will affect balance tendency. As an example, assume the following initial structure: $-PO$, $+PX$, $+OX$. P can satisfy not only the balance principle, but also the positivity and interpersonal change biases by changing to $+PO$. But if the message (from O) telling P that O's opinion of X was extreme, a change to $+PO$ is less likely than if the message were moderate. *Note that in this way, the extremity bias can counteract the operation of the positivity and interpersonal change biases.* Although the Feather (1967a) and Feather-Jeffries (1967) studies did not measure change, the following conditional proposition can be tentatively stated:

CP 8 *(Extremity and Change): An extremely worded message from O to P will make an increase in P's liking for O less likely than a moderately worded message. To the extent that an increase in liking would result in a change toward balance, to that extent extremity of the message prevents a tendency toward balance.*

A recent investigation by DeSoto et al. (1968) provides some limited evidence in favor of a *completeness* bias. This bias, introduced by Harary (1959), postulates that the focal person will prefer complete structures over incomplete ones, independently of balance–unbalance. Namely, it is conceivable that a structure *which is unbalaned* but complete could be preferred over an incomplete (vacuous) structure. For the most part, the DeSoto et al. data do show that complete structures (all relations stated) are easier to learn than (are "preferred over") incomplete structures, where one or more relations are left ungiven or unstated. The DeSoto et al. data do not, however, indicate whether a preference for completeness can *exceed* a preference for balance. There is no evidence (in this or in any other study) that, for example, complete unbalanced structures are easier to learn than incomplete ones. Such a finding would indicate a preference for completeness *instead* of preference for balance.

The evidence in favor of a completeness bias is very fragmentary. As a matter of fact, Morrissette (1966) has obtained results against the operation of a completeness bias: He found that an index of balance which ignored vacuous cycles constituted a better predictor of tension than an index of balance which did incorporate incomplete (vacuous) cycles. The inference is that the presence or absence of incomplete cycles in a structure makes no difference to a person in terms of tension. The results of this latter study are discussed more thoroughly in the next chapter.

If a completeness bias is operative, if only minimally, then there are implications regarding the graph-theoretic convention of treating vacuous structures or cycles as vacuously "balanced." If people do in fact learn complete structures with fewer errors than incomplete ones, then it would not make sense to say that incomplete structures are psychologically "balanced," as implied by the concept of "vacuous balance." The term "vacuous balance," may be a misnomer; perhaps substituting the term "vacuous structure" is advisable. The use of the term "balance" implies both preference and stability, an implication questioned by the DeSoto et al. data. Yet, the Morrissette (1966) results, using tension as the dependent variable, lead to the conclusion that the presence-absence of vacuous cycles in a structure is not psychologically meaningful (i.e., it makes no difference in terms of tension). Clearly, additional research is necessary in order to resolve this problem.

It is possible, however, to state a conditional proposition on completeness and preference, given the results of DeSoto et al. Since there is no evidence one way or the other in regard to completeness and change, no conditional proposition treating change as the dependent variable can be stated.

CP 9 *(Completeness and Preference): Independently of the balance–unbalance of complete structures, complete structures tend to be learned with fewer errors than incomplete structures. From this one may infer a preference for structural completeness over structural incompleteness.*

The postulation of independent effects of cognitive biases leads one to pose a crucial question: Under what kinds of conditions can one obtain effects of cognitive biases which are stronger than the effects of balance–unbalance? If the effects of the cognitive biases themselves are sufficient to explain one's findings, then one need not refer to the balance principle at all. In this respect, a recent study of the interpersonal-hypothetical type by Zajonc and Sherman (1967) on POQ (triadic) structures deals a severe blow to the balance principle. As in previous studies by Zajonc and Burnstein, the number of errors in learning a structure was the dependent variable. It was found that the balance–unbalance of the structure was unrelated to learning. The effects of balance were not significant. As a matter of fact, there was a slight tendency (though not statistically significant) for *unbalanced* structures to be learned with fewer errors (to be easier to learn) than balanced structures. Taking number of errors *per relation* as the dependent variable, strong effects of the positivity and reciprocity biases were noted. Namely, these latter two biases explained errors in learning, whereas the balance–unbalance of the structure did not.

The investigators cite two possible reasons why no effects of balance–unbalance were observed. First, the task was set up in such a difficult way that the subject's perceptions may not have been in terms of balance–unbalance at all; the difficulty of the task might have suppressed any balance effects. However, the investigators replicated the study using a fewer number of structures (thus making the subject's task easier), but still no effects of balance–unbalance were observed.

There is a second possible explanation for the negative findings obtained. When learning each of the POQ structures, the subject was not asked to "identify with" one of the persons (P) in the structure. This is in contrast to other studies using the interpersonal-hypothetical design, where the subject is often (though not always) asked to "be P." Since the subject was not part of the "group" being learned, it might be reasonable to suspect that balance–unbalance should have no effect. It seems necessary that the focal person "be" a member of the structure that is being learned, or that at least this condition be approximated as much as possible if the interpersonal-hypothetical design is used. This is one advantage of concrete designs over hypothetical ones. It is important to note, however, that in the previously-cited studies by Zajonc and Burnstein (1965a, 1965b), which did obtain effects of balance–unbalance, the subject was not asked to identify with one of the persons represented in the structure. This latter point places even greater weight on the findings of Zajonc and Sherman.

The results of the Zajonc-Sherman study cannot be ignored. Their findings suggest that the conditional propositions postulating independent effects of the positivity and reciprocity biases are "strong" propositions, and that the balance principle, itself a type of cognitive bias, should not continue to enjoy the privileged position that it now has in social psychology. If other biases explain results not only in addition to but better than the balance principle, then it would seem that the balance principle has only minimal explanatory power.

As will be seen a bit later when the effects of cognitive bias upon tension are considered, this latter statement gains additional weight. The investigators themselves (Zajonc and Sherman, 1967, p. 649), in the light of the findings of their study plus previous studies by Zajonc and associates, state that "The results . . . suggest that the explanatory power of the balance principle, when confronted by empirical results, does not surpass other sources of cognitive bias that operate in the perception of social relations."

The Zajonc-Sherman data also reveal the presence of an *agreement* bias, though the results in regard to this latter bias are not as impressive as the results that pertain to the positivity and reciprocity biases. Since their study focused on the POQ rather than the POX unit, "agreement" can be defined as the similarity in sign between the PQ and OQ relations. "Disagreement" constitutes dissimilarity between the PQ and OQ signs. *Note, in addition, that two other types of "agreement" are possible:* The similarity-dissimilarity between the signs of the PQ and PO relations, and the similarity-dissimilarity between the signs of the PO and OQ relations. Thus, there are three pairs of comparisons that one can make. This latter kind of comparison involves *lateral symmetry* (Newcomb, 1968), and is analogous to the concept of agreement in the POX unit. (Note that the concept of lateral symmetry is not limited to the POQ unit, but can apply to the POX unit as well. There are three pairs of comparisons: PX/OX ["agreement," as typically defined], PX/PO, and PO/OX.) Generally, a pair of relations is laterally symmetric if they are of the same sign, and laterally asymmetric if they are of opposite sign.

The results of Zajonc and Sherman (1967), and a re-analysis by Newcomb (1968) of data gathered by Zajonc and Burnstein (1965a, 1965b), suggests that "ease of learning" a structure is at least in part explainable on the basis of lateral symmetry. There is a tendency for ease of learning to increase as a function of the number of laterally symmetric pairs in the structure. Although the evidence is limited, it does permit the tentative statement of a conditional proposition on the independent effects of lateral symmetry (agreement) upon preference:

CP 10   *(Agreement [Lateral Symmetry] and Preference): Independently of the balance–unbalance of a structure, there is a slight tendency for ease of learning the structure to increase as the number of laterally symmetric pairs of relations in the structure increases. From this, one may infer a preference for lateral symmetry (agreement) over lateral asymmetry (disagreement).*

There is further evidence, provided by Rodrigues (1967; cf. Rodrigues, 1968) in a study of the POX structure, that agreement explains change independently of balance–unbalance. After being presented with the "basic eight" POX structures, subjects were asked to indicate which relations in which structures they wished to change. Independent effects of agreement were found, particularly in regard to the subject's desire to change the *OX* relation.

CP 11 *(Agreement and Change): Independently of the balance–unbalance of a structure, the focal person will tend to change one attitudinal relation in the direction of the other attitudinal relation. Thus, there is a tendency to make the PX and OX relations similar in sign, independently of the sign of the PO relation (i.e., independently of balance–unbalance).*

There is no evidence that lateral symmetry in the *POQ* structure exerts independent effects upon change. In addition, it should be stressed that the evidence favoring an independent agreement effect on *both* preference and change is rather limited. CP 10 and CP 11 are therefore to be taken as tentative. In a following section, however, it will become clear that the independent effects of agreement upon *tension* are quite marked. Thus, while the agreement bias is strongly operative in explaining tension, it appears to be less operative in explaining preference and change.

Least Cost

Introduced by Abelson and Rosenberg (1958; also Rosenberg and Abelson, 1960, and Harary, 1959), and deduced from Hilgard's (1948) general psychological principle of least effort, the least cost hypothesis pertains to the *means* which the focal person can use to attain balance. The postulation of this bias therefore presumes a balance tendency, though the bias itself is not deducible from the balance principle. Evidence favoring it would modify the Balance Tendency hypothesis. The primary purpose of this section is to examine how the least cost bias interacts or combines with the other cognitive biases, and under what kinds of conditions a least cost or "minimal change" effect does *not* operate.

In an impressive study of the subject's tendency to "restructure" (change or alter) relations in structures, Burnstein (1967, cited above) explored the way in which the least cost bias could interact with the biases of positivity, reciprocity and interpersonal change. The structures diagrammed in Figure 1 represent the structures presented to the subjects in Burnstein's interpersonal-hypothetical design. There are sixteen *POX* structures altogether, each containing four relations which are either positive or negative. Note that certain structures (the unnumbered ones) were treated as isomorphic to others, yielding nine "basic" structures. The structures were presented to the subjects verbally (not in picture form), and each subject was to indicate (a) which relations he would change, if any, and (b) the direction (positive or negative) of that change. Subjects were not asked to identify with the "*P*" position in the structure.

This study is important because it provides detailed data on how the various cognitive biases combine with each other, and how least cost is affected by the other biases. Although mentioned above, the findings on balance, reciprocity, positivity, and interpersonal change respectively can be listed before least cost is discussed. (a) Unbalanced structures were more likely to be altered than balanced ones, and alterations tended to result in a balance structure; (b) initially non-reciprocal relations between P and O were changed toward reciprocity; (c) initially negative relations, whether interpersonal or attitudinal, were changed in the positive direction, and initially positive relations were kept positive (and thus, changes were in the direction of positive reciprocity between P and O); and (d) interpersonal relations were more frequently altered than attitudinal relations.

The lucid findings of Burnstein show that with certain structures, the subject will satisfy a number of biases together, but for other structures, he will yield to certain biases and not others. Let us consider examples of the first instance. Clearly, in structure 1 (Figure 1), the subject can satisfy three biases (beside balance) by doing nothing: Positivity (all relations are positive), reciprocity (the PO relation is already one of positive reciprocity) and least cost (no changes at all are necessary). In structure 2 (note also its isomorph), which is unbalanced, both positivity and least cost demand change of the $-OX$ relation to $+OX$. (Neither the reciprocity nor the interpersonal change biases apply.) Burnstein found that this is exactly what happened. In structures 3 and 7, note that changing the $-OP$ relation to $+OP$ satisfies not only balance tendency but *four* biases together: positivity, reciprocity, interpersonal change and least cost. In structure 7, changing to $+PX$, $+OX$ and $+OP$ (making three changes) would satisfy balance and the biases of positivity, reciprocity and interpersonal change, but would violate least cost. Hence, only the OP relation is changed (to $+OP$) — thus satisfying all four biases—and the negative PX and OX relations are retained.

With other structures, however, the least cost bias yields to other biases. This suggests that the least cost bias has less "power" than some of the others; that there is a "cognitive hierarchy" of biases which are evoked by the focal person—where the higher one is more frequently evoked—and the least cost bias occupies a relatively low position in this hierarchy. Take as an example structure 6. Clearly, the subject can satisfy both balance and least cost by changing $+PX$ to $-PX$ (or $+OX$ to $-OX$). Burnstein finds, however, that the subject actually changes $-PO$ and $-OP$ to $+PO$ and $+OP$ (thus making two changes instead of one—the minimum necessary), hence violating least cost, but satisfying positivity, reciprocity and interpersonal change.

Likewise, in structure 9, least cost (and also positivity) can be satisfied by changing $-PX$ to $+PX$. But the subjects did not do this. They change to $+PO$ and $+OP$, violating least cost but satisfying positivity and interpersonal change and also the bias toward positive reciprocity. Since positivity is satisfied

FIGURE 1   STRUCTURES USED IN THE BURNSTEIN STUDY*

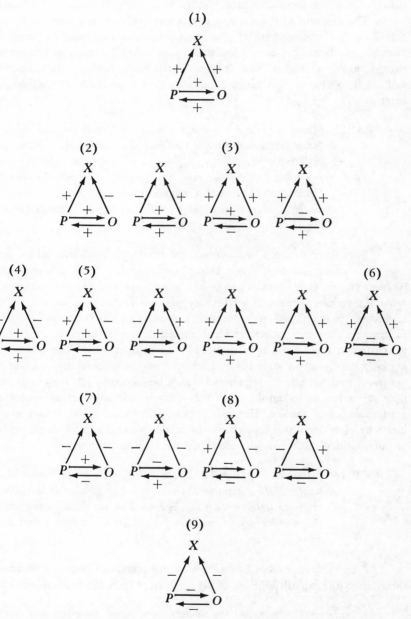

* Adapted from Burnstein (1967), p. 38. Isomorphs are unnumbered. In the first row, the structure contains four positive relations; in the second row, three positives and one negative; in the third row, two positives and two negatives; in the fourth row, one positive and three negatives; and in the fifth row, four negatives.

in both instances, this finding suggests that the interpersonal bias is a relatively powerful one and occupies a high position in a cognitive hierarchy of biases.[3]

The meaning of these results is that the least cost bias seems to operate only if other biases occupying higher positions in the focal person's "cognitive hierarchy" of biases can be satisfied at the same time. If a minimal (least cost) change violates a "higher" bias (such as interpersonal change), then least cost will not be operative. This places a limitation on the generality of the least cost effect.

> CP 12 *(Least Cost and Change): Under the condition that minimal (least cost) change toward balance also satisfies other biases such as interpersonal change, positivity and reciprocity, then the focal person will achieve balance through the fewest possible changes. Under the condition that minimal change will violate these other biases, then the focal person will not achieve balance through the fewest possible changes.*

Though undiscussed by Burnstein, the intriguing implication of his findings—as implied above—is that a hierarchy of cognitive biases relevant to the problem of balance maintenance in groups is operative, and the focal person will evoke the various biases with a frequency which is in direct proportion to their hierarchical position. Although Burnstein's own design was not sensitive enough to permit a convincing statement on this matter, it would no doubt be possible to construct a study or series of studies to test such speculation. The evidence of not only the Burnstein study but also other investigations cited suggests that the positivity, reciprocity and interpersonal change biases occupy relatively high positions in the hierarchy, and that least cost—though definitely operative—occupies a relatively lower position. Hence, it is possible to postulate the existence of a hierarchy of biases which supplement the balance process and which are evoked to differing degrees, depending upon their hierarchical position.

> CP 13 *(Hierarchy of Biases): There exists a cognitive hierarchy of biases which determine the way in which balance is maintained in group settings; each bias is evoked by the focal person with a frequency which is in direct proportion to its hierarchical position.*

Clearly, there is room for research on this postulated hierarchy. What are the relative hierarchical positions of all the biases? Does the balance bias itself

---

3. Burnstein (1967) treated the subject's own attitude toward X as a type of cognitive bias. But this is only because the subject was not asked to identify with P (to "be P") in the structure. If the subject is asked to identify with P, his own attitude becomes a relation in the structure (the PX relation). To call the subject's attitude a "bias" seems misleading.

fit somewhere in this hierarchy—such that it can be violated by other biases holding a higher relative position (witness the findings of Zajonc and Sherman [1967], cited earlier)? Does the hierarchy operate in a different way or take a different ordering, depending upon whether the structure is dyadic or triadic? Does least cost tend to become *more operative* as the *size* of the group increases? In regard to this last question, it would seem that as the number of persons in a group increases, least cost will tend to occupy a higher hierarchical position, since the number of possible changes (the number of relations) will increase geometrically. *This would illustrate the dependence of such a "cognitive" hierarchy upon the structural properties of groups. Namely, the focal person would not maintain an invariant hierarchy, but he would shift and modify it, depending upon the size of the group and/or the number of relations in the group's structure.*

The Effects of Cognitive Bias upon Tension

Much research has been devoted to the effects of positivity and agreement upon tension. Although predictions can be made about the effects of reciprocity upon tension (non-reciprocity produces more tension than reciprocity), such a prediction has not yet been directly tested. The interpersonal, extremity and least cost biases do not apply directly to the Tension hypothesis, and for this reason are not discussed in this section. Evidence pertaining to completeness and tension is somewhat inconclusive, although Morrissette (1966) has obtained evidence that the presence-absence of incomplete cycles in a structure does not affect tension.

The first inklings that the sign of a relation could affect tension independently of balance–unbalance were found in the early Jordan (1953) study discussed in the previous chapter. After presenting sixty-four structures to subjects for "pleasantness" ratings, it was found that as the number of positive relations in the structure increased, the structure was rated as more pleasant. Systematic study of the effects of biases upon tension was not undertaken until recently. In Rodrigues' (1965) interpersonal-hypothetical design, subjects were presented with structures which varied in balance (balance, unbalance), sign of PO (positive, negative), importance of X (important, unimportant), and strength of relations (only a distinction between "strong" and "weak" was made). Each structure was rated by the subject on a seven-point scale indicating the amount of "tension, discomfort or uneasiness" he would experience if he were "faced with such situations." It was found that as predicted, balance produced less tension than unbalance, and that independently of balance, negative interpersonal relations were a greater source of tension than positive ones, suggesting an independent positivity bias. It was also found that regardless of balance–unbalance, important issues were a source of greater tension than unimportant ones. In addition, as the number of "strong" (as opposed to "weak") relations increased, tension also increased.[4] It appeared that agreement also affected tension independently of balance–unbalance, but the results were not conclusive.

More conclusive results on the effects of both positivity and agreement were provided in a second study by Rodrigues (1967). The "basic eight" Heider structures were presented to the subjects; hence, only balance, positivity and agreement were varied. Tension was measured by means of a millimeter scale of pleasantness. As expected, it was found that structures containing agreement $(+PX, +OX;$ or $-PX, -OX)$ were rated as more pleasant than structures containing disagreement $(-PX, +OX;$ or $+PX, -OX)$. Structures containing $+PO$ were rated as more pleasant than structures containing $-PO$. Both effects were independent of balance–unbalance.

Further support for the independent effects of positivity and agreement upon tension is provided by Taylor (1968). Additional evidence and discussion of these data is given in the seventh chapter of this text. A brief account of the findings on positivity and agreement can be stated, however. First, Taylor's method of measuring tension did not employ a questionnaire technique, where the subject indicates his own feelings, as in other studies. The behavior of each subject in an interaction situation was observed and recorded by means of Bales' (1951) scheme of Interaction Process Analysis (IPA). One of the observation-categories of this scheme allows the observer to code "tension behavior" of the subject. Second, an interpersonal-concrete design was used; each subject (P) discussed an issue (X) with a role player (O) for a period of thirty minutes. Four experimental conditions were used; P likes O and agrees with him (balance), dislike-disagree (balance), dislike-agree (unbalance), and like-disagree (unbalance).

As predicted, a very strong effect of balance–unbalance was observed. Subjects under the balance conditions revealed far less tension than subjects under the unbalance condition. Both positivity and agreement independently affected tension, such that liking resulted in less tension than dislike, and agreement resulted in less tension than disagreement. The lowest tension appeared in the like-agree condition, showing a significant interaction effect.

From the evidence of these studies, conditional propositions on the independent effects of positivity and agreement can be stated.

CP 14　*(Interpersonal Positivity and Tension): Independently of balance–unbalance, if the focal person likes the other, he will experience less tension than if he dislikes the other.*

This proposition refers explicitly to the effect of *interpersonal* positivity.

---

4. A detailed discussion of importance of X appears later in this chapter. The problem of strength of relations is discussed under "Polarity and the Congruity Model" (in this chapter) and again in Chapter 6.

It has been implied in the literature that *attitudinal* positivity (i.e., the sign of the PX or the OX relation) can also independently affect tension, but no concrete results to this effect have yet appeared.

While the sign of a single attitudinal relation alone may not affect tension, the evidence clearly supports the view that the PX and perceived OX attitudes combined do affect tension:

> CP 15 *(Agreement and Tension): Independently of balance–unbalance, if the attitudinal PX relation is of the same sign as the perceived OX relation (agreement), then the focal person's tension is less than if the relations are of opposite sign (disagreement).*

Although the preponderance of evidence shows that both positivity and agreement affect tension independently of balance, the re-analysis of data gathered in at least one study implies, at first glance, that positivity and agreement have limited effects upon tension. The study in question was done by Price, Harburg and McLeod (1965); independent effects were obtained. However, Jordan's (1966b) re-analysis of the Price et al. data showed absolutely no effects at all. Let us take a close look at both the study and the critique.[5]

Price et al. used an interpersonal-concrete design. Each subject was asked to name two of his "best friends" (O and Q) whom he "strongly liked" (thus getting a score of +3), two more friends whom he "mildly liked" (+2), and two more whom he "slightly liked" (+1). Hence, the triadic structure was the unit of analysis, and the *strengths* of the liking relations were measured. Although negative PQ and OQ relations were considered in the design (−3, −2, −1), *only positive PO relations* (of varying strengths) were used. Structures containing −PO, of whatever strength, were not studied. The tension variable was defined in terms of "positive affect" ("pleasant") and "negative affect" ("uneasy"). The subject (P) indicated his "affect" by checking a point on a millimeter scale with the words "pleasant" and "uneasy" appearing at each end.

The predictions of interest in this study are as follows: (a) The variation in affect is a function of PQ/OQ *discrepancy*, if the PO relation is held constant. Discrepancy is defined as the difference between the *strengths* of the PQ and OQ relations (for example, if PQ and OQ were +2 and +3 respectively, discrepancy = 1; if these two relations were −1 and +4, discrepancy = 5, showing that the algebraic and not the absolute difference is taken). Any variation in affect with the strength of PO held constant would demonstrate an independent

---

5. Newcomb (1968) has also recently questioned the findings that positivity and agreement independently affect tension. His argument is tied in with his three-category scheme of balance, non-balance and unbalance. Since data gathered by the present author question his three-category scheme (Taylor, 1967; Taylor, 1968; Chapter 7 of this text), and in addition, reveal independent effects of both positivity and agreement (as have the other researchers cited), a detailed treatment of Newcomb's three-category scheme will be undertaken in Chapter 7.

effect of discrepancy. (b) Variation in affect is a function of the strength of the +PO relation, if discrepancy is held constant. This would demonstrate an independent effect of positivity (the strength of +PO). The results appeared, at the time, to support the predictions. The investigators concluded that affect is a function of the strength of the +PO relation (with discrepancy constant), and a function of discrepancy (with strength of +PO constant).

By systematically examining pairs of triads each containing three relations of varying strengths, Jordan (1966b) was able to demonstrate that the Price et al. data did not support the two predictions. Jordan's procedure was as follows: Note the following set of triadic structures, in which the PO relation varies, but the PQ and OQ relations (discrepancy) are constant:

a. +1 PO, +3 PQ, +3 OQ
b. +2 PO, +3 PQ, +3 OQ
c. +3 PO, +3 PQ, +3 OQ

The symbol "+1 PO" means that "P likes O with a strength of +1"; "+2 PO" means "P likes O with a strength of +2," and so on. The mean affect rating for each triad was recorded. Three statistical tests of difference are possible: a versus b, b versus c, and a versus c. By systematically examining in this way all possible triad comparisons, Jordan was able to determine if, in fact, affect varied as a function of liking (with discrepancy constant) and as a function of discrepancy (with liking constant).

There were fifty-four sets of three comparisons possible (thus giving 54 × 3 or 162 separate paired comparisons), but only forty-one of these could be tested. This was true because some sets had been eliminated by Price et al. (without clearly stating why). Of these forty-one sets (a "set" consists of three paired comparisons), only six supported the predictions, thirty-four disconfirmed the predictions, and one was ambiguous. Jordan thus concluded that discrepancy *does not* determine affect if the strength of the +PO relation is constant, nor does the strength of the +PO relation determine affect if discrepancy is constant. Thus, it would not appear that discrepancy (cf. agreement) and strength of PO (cf. positivity) constitute independent cognitive biases, as stated in the conditional propositions above.

Despite the admirable sophistication and clarity of Jordan's re-analysis, his own conclusions must be placed in the light of other studies on the effects of positivity and agreement upon tension. Why should Jordan's inferences from the re-analysis be in conflict with the results of Rodrigues (1965), Rodrigues (1967), Taylor (1968), and Jordan's own early study (Jordan, 1953)—all finding that agreement and positivity affect tension independently?

There are several reasons why the Jordan re-analysis conflicts with these other studies. First and most importantly, it will be recalled that while Price et al. examined both positive and negative PQ and OQ relations, only the +PO type of structure was studied; structures containing −PO were not part of the study. Therefore, any variation in affect (or lack of it) could certainly not be attributed to the variable "like-*dislike*." Varying the *strength* of $+PO$ is clearly not the same as contrasting like with dislike, as other investigators have done.

Second, "discrepancy" is not the same as "agreement." Discrepancy can exist even though the PQ and OQ (or PX and OX) relations are identical *in sign* (such as the difference between $+1$ PQ and $+3$ PQ). Generally, *agreement* refers to similarity in sign, whereas *discrepancy* refers to differences in strength. Overall, the evidence seems to strongly favor an independent effect of agreement upon tension, but much less, if any, of an independent effect of discrepancy upon tension. Rodrigues (1965) does vary the strength of relations (and finds an independent effect of strength), but his explanatory variable is "number of strong relations in a structure" rather than "strength of a *given* relation." Hence, even though he measured tension, a direct test of the independent effects of discrepancy as defined above was not possible. His results are only suggestive.

Before continuing with our discussion of the Jordan critique, a statement of the relative effects of agreement versus discrepancy upon tension seems to be in order. The evidence shows that:

> CP 16   *(Relative Effects of Agreement and Discrepancy Upon Tension):*
> *While tension will vary according to whether or not the PX and OX (or PQ and OQ) relations are of the same sign (agreement), tension is less likely to vary according to the degree to which PX and OX (or PQ and OQ) relations of the same sign differ in strength (discrepancy).*

It must be carefully noted that discrepancy in this conditional proposition refers to the difference in the strengths of two relations *which are of the same sign*. Clearly, two relations can differ in both sign *and* strength. The combined effects of discrepancy and agreement should be quite marked. For example, the following two relations in the same structure should yield the maximum tension: $+3$ PX and -3 OX. In this instance, discrepancy is maximal (if $+3$ and -3 are the maximum scale values) and there is disagreement rather than agreement.

Just as the relative effects of agreement and discrepancy upon tension can be compared, so can the relative effects of sign of the PO relation ($+PO$ versus $-PO$) and *strength* of the PO relation ($+3$ PO, $+2$ PO, etc.). The evidence suggests that the strength of the PO relation (of a given sign) does not predict tension as well as the sign of the PO relation.

> CP 17   *(The Relative Effects of Sign and Strength of the Interpersonal Relation upon Tension): While tension will vary according to the sign of the interpersonal relation, the degree to which tension varies as a function of the strength of the interpersonal relation (of a given sign) is less.*

Hence, if one is comparing *two* structures containing +1 *PO* and +3 *PO* (where discrepancy is the same in both structures), the differences in tension between the two structures, if any, will be slight. The difference should be maximal in the case of +3 *PO* versus −3 *PO*, illustrating that the combined effects upon tension of sign and strength should be quite marked.

So far, then, there are two possible reasons why Jordan's re-analysis of the Price et al. study conflicts with the conclusions of other studies: (1) Price et al. examined only +*PO* (liking) structures; and (2) the concept of "discrepancy" is not equivalent to the concept of "agreement," nor is the "strength of *PO*" equivalent with "sign of *PO*." There is a third possible reason for the conflicting interpretations. Recall that the Price et al. operational definition of tension ("affect") differs greatly from the definitions of tension used in the Jordan (1953), Rodrigues (1965; 1967) and Taylor (1968) studies. "Positive affect" (cf. "low tension") was equated with "pleasantness," whereas "negative affect" (cf. "high tension") was equated with "uneasiness." But the terms "pleasant-unpleasant," if they were to appear as antonyms at the ends of a questionnaire scale, may not be equivalent to the terms "easy-uneasy." Hence, "pleasant" may not be the same thing as "easy," and "unpleasant" may not be the same as "uneasy." The operationalization in terms of "pleasantness" may measure a different concept than the operationalization "uneasiness." Furthermore, neither of the two kinds of pairs may reflect positive or negative "affect," as intended in the Price et al. study.

This difficulty reflects a broad problem existing in the balance literature: The meaning and use of the term "tension" is not clear. Tension has been defined in so many different ways. It has been variously defined operationally in terms of "pleasantness," "discomfort," "uneasiness," "anxiousness," "negative affect," and GSR deflections. Differing conceptual definitions of tension have caused the concept to be operationalized by a number of non-equivalent procedures, thus casting doubt on the *validity* of measures of tension. The results of two or more studies are often not directly comparable because different measures of tension are used. For this reason, the Price et al. study, and the Jordan re-analysis, is not directly comparable to other studies. Interestingly, one has yet to find a study in balance which presents data on the validity of the measures of tension employed. Most indicators used are assumed by the investigator to have "face" validity, but no actual validation procedure is ever carried out. Since this diversity in measures of tension throws some doubt on the validity of tension measures used in studies of balance, thus making any systematic comparison of studies difficult, the conditional propositions just stated (CP 16 and CP 17)— which *do* involve the comparison of studies—must be taken as tentative.

A Note on the Sources of Cognitive Bias

The section on cognitive bias should not be closed without making a brief reference to the possible origin or sources of such biases. Why should a person prefer positive to negative relations, agreement to disagreement, reciprocity to non-reciprocity? Where does the focal person acquire such "biases" in the first place? Such questions are rarely raised in the cognitive bias literature, yet—as we shall see—significant implications arise from such questions. The position may be taken that the origin of a cognitive bias lies in the norms or behavioral expectations that are learned from parents, friends, superiors, peers, mass media, and the like. The process through which one learns norms—the socialization process—can be seen as the source of what the literature refers to as "cognitive bias."

For example, there is a "norm of reciprocity" that we all learn, through the socialization process, almost from childhood. One favor deserves another favor in return; one insult deserves another; you scratch my back and I'll scratch yours; an eye for an eye, and so on. Such maxims are the rules for behavior in society and in groups; they are the norms which guide our social relations with others. As a result of the socialization process, we *internalize* the norms of society, and take them with us into a large number of social situations and groups. It is not at all surprising, therefore, that a "cognitive bias" of reciprocity shows up in an experiment on balance: The subject, a product of the socialization process, prefers reciprocal interpersonal relations in the abstract structure placed before him by the experimenter, just as he has always preferred reciprocity in his everyday contact with people.

In this respect, the operation of biases in experiments on balance can be seen as a direct result of the norms of society which the subject has successfully internalized and brought into the experiment with him. Hence, a cognitive bias can be defined as a type of internalized norm. The interesting question to raise, then, is what will happen to an experimental subject who has *not* internalized a particular bias? Gang members are notorious for developing and then internalizing norms which are directly contrary to the norms of society (Cohen, 1955; Yinger, 1960). What if, through membership in a gang, one has learned to view everything as negative—that disliking someone is generally better than liking him and that disfavoring any issue is generally better than favoring it? Under such conditions, one might expect a cognitive bias toward "negativity" rather than positivity.

The implication here is that balance researchers, particularly those favoring the cognitive bias framework, must begin to consider the sources of such biases and the consequences of the *failure* of an experimental subject to internalize a norm that he, as experimenter, had assumed was internalized successfully. The subject may prefer negative relations to positive relations, disagreement to agreement, non-reciprocity to reciprocity, and greater-than-minimal change to minimal change. Perhaps the balance researcher ought to *measure* the extent to which a bias is internalized.

It is important to note that researchers using the cognitive bias frame of reference treat a given bias as a constant rather than as a variable in their research. Results are explainable on the basis of cognitive bias if one assumes that people prefer positive relations to negative relations, agreement to disagreement, and so on. If one makes no such an assumption—if one measures *whether or not* a subject "prefers" positive to negative relations, then a particular bias is translated into a variable rather than left to remain as an implicit constant. Research on subjects other than college sophomores—who have generally been quite successful in internalizing norms or biases—seems advisable. Perhaps balance research on gang members would yield strikingly different results in regard to the operation of cognitive bias.

5 • 1b   *Importance of X*

Any statement or proposition taking into account the degree of importance of X to the focal person is a "corollary" to one or more of the general propositions of balance theory. The variable "importance" pertains to an object (X) which is part of the structure under study; it is therefore a parameter variable. Importance of X can affect balance preference, balance tendency (change), and tension, thus modifying the Preference, Tendency and Tension hypotheses:

> CP 18   *(Importance and Preference): Under the condition that the object X is important to P, the P will prefer balance to unbalance. Under the condition that X is not important to P, then P will be less likely to prefer balance to unbalance.*

> CP 19   *(Importance and Change): If the object X is important to P, then initially unbalanced conditions will cause P to change one or more relations in the direction of balance. In contrast, if the object X is unimportant to P, then initially unbalanced conditions are less likely to result in changes in the direction of balance on the part of P.*

This latter proposition follows from the next one, where unbalance is expected to produce tension only if X is important:

> CP 20   *(Importance and Tension): Under the condition that the object X is important to P, unbalance will produce more tension than balance. However, under the condition that X is unimportant to P, then conditions of balance and unbalance are less likely to differ in tension.*

Results partially supporting CP 18 (Importance and Preference) are provided by Byrne (1961). The independent variable of the study was perceived similarity between the subject and a hypothetical other. Similar others were rated by the subject as more attractive in terms of personal feelings, desirability as a work partner, intelligence, knowledge of current events, morality, and "adjustment." However, importance of the attitude object affected ratings only on personal feelings, morality and adjustment. Namely, ratings on only these three dependent measures were higher if the other was perceived as similar on important issues than if he was perceived as similar on *un*important issues.

More conclusive findings were obtained in a learning study discussed earlier by Zajonc and Burnstein (1965a). The number of errors made in learning balanced and unbalanced structures was measured. Conditions of balance and unbalance did not differ in errors made; the effects of balance–unbalance of the structure were not statistically significant. When importance of X was taken into account, a different picture emerged: If X was important (favoring or disfavoring integration), balanced structures were easier to learn than unbalanced ones, but if the issue was unimportant (favoring or disfavoring *Newsweek* magazine), balanced and unbalanced structures did not differ in ease of learning. This supports the view that balance is preferred (balanced structures are easier to learn) only if the X-object in the structure is important to P.

There is more research evidence supporting CP 18 and CP 20 than CP 19, even though CP 19 seems straightforward. While there is no evidence to contradict it, results in support of it have been only mildly suggestive. Taylor (1966), using a group discussion (interpersonal-concrete) situation, found that under given conditions of initial unbalance, P is more likely to change his attitude toward X and his liking for O in the direction of balance if the issue is important. He is less likely to do so if the issue is unimportant. The effects of importance only approached statistical significance, however. The findings of Zajonc and Sherman (1967) lead to some support of CP 19. Due to the lack of direct tests of CP 19, or some similar proposition involving tendency or change as the dependent variable, it should remain a tentative proposition.

Evidence strongly favoring CP 20 (Importance and Tension) has been presented by Rodriques (1965). It was found that unbalanced structures were rated as more "tense" and "uncomfortable" than balanced structures. The effect of balance–unbalance was *magnified,* however, if X was important: Larger differences in tension between balance and unbalance are obtained if X is important than if X is unimportant. Thus, both balance and importance interact upon tension; the greatest tension is found under conditions of unbalance involving an important X.

Despite evidence suggesting that importance be taken into account in any study of the balance process, there have been some studies suggesting that importance is not "as important" as is generally assumed. Byrne and Nelson (1964) find that attitudinally similar others are rated as more attractive than dissimilar others, regardless of the importance of the attitude object, X. The failure of importance to have any effect on the similarity-attraction relationship was attributed to the range of attitude topics used in the study. It was thought that the differentiation in terms of importance was not sufficient. For this reason, the study was repeated (Byrne and Nelson, 1965b), using a greater range of topics, from highly important issues (for example, belief in God, racial integration in public schools, and birth control) to trivial ones (for example, gardening, the custom of tipping). Still, importance of X did not affect the relationship between similarity and attraction; importance had no independent effect on attraction, nor did importance and similarity interact. Similar others were rated as attractive, and dissimilar others as unattractive, regardless of importance.

Note that the two Byrne-Nelson studies pertain to the matter of preference (CP 18), as does the study by Zajonc and Burnstein (1965a). It was found that importance made a difference in the latter study, but not in the two Byrne-Nelson studies. Both studies were done using designs of the interpersonal-hypothetical variety, so that the concrete-hypothetical distinction that we have drawn before would not explain the contrasting results. We note, however, that "ease of learning" is the dependent variable in the Zajonc-Burnstein study, whereas the similarity-attraction relationship is the major focus in the Byrne-Nelson studies, thus making attraction the dependent variable. The inference to be drawn from these two sets of results is that while importance of X affects the learning of structures, it has less effect on the similarity-attraction relationship. As Byrne and associates have attempted to show, the similarity-attraction relationship is independent of a number of factors, of which importance of X is one (see section 4.2b in Chapter 4). Thus, if the matter of "balance preference" is stated in terms of "ease in learning a structure," then importance of the X-object does make a difference, and CP 18 is upheld. If, however, the matter of preference is thought of in terms of the similarity-attraction relationship, then the evidence shows that importance of the X-object makes little difference. The results of the two sets of studies (Zajonc-Burnstein and Byrne-Nelson) are not necessarily contradictory; it is just that the formulation of the Balance Preference hypothesis is different in each case.

5 • 1c   Polarity and the Congruity Model

The reader will remember that two broad *theoretical perspectives* are revealed in the literature on balance. One was the *interpersonal perspective*, where the unit of analysis consists of at least two persons and at least one X (or Q). The models of Heider and Newcomb are generally regarded as reflecting the interpersonal perspective. The second perspective is intra*personal rather than inter*personal; only one person need be part of the unit of analysis. This second perspective, the *cognitive perspective*, is embodied in Osgood's model of attitude congruity (Osgood and Tannenbaum, 1955; Osgood et al., 1957; Osgood, 1960), which was briefly discussed in Chapter 2, and which was contrasted with the Heider and Newcomb models. With the Osgood Model, the objects are typically a focal person (P), and a source (S) of an assertion about an object or "concept" (C). (The symbol "C" for "concept" will be used instead of the symbol "O" for "object of assertion," in order to avoid letting "O" erroneously stand for "other.") The Osgood congruity model posits a preference for and a tendency toward consistency (congruity) among three variables: the *source attitude* (P's attitude toward the source of assertion, S), the *concept attitude* (P's attitude toward the concept, C), and the *assertion* linking the source with the concept (the sign of S's statement or communication about the concept, C). Hence, the Osgood model differs from the Heider and Newcomb models in that the former focuses upon attitudinal relations alone, whereas the latter theorists focus upon both attitudinal and interpersonal relations. Even though the Osgood formulation is a model of attitudinal rather than attitudinal and interpersonal preference and change, certain aspects of the Osgood model are highly relevant to interpersonal processes. It is the purpose of this section to point out certain of these areas of relevance.

Detailed discussion of the Osgood model and the cognitive perspective has been deferred until now for two reasons. First, although part of the theory of "cognitive consistency" (Abelson et al., 1968; Feldman, 1966; Brown, 1965; Zajonc, 1960), the Osgood model is not completely isomorphic with the Heider and Newcomb interpersonal models. In the case of the Osgood PSC unit, only three "basic" relations are considered (source attitude, concept attitude and assertion), since the source and the concept cannot have orientations toward the person. In the dyadic interpersonal (POX) condition, O can have an orientation or relation to P. And in the triadic interpersonal (POQ) condition, other relations besides the "basic" PO, PQ and OQ relations are possible. The implications of this were discussed in part in the previous chapter in section 4.3c, "Dyads versus Triads." In addition, the Osgood and Heider-Newcomb models can yield differing predictions, as pointed out in Chapter 2. For these reasons, the cognitive and interpersonal models cannot be taken as completely similar, as some authors (e.g., Pepitone, 1966, p. 258) have recently implied.

Second, one of the primary contributions of the Osgood model and research following it has been what is now called the *polarity corollary,* the major topic of this section. Because a fair amount of research has been carried out in regard to the polarity corollary, because findings in regard to it are relevant to the matter of the *strength* (in addition to the sign) of a relation between a focal person and other objects of orientation (whether person or non-person), and because the polarity corollary (and recent modifications of it) is a source for conditional propositions which modify the general propositions of balance theory, a treatment of the congruity model and the polarity corollary is appropriate.

What, then, is the "polarity corollary?" The literature reveals two quite distinct interpretations. The first interpretation concerns the problem, "How much will an attitudinal relation change or shift, given that we know its *initial strength* or *polarity?*" Hence, the initial strength of the attitude is "given" or "known." In contrast, the second interpretation involves predicting an "unknown" attitude on the basis of *other* known, or given, attitudes. For example, predicting the strength of the source attitude (the *PS* relation) from knowledge about the strength of the concept attitude (the *PC* relation) and the sign of the assertion (the *SC* relation) involves the second interpretation of the polarity corollary. In general, both interpretations hold that the *strengths* of attitudes (in addition to their signs) are important for predictions pertaining to either a preference for or a tendency toward congruity.

Let us take a closer look at the two interpretations. The first interpretation states that a "strong (high polarity) attitude is less likely to change than a weak (low polarity) attitude." Take as an example the following structure:

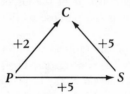

In this case, the *PC* attitude has a strength or polarity of +2; the *PS* attitude, of +5, and the *SC* assertion, of +5. This is an incongruent structure, since the polarities of the relations are not equivalent. (Note that this structure is "sign-balanced" according to the Heider model, since the product of the signs is positive. It is "asymmetric" by Newcomb's formulation, due to the *discrepancy* in the *PC* and *SC* relations.) Due to the incongruity, the *PC* and *PS* attitudes are expected to change toward congruity—if the *SC* assertion (and *P*'s perception of it) is assumed to remain constant.[6] But which of the two attitudes is more likely to change? On the basis of the polarity corollary, one would predict that the weaker attitude (the *PC* attitude) is more likely to change than the stronger one (the *PS* attitude). Hence, one may state generally that the *less the polarity of an attitude, the greater its likelihood of its changing or shifting in the direction of congruity.*

There is an additional implication of the first interpretation of the polarity corollary. Not only is a weaker attitude *more likely* to change, but in addition, the *degree or magnitude of change* in an initially weak attitude will be greater than the degree of change in an initially strong attitude. Hence, in the above structure, if both the *PS* and *PC* attitudes change, the magnitude of change or shift in the latter will be greater than the magnitude of change in the former. This means that if both attitudes change together, *each is expected to change with a magnitude which is in inverse proportion to its respective polarity.* This interpretation of the polarity corollary (the first interpretation) has been responsible for a

---

6. The matter of assuming a constant assertion is discussed later in this section.

formula developed by Osgood and his associates. This formula, and modifications of it, are discussed on the following pages.

The first interpretation of polarity, then, is concerned with the issue of predicting both the likelihood and the magnitude of change in an attitude of a strength or polarity which is initially known. The second interpretation, in contrast, is concerned with predicting the strength of an *unknown* attitude, if certain other attitudes are known or taken as given. Examine the following structure:

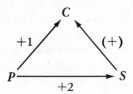

Given the strengths of the *PC* and *SC* relations, what will be the *strength* of the *PS* relation? Note that the *sign* of the *PS* relation is expected to be positive; the Heider, Newcomb and Osgood models all predict this. But predicting the strength is problematical. There have been a number of procedures used. These are reviewed below.[7] The point being made here is that the second interpretation of the corollary involves predicting the strength of an unknown attitude when the strengths of other attitudes or relations in the structure are known.

The First Interpretation: Predicting the Degree of Change in a Given Relation

There is some evidence that for interpersonal structures, stronger relations are less likely to change than weaker ones. In a study of triadic *POQ* structures, Davol (1959) found that given an unbalanced structure containing strong relations, that structure was less likely to change than an unbalanced structure which contained weak relations. It was speculated that "when . . . relations were strong, they were evidently more able to resist tensions brought about by unbalance . . . but when the relations were weak, the tensions due to unbalance were sufficient to bring about balanced triads" (p. 395).

Most of the research on the first interpretation of the polarity corollary has been carried out on cognitive, rather than interpersonal, structures. Of importance in the evaluation of this research is an understanding of Osgood's "Semantic Differential" questionnaire, a popular instrument used for the measurement

7. At least *six* different procedures for predicting the strength of an "unknown" relation in a structure have appeared in the literature. Two of these procedures are discussed in this chapter. Since a complete treatment of these six procedures involves formalization, the remaining four are discussed later, in the next chapter.

of attitudes (Osgood et al., 1957, pp. 189–216). This instrument involves the use of seven-point Likert scales. Each scale is used to measure a person's attitude toward a concept (C). The following set of scales, for example, can be used to rate one or more concepts:

good	+3	+2	+1	0	−1	−2	−3	bad
fair	+3	+2	+1	0	−1	−2	−3	unfair
foolish	−3	−2	−1	0	+1	+2	+3	wise

The middle space is to be checked by the person if he feels that the particular scale does not apply to the concept, if his feeling is neutral, or if he feels that each adjective applies equally to the concept. The scale value, or *polarity,* in this instance is zero. Checking the +1 or the −1 space, on the good-bad scale for example, would indicate "slightly good" or "slightly bad," respectively. The +2 or −2 values are interpreted as "quite good" and "quite bad," and the +3 and −3 values are interpreted as "very good" and "very bad." Once the subject has checked all scales that are given on his questionnaire form, his responses are averaged, yielding a general attitude score which reflects both strength (polarity) and direction (sign).

Osgood et al. (1957) find that at least three dimensions or *factors* underly the inventory of Semantic Differential scales. One dimension is the "potency" of the concept being rated. The potency dimension is reflected in such scales as "strong-weak," "hard-soft," and "masculine-feminine." A second dimension is "activity," exemplified by scales such as "active-passive," and "fast-slow." The third and major dimension is called the "evaluative" dimension; it is this latter dimension that represents *attitude* and is reflected by scales such as "good-bad," "fair-unfair" and "wise-foolish." Consequently, if one is interested in measuring a person's attitude, only the scales which are intended to reflect the evaluative dimension are used. Namely, the scores on the evaluative scales are averaged, and this average score is treated as the measure of the person's attitude toward the concept.

Much controversy has arisen over Osgood's formula for predicting the magnitude of change in an attitude on the basis of its initial polarity as measured by Semantic Differential scores (Osgood and Tannenbaum, 1955; Osgood et al., 1957; Osgood, 1960). The formula is as follows:

$$d_{cs} = \frac{|d_c|}{|d_c| + |d_s|}\,(d_c) + \frac{|d_s|}{|d_c| + |d_s|}\,(d_s)$$

where

$d_{cs} =$ the degree or magnitude of change in *both* the source and concept attitudes. This is the dependent variable; it is what is being predicted.

$d_c, d_s =$ the polarity (strength, or deviation from neutrality) of the concept and source attitudes with respect to sign; and

$|d_c|$, $|d_s|$ = the polarity of the concept and source attitudes *ignoring* their signs.

In order to understand how this formula works, take the case of two positive attitudes of unequal polarity and a positive assertion:

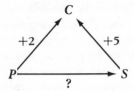

This is an incongruent (but balanced) condition. Both the source and concept attitudes are expected to change. Since the assertion is positive, both attitudes are expected to change *toward* one another—there will be a tendency for these attitudes to "regress" toward each other. Furthermore, the PC attitude (the weaker attitude) is expected to shift more than the PS attitude (the stronger attitude).

If, on the other hand, the assertion is negative, the two attitudes are expected to change *away* from each other:

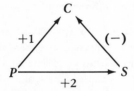

The magnitude of change in each attitude will be in inverse proportion to their respective polarities: The PC attitude will shift more than the PS attitude.

The principal difficulty with this formulation is that it confuses the *relative polarity* of an attitude with its *relative salience or importance* (Brown, 1965, p. 572). It is not true that a "strong" attitude is necessarily "important" to P, or that a "weak" attitude is relatively "unimportant." Assume that P has an attitude toward the war (C) which is of weak polarity (say, +1). Assume further that the President (S) makes a negative assertion about the war, and that P has an attitude of strong polarity toward the President (+3). This is an incongruent structure. The Osgood formulation predicts that P's attitude toward the war will change to a greater degree than will his attitude toward the President, since the former attitude is of lower polarity. But what if P regards war as a more important matter than the President—the salience of his attitudes about wars in general is high? Although P may have only a moderately favorable attitude toward the war, the salience of the attitude might be quite strong (P's son might have participated in the Vietnam war, for example); hence, P will not be likely to change that attitude, or if he does change it, the magnitude of change will be slight. If P's attitude toward the President is of high polarity ("I really like what the President is doing"), but *relatively* less salient ("I would still rather change my opinions toward the President than toward something as major and as important as wars"), then P's attitude toward the President—even though it is of the higher polarity—might be more likely to change. This is the direct opposite from what would be predicted by the Osgood formulation of the polarity corollary.

In the light of the difference between polarity of an attitude and salience of an attitude, an important modification to the Osgood formula was introduced by Rokeach and Rothman (1965). Both polarity and salience (importance) were considered in this study. The investigators argued as follows: The magnitude of change in both the source attitude and the concept attitude will depend upon two factors, their respective polarities and the degree to which each attitude is important to P. Hence, the degree of change in each attitude is a result of both factors; one must *weight* the polarity of each attitude according to its relative importance. This "weight" was defined as follows:

> $w =$ the degree of importance of the *concept attitude,* expressed
>   as a proportion; and
> $1 - w =$ the degree of importance of the *source attitude.*

If maximal importance is defined as 1 (or 100 percent), then $w + (1 - w)$ will always be 1 (or 100, if w is expressed as a percent instead of a proportion). Hence, the importance of each attitude is defined as *relative* to the importance of the other. For this reason, the expressions w and $1 - w$ give the *relative importance* of the concept and source attitudes, respectively. If the importance (w) of the concept attitude is .70, then the relative importance of the source attitude $(1 - w)$ will be .30. If both attitudes are of equal importance, then $w = 1 - w = .50$. The Rokeach-Rothman formula, expressing the expected magnitude of shift in both attitudes as a function of both the relative importance and the polarities of the concept and source attitudes, is:

$$d_{cs} = (w)d_c + (1 - w)d_s$$

where

> $d_{cs} =$ the degree of change in both the source and concept
>   attitudes;
> $d_c =$ the polarity of the concept attitude;
> $d_s =$ the polarity of the source attitude;
> $w =$ the relative importance of the concept attitude; and
> $1 - w =$ the relative importance of the source attitude.

The attitude with the strongest polarity *and* the greatest relative importance is expected to change the least. If the product $(w)d_c$ is equal to the product $(1 - w)d_s$, then each attitude will change to the same degree. If the relative polarities are unequal (say, $d_c > d_s$) but the relative importance of both attitudes are equal ($w = 1 - w = .50$), then the "pressure" toward change that is exerted by the factor of relative importance is the same, and the source attitude will change more than the concept attitude, due to its smaller polarity. If the polarities are equal, then the factor of relative importance exerts the "pressure" toward change, the attitude having the least relative importance being most likely to change. In short, this formulation tells us that the magnitude of change in both attitudes is a function of a combination of two factors, polarity and relative importance.

The investigators tested both the original Osgood formula and their own formula against each other, and simply determined which came closer to predicting the degree of shift in both the source and concept attitudes using actual subjects. The study involved giving the subject different word combinations, and getting a separate measurement of polarity and relative importance of the source and concept attitudes. The dependent variable was the degree of shift in both attitudes (d_{cs}). The results showed that the Rokeach-Rothman formula was three times more accurate in predicting empirically obtained values in attitudinal shifts than was the Osgood formula. The conclusion from the Rokeach-Rothman study is that attitudinal change is a function of *both* the initial polarity and the initial relative importance of the given attitudes, and not just a function of polarity. The results are not a complete refutation of the Osgood formula, but a substantial refinement of it.

In regard to the first interpretation of the polarity corollary, the evidence suggests that given a cognitive *PSC* unit consisting of a source attitude, a concept attitude and an assertion, the magnitude of change in both attitudes depends upon the polarity and relative importance of each attitude:

> CP 21 *(Polarity, Relative Importance, and Change): Given a source attitude and a concept attitude of known values, and given incongruity among these attitudes and an assertion, the degree of shift in both attitudes will depend upon their polarities and their relative importance to P.*

Note that when the two attitudes and the assertion form a *congruent* structure, no change at all is expected. Hence, this conditional proposition presumes a tendency toward congruity; it is therefore a "weaker" modification of the general theory than are certain of the cognitive bias propositions stated earlier, since certain cognitive biases can explain attitude change in addition to a consistency (balance or congruity) principle—they do not presume a tendency toward consistency.

In the previous section of this text, the variable "importance of X" in the POX interpersonal unit was discussed. An important implication of the Rokeach-Rothman study is apparent if their insights are applied to dyadic (and even triadic) interpersonal structures. *An analog of the "relative importance" of C and S to P would be the importance of X to P relative to P's commitment to or involvement with O.* The literature reviewed under "importance of X" above considers X in a vacuum—the salience or importance of X is not considered in light of the relative commitment or involvement that P may have with O. P may like O moderately ($+1$) but be highly committed to the relationship— they may occupy the same office, or even be members of the same family. Hence, P would not be likely to change his liking for O, despite the low polarity of the PO relation (liking). Conversely, P may like O very much ($+3$), but be *more willing* to change that relation rather than change the PX relation because of the great importance of X (and hence *less relative commitment* to O). The "importance of X" relative to P's commitment to O should be a major factor in predicting the magnitude of change in both the PO and PX relations. This factor may be labeled the *importance/commitment factor,* and is directly analogous to the Rokeach-Rothman factor of relative importance.

Thus, magnitude of change in attitudinal (PX) and interpersonal (PO) relations can be seen as a function of two variables: the polarity of the particular relation (the polarity factor), and the importance/commitment factor:

CP 22   *(The Importance/Commitment Factor, Polarity, and Change in the PX and PO Relations): Given an unbalanced (and therefore incongruent) structure, the degree to which the PX (attitudinal) and PO (interpersonal) relations will change will depend not only upon the relative polarities of the two relations (the polarity factor), but also upon the importance of X to P in relation to P's commitment to or involvement with O (the importance/ commitment factor). This means that the particular relation will change with a magnitude which is inversely proportional to the product of its polarity and the relative importance of (commitment to) the object.*

Thus, a relation of high polarity and high importance (commitment) is least likely to change. A relation of low polarity and low importance (commitment) is most likely to change. If the two relations differ in polarity but the importance of X is equal to P's commitment to O, then the factor of polarity determines change, and the relation of the lesser polarity will change the most. If the two relations differ in terms of importance (of X) and commitment (to O) but the polarities of the two relations are equal, then it is the importance/commitment factor, and not the polarity factor, that determines change, and the relation having the lesser importance (commitment) will change the most.

It would be possible to quantify the polarity and importance/commitment factors in a manner similar to that used by Rokeach and Rothman. The polarities of the *PX* and *PO* relations could be ascertained, as could the degree to which *P* thinks that *X* is important (*w*) and the *relative* degree to which *P* is committed to his social relationship with *O* (which would then become 1 − *w*). The expected magnitude of change in the *PX* relation could then be defined in terms of the product of the strength of the *PX* relation times *w*, and the expected magnitude of change in the *PO* relation could be defined in terms of the product of the strength of the *PO* relation times 1 − *w*. The resulting formula would have to express the expected magnitude of change in each relation as an *inverse* function of the product of strength and importance (commitment).

There is, of course, no conclusive evidence that directly tests CP 22; the Rokeach-Rothman findings are only suggestive. It is not known whether the Rokeach-Rothman formula, which was applied to word associations, is generalizable to the interpersonal *POX* unit. The above proposition must be taken as tentative for an additional reason. Recall that in applying the Osgood formulation to predict changes in the *PC* (concept) and *PS* (source) attitudes, one must assume that the *assertion* linking *S* to *C* is constant through time. The same thing applies to the Rokeach-Rothman modification. Note that the *OX* relation in the interpersonal model is the analog of the *SC* assertion in the congruity model. Hence, the above proposition (CP 22) requires that one assume a constant perception of the *OX* relation on the part of *P*. Clearly, this assumption is not always warranted; any design testing it (and there have been none so far) would therefore have to either "block off" the alternative of altering this perception, or introduce a statistical control for it.

In regard to the matter of the assertion linking *S* to *C* in the *PSC* cognitive structure, a principle of an "*assertion constant*" is generally cited in discussions of Osgood's model. There are two different meanings of this term. The first meaning is stated immediately above: that in order to predict change in the concept (*PC*) and source (*PS*) attitudes, one must assume that the assertion linking *S* to *C* will remain constant over time. If this is done, however, errors in interpretation of results can arise. For example, assume the following initially incongruent structure: −1 *PC*, +3 *PS*, and +*CS* (the assertion). If *P* changes from −1 *PC* to +1 *PC* (a shift in the concept attitude toward the positive) and at the same time does not change the source attitude, then the change in the concept attitude would be interpreted as a change toward (rather than away from) congruity. But what if at the same time *P* altered his perception of the assertion that *S* made about *C*? What if this perception shifted in the negative direction? This would—in conjunction with the previous shift in the concept attitude—constitute a change toward incongruity, and a negative finding under the hypothesized tendency toward congruity. It is quite possible that some of the earlier studies by Osgood and associates were subject to this kind of error in interpretation, although recent studies (see Tannenbaum, 1967) have taken it into account.

There is a second meaning of the term "assertion constant," as used with the Osgood model. Brown (1962, p. 26) interprets the term to mean that there tends to be "a greater force" acting on the concept than on the source. Hence, given a condition of incongruity and equal polarities of the source and concept attitudes, the concept attitude would change more than the source attitude. Rokeach and Rothman (1965) hypothesized that attitude change was a *joint* function of polarity and relative importance, rather than of polarity alone and a "constant" force or pressure acting on the concept. Thus, they rejected Osgood's idea of an assertion constant. As we have seen, the Rokeach-Rothman interpretation led to more accurate empirical results. For this reason, their results can be taken as a refutation of this second meaning of the "assertion constant."

The Second Interpretation: Predicting the Strength of an Unknown Relation

The first interpretation of the polarity corollary concerns the problem of predicting the degree of change or shift in an attitude, the initial strength (polarity) of that attitude being known. The second interpretation deals with the matter of predicting the polarity of an *unknown* attitude when the polarities of other attitudes in the same structure are known. An example would be predicting the strength of the source *(PS)* attitude when the polarity of the concept *(PC)* attitude and the strength (not only the sign) of the assertion *(SC)* are known. The potential pragmatic applicability of such a procedure could prove interesting—for example, predicting a person's attitude toward a political candidate *(S)* who makes an assertion about an issue *(C)*, when only the attitude of the person toward the issue is known.

Research by Osgood and associates (Osgood and Tannenbaum, 1955; Osgood et al., 1957) has generally supported the prediction that the polarity formula (p. 150, above) can be used to predict the strength of an unknown attitude. It has been maintained by Fishbein and associates (Triandis and Fishbein, 1963; Fishbein and Hunter, 1964) that the Osgood formulation implies that an unknown attitude or relation is a function of the *average* of the strengths of known relations in a structure. Take as an example the following configuration, where the symbol "R" signifies "the sign and strength of a relation":

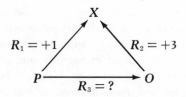

Assume that one is interested in predicting the *sign and strength* (polarity) of R_3. The sign is expected to be positive, since to be balanced (and also congruent), the sign of R_3 must be positive. But what about the strength of R_3? According to Fishbein and associates, the Osgood "averaging" procedure implies obtaining the sum of the values of the known relations, and then dividing by the number of known relations:

$$R_3 = \frac{\sum\limits_{i=1}^{K} |R_i|}{K}$$

where

$|R_i|$ = the absolute value (ignoring the sign) of a given relation; and
K = the number of known relations.

In the example,

$$R_3 = \frac{1+3}{2} = \frac{4}{2} = (+) \ 2.$$

Fishbein and associates, however, advocate a "summation" procedure for predicting R_3, namely, simply adding up the absolute strengths of the known relations:

$$R_3 = \sum_{i=1}^{K} |R_i|.$$

In the example,

$$R_3 = 1 + 3 = (+) \ 4.$$

The *expected value* of R_3 would therefore be 4 with the summation (Fishbein) procedure, but 2 with the averaging (Osgood) procedure. Which procedure best predicts empirically obtained results on actual subjects?

Fishbein and Hunter (1964) present evidence favoring a summation procedure. In a study of word associations, they structured a design so that as a number of *given* relations in the structure increased, the predicted strength of the *unknown* relation would *increase* if a summation procedure were applied, but *decrease* if an averaging procedure were applied. Table 1 illustrates how this was done. Note that the expected value of the unknown relation (R_o) increases across the three experimental treatments if summation is applied, but decreases if averaging is applied. All that remained was to see whether the predicted value of R_o in fact increased or decreased as a function of experimental treatment condition.

The results strongly supported the summation procedure. The obtained values of R_o increased across the three experimental conditions rather than decreased, and markedly so. These results were interpreted as casting doubt upon the averaging procedure implied in the Osgood model. This led the investigators

TABLE 1   DESIGN OF THE FISHBEIN-HUNTER STUDY[a,b]

	CONDITION I	CONDITION II	CONDITION III
	$R_1 = +3$	$R_1 = +3$	$R_1 = +3$
		$R_2 = +2$	$R_2 = +2$
			$R_3 = +1$
			$R_4 = +0.5$
$R_o = \Sigma\,\lvert R_i \rvert$ (Summation)[c]	$R_o = +3$	$R_o = +5$	$R_o = +6.5$
$R_o = \dfrac{\Sigma\,\lvert R_i \rvert}{K}$ (Averaging)[c]	$R_o = +3$	$R_o = +2.5$	$R_o = +1.6$

[a] Adapted from Fishbein and Hunter (1964).
[b] The expression R_o refers to the *expected value of the unknown relation.*
[c] The summation procedure demands adding the absolute values of each R_i. The averaging procedure demands dividing this sum by K, the number of known relations.

to advocate a summation "theory" over the congruity model. The results confirmed those obtained in an earlier cross-cultural study by Triandis and Fishbein (1963), in which the person's attitude toward an object was found to be a function of the summation, rather than the average, of other attitudes and *beliefs* in the person's cognitive structure. An attitude was defined as the evaluative dimension of orientation toward an object, whereas a belief is an orientation made in terms of "likelihood" or "probability" (Fishbein and Raven, 1962).

Although it remains questionable whether the Fishbein studies are as rigorous a test of the Osgood polarity formulation as other studies (such as the Rokeach-Rothman (1965) study discussed above), the "averaging" versus "summation" question cannot be dismissed as a mere artificial distinction. There is a deeper question at stake here: Is the perception of inconsistency or unbalance a result of the "psychological adding" of inconsistent cognitions, or of "psychologically averaging" them in some way? Is the *impact* of inconsistent relations upon the person so severe as would be implied by adding the values of the relations, or is the impact weaker—as implied by averaging them? The evidence of Fishbein suggests that the psychological impact of inconsistency upon the focal person is so strong as to advocate a summation procedure, implying that the focal person "goes to extremes" in his attempts to resolve inconsistencies. Less of an extreme "resolution" of inconsistency is implied by the averaging procedure.

The summation-averaging controversy gains greater importance when one realizes that there are other procedures available (besides averaging or summation) for predicting the strength of an unknown relation in a structure. No fewer than *six* separate procedures have appeared in the literature! Detailed discussion of them will require graph-theoretic analysis, and for this reason, the problem is treated in the next chapter. A brief listing of these six procedures at this time is worthwhile, however. The strength of an unknown relation in a structure has been variously predicted on the basis of: (a) The *discrepancy* among the known relations in the structure (this procedure is derivable from Newcomb's model); (b) the *product* (through multiplication) of the strengths of the given relations in the structure (this procedure is derivable from the original Cartwright-Harary definition of balance, and Morrissette's extension of it); (c) the *sum* of the strengths of the given relations in the structure (advocated by Fishbein and associates); (d) the *average* of the strengths of the given relations (derivable from the Osgood formulation, according to Fishbein and associates); (e) the known relation of *maximum strength* in the structure; and finally (*f*) the strength of any *interpersonal relation* in the structure. All six procedures imply different meanings of the concept of inconsistency (unbalance or incongruity).

5 • 2   THE EFFECTS OF PERSONALITY VARIABLES UPON THE BALANCE PROCESS

The previous major section was concerned principally with "corollaries" to the theory of balance. A corollary was defined as any conditional proposition which modifies one or more of the general propositions of the theory, with the additional stipulation that (a) the corollary itself is not deducible from balance theory (i.e., from one or more of the general propositions), but from some general non-balance principle, such as a principle of least effort, a preference for positivity, a preference for completeness, etc.; *or* (b) they employ, in one way or another, a "parameter" variable or relation—an attribute of the structural unit under study. Certain cognitive biases were seen as reflecting this latter stipulation. The Osgood polarity corollary and modifications of it are based on the strengths of parameter relations or variables in a cognitive structure.

To the extent that any *personality* variables affect the operation of the balance process, to that extent personality variables constitute a source of conditional propositions. A personality variable is any "predispositional" variable which is not part of the abstract structural unit under study. A person's high or low propensity to be "authoritarian," his intelligence, his fears and ego defenses—all these represent examples of personality variables which can potentially affect his preference for or tendency toward balance.

Although it is clear that variations along personality dimensions constitute potential sources for conditional propositions, any conditional proposition using a personality variable as the source of the inference will not be called a "corollary," but simply a "conditional proposition" or "conditional relationship." This distinction is made primarily because the empirical literature presents at least a minimally unified picture in regard to corollaries, a picture we tried to draw in section 5.1. No such coherent picture emerges in regard to the effects of personality variables. Literature which evaluates the effects of personality variables on the balance process is heterogeneous; no unified scheme or taxonomy can be seen. It is for this reason that the effects of personality dimensions are considered in a separate section of this book. No claim is being made here that the discussion is exhaustive. Only when an empirical study yields a clear interpretation, and when it is demonstrated that in fact variation along a particular personality dimension affects balance preference and tendency, will a discussion of that particular personality variable be undertaken. The effects of four personality variables are cited: self-evaluation, authoritarianism and intolerance for inconsistency, affiliation need, and cognitive complexity. The effects of a few additional ones are discussed at the end of this section.

A word of caution should be given regarding the possible confusion between a "cognitive bias," on one hand, and a "personality variable," on the other. A cognitive bias, such as the preference for positivity, or the preference for balance itself, is assumed to be a *constant* propensity or tendency. The theoretical and empirical literature postulates that all people generally prefer positive relations to negative relations, balance to unbalance, and so on. In contrast to a cognitive bias, a personality "variable" is treated as an attribute which *varies* from person to person: Some people are highly authoritarian, others less authoritarian; some people have a high need to affiliate with others, whereas for other people this need is less; some people have a favorable opinion of themselves, while others have an unfavorable self-opinion. All these attributes are assumed to take on different values across different persons in a population, whereas a "bias" is *assumed* to be an attribute which maintains a relatively constant value.

5 • 2a   Self-Evaluation

Any postulated tendency for a person to think or act in a certain way may be dependent upon that person's own opinion of himself. Under the condition that the person evaluates himself favorably, then one would be willing to predict that he will love another who loves him. But what if the person hates himself? Would he then be just as likely to return the love of another—another who erroneously loves the despised self? That men attempt to sustain, nourish and fondle objects of their love appears unarguable; yet, man will extinguish, starve and reject the objects of his affections. Such paradoxes are as commonplace as their opposites, and we cannot help feeling a great profundity and "deep truth" is expressed when Oscar Wilde (*The Ballad of Reading Gaol*) says that "Each man kills the thing he loves."

Many puzzling phenomena of everyday life appear more understandable if one assumes that the person involved evaluates himself or herself unfavorably rather than favorably. Thus, it is difficult ordinarily to understand why a girl may reject a man who loves her and love a man who rejects her, or why a man beats his wife, or why the businessman feels a sense of comfort upon experiencing failure and feel uncomfortable when he has been victorious or successful, or why a child may seek rather than avoid punishment. If we assume that the girl, the wife-beater, the businessman and the child all evaluate themselves negatively rather than positively, the bewildering quality of their actions disappears; their actions seem comprehensible. Perhaps the actions of persons which seem "irrational" have at their roots a self-evaluation which is counter to that which we, as the observers of such actions, assume it to be.[8]

The balance principle states quite flatly that if P thinks O likes him, then P will like O. Interestingly, through the application of the balance principle itself, it can be shown that this will be true only if P evaluates himself positively. If he evaluates himself negatively, then the reverse will be true. It thus can be demonstrated that the Balance Preference and Balance Tendency hypothesis must assume a positive self-evaluation on the part of P in order to be empirically accurate. Heider himself recognized this condition (Heider, 1958, p. 181). Take as an example the structures graphed in Figure 2. The symbol "P" represents the focal person, the symbol "P'" represents P's "self," and the PP' relation (arrow) represents P's self-evaluation, which is either favorable (+) or unfavorable (−). The graph in Figure 2A represents a condition where P likes O and O likes "P's self" (i.e., O likes P), a balanced condition. But note Figure 2B; P still likes O and O still likes P, but because of P's negative self-evaluation (−PP'), the structure is unbalanced. *What would otherwise appear to be a balanced structure (if self-evaluation were positive) is actually unbalanced in the case of negative self-evaluation.* The structure in Figure 2C, where O likes P but P dislikes O, would be unbalanced if P's self-evaluation were positive, but is in fact balanced, since self-evaluation is negative. The "paradoxical" situation where a girl (P) rejects a man (−PO) who loves her (+OP') is less paradoxical and therefore more understandable (it is balanced) if we assume the girl actually hates herself (−PP').

By similar graph-theoretic procedures, the proverbial POX structure can be subjected to a self-evaluation analysis (Figure 2D, E and F). Conditions of +PO, +PX and +OX (balance) are balanced if self-evaluation is positive (Figure 2D) but unbalanced if self-evaluation is negative (Figure 2E). Similarly, a seemingly unbalanced structure involving P, O and X (+PO, −PX and +OX) is actually balanced if self-evaluation is negative (Figure 2F). The reader can easily convince himself that similar graph-theoretic analysis can be applied to other types of units ($POQX$, $ABCDE$, etc.). Note that any balanced cycle (assuming positive self-evaluation) is unbalanced if self-evaluation is negative, and that any unbalanced cycle (assuming positive self-evaluation) is balanced if self-evaluation is negative. This can be verified by remembering that a cycle is balanced if it contains an even number of negative lines (relations). Adding one

8. Parts of the foregoing paragraph are paraphrases from Deutsch and Solomon (1959), pp. 96–97.

FIGURE 2   A GRAPH-THEORETIC ANALYSIS OF NEGATIVE SELF-EVALUATION

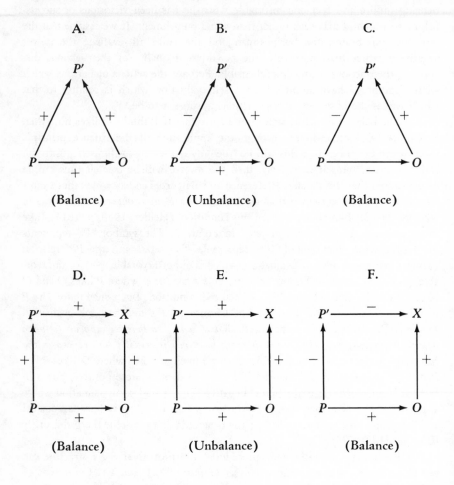

negative line (the line representing negative self-evaluation) will make the number of lines odd and hence make the cycle unbalanced. If the cycle contains an odd number of lines to begin with (therefore making it unbalanced), the addition of the negative self-evaluation line will make the cycle balanced. It should be pointed out that heretofore, no acceptable model for the analysis of the effects of self-evaluation has been presented in the literature (Zajonc, 1968). The present graph-theoretic interpretation is offered as an attempt to clarify the effects of self-evaluation. The applicability of this kind of model will become apparent in our following consideration of empirical studies.

The striking implication here is that *under conditions of negative self-evaluation, balanced structures are to be treated as though they are unbalanced, and unbalanced structures are to be treated as though they are balanced.* If self-evaluation is negative, then a preference for or a tendency toward balance would exist under initially *balanced* structures; preference or tendency toward balance would be *less* for *un*balanced structures. Hence, under the condition of negative self-evaluation on the part of *P*, the predictions of the Balance Preference and Balance Tendency hypotheses are completely reversed. A review of empirical findings shows this to be true.

It an experiment by Deutsch and Solomon (1959), the subject's (*P*'s) evaluation of himself was measured by means of a "self-concept scale," and subjects were then divided into two categories on the basis of their own self-image (favorable or unfavorable). The extent to which the other (*O*) liked or disliked the subject was experimentally manipulated by means of falsified notes which a given subject believed came from another subject with whom he had worked on a task. Thus, a 2 × 2 design was created: (a) favorable self-evaluation, *O* likes *P* (favorable note); (b) favorable self-evaluation, *O* dislikes *P* (unfavorable note); (*c*) unfavorable self-evaluation, *O* likes *P*; and (d) unfavorable self-evaluation, *O* dislikes *P*. The dependent variable was *P*'s rating of his attraction toward *O*. The study thus can be treated as testing a deduction from the Balance Preference hypothesis.

It was found that subjects who received negative notes from *O* rated those note writers unfavorably (i.e., as unattractive) if they (the subjects) had a positive self-evaluation, but favorably if they evaluated themselves negatively. The subjects who received positive notes rated the note-writers as favorable if they thought positively of themselves, but unfavorably if they thought negatively of themselves. Hence, liking the other is reciprocated only under conditions of favorable self-evaluation. Liking tends to be non-reciprocal (asymmetric) under conditions of unfavorable self-evaluation.

Although it was not attempted in the Deutsch-Solomon experiment, a straightforward graph-theoretic analysis of the results can be done, and clarifies the findings they obtained. Figure 3A presents four incomplete graphs corresponding to the four experimental conditions used. The signs of the *PP'* and *OP'* relations are given, and the sign of the *PO* relation (the dependent variable of the study—this is what is being predicted) is left ungiven. If self-evaluation is positive (+*PP'*), one would predict that *P* will like *O* (+*PO*) if *O* likes *P* (+*OP'*) (Condition I), and *P* will dislike *O* if *O* dislikes *P* (Condition II). Both of these predictions lead to a balanced structure. These predictions were confirmed by Deutsch and Solomon. If, however, self-evaluation is negative, then in order for the structure to be balanced, *P* will dislike *O* if *O* *likes* *P* (Condition III), and will like him if he *dislikes* *P* (Condition IV). The Deutsch-Solomon findings support this prediction also. Hence, the predictions of the Balance Preference hypothesis are confirmed if self-evaluation is positive, but completely reversed if self-evaluation is negative.

FIGURE 3   A GRAPH-THEORETIC ANALYSIS OF THE DEUTSCH-SOLOMON
AND KIND EXPERIMENTS

A. *The Deutsch-Solomon (1959) experiment:*

Induced liking, *O* of *P*:

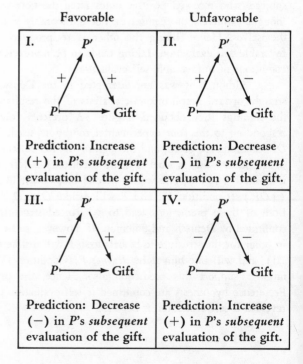

B. *The Kind (1965) experiment:*

Initial evaluation of the gift:

Results similar to those obtained by Deutsch and Solomon were obtained by Kind (1965, cited in Pepitone, 1966). As with the Deutsch-Solomon study, a graph-theoretic analysis of the experiment clarifies the results. While the Deutsch-Solomon experiment involved an interpersonal (P and O) situation, the Kind study examined the way in which the subject's initial evaluation of gifts (prints of paintings) would subsequently change after self-evaluation was manipulated. Hence, the study tested a deduction from the Balance Tendency hypothesis (rather than the Balance Preference hypothesis), since change was measured. Self-evaluation was manipulated by leading the subjects to believe that they were high in their "esthetic ability" to judge paintings (the favorable self-evaluation induction) or low in this ability (the unfavorable self-evaluation induction). The subject's initial evaluation of the gift (a painting) was measured, thus creating the four conditions represented in Figure 3B. The dependent variable was whether or not the subject increased his evaluation of the gift after making the initial evaluation. The induction of self-evaluation came after the subjects made these initial evaluations of the gifts. The appropriate predictions are indicated below each graph in Figure 3B.

The results of the study were as follows: 80 percent of the subjects under Condition IV increased their evaluations of the gift (the "$P/gift$" relation), and 60 percent of the subjects under Condition I increased their evaluation. In contrast, only 44 percent of the subjects under Condition III increased their evaluation of the gift, and only 20 percent under Condition II did so. The results support the predictions.

The evidence from the Deutsch-Solomon and Kind studies, and our own graph-theoretic analysis of the results, permit the statement of two "strong" conditional propositions. The propositions are strong modifications of the Balance Preference and Balance Tendency hypotheses, since under conditions of negative self-evaluation, the predictions of these two hypotheses are completely reversed. The first (CP 23) is based on the results of the Deutsch-Solomon experiment (preference); the second (CP 24) is based on the results of the Kind experiment (tendency):

> CP 23 *(Balance-Unbalance, Self-Evaluation and Preference): Under conditions of positive self-evaluation, balance structures are in effect balanced, and unbalanced structures are in effect unbalanced. Hence, the predictions of the Balance Preference hypothesis, or any deductions therefrom, remain as originally stated. In contrast, under conditions of negative self-evaluation, balanced structures are in effect unbalanced, and unbalanced structures are in effect balanced. Thus, the predictions of the Balance Preference hypothesis, or any deductions therefrom, are reversed: If self-evaluation is negative, the focal person will exhibit a greater preference for UNbalance than for balance.*

The predictions of this conditional proposition become clear if one interprets the phrase "in effect balanced" or "in effect unbalanced" in light of the graphs given in Figure 2. For example, an otherwise balanced PO structure involving mutual liking ($+PO$, $+OP$) is "in effect" unbalanced if self-evaluation is negative. Similarly, an otherwise unbalanced PO structure involving asymmetric liking ($-PO$, $+OP$) is "in effect" balanced if self-evaluation is negative. This will generally be the case regardless of how many lines a structure (or more accurately, a cycle) contains. The predictions of the Balance Preference hypothesis are reversed because if self-evaluation is negative, P will *appear* to prefer unbalance to balance.

Similar reasoning applies to the issue of Balance Tendency (change over time):

CP 24   *(Balance-Unbalance, Self-Evaluation, and Change): Under conditions of positive self-evaluation, balanced structures are in effect balanced, and unbalanced structures are in effect unbalanced. Thus, balanced structures are more stable (less likely to change) than are unbalanced structures. In contrast, under conditions of negative self-evaluation, balanced structures are in effect unbalanced, and unbalanced structures are in effect balanced. Hence, contrary to the Balance Tendency hypothesis, or any deductions therefrom, balanced structures will be less stable (more likely to change) than unbalanced structures, if self-evaluation is negative.*

Zajonc (1968) presents an intriguing problem involving negative self-evaluation and the Heiderian concept of the unit relation. Note that if P evaluates himself negatively, then unbalance is already present, since he is clearly bound with his "self"—he evaluates negatively something with which he has a positive unit relation. Given this special kind of unbalance, we would predict some change or alteration in the direction of balance on the part of P. Although Zajonc does not go into this question, one alternative available to P would be to sever the bond (i.e., the unit relation of "belonging") between himself (P) and "his self" (P'). Clearly, according to Heiderian theory, this would represent a change toward balance—P disconnects or severs himself from an object (P') which he disfavors. Simply stated, P develops a "split personality." By this interpretation, instances of split personalities can be seen as (among other things) a type of tendency toward balance!

5 • 2b   *Authoritarianism and Intolerance for Inconsistency*

It stands to reason that a person who has a low tolerance for inconsistencies, imbalances, incongruities, asymmetries and the like, is expected to exhibit a greater preference for balance than a person with a higher tolerance for inconsistency. "Authoritarian personalities" are generally thought of as being lower in their tolerance and ability to withstand disorder, disharmony, and inconsistencies than are relatively non-authoritarian persons (Adorno et al., 1950). Hence, one would expect a person high in authoritarianism to exhibit a greater preference for balance than a person low in authoritarianism. Newcomb (1963) finds that high-authoritarian persons (as defined by the Adorno et al. "F-Scale," an instrument for measuring authoritarianism) tend to overestimate their attitudinal agreement with a liked other. High authoritarians desire balance among their attitudes, their perception of others' attitudes and their liking for others even at the expense of accurately perceiving the other's attitude. Such autistic perceptions were found to be less likely among low authoritarians. In contrast to high authoritarians, the low authoritarians sought "realistic" alternatives—for example, adjusting their liking for the other in accordance with their realistic assessment of agreement, rather than increasing perceived agreement with a liked other in excess of actual agreement.

An interesting study by Feather (1964a) explored the degree to which a person's intolerance for inconsistency would affect his preference for consistency between his own attitudes toward religion and an attitude expressed in a verbal argument. Intolerance for inconsistency was measured by the Rokeach Dogmatism Scale (Rokeach, 1960) and the Budner Intolerance for Ambiguity Test (Budner, 1962). Persons high in dogmatism and intolerance for ambiguity were assumed to reflect a high intolerance for inconsistency. Sets of verbal arguments, in the form of syllogisms, were given to the subjects. Feather was able to construct his design so that a subject could (a) choose a conclusion to the syllogism which was logically valid, but inconsistent with (different from) his own attitude toward religion; or (b) choose a conclusion which was logically invalid, but consistent with (the same as) his own attitude toward religion.

The results showed that persons high in intolerance for inconsistency were more likely to select the latter alternative (attitudinally consistent but logically invalid) than were persons who scored less in intolerance. The results are in line with those of Newcomb (1961; 1963), suggesting that intolerant persons (and high authoritarians) tend to resist perceptions which are inconsistent with other attitudinal components of their cognitive structures, and that they elect autistic (rather than realistic) alternatives to the resolution of inconsistency and unbalance. Generally:

CP 25 *(Authoritarianism, Intolerance for Inconsistency, and Balance Preference): Persons high in authoritarianism (and in intolerance for inconsistency) are likely to exhibit a greater preference for balance than are persons low in authoritarianism (and in intolerance). Furthermore, the former type is more likely to prefer balance by "autistic" perceptions rather than by "realistic" perceptions.*

High authoritarians are also more likely to *change* their attitudes in a direction of balance than are low authoritarians. In a study of the *POX* dyadic unit, and using an interpersonal-concrete situation, McLeod et al., (1966) measured the subject's liking for a partner, and the subject's attitude toward a variety of issues such as loyalty oaths for college professors, capital punishment, and visiting hours in women's dormitories. It was found that during a subsequent group discussion, persons high in authoritarianism (as measured by the Adorno F-Scale) were more likely to shift their attitudes in the direction of the attitude of a liked other than were non-authoritarians. In addition, high authoritarians were more likely to increase their liking for their partner, and to increase the degree to which they thought their partner liked them (perceived liking). Hence, authoritarians were more likely to shift or "yield" on three variables: attitude, liking, and perceived liking. Interestingly, persons shifting their attitudes in the direction of the attitude of a liked other were more likely to come from religiously ritualistic homes and low socioeconomic backgrounds.

> CP 26 *(Authoritarianism and Balance Tendency): Persons high in authoritarianism are more likely to change attitudinal and interpersonal relations in the direction of balance (given initial unbalance) than are persons low in authoritarianism. Specifically, they are likely to exhibit a greater tendency to change the following variables in the direction of balance: attitude, liking, and perceived liking.*

Although there is no evidence to contradict the conditional proposition on authoritarianism and tendency (CP 26), certain researchers have found authoritarianism to be independent of the focal person's preference for balance— i.e., they have presented evidence that would appear to contradict CP 25 on authoritarianism and preference. Utilizing an interpersonal-hypothetical design, where *P* was given attitudinal information about a fictitious *O*, Byrne (1965) and Sheffield and Byrne (1967) found the similarity-attraction relationship to be independent of authoritarianism of the focal person. Namely, others who were perceived as attitudinal similar were rated as more attractive than others who were perceived as attitudinally dissimilar, regardless of the authoritarianism of the person (*P*) doing the rating. Attraction was explained neither by authoritarianism nor by the interaction of similarity and authoritarianism.

There are several explanations for these findings. It seems that an explanation is necessary, inasmuch as they are in disagreement with research supporting CP 25 (on authoritarianism and preference). First, the methodology used in the two Byrne studies grossly differs from the methodology used in studies lending support to CP 25. While Newcomb's (1961, 1963) results (as those of McLeod et al., 1966) were obtained in actual interpersonal situations, the Byrne studies used a "hypothetical other" (interpersonal-hypothetical) design. Coming face-to-face with and communicating with a disliked other are more likely to affect the focal person's perceptions of the other than if he does not actually see the other "in the flesh." To the extent that balance forces can be seen as more operative in interpersonal-concrete than in interpersonal-hypothetical situations, and to the extent that high authoritarians are more sensitive to balance forces, then to that extent high authoriarians will reveal a greater preference for balance than non-authoritarians *given* an interpersonal-concrete situation. This would explain why Byrne and associates did not find any effect of authoritarianism in their interpersonal-hypothetical experiment.

A second possible reason for the contrasting results is that Byrne's measure of attraction differs from that used in the other studies by Newcomb and McLeod et al. Byrne's definition of "attraction" is quite wide in scope. The subject is asked to rate the other on such diverse "attraction" dimensions as intelligence, knowledge of current events, morality, adjustment, and desirability as a work partner (Sheffield and Byrne, 1967). This differs greatly from Newcomb's delineation of the types of attraction (Newcomb, 1960, 1961, 1963) and from the liking measure employed by McLeod et al., (1966). Third, the investigators (Sheffield and Byrne, 1967) used the Adorno F-Scale to measure authoritarianism. They suspected that another measure of authoritarianism and/or intolerance, such as the Rokeach "dogmatism" scale, might be a more sensitive measure. If used, the hypothesized effects of authoritarianism upon the similarity-attraction relationship might have been obtained. We noted that Feather (1964a) used the Rokeach scale and did find that his results were affected by high-low intolerance. In sum, it does appear that authoritarianism affects both balance preference and balance tendency in face-to-face (interpersonal-concrete) situations. The effect of authoritarianism on the *similarity-attraction relationship* in the *interpersonal-hypothetical* situation appears to be less.

5 • 2c   Affiliation Need

People vary in the extent to which they want close, affective contacts with others—they vary in their "need for affiliation" with others. Past studies have shown that persons high in affiliation need are more likely to seek positively affective responses from others and to be attracted toward others than are those with a low affiliation need (French and Chadwick, 1956; Lansing and Heynes, 1959). Persons high in affiliation need are more likely to want to like others and to have others like them. Since attraction is one of the parameter variables of the balance model, it follows that affiliation need can affect a person's preference for balanced interpersonal structures.

Two studies by Byrne and associates evaluate the effects of affiliation need on the similarity-attraction relationship. As in all of the Byrne studies, attraction is the dependent variable, and perceived similarity is the independent variable. Affiliation need was measured by means of Thematic Apperception Test (TAT) protocols. In the first study, Byrne (1961) found that, as expected, similar hypothetical others were rated as more attractive than dissimilar others, but affiliation need ("high" versus "low") did not affect attraction. However, a significant interaction affect of similarity and affiliation need upon attraction was obtained: If affiliation need is low, differences in attraction on the basis of similarity-dissimilarity are slight. If affiliation need is high, differences in attraction due to similarity-dissimilarity are very marked; similar others are rated as far more attractive than dissimilar others. Stated another way, a high need for affiliation does not by itself result in high attraction toward the other; it does so only if the other is perceived as attitudinally similar. If the other is perceived as dissimilar (by one who scores high in affiliation need), then the *lowest* attraction rating is found.

While similarity-dissimilarity affects attraction independently of affiliation need, affiliation need does not affect attraction independently, and similarity and affiliation need interact to produce larger differences in attraction under conditions of high affiliation need. Specifically, persons high in affiliation need are more likely to like similar others and *dislike dissimilar others* than are persons who are low in affiliation need. These results can be interpreted as follows: The effect of similarity-dissimilarity upon attraction is *magnified* in the case of high affiliation need relative to the case of low affiliation need. This suggests that persons high in need for affiliation are more *sensitive* to balance forces than persons low on this characteristic. They are more prone to bring their liking for the other into balance with their perceptions of the attitudinal similarity of the other. Hence, the evidence suggests that persons high in need for affiliation are more likely to prefer balanced structures than are persons low in affiliation need.

A later replication by Byrne (1962), using three categories of affiliation need (high, medium and low), yields similar results. Affiliation need does not affect attraction independently of similarity, yet similarity and affiliation need interact such that the greater the subject's need for affiliation, the more likely he is to like similar others and dislike dissimilar others. Generally, as affiliation need increases, there is a proportionately greater tendency to balance liking with similarity.

CP 27   (*Affiliation Need and Balance Preference*): Persons high in *affiliation need are more likely to balance attraction with perceived similarity than are persons low in affiliation need. The tendency for them to like similar others and dislike dissimilar others is greater than for persons low in affiliation need. Hence, persons high in this characteristic are more sensitive to balance forces; a high need for affiliation magnifies the effect of similarity-dissimilarity on attraction.*

5 • 2d   Cognitive Complexity

Although only indirectly relevant to issues involving balance in inter-personal situations, a study by Scott (1963) suggests that the "cognitive complexity" of a person will affect his preference for balance. In Scott's study, subjects were requested to place nations into groupings on the basis of characteristics the nations had in common (type of governmental system, political ideology, etc.). The "cognitive complexity" of the subject was defined as the number of characteristics or criteria used in grouping the nations. Persons using a greater number of criteria were defined as more "cognitively complex" than persons using relatively fewer criteria. Next, the subjects were asked to indicate whether they felt that the nations in a particular grouping would be "friendly" or "unfriendly" toward each other. Scott's measure of balance preference on the part of the subjects (the dependent variable) was the number of friendly pairs of nations that appeared in a grouping. For example, a grouping consisting of nations all rated as friendly toward one another would be a "balanced" grouping.[9] It was found that the subjects, in general, preferred balanced rather than unbalanced groupings. However, it was also discovered that the greater the number of criteria the subject used in classifying the nations, the less the number of balanced groupings he formed. The greater the cognitive complexity of the subject (the greater the number of criteria used in classifying the nations), the less his preference for balanced groupings.

Although the results of Scott's experiment are of only indirect relevance to the matter of balance in interpersonal structures, his results do provide some insights. The finding that cognitively complex persons are less likely to prefer balance can be interpreted as follows: Cognitively complex persons may be thought of as exhibiting a distaste for simplicity. They are predisposed toward perceiving objects in their environment, and the relations between those objects, as intricate rather than as simplistic and straightforward phenomena. A person of less complexity is predisposed toward simplifying and stereotyping. Now, to the degree that balanced structures may be characterized as simple and stereotyped, and to the degree that unbalanced structures are relatively more complicated and even perplexing, then to that degree cognitively "simple" persons will be more likely to prefer balanced structures than cognitively complex persons. One may state generally that persons who use many (as opposed to rela-

9. Scott's measure of the "balance" of the groupings (derived from Abelson and Rosenberg, 1958) is not as one might suspect. Although a grouping was defined as balanced if only "friendly" pairs of nations were found in a grouping, the grouping was also defined as balanced if *only negative* relations between pairs of nations appeared. This is clearly in conflict with the general definition of balance: A three-nation group, containing three negative relations, could not be defined as a "balanced" grouping. Because of the unique way in which balance was measured, Scott's results are only suggestive. His measure of "balance" seems more in line with the graph-theoretic property of *clustering* (Harary, 1959; Davis, 1967; Abelson, 1967), to be discussed at length in the next chapter.

tively fewer) *criteria* for evaluating objects of orientation (i.e., "complex" persons) are less likely to prefer balance among those objects.

CP 28   *(Cognitive Complexity and Balance Preference): The greater the cognitive complexity of the person (the greater the number of criteria he uses in evaluating objects of orientation), the less will be his preference for balance among those objects of orientation.*

It is interesting to note that Scott (1963) found that the subject's preference for balanced groupings among nations was not related to general intelligence (measured, perhaps invalidly, as the extent of the subject's knowledge of current events). Similarly, Schrader and Lewit (1962) find that the tendency for subjects to complete graphs in a balanced fashion is not related to general intelligence (Schrader and Lewit do not give the measure of intelligence in their article). Thus, although "cognitive complexity" is related to balance preference, there is no evidence that intelligence is. One inference to be made is that contrary to what we might suspect, "cognitive complexity," as defined in the Scott study, is not related to intelligence.

5 • 2e   *Other Personality Variables*

Not much research has been carried out on the effects of personality or predispositional variables upon the balance process. There remain a large number of important personality dimensions besides those discussed above which could have major effects on the focal person's preference for or tendency toward balance. Although there is fragmentary evidence that general intelligence does not affect balance preference (Scott, 1963; Schrader and Lewit, 1962), additional research is needed. The effects of additional and potentially critical variables need to be considered: manifest anxiety (a high general anxiety level might increase a person's resistance to the tensions of unbalance), sadomasochism (a masochist may be more likely to prefer the "pain" of unbalance), propensity to be defensive (a person prone to using ego defense mechanisms might be more likely to evoke one or more "microprocesses," such as denial or segregation, as an alternative to attitudinal or interpersonal change), compulsiveness (the compulsive, "anal" person will exhibit a greater preference for the order of balanced states), and ego strength ("stronger" personalities might be more likely to resist the tensions brought about by unbalance), to mention only a few.

That the listing of variables in this entire section seems heterogeneous only reflects the condition of the literature; studies on balance have yet to yield a coherent taxonomy of personality variables affecting the balance process. A study by Harari (1967) is a case in point. The effects of seven "predispositional" variables on subjects' preferences for balance was ascertained; the variables were: desire for support, conformity, recognition, independence, benevolence, leadership, and moderation. It was found that only independence and moderation affected balance preference. Persons predisposed toward being "independent" and persons predisposed toward being "moderate" in making judgments of others were more likely to prefer balanced *POX* structures. Although Harari stressed the necessity for considering personality variables in the balance model, he presents only a heterogeneous listing of such variables; no scheme for classifying personality dimensions is suggested, nor are convincing explanations given as to why certain of the personality variables and not others should be related to balance preference. In addition, he largely ignores important research on variables such as self-evaluation and intolerance for inconsistency.

Generally, any given study considering the effects of one or more personality variables is likely to ignore other studies of balance which employ personality variables. Clearly, there is a need for unified research in this area. Furthermore, the necessity of locating crucial conditional variables (such as self-evaluation) cannot be overemphasized.

5 • 3   THE EFFECTS OF SOCIAL-STRUCTURAL VARIABLES UPON THE BALANCE PROCESS

Perhaps because the vast majority of studies on the balance process have been conducted by social psychologists trained as psychologists rather than by social psychologists trained as sociologists, investigations which evaluate the effect of social-structural variables upon balance preference and tendency are almost nonexistent. Broadly defined, a social-structural variable is any attribute or characteristic of the group and/or societal context within which the individual is placed. A social-structural variable is to be thought of as distinct from a personality variable. Competition-cooperation is one kind of social-structural variable. Whether or not *P* and *O* are engaged in cooperative or competitive activity is a property of group structure rather than of personality. A different kind of social-structural variable would be, say, the socio-economic status of *P*. The fact that *P* is "upper class," "middle class" or "lower class" is to be regarded as an attribute of social structure or social organization.

In contrast to a social-structural variable, a socio-*cultural* variable is any attribute (a) of the culture peculiar to the small group under study, such as the norms or rules for social behavior that have developed since the group's formation; or (b) of the culture of society at large—for example, any norm or rule of behavior which the person has "internalized" and which can as a result affect his attitudes, likes-dislikes, and behavior in any small group of which he is a member.

The "cognitive biases" of positivity, agreement, and so on can, to a great degree, be seen as a result of this internalization process. This sociological position and implications of it were discussed earlier, at the end of the section on cognitive bias.

This text reflects, if only minimally, the analytical sociological distinction between three broad "levels of analysis": personality, social structure, and culture. This tripartite distinction is revealed in the discussion of the effects of personality characteristics on the balance process in the previous section, by the limited treatment of social-structural variables in the present section, and by the postulation of cognitive biases as reflecting internalized norms (culture) in an earlier section.

On the following pages, two *classes* of social-structural variables are considered: *experimental-situational* variables and *socio-economic* variables. An experimental-situational variable is any attribute or characteristic of the experimental setting or context. Competition-cooperation between P and O is an example. In contrast, a socio-economic variable is not to be thought of as "situational," but is some characteristic that P (and/or O) has as a result of his occupational, educational, economic and/or social position in the broader structure of society. His social class position is an example.

5 • 3a   *Experimental-Situational Variables*

Competition-Cooperation

For many years, small group researchers have been interested in the relative effects of cooperation and competition upon group process (cf. Miller and Hamblin, 1963). Only recently has this variable been applied to the propositions of balance theory. A study by Lerner et al. (1967) shows that competition-cooperation is a highly important social-structural variable which can determine the way in which perceived similarity and attraction are related. Studying the POX unit, they created the following two experimental conditions:

1. The *anticipated competition* condition, where the subject (P) was led to believe that he would work on a task with another subject (O), but that each would have to "trap or maneuver the other into making an error," and that the "winner" (the one who made the fewer errors) would receive a "substantial amount of money." Thus, the induction of anticipated competition was accomplished by leading the subject to believe that the other's loss was equal to his gain—a condition referred to in small group studies as a *zero-sum game*. The more mistakes or errors made by the other, the greater the monetary reward to the subject.

2. The *anticipated cooperation* condition, where the subject was told that the object of the task was to *help* the other to collect as many "points" as possible, and that the other would in turn help him. As compensation for points gained, each subject (P and O) would receive equal amounts of money, and one could therefore not gain by preventing the other from successfully completing the task.

The two dependent variables of the study were the perceived attitudinal similarity of the other and attraction toward the other. Perceived similarity was measured by means of P's own ratings on a "ways to live" scale in comparison to his expectations of O's ratings. Items on this scale concerned religious and ethical issues. Attraction of P to O was assessed by fifteen bipolar scales in Semantic-Differential format. Some examples: the other is likeable-unlikeable, mature-immature, responsible-irresponsible.

The investigators found that: (a) Anticipated cooperation resulted in higher attraction ratings (P of O) than did anticipated competition. Hence, if P anticipates cooperation with O, he finds O more attractive than if competition is anticipated. (b) Generally, attraction and perceptions of attitudinal similarity-dissimilarity were not related to each other. Although the other is rated as attractive as a result of anticipated cooperation, he is *not* necessarily perceived as attitudinally similar—perceptions of similarity were unaffected by anticipated cooperation.

Why should anticipated cooperation result in increased attraction, with perceived similarity being unaffected? The explanation lies in whether or not P expects that O will be instrumental in obtaining a reward for the self (P). Recall that under conditions of competition, O could *prevent* P from getting a monetary reward. In contrast, under conditions of anticipated cooperation, P expected that O would *help* him in gaining the reward. It has been proposed by Newcomb (1953, 1956, 1959, 1961) and by Byrne and associates that if P anticipates a reward from O, or if O can be instrumental in gaining reward for P, then P is more likely to be attracted toward O. Since anticipated cooperation results in anticipation of greater reward through O's actions than does anticipated competition, it follows that greater attraction of P to O will result from anticipated cooperation. Similar reasoning is found in early work on the effects of competition-cooperation upon liking by Deutsch (1949).

This reasoning is important when one considers that perceived similarity of the other is also hypothesized to be a type of reward: P's discovery that O agrees with him on important issues is rewarding, and we like those who reward us. Why, then, did Lerner et al. (1967) find that similarity, a type of reward, is *not* necessarily desired under conditions of cooperation? The answer lies in the salience or importance of the type of reward: Discovering that the other is similar may be rewarding to a degree, but a *monetary* reward is certainly a far more important kind of reward, particularly for poverty-stricken sophomore undergraduates. The fact that attitudinal similarity may constitute a reward is negligible. This explanation gains weight if one realizes that the subjects in the Lerner et al. study were informed that their monetary gain would be very large. Generally, *if P anticipates that O will be instrumental in gaining reward for him (P), and if that reward is of greater salience to P than the perception of attitudinal similarity with O, then P's attraction toward O will be a function of the anticipation of that reward rather than a function of perceived similarity.* Since under the cooperation condition, P expected that O would help him in gaining a monetary reward (and under the competition condition, O could prevent this), it follows that anticipated cooperation will result in greater attraction than anticipated competition, and that the perception of attitudinal similarity of the other is irrelevant.

The findings of Lerner et al. and the above explanation for their results permit the statement of two "strong" conditional propositions. They are strong because the conditional variable, competition-cooperation, reduces the relationship between similarity and attraction. The first conditional proposition introduces, as a conditional variable, the presence and/or availability of rewards from O to P other than perceived similarity. The second proposition below cites the specific effects of cooperation-competition.

CP 29 *(Rewards Other than Similarity, and Attraction): If P can obtain from O important rewards other than the perception of attitudinal similarity, then P will tend to like O regardless of whether O is perceived as attitudinally similar or dissimilar.*

Stated in another way, as the availability of important rewards from O (other than attitudinal similarity) increases, P's liking for O will also increase in direct proportion, regardless of the perceived attitudinal similarity of O.

Under the condition that cooperation between P and O results in greater reward for P than does competition, then it follows (from CP 29) that cooperation results in greater attraction of P to O than does competition. This is exactly what Lerner et al. (1967) found. Thus:

CP 30 *(Competition-Cooperation, Attraction, and Perceived Similarity): Independently of P's perception of the attitudinal similarity of O, cooperation between P and O results in greater attraction (P to O) than does competition.*

The Lerner et al. findings and the above strong conditional propositions based on them have important implications in regard to the similarity-attraction relationship. This suggests a broad hypothesis—that whether or not perceived similarity is related to attraction is dependent upon the *social-structural context* within which P and O find themselves. Competition-cooperation is only one among many properties of the social context. The Lerner et al. findings seriously question the advisability of labeling the similarity-attraction relationship as a "law," as Byrne and associates have done. The relationship does not appear to be a law at all, but one which depends heavily upon both the personality predispositions of the group members (such as self-evaluation) and upon the social-structural properties of the context within which P and O are interacting. Additional research is needed to discover just what other critical social-structural variables there are. Below, some suggestions are made in regard to two such social-structural variables: restrictions on communication and "task" versus "process" orientation. In the main, however, research in balance has not even begun to consider the vast range of such contextual attributes which can potentially affect the operation of balance dynamics.

Plausibility and Differentiability of the Structure

There are certain structural variables that are "situational" and which at the same time are properties of the *POX*-type unit itself, but which are properties other than balance–unbalance. Such properties can affect the operation of the balance process. Two such intriguing concepts, identified by Schrader and Lewit (1962), are the *plausibility* and *differentiability* of a structure. The plausibility of a structure is determined by asking, "What is the *maximum* degree of balance that a particular structure can attain?" The differentiability of the structure is determined by asking, "How many different *ways* can one attain a maximal degree of balance in a particular structure?" Plausibility is the maximum attainable degree of balance of an incomplete structure, and differentiability is the number of ways to attain that maximal degree of balance. Both concepts presume a preference for or a tendency toward balance. Although they are not in any way "measures" of the extent of balance–unbalance of a structure, they are "structural" inasmuch as they refer to sentiment or attitudinal relations between objects, and they are "experimental-situational" inasmuch as they pertain to conditions in the experimental setting.[10]

Schrader and Lewit presented a number of incomplete structures to subjects. An incomplete structure is one which contains one or more missing or unstated relations. All structures differed in their plausibility and differentiability. The objects (four) in each structure were intended to represent co-workers on a research staff, and the subject was to imagine himself as being one person in the structure. Each subject was then requested to fill in the missing relations. The degree of balance of the structure completed by each subject was then ascertained. The comfort-discomfort (tension) that the subject expected to experience if he were in the situation was also measured. It was found that: (a) the more plausible the structure, the more likely the subject was to maximally balance it. Stated in another way, the greater the maximum *possible* degree of balance for a particular structure, the greater the degree of balance of the structure completed by the subject. (b) The greater the differentiability of the structure, the more likely the subject was to maximally balance it. This means that the greater the number of ways there are to maximally balance a structure, the more likely the subject was to find one of those ways. The less the number of ways to balance

10. Any property of a sentiment or attitude structure *other than* balance–unbalance is called an *extrabalance property*. These are discussed in the next chapter. The concepts of plausibility and differentiability are not discussed then because, although they are properties other than balance–unbalance, they presume a preference for and a tendency toward balance (and consequently, both concepts are defined in terms of balance–unbalance). Hence, plausibility and differentiability are not, in the strictest sense, "extrabalance" properties.

the structure (the less the differentiability), the less likely the subject was to find a way to maximally balance the structure, and the less the resulting degree of balance of the structure. (c) Less tension was associated with structures of high plausibility and differentiability. Hence, the greater the maximum attainable degree of balance for a structure (plausibility), and the greater the number of ways to maximally balance a structure (differentiability), then the less the degree of tension that the subject expected to experience as a member of the structure.

> CP 31 *(Plausibility, Differentiability, Balance Preference and Tension): The greater the plausibility and/or differentiability of a structure, the more likely the focal person will be to maximally balance that structure. Furthermore, the greater the plausibility and/or differentiability of a structure, the less the amount of tension the focal person will experience as a member of that structure.*

Other Situational Variables

It would be worthwhile for future studies to examine the effects of additional situational variables (besides cooperation-competition, plausibility, and differentiability) upon the balance process. Recent work in *communication networks* (Shaw, 1964) might be applied to the Balance Tendency hypothesis. If unbalance among three or more persons will generate forces toward communication and resulting attitudinal and interpersonal changes in the direction of balance—as Newcomb had maintained—then to the degree that communication is *restricted* by allowing some of the group members to communicate and preventing others from communicating, then to that degree a tendency toward balance may be prevented. We noted on page 129 that under the condition that an interpersonal change can result in balance, communication would not be necessary in order to achieve balance. Hence, we might predict that the restriction of communication will affect changes in attitudinal relations but not affect changes in interpersonal (sentiment or liking) relations.

A second situational variable which could determine the relative likelihood of changes in attitudinal and sentiment relations is *task orientation* versus *process orientation* (Olmstead, 1954; Bales, 1951; Mills, 1967). Under situational conditions of task orientation, the group members focus upon non-interpersonal, non-affective issues; attention is directed toward the discussion and resolution of instrumental, "external" matters. The group is businesslike and calculated, and not concerned with issues involving the personal problems of the members. Classroom discussions, seminars, board meetings and the like constitute typical examples of task-oriented groups. In terms of the *POX* paradigm, this means that the focus of attention is on *PX* and *OX* attitudinal relations, and less on *PO* interpersonal relations. In contrast, conditions of *process orientation* demand "self-analysis"—the focus upon emotional issues, interpersonal and personal problems, and the like. "Self-analytic" groups are characterized on the basis of process orientation (Slater, 1962; Mills, 1964b). Therapy groups and training groups (also called "T" groups or "sensitivity-training" groups) are the best examples of extreme process orientation.[11]

It seems likely that under conditions of task-orientation, attitudinal relations are more likely to change, whereas under conditions of process orientation, interpersonal relations are more likely to change. Evidence to this effect would question the applicability of the "interpersonal cognitive bias" discussed earlier: There is no constant or standard preference for interpersonal change over attitudinal change; whichever is most likely will depend upon the type of general orientation (task versus process) of the group members. Hence, the task-process distinction can be seen as a set of contextual conditions which affect the operation of cognitive biases and as a result the operation of the balance process itself.

5 • 3b   Socio-Economic Variables

A very limited amount of research has been done on the extent to which socio-economic variables can affect the balance process. McLeod et al. (1966) measured the socio-economic status (SES) of the subject (a college student) as a member of a POX unit by means of the subject's perception of his social class position, his family income, and his father's education. The SES score of each subject was determined by averaging these three indicators. It was found that subjects from lower-status families were more likely to change their attitudes toward X in the direction of the perceived attitude of a liked other than were subjects from higher-status families. Thus, low SES subjects exhibited a greater tendency to change the PX attitude toward balance than did high SES subjects. This may be explained by the fact that lower SES persons tend to score higher on authoritarianism and intolerance for inconsistency than higher SES persons. Since authoritarian persons tend to exhibit greater tendencies toward balance on both attitudinal and interpersonal variables (see CP 25 and CP 26, discussed earlier), it follows that lower SES persons show a greater tendency to balance the PX attitude with the perceived OX attitude and the PO interpersonal relation.

> CP 32 *(Socio-economic Status of P and Balance Tendency): Persons of lower socio-economic status are more likely to change their attitudes toward X in the direction of their perception of the attitude of a liked other than are persons of relatively higher socio-economic status.*

11. Another way to conceptualize the task-process distinction is to postulate that any group possesses both components. Thus, although a meeting of businessmen may appear to be "task-oriented," many emotional issues and "latent" problems may be present, yet undiscussed. W. R. Bion's (1959) concept of the "basic assumption" (a "shared unconscious") reflects this view, as does Mills' (1964a) concept of "group emotion."

The McLeod et al. study treated the X-object in the POX unit as an attitude-object, and the similarity of P and O with respect to that object was determined. Similarity between P and O with respect to socio-economic status can be taken as the independent variable, and the attraction of P to O can be predicted on the basis of status similarity. Thus, "similarity-dissimilarity with respect to X" becomes "similarity-dissimilarity with respect to status," and the X-object becomes status. Early research shows that positive sociometric choice (high attraction) tends to exist among persons of similar rather than dissimilar socioeconomic status (Bonney, 1946; Lundberg and Beazley, 1948; Longmore, 1948). Recently, Byrne, Clore and Worchel (1966) found that subjects are more attracted toward others perceived as similar in SES than toward others who are perceived as dissimilar. However, if P perceived that O was dissimilar but *higher* than himself in status, then O was rated as more attractive than if O was perceived as dissimilar but *lower* in status. This constitutes evidence for a "status seeking effect" on the part of P, even if O is perceived as dissimilar in status.

When *both* the attitudinal similarity of P and O and the SES of O are measured, a different picture emerges. Byrne, Griffitt and Golightly (1966), in a refinement of the study just cited, led P to believe that a hypothetical O was either high in occupational status (physicist), middle (electrician), or low (janitor). The occupational (or family) status *of* P was not measured in the study. Perceived attitude similarity was manipulated. It was found that only attitudinal similarity affected P's attraction toward O. Neither the occupational status of O nor the interaction of similarity and occupational status of O was statistically significant.

The results were explained by the investigators in the following way: If P has information about O which pertains to O's attitudes toward important issues, then only perceived attitudinal similarity is relevant for predicting P's attraction toward O, and the perceived status of O is irrelevant. In comparison to the results of Byrne, Clore and Worchel (1966) cited above, this means that the status of O predicts P's attraction toward O *only if* no attitudinal information about O is available to P. Occupational or class stereotypes are only relevant in the absence of more specific, attitudinal information. These conclusions (and hence the following conditional proposition) are tentative, since the occupational status *of* P (or his family's status) was not measured in the second study by Byrne, Griffitt and Golightly.

CP 33   *(Socio-Economic Status of O and Balance Preference): Under the condition that P has no attitudinal information about O, then the perceived socio-economic status of O will affect P's attraction toward O. If P does have attitudinal information on O, then the perceived socio-economic status of O will not affect P's attraction toward O.*

5 • 4   SUMMARY

This chapter was concerned with research findings which justified the statement of *conditional propositions*—propositions which modify, refine, broaden, extend, or even cancel or completely reverse the predictions of one or more of the four general propositions of balance theory. The treatment of conditional propositions was divided into three main classes:

1. Conditional propositions which concerned *corollaries* to the theory—namely, conditional propositions based on parameter variables. Three types of corollaries were treated: Those concerning cognitive bias, importance of the X-object, and the polarity corollary of the Osgood model of attitude congruity. In regard to the matter of cognitive bias, it was pointed out that five of the seven biases are "true" modifications of balance theory, since they are not themselves deducible from the concept of balance: positivity, completeness, extremity, least cost, and interpersonal preference or change. (The further stipulation was added that although the least cost and interpersonal biases are not deducible from the balance concept, they nevertheless *presume* a preference for or a tendency toward balance.) Two additional biases, reciprocity and agreement (lateral symmetry), were regarded as being deducible from the balance concept, and are therefore not true modifications of the general theory in the way that the former biases are.

2. Conditional propositions arising from the consideration of *personality variables*. The major focus was upon concrete research evidence concerning the effects of personality on balance.

3. Conditional propositions arising out of the consideration of *social-structural variables*.

It is difficult to summarize concisely what has been said in the totality of this rather long chapter. The thirty-three enumerated conditional propositions themselves constitute a summarization of the relevant research findings. Nonetheless, to the degee that it is possible, the salient conclusions of the foregoing chapter are presented in the following fifteen points:

1. (The effects of positivity.) Independently of the balance–unbalance of a structure, positive relations, especially if they are interpersonal (as opposed to attitudinal), are learned with fewer errors than (are "preferred over") negative relations (CP 1). Furthermore, a subject is more likely to alter or change a negative relation in the positive direction, and will tend to keep a positive relation positive (CP 4). There is strong evidence that the presence of negative *interpersonal* relations in a structure is a greater source of tension than is the presence of positive interpersonal relations (CP 14).

2. (The effects of reciprocity.) Reciprocal interpersonal relations are easier to learn than non-reciprocal interpersonal relations (CP 2), and changes are

more often in the direction of reciprocity than in the direction of non-reciprocity (CP 5). Furthermore, relations of *positive reciprocity* are easier to learn than relations of *negative reciprocity* (CP 2), and changes tend to be in the direction of positive rather than negative reciprocity (CP 5).

3. (The effects of the interpersonal bias.) Independently of the balance–unbalance of a structure, interpersonal relations are easier to learn than attitudinal or unit relations (CP 3), and subjects are more likely to alter or change interpersonal rather than attitudinal relations (CP 6). There is evidence that interpersonal relations, rather than attitudinal or unit relations, constitute "anchors" or "cues" which people use to form perceptions about the sum total of relations in structures.

4. (The "extremity effect.") An "extreme" (strongly worded) message from O to P results in less liking for P of O than a moderately worded message (CP 7). To the extent that an increase in liking will result in a change toward balance, to that extent extremity of communication prevents a tendency toward balance (CP 8).

5. (The completeness bias.) There is some evidence that complete structures (all relations given) are learned with fewer errors than incomplete ones (one or more relations ungiven) (CP 9), but the completeness-incompleteness of a structure does not appear to affect tension, as had been previously hypothesized.

6. (The effects of agreement and lateral symmetry.) Independently of the balance–unbalance of a structure, the variable agree-disagree (cf. lateral symmetry) affects learning (CP 10) (structures containing laterally symmetric pairs of relations are easier to learn), change (CP 11) (there is a tendency to make the PX and OX signs similar, regardless of the sign of the PO relation), and tension (CP 15) (dissimilarity in the signs of the PX and OX relations is a greater source of tension than similarity in the signs).

7. (Relative effects of bias versus balance.) There is recent evidence that the effects of balance–unbalance upon learning (preference) can be exceeded by the effects of certain biases; among them: positivity, reciprocity, and lateral symmetry (agreement). This suggests that when "ease of learning" is taken as the dependent variable, the balance concept does not have the same explanatory power as do other types of biases, and that perhaps the balance principle itself should be regarded as simply one among several cognitive biases that operate in the perception of structures of interpersonal and attitudinal relations.

8. (Relative effects of sign and strength of the PO relation upon tension.) While there is considerable evidence that the *sign* of the PO relation affects tension (negative interpersonal relations are a greater source of tension than positive interpersonal relations), there is no evidence that the *strength* of an interpersonal relation *of a given sign* affects tension (CP 17).

9. (Relative effects of agreement versus discrepancy upon tension.) While the similarity in *sign* of the PX and OX relations (agreement) affects

tension, there is no convincing evidence that the *discrepancy* between the PX and OX relations affects tension, when the strength of the PO relation is held constant (CP 16). (Discrepancy is the algebraic difference between the strengths of the PX and OX relations.)

10. (Least cost, and the hierarchy of biases.) There is evidence that if the least cost (minimal change) bias does not violate other biases such as interpersonal change, positivity, and reciprocity, then balance will be achieved by means of the minimum necessary changes. But if the least cost bias does violate these other biases, then balance will *not* be achieved through the minimum necessary changes (CP 12). This suggests that a *hierarchy of biases* determines the ways and means through which balance is maintained in groups, and that the least cost bias occupies a relatively low hierarchical position (CP 13). It was expected that the least cost bias will become more operative and thus attain a higher position in this hierarchy as the number of objects and/or relations in the structure increases. *This suggests that the focal person's "cognitive" hierarchy is not an invariant, constant one, as previously implied in the literature, but that it is modified depending upon certain structural properties (such as the number of objects and/or relations in the total structure).*

11. (The effects of importance.) There is evidence that importance of the X-object affects preference (CP 18) and tension (CP 20), but the available evidence favoring an effect of importance upon change is very fragmentary (CP 19).

12. (Polarity, the relative importance factor, and the importance/commitment factor.) Both the *likelihood* and *magnitude* of change in an attitudinal relation is a function of both the strength of that attitude (the polarity factor) and the *relative salience* of that attitude in comparison to another attitude which is part of the same structure (the relative importance factor) (CP 21). The evidence implies that the likelihood and magnitude of change in the PX and PO relations in an interpersonal (POX) structure depends not only upon the strengths of each relation (the polarity factor) but also upon the importance of X *relative to* P's involvement with or commitment to O (the importance/commitment factor) (CP 22). In predicting change in the PS and PC attitudes (in the Osgood PSC structure), or in predicting change in PO liking or in the PX attitude (in the interpersonal POX structure), one must assume that the SC *assertion* (in the Osgood model), or the *perceived OX attitude* (in the interpersonal model) is constant through time.

13. (The effects of personality variables.) Certain personality variables affect the operation of the balance process. In the instance of negative self-evaluation, the predictions of balance preference and balance tendency are completely reversed (CP 23 and CP 24). A graph-theoretic re-interpretation of the results of two studies on self-evaluation was presented, and shows why this "reversal" takes place. Other personality variables that affect the balance process are: Authoritarianism (high authoritarians exhibit a greater preference for (CP

25) and tendency toward (CP 26) balance, particularly "autistic" balance); affiliation need (a high need for affiliation *magnifies* the effect of perceived attitudinal similarity upon attraction (CP 27)); and cognitive complexity (the greater the number of criteria a person uses to evaluate or classify objects of orientation (the greater his cognitive complexity), the less likely he is to prefer balance among those objects (CP 28)).

14. (The effects of situational social-structural variables.) If P can obtain rewards from O other than the perception of attitudinal similarity of O, then P will tend to like O, regardless of whether O is perceived as attitudinally similar or dissimilar (CP 29). Since cooperation between P and O is a source of greater reward for P than is competition, it follows that cooperation results in greater liking (P of O) than does competition, regardless of the perceived attitudinal similarity of O (CP 30). Hence, the situational social-structural context within which P and O interact can affect balance preference. Two other structural variables which can affect both preference and tension are the plausibility and differentiability of a structure (CP 31). It was pointed out that much more research into the effects of situational-structural variables on the balance process needs to be carried out.

15. (The effects of socio-economic variables.) The socio-economic status *of P* affects his tendency to balance a structure, such that persons of lower socio-economic status are more likely to change their attitude toward X in the direction of balance with other relations in the structure than are persons of relatively higher socio-economic status (CP 32). The perceived socio-economic status *of O* can affect P's liking for O, *unless* attitudinal information about O is available to P (CP 33).

To the extent that it can be done succinctly, it is worthwhile to state the classes of "strong" conditional propositions that have been encountered in this chapter. *There is clear evidence that certain cognitive biases, certain personality variables and certain social-structural variables have profound effects on the balance process, thus making the fundamental predictions of balance theory heavily conditional.* Specifically, the following classes of conditional propositions place strong modifications upon the four propositions of balance theory, and for this reason they constitute blows to the explanatory power of the concept of balance in social psychology and in small group research:

1. The propositions concerning cognitive bias, *taken collectively*. Evidence is rapidly accruing that the ease of learning a structure, the preference for perceiving the combinations or relations in a structure in a certain way, the likelihood and magnitude of change in a relation and the amount of tension aroused in the focal person, can all potentially be explained by the operation of various cognitive biases, particularly the positivity, reciprocity, agreement, and interpersonal biases. Since the positivity and interpersonal biases are not simply re-statements of the balance principle (as are the reciprocity and agreement

biases), these two types of bias in particular present the severest challenge to the explanatory power of the balance concept.

2. The two propositions concerning the way in which the least cost bias interacts with the other biases, and the relative position of the various biases in a cognitive hierarchy. It is hypothesized that the ordered position of the biases in this hierarchy is not invariant and constant, but that the hierarchical positions of biases depends upon certain structural conditions, such as the number of objects and/or relations in the structure, and possibly upon other structural properties.

3. The propositions concerning the *lack* of effects of relation *strength* upon tension, as opposed to the effects of the *signs* of relations upon tension.

4. The propositions concerning the effects of polarity and relative salience (and importance/commitment).

5. The effects of the personality variable, self-evaluation. The two propositions concerning the effects of this variable lead to the suspicion that there are *other* unknown personality variables which can exert similar profound effects upon the balance process.

6. The effects of the social-structural variable, competition-cooperation, and the proposition concerning the availability of rewards to *P that are provided by situational-structural conditions* and which are rewards other than *P*'s perception of attitudinal similarity of *O*. The broad implication is that there are other, unexplored variables which are situational-structural in nature (which are not attributes of personality, nor parameter variables), and which can exert marked effects upon balance dynamics in small groups.

Before proceeding to the next chapter, it should be made crystal-clear to the reader that the present chapter by no means exhausts our discussion of findings which limit the explanatory ability of the concept of balance. There are other considerations which lead to strong modifications of the theory. Although this entire issue is examined again in the last chapter, certain limiting considerations are raised in Chapter 6, which concerns graph-theoretic formalization of the theory of balance.

6......

Issues Involving Formalization

In Chapter 3, an introductory discussion of graph-theoretic models of balance was presented. The reader may wish to go back and review the material at this time. A cognitive or interpersonal structure can be represented as a number of *lines* (representing relations) connecting two or more *points* (representing either persons or non-person cognitive objects or elements). Each line may be directed (for example, $P \rightarrow O$) or non-directed ($P—O$). In the latter instance, the relation is treated as symmetric. Each line can be labeled in sign only, or in terms of both sign and strength. Any set of points and lines is a *graph*. A graph where $T = 1$ (a Type I graph) contains only one class of line (for example, lines representing interpersonal relations only). A graph where $T = 2$ (a Type II graph) contains two classes of lines (for example, two types of lines representing attitudes and perceived attitudes, or attitudinal and interpersonal relations, or sentiment and unit relations). Graphs where $T > 2$ contain three or more classes of relations.

A *path* consists of two or more lines connecting consecutive points. A *cycle* is any path returning to the point of origin, namely, any recursive path through any given point.[1] The *length of a cycle* is the number of lines in it. A two-line cycle, or more succinctly a 2-cycle, is the smallest possible cycle, and contains two lines; a 3-cycle contains three lines, and so on. Three methods for counting cycles were reviewed in Chapter 3. Only "Method 1" (the Cartwright-Harary method) will be used to count cycles in our discussion in this chapter.

A cycle is *balanced* if the algebraic product of its lines is positive, which is equivalent to saying that it contains an even number of negative lines. A graph is "completely balanced" only if all of its cycles are positive. A theorem, the *decomposition* or *structural* theorem, tells us that a graph is completely balanced

---

1. As stated in the third chapter, the terms *cycle* and *semicycle* will be used as synonymous. A semicycle is any nonrecursive closed path. For example, the path $A \rightarrow B$, $B \rightarrow C$, and $C \rightarrow A$ is a cycle. The path $A \rightarrow B$, $B \rightarrow C$, and $A \rightarrow C$ is a semicycle.

if it can be partitioned into *two* subsets, such that each positive line joins points within a subset, and each negative line joins points from different subsets (a single point can be a subset). In the application of the decomposition theorem, missing lines are ignored (missing lines can appear either within or between subsets). The decomposition theorem will be shown to be a special case of another and very interesting theorem, the *cluster theorem,* to be reviewed below. (It will also be demonstrated that the concept of balance itself is a special case of another concept, the concept of *clustering.*)

The purpose of the present chapter is to review current and largely unresolved empirical issues involving graph-theoretic formalization. Four sets of issues are discussed. First, five *indices* of degree of balance are contrasted, and evidence pertaining to the empirical accuracy of each will be presented. Second, formal properties of structures other than balance—*extrabalance properties*—will be introduced and discussed, particularly the property of *clustering.* Third, a set of problems pertaining to *cycle length* and *non-local cycles* will be outlined. Finally, a six-fold controversy for predicting the *strength of an unknown relation* in a cycle will be outlined, and empirical evidence relevant to this controversy will be reviewed.

6 • 1   INDICES OF BALANCE

A graph or structure is completely balanced only if all of its cycles are positive. However, a structure may be described in terms of its *degree* of balance. The Cartwright-Harary index of degree of balance, reviewed in Chapter 3, is as follows (Cartwright and Harary, 1956; Harary, 1959; Harary et al., 1965):

Index 1 (Cartwright-Harary): $b(G) = \dfrac{+c(G)}{c(G)}$

where

$b(G)$ = the degree of balance of the structure (graph);
$+c(G)$ = the number of positive (balanced) cycles in the structure; and
$c(G)$ = the total number of cycles in the structure, both positive (balanced) and negative (unbalanced).

Hence, the degree of balance of a total structure, ranging from 0 (complete unbalance) to 1.00 (complete balance), is the ratio of positive cycles in the structure to the total number of cycles in the structure.

The principal difficulty with this index is that it does not consider the *strengths* of relations (lines) in a structure. Morrissette (1958) introduced an index which expresses the degree of balance in terms of the strengths of relations. Let σ be the strength of a cycle (the elgebraic product of the strengths of the lines in the cycle), let each cycle be designated as Z_k, and let r represent the number of cycles. The expression σZ is the strength of a given cycle, and $p\sigma Z$ is the strength of a positive cycle. The degree of balance of the structure, $b(G)$, becomes:

Index 2 (Morrissette):
$$b(G) = \frac{\displaystyle\sum_{k=1}^{r} p\sigma Z_k}{\displaystyle\sum_{k=1}^{r} |\sigma Z_k|}$$

which is read and interpreted thus: The degree of balance of the total structure is the sum of the strengths of all positive cycles divided by the absolute sum (ignoring signs) of the strengths of all cycles. This index was discussed in Chapter 3.

A third index recently introduced by Morrissette (1966), to be referred to as the Morrissette $\gamma(G)$ index, considers *vacuous* cycles in a structure. A *vacuous cycle* is any *incomplete* cycle. For example, if P likes O ($+PO$), P likes Q ($+PQ$), but O and Q have no relation to each other (for example, they do not know each other), the cycle thus formed is vacuous. If the structure contains four or more persons (points), or if two or more *classes* of relations appear in the structure (i.e., if $T > 1$), many vacuous cycles can appear. *It should be noted that the two indices just cited (Index 1 and Index 2) count only complete cycles, and ignore vacuous cycles.* Hence, degree of balance may be expressed in a way which incorporates vacuous cycles (Morrissette, 1966):

Index 3 (Morrissette):
$$\gamma(G) = \frac{+c(G)}{c(K_p)}$$
where

$\gamma(G)$ = the degree of balance of the structure, taking into consideration vacuous cycles;

$+c(G)$ = the number of positive complete cycles in the structure; and

$c(K_p)$ = the total number of cycles that *would exist* if the structure were complete (complete cycles plus vacuous cycles).

This index gives the ratio of positive complete cycles to all cycles that would exist if the structure were complete (which will be the number of vacuous cycles plus the number of complete cycles, both positive and negative). Note that this index does not consider the *strengths* of relations. Note also that if one or more relations are not present (or if they are present but of zero value)—if the structure is incomplete—$\gamma(G)$ will always be less than 1.00; the structure will always be treated as less than completely balanced. If the structure is complete, then $\gamma(G)$ can become 1.00 (if all cycles are positive).

By inference from this index, we note that any vacuous cycle is not balanced. This conflicts with the previously discussed convention that a vacuous cycle is to be treated as "vacuously balanced" (Cartwright and Harary, 1956; Berger et al., 1962). The greater the number of vacuous cycles, the less will be the maximum attainable degree of balance, $\gamma(G)$, of the total structure. The underlying purpose of this index is to take into account the *completeness* cognitive bias. The logic is that a structure which contains one or more incomplete (vacuous) cycles cannot be called "stable" (balanced), because it violates the completeness bias. Hence, any structure containing one or more incomplete cycles will always be less than balanced—$\gamma(G)$ will always be less than 1.00.

A vacuous cycle is a cycle which contains one or more absent lines, but an "absent line" can represent either one of two things: (1) that there is *no relation* between the two points—suggesting, for example, that the two persons represented *do not know* each other; (2) that there is a relation between the two points but it is of *zero value*. For example, P may know O, but feel completely neutral toward him. The former is called "no relation" or an "absent" relation; the latter is called "a relation of zero value" or a "null relation." One may raise the question whether it is meaningful to distinguish one from the other in graph-theoretic representation. Morrissette (1967) showed that in terms of tension, it makes no difference. This was demonstrated by having subjects rate interpersonal structures which were alike in all respects, except that one set contained an absent relation, whereas another set contained one relation of zero value. The two kinds of structures did not yield significantly different tension ratings. This evidence can be interpreted to mean that the graph-theoretic convention of letting an absent line indicate *either* "absent relation" or "relation of zero value" is justified. In terms of tension, the distinction is not psychologically meaningful.

Studies which test the empirical workability of the three indices just defined are relatively sparse. Morrissette's (1958) original study used Index 2 (which considers the strengths of relations). Subjects were presented with three-object structures (representing three persons, with both sentiment and unit relations appearing between them), and also four-object structures (four persons). The subject was asked to "be" one of the persons (represented by point P) in any structure he rated. The subject's ratings were in terms of tension, as indicated by ratings of "discomfort," "difficulties," and "pressures to change the relations"—more probably a measure of desire to change (stability) than a measure of tension. Generally, it was found that tension rating was inversely related to degree of balance. However, for four-object structures, only the degree of *local balance* (considering only cycles passing through point P—the point representing the subject doing the rating) predicted tension. Degree of *total balance* (considering all cycles in the structure) did not. The implications of this latter finding are discussed later in detail, since they concern the problem of local versus nonlocal cycles in a total structure.

To the author's knowledge, this initial study by Morrissette is the only one to utilize Index 2. Hence, it has not been determined whether it predicts tension (or change) better than the other two indices. Note that Index 1 *can* be computed even if strengths of relations are given, and so can Index 3. Thus, the empirical workability of Index 2 can be potentially contrasted with Indices 1 and 3, but it has not yet been done. However, Indices 1 and 3 have been contrasted against each other in a recent study by Morrissette et al. (1966). Subjects were asked to rate three-object structures, all of which were incomplete. It was therefore possible to test Index 1, which ignores vacuous cycles, against Index 3, which incorporates vacuous cycles. It was found that the subjects' tension ratings were predicted by Index 1 but not by Index 3. These results are congruent with those obtained in a later study in which only Index 1 was used (Morrissette et al., 1967).

The inference to be made here is that the presence or absence of vacuous (incomplete) cycles in a structure does not affect the focal person's tension; only the balance–unbalance of complete cycles does. Furthermore, Morrissette interpreted his results as indicating no cognitive bias toward completeness. We note in passing that this inference conflicts with the results of other studies finding effects of a completeness bias, such as the one by DeSoto et al. (1968), discussed in Chapter 5. It would seem that Morrissette's evidence is inconclusive, not only because of the more recent results of DeSoto et al. but also because his design did not permit a test of preference. For example, by presenting subjects with three sets of structures, some complete and balanced, some complete and unbalanced, and some incomplete, not only could a preference or non-preference for completeness be isolated, but the effects of completeness *versus* the effects of balance could be ascertained. To date, the evidence in regard to the operation of a completeness bias remains inconclusive, as indicated in the foregoing chapter.

The Rosenberg-Abelson least cost hypothesis can be translated into an index of balance (Abelson and Rosenberg, 1958; Rosenberg and Abelson, 1960; also Harary, 1959). The degree of balance of a structure can be defined as the minimum number of changes necessary to achieve complete balance. The greater the number of required changes, the *less* the degree of balance of the total structure. This is identical to Harary's *line index* of degree of balance, λ, the number of lines in a deletion-minimal or negation-minimal set of relations. Recall from the third chapter that a deletion-minimal set of lines (relations) is the fewest number of lines the removal or deletion of which results in complete balance, if vacuous cycles are ignored. A negation-minimal set is the fewest number of lines the negation of which results in complete balance. Negation means changing a positive line to negative, or a negative line to positive. Remember that the lines in a deletion-minimal set *are the same lines* in a negation-minimal set. It should be mentioned that for small structures, finding the minimal negations (or deletions) is not difficult, but for even moderately large structures, no suitable procedure for calculating the minimal negations (deletions) has appeared in the literature.

Index 4

(Rosenberg-Abelson-Harary) :   The fewest number of negations (or deletions) needed to achieve complete balance of the total structure.

A recent study by Phillips (1967) contrasts Index 4 with Index 1. It was found that Index 4 ordered the data better than did the original Cartwright-Harary index, Index 1. Phillips' study focused upon cognitive change, and his findings suggest that Index 4 is a better index of changes than Index 1. Indices 2 and 3 were not computed in the study, although they could have been. In addition, a fifth index (developed by Phillips) was used, and it ordered the data best of all. A detailed description of Phillips' methodology is necessary before his complex index can be defined.

Phillips sought to investigate the way in which cognitive elements and the relations between the elements combine in the minds of persons, and how these combinations change over time. The "cognitive elements" were not person-objects, however. In one experiment, the elements were defined as cognitive concepts such as "disease" and "germs" (two elements), "antibiotics" and "disease," or "hill" and "dress." Pairs of such elements were presented to subjects by means of cards. Each subject was given several trials (up to five) on a number of such paired elements. The relation between any pair of elements could be positive, neutral, or negative. The subject indicated which of these three he thought it was, or perceived it to be. For example, the relation between "disease" and "germs" would probably be perceived as positive (one causes the other); the relation between "antibiotics" and "disease," as negative (one prevents the other); and the relation between "hill" and "dress," as neutral (each is irrelevant to the other). For a given trial, all possible pairs of seven elements (giving twenty-one pairs) were presented to subjects on cards. The reader should recognize that most pairs of elements would be open to the subject's interpretation, and would not be as obvious as the examples just cited.

In another experiment, a "trial" consisted of a discussion session between the subject and a role player on various aspects of the issue "capital punishment." A cognitive element was defined as a particular aspect of the issue. (Note carefully that the objects in the "structure" that Phillips studied here are not the subject, role player, and an "aspect" of the capital punishment issue. The objects in this strictly cognitive structure consisted of only the aspects of the issue. The relation is the positive, negative or null relation between the aspects of the issue themselves. The subject and the role player were not part of the abstract structure under study.) Six aspects of the capital punishment issue were discussed at each trial or discussion session. For each session, the subjects' judgments of the relations (positive, negative or null) between the aspects was ascertained.

The purpose of the study was to determine if the degree of balance among cognitive elements (word-concepts in one experiment, aspects of the capital punishment issue in another) increased over time—over the different trials. Hence, Phillips computed a given index of balance among cognitive elements *for each subject at each trial,* and simply observed the changes in the indices— whether they increased, decreased, or did not change. His own index (we will call it Index 5) was then compared to the Cartwright-Harary index (Index 1) and to the Abelson-Rosenberg index (Index 4). Each index was computed on each subject for each trial.

In order to understand how Phillips computed his index, and in order to interpret it intuitively, it is necessary at this time to introduce the concept of the *adjacency matrix* of a graph (Harary et al., 1965). Refer to Figure 1. In this figure, *positive* relations are indicated by solid lines, *negative* relations are indicated by broken lines, and *neutral* relations are indicated by absent lines. (Note that this differs from the convention used in Chapter 3.) The graph in Figure 1A represents six relations (two positive and four negative) between four *cognitive elements* (*A, B, C* and *D*). The structure is completely balanced according to the decomposition theorem. The matrix in Figure 1B records the relation between adjacent points in the graph in Figure 1A. A $+1$ entry means that the relation between any two elements is positive. For example, the relation between element *A* and element *B* is positive; hence, the entry in row *A*–column *B* of the matrix as $+1$ (as is the entry in row *B*–column *A,* since any non-directed line is treated as symmetric). A -1 indicates a negative relation, and a zero would indicate a null (or absent) relation (see Figure 1E and F). Generally, any entry in the matrix corresponding to row *i* and column *j* represents the relation between element *i* and element *j* in the graph.

Each adjacency matrix represents the perceived relations among elements for a particular subject at a particular trial. Phillips' procedure for ascertaining the degree of balance of the graph involved the factor-analysis of the graph's adjacency matrix according to Jacobi's method as discussed by White (1958). An *eigenvector* of a matrix represents a "cluster" or "underlying dimension" of a matrix. The *eigenvalue* of a matrix, λ (not to be confused with Harary's line index, λ), reflects the percent of variance explained—the "strength" of the cluster. There are as many eigenvectors (and eigenvalues) as there are clusters. The matrix in Figure 1B and its corresponding graph show two clusters; hence, two eigenvalues describe the matrix. Readers familiar with factor analysis will recognize that two factors describe the entire matrix. Both eigenvalues (and therefore both factors) are of equal *size*—the "percent variance explained" is the same for both clusters, since two elements and one relation are involved in each cluster, and the strengths of the relations in each cluster are equal ($+1$). The term *strength of a cluster* will hereafter be used as the intuitive definition of "percent variance explained by a factor," which is directly analogous to the *size* of the eigenvalue.

Phillips' argument, which derives from the decomposition theorem and from Abelson and Rosenberg's matrix-formulations of balance (Abelson and

FIGURE 1   AN ILLUSTRATION OF PHILLIPS' INDEX

A.

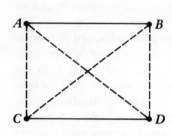

B.

	A	B	C	D
A		+1	−1	−1
B	+1		−1	−1
C	−1	−1		+1
D	−1	−1	+1	

C.

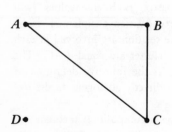

D.

	A	B	C	D
A		+1	+1	−1
B	+1		+1	−1
C	+1	+1		−1
D	−1	−1	−1	

E.

F.

	A	B	C	D
A		+1	+1	0
B	+1		+1	0
C	+1	+1		0
D	0	0	0	

Rosenberg, 1958), is that the *size* of an eigenvalue (the strength of a cluster) indicates the degree of balance of a matrix, and hence the degree of balance of its corresponding graph. A graph which contains only positive relations will have one eigenvalue, and it will be of maximum size, indicating complete balance. A matrix representing a positive relation between A and B, a positive relation between B and C, but a negative relation between A and C will have a smaller eigenvalue; the strength of the cluster is less, indicating that it is less balanced.

The graph in Figure 1C and its adjacency matrix (Figure 1D) show two clusters (note that point D is to be treated as a "cluster"). Likewise, so does the graph and matrix in Figure 1E and F. Both graphs are completely balanced according to the decomposition theorem. But the *size* of one cluster (the number of points in it) is greater; the ABC cluster is greater in size than the cluster containing the single point, D. In addition, the *strength* of the ABC cluster (the "percent variance explained" by the factor describing that cluster) is greater. The adjacency matrix will yield two eigenvalues, one larger than the other. According to Phillips, *the degree of balance of a matrix (and hence its graph) is indicated by the size of the largest eigenvalue of the matrix.* The size of the largest eigenvalue indicates the strength of the strongest cluster. The larger the *largest* eigenvalue, the greater the degree of balance. By this definition, the matrix in Figure 1D (and also the matrix in Figure 1F) is *more balanced than* the matrix in Figure 1B. The strength of the ABC cluster in Figure 1D (the size of the largest eigenvalue) is greater than the strength of either of the two clusters (which are themselves of equal strength) in Figure 1B.

Abelson (1967, pp. 16–17), independently of Phillips, has suggested a strikingly similar factor-analytic conceptualization of a degree of balance index, although his treatment is suggestive and undetailed. Abelson defines a factor-index of degree of balance as the "proportion of the total sum of squares explained by the first [largest] factor" (p. 17), which is directly analogous to Phillips' definition of degree of balance of a matrix as the size of the *largest* eigenvalue.

Letting λ_1 represent the size of the largest eigenvalue of an adjacency matrix, Phillips' index of degree of balance (Index 5) becomes:

Index 5 (Phillips): $b(G) = \lambda_1,$

where

$b(G)$ = the degree of balance of the matrix of a particular subject at a particular trial; and

λ_1 = the largest eigenvalue (the "strength" of the strongest cluster) of the matrix of the particular subject at a particular trial.

It seems clear that Phillips' definition of balance conceptually departs from the typical formal definitions used by Heider (1946, 1958), Cartwright and Harary (1956), and Harary et al. (1965). Phillips' definition differs in at

least two respects. First, by Phillips' procedure, the graph in Figure 1C is characterized by a *higher degree of balance* than the graph in Figure 1A. But by
the typical procedure, both graphs are completely balanced according to the
decomposition theorem, and $b(G) = 1.00$. *It is important to note that Indices
1, 2, 3, and 4 all give the degree of balance of both graphs as perfect* (1.00 in
the case of Indices 1, 2 and 3; zero (no changes required) in the case of
Index 4).[2] Second, the graph in Figure 2 below would be considered quite highly
balanced by Phillips' procedure (note the strong *ABC* cluster), but unbalanced
by the decomposition theorem, which tells us that a graph is completely balanced
if it is decomposed into *two* positive subsets or clusters (there are three positive
subsets or clusters in the graph in Figure 2). Phillips' procedure, which determines the number of clusters and the strength (eigenvalue) of the largest cluster
in a matrix (and its graph), is very similar to the logic which underlies Harary's
(1959) and Davis' (1967) concept of *clustering,* which will be discussed later
in this chapter.

Phillips tested Index 1, Index 4 and Index 5 (his own index) against
each other. The hypothesis predicted that both Indices 1 and 5 will *increase* over
time (over a number of trials for each subject), and that Index 4 will *decrease*
(the number of changes required to achieve complete balance will decrease over
the trials.) He found that (a) Index 1 reflected no changes at all; (b) Index 4
tended to decrease to a certain extent, as predicted; and (c) the largest change
(increase) was reflected by Phillips' index (Index 5). It was therefore concluded
that this latter index was superior to the other two in describing changes in the
degree of balance of a cognitive structure over time.

Index 3 (Morrissette's $\gamma(G)$) was not computed, and therefore could not
be contrasted with the others. Note that it would have been useful to compute
this index, since on each trial some relations were neutral, and hence vacuous
cycles could appear in the graph for a particular trial. Index 2 was not directly
applicable, since Phillips did not measure the *strengths* of perceived relations
between cognitive elements. Since relations were expressed as $+1$, 0, or -1,
Index 2 would give the same results as Index 1.[3]

---

2. Index 1 (Cartwright-Harary) gives $b(G) = 1.00$ since all cycles are positive
in both graphs. Index 2 (Morrissette) would give the same result, since the strengths of
relations are given as $+1$ or -1. Index 3 (Morrissette's $\gamma(G)$) gives a degree of balance
of 1.00, since all cycles are positive in both graphs, and neither graph contains vacuous
cycles. (This would not be so for the graph in Figure 1E, however.) Index 4 (Rosenberg-
Abelson-Harary), the minimum number of changes required to attain complete balance, is
zero (no changes required).

3. Part of Phillips' study entailed measuring the subject's *evaluation* of the cognitive element—i.e., the subject-to-element relation rather than the element-to-element
relation. Evaluation was expressed in terms of strength. However, his index, λ_1, was computed only for the matrix of relations among elements, not for the matrix where the subject-
to-element relation was a given entry. Hence, the strength of a relation is not a component
of the λ_1 index.

FIGURE 2   AN UNBALANCED STRUCTURE SHOWING A STRONG CLUSTER

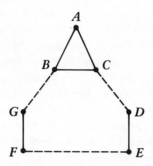

It would appear that Phillips' procedure reflects both the number of "clusters" that are formed over time in the person's cognitive structure, and the strength of the strongest cluster (as indicated by λ_1), and how it changes over time. This does not appear to be a measure of balance, as Phillips maintains, but a measure of extent of clustering. A clustered structure is not necessarily a balanced structure (see Figure 2). *The fact that Index 1 did not change over time but Index 5 increased may only reflect that the cognitive structures were balanced to begin with and remained so, but the degree of clustering increased.* Phillips did not show the mean values of Index 1 for each trial. It was therefore quite possible that Index 1 was high to begin with (indicating a high degree of balance), and this is why it did not increase. This kind of potential danger is called "regression effect," and should always be accounted for or controlled in studies of change. While the degree of balance over trials might have remained high and constant (which is very possible, since according to the Balance Preference hypothesis, the subjects' cognitive structures could have been balanced on the *first* trial), the degree of clustering increased. But one cannot infer from this, as did Phillips, that Index 5 is a better index of "balance." For these reasons, Phillips' inferences on the relative superiority of indices of balance are inconclusive.

It should be pointed out that while Phillips' index is highly imaginative, the formal properties and implications of a factor (eigenvalue) index of balance are not, to be sure, well understood. The idea is very new. Much more empirical work, oriented toward discovering the intricate attributes of such a complex index, is sorely needed. Although exploratory, Phillips' study does provide intriguing leads, and it lays the groundwork for further investigations which utilize factor-indices of degree of balance.

To summarize: Phillips' Index (Index 5) appears to order change data better than Index 4, and Index 4 ordered Phillips' data better than Index 1. The results are to be taken as tentative for the following four reasons: (1) Index 3, which could have been computed, was not; its merits relative to the others was therefore not ascertainable. (2) Phillips' definition of balance departs conceptually from that typically used by graph theoreticians. His index appears to measure degree of *clustering* in a structure rather than degree of balance. Clustering is not the same as balance, as we will see even more clearly in a discussion of clustering in the next section of this chapter. (3) He did not measure the *strengths* of relations between cognitive elements; hence, Index 2 could not have been used in his study. (4) Phillips' study focused upon relations between nonperson (strictly cognitive) elements, and any generalizations one wishes to make from his results to group structures must be tentative ones. In general, until a single study (preferably of interpersonal structures) contrasts all five indices against each other, the superiority of one over the other cannot be definitely established. Such a study has yet to be conducted.

6 • 2   EXTRABALANCE PROPERTIES

6 • 2a   *The Importance of Extrabalance Properties*

It should be quite clear to the reader by this time that the property of balance is only one among many formal properties of cognitive or interpersonal structures. There are others. DeSoto et al. (1968) refer to such properties as *extrabalance properties*. Whether or not a structure is *transitive* is an extrabalance property. For example, if P likes O, O likes Q and P likes Q (all three relations are directed and asymmetric), the structure is transitive. If the relations (arrows) were to mean "is of higher status than," then a structure formed by $P \rightarrow O$ (which means "P is of higher status than O"), $O \rightarrow Q$, and $P \rightarrow Q$ is a transitive structure. If $P \rightarrow O$ (P is higher than O), $O \rightarrow Q$ (O is higher than Q) but $Q \rightarrow P$ (Q is higher than P), then the structure is *intransitive*. (Note that any three-line transitive structure is, strictly speaking, a *semicycle* rather than a cycle.) DeSoto (1960; cf. Mosher, 1967) finds that transitive structures are easier to learn than intransitive structures, suggesting that people have a "preference" for transitive over intransitive structures.

Other extrabalance properties were discussed in Chapter 5 under "Cognitive Biases." Note that certain "cognitive" biases can be translated into formal properties of graph structures. The property of *completeness* has been discussed before. Generally, it is found that complete structures are easier to learn than (are preferred over) incomplete or vacuous structures (DeSoto et al., 1968), but the hypothesis that incomplete structures produce greater tension than complete structures has been questioned by Morrissette (1966). The property of *positivity*, discussed earlier as a cognitive bias, can be defined as an extrabalance structural property (the number or proportion of positive relations in the structure). The evidence, reviewed earlier, strongly suggests that (a) positive relations are easier to learn than negative ones; (b) subjects tend to change negative relations to positive ones, and tend to keep positive relations positive; and (c) the presence of negative relations in a structure tends to produce greater tension than the presence of positive relations. Whether or not the structure consists of *interpersonal* relations alone, or of interpersonal plus attitudinal (or unit) relations, can affect both preference and tendency. Evidence reviewed in Chapter 5 shows that interpersonal relations are easier to learn than attitudinal relations (preference), and that persons are more likely to alter or change interpersonal relations than attitudinal relations (tendency).

The properties of *plausibility* and *differentiability* of a structure are not in the strictest sense "extrabalance" properties, since they presume a balance preference and tendency, and are defined in terms of the balance concept. Plausibility is the maximum attainable degree of balance of an incomplete structure, and differentiability is the number of different ways to attain that maximal balance. Still, however, these two concepts are obviously not *identical* to the concept of balance, and to that degree they complement the general theory. The evidence shows that plausibility and differentiability are both inversely related to tension.

The property of *symmetry (reciprocity)* is sometimes treated in the literature as though it were an extrabalance property, but because by definition a symmetric relation is a balanced 2-cycle, the property of symmetry is a sub-type of the balance concept itself. Likewise, we have taken the position before that the property of *agreement* can be treated as a sub-type of the balance concept. Some investigators (e.g., Newcomb, 1968) have implied that the property of *lateral symmetry* can be regarded as an extra-balance property. But lateral symmetry, in both the *POX* and *POQ* types of unit, is the same as agreement. Lateral symmetry involves comparing the sign of *PX* to the sign of *PO*, or the sign of *PX* to the sign of *OX*, or the sign of *PO* to the sign of *OX*. With three relations, there are three possible comparisons involving lateral symmetry. If the two relations in the paired comparison are like-signed, there is lateral symmetry. If the two signs are unlike, there is lateral asymmetry. Evidence reviewed in Chapter 5 shows that agreement (lateral symmetry involving the *PX* and *OX* relations in the *POX* structure, and the *PQ* and *OQ* relations in the *POQ* structure) definitely affects tension. There is some evidence, though less convincing, that the number of laterally symmetric pairs of relations in a structure affects preference (learning) and change. In sum, to the extent that agreement and lateral symmetry can explain one's results *in addition to* the balance concept, then agreement and lateral symmetry are, *empirically* speaking, "extrabalance" properties. *Formally* speaking, they are not.

One should not confuse, at least conceptually, the distinction between a formal property of a structure, on the one hand, and a "cognitive bias," on the other. The distinction, however, seems academic. Of the seven types of cognitive bias discussed in Chapter 5, the following six can also be translated into formal properties of structures: positivity, interpersonal versus attitudinal relations, completeness, symmetry (reciprocity), agreement and lateral symmetry, and least cost. (We note the further stipulation that the last three, although they can be translated into formal structural properties, are not *extra*balance properties. Symmetry, agreement and lateral symmetry are sub-types of balance; likewise, least cost can be translated into a *balance* property—recall our treatment of Index 4 above.) The remaining bias, the bias against "extremity" of communication, cannot be thought of as a formal structural property, but only as a strict cognitive bias.

By way of summary, one might ask, what is the importance of considering extrabalance properties in the theory of balance? The "role" of extrabalance properties in the theory can be summarized succinctly. (1) Empirical investigations which employ one or more extrabalance properties can use such properties to account for findings that are not accounted for by the property of balance To the degree that *both* balance and extrabalance properties explain one's findings, extrabalance properties *complement* the explanatory power of the balance property. (2) The current "state of affairs" in the literature suggests that certain properties other than balance can potentially account for findings *instead of* having the balance concept account for the findings. Thus, there is the danger that certain extrabalance concepts may eventually replace the balance concept altogether; that other concepts besides balance will become the ones in vogue in social psychology, and will explain all that balance can explain, and more. As will be seen in the next section, the extrabalance concept of *clustering* has the potential for replacing the balance concept as an explanatory one in the social psychology of small groups and cognitive structures. Findings reviewed earlier by Zajonc and Sherman (1967), who found no effects at all of balance but only effects of positivity and *PO* reciprocity, constitute another case-in-point.

6 • 2b   *Clustering*

Perhaps the most intriguing of all extrabalance properties of structures is that of *clustering,* introduced in formal graph-theoretic terms by Harary (1959) and developed by Davis (1967). Davis' formulation is intended to apply to interpersonal structures, although its applicability to cognitive structures will become quite apparent in the course of the discussion to follow.

Davis (1967) notes the well established fact that groups often tend to polarize or split into "cliques" or clusters, or into one or more cliques and one or more "isolates." A *cluster* is defined as a subset of two or more points connected by positive lines, and only negative lines, or the absence of a line, may appear between clusters. Absent lines may also appear within a cluster. A single point having only negative lines (or absent lines) to or from it is also defined as a cluster. By the decomposition theorem, a structure which is partitioned into *two* clusters is balanced. The relations represented are hypothesized to be stable, not likely to change. But what if an interpersonal structure contains three or more distinct clusters? Davis hypothesizes that if the structure is *completely clustered* (only positive lines within clusters, only negative (or absent) lines between clusters), it is stable and therefore not likely to change. But since some completely clustered structures are not balanced (visualize the simple structure consisting of three points connected by three negative lines), the implication is that *a structure can be unbalanced, yet stable.*

It can be easily seen that a structure which is partitioned into three or more clusters *can* be unbalanced. The simple case of three points connected only by negative lines illustrates this—it is completely clustered but unbalanced. As another example, note the graph in Figure 3. Three clusters are evident; only positive lines appear within a particular cluster, and only negative (or absent) lines appear between clusters. By the decomposition theorem, the graph is unbalanced. This can be verified by noting that some of the cycles in the total structure are unbalanced, since they contain an odd number of negative lines: the *ACGHEA* cycle and the *ABDFHGCA* cycle, for example. However, a graph partitioned into three or more clusters is *not necessarily* unbalanced. A graph can contain four clusters and still be balanced, even though the decomposition theorem would be of no assistance in telling us that it is balanced. For example, visualize a graph of four clusters containing the following relations: $+AB$, $-BC$, $+CD$, $-DE$, $+EF$, $-FG$, $+GH$, $-HA$. This single cycle contains an even number of negative lines (four) and is therefore balanced.

FIGURE 3   A PERFECTLY CLUSTERED BUT UNBALANCED STRUCTURE

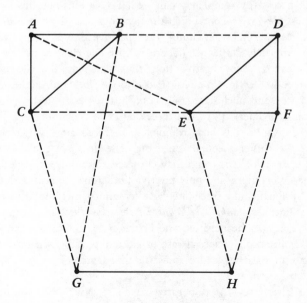

Davis notes that *a graph is completely clustered if none of its cycles contains exactly one negative line.* This may be referred to as the *cluster theorem* (Davis, 1967, p. 181). This theorem provides us with a kind of "shortcut" in determining whether or not a graph is completely clustered. Having no cycles containing exactly one negative line is both a *necessary and sufficient* condition for complete clustering. If a graph is in fact completely clustered, then it will have no cycles containing exactly one negative line. Hence, if there are no cycles containing one negative line, then it follows that either (a) all points in the entire graph are joined by positive lines (in which case there is only one cluster); or (b) each subset of points contains only positive lines, with only negative (or absent) lines appearing between subsets (a single point can be a "subset"). In both of these cases, the graph is completely clustered.

It is interesting to note that the decomposition theorem is a special case of the cluster theorem. A graph containing two perfect clusters is both balanced and completely clustered; clearly, a graph containing two clusters cannot have any cycles containing exactly one negative line. A graph with three or more perfect clusters may or may not be balanced, but it is nevertheless completely clustered.

Since a graph with three or more clusters can be completely clustered but not balanced (decomposed into two clusters), it follows that the decomposition theorem is a special case of the cluster theorem, and not vice versa.

It can be demonstrated that complete balance of *any* type is a special case of complete clustering. Namely, any graph which is completely balanced is also necessarily completely clustered. In addition, a graph which is completely clustered is not necessarily completely balanced. Let us illustrate this by examining the four possible cycles containing three points and three nondirected lines. (1) Any three-line cycle containing three positive line is both completely balanced and completely clustered. (There is only one cluster, and the cycle does not contain exactly one negative line, thus satisfying the cluster theorem.) (2) Any three-line cycle containing two positive lines and one negative line is both unbalanced and unclustered. (It is unclustered because the cycle *does* contain one negative line.) (3) Any three-line cycle containing one positive line and two negative lines is both completely balanced and completely clustered. (It satisfies the cluster theorem, since the cycle does not contain one negative line—it contains two. It is completely clustered since only negative lines appear between the two clusters, and only positive lines (one) appear within the single cluster.) (4) Finally, any three-line cycle containing three negative lines (hence no positive lines) *is unbalanced but completely clustered.* (Each point is a cluster; there is not one negative line in the cycle, but three.) This latter case shows us that balance is a special case of clustering, rather than clustering being a special case of balance. It also shows us that a graph can be completely clustered but unbalanced.

This latter case—the all-negative triadic structure—was also regarded as a peculiarity by Heider. He noted that this type of structure was "not as unbalanced (unstable) as" the other types. The Davis hypothesis that completely clustered structures are stable fits in with Heider's suspicion. Hence, according to the clustering formulation, it is possible for a triadic structure to be unbalanced, yet stable (if it is clustered).

In general, the following statement is true for structures of any size containing any number of cycles of varying lengths: *All completely balanced structures are necessarily completely clustered, but all completely clustered structures are not necessarily completely balanced.* Hence, the concept of balance is a subtype of the concept of clustering. The fact that all completely balanced structures are necessarily completely clustered can be proved by noting that a graph with an even number of lines in all of its cycles cannot have any cycle containing exactly one negative line. (Remember that one way to tell whether or not a graph is completely balanced is to note whether or not all of its cycles contain an even number of negative lines.) The fact that a completely clustered structure is not necessarily balanced was illustrated in Figure 3 and also in the case of the all-negative triad. The statement that all completely clustered structures are not necessarily balanced is proved by noting that a single cycle containing, say, three negative lines *can* be clustered, but it cannot possibly be balanced.

This latter insight is an important one for the general theory of balance. Since it is true that all structures which are completely balanced are necessarily completely clustered, but that all completely clustered structures are not completely balanced, then the formal concept of clustering is more general—it is broader in scope—than the formal concept of balance. In this sense it is an "extrabalance" property. The immediate implication is that a *greater range* of empirical phenomena can be explained by the concept of clustering than by the concept of balance. Specifically, *that which is explainable by the concept of balance is also explainable by the concept of clustering, and the concept of clustering explains more than the concept of balance.* This was implied above, when it was noted that clique formation can be explained by the concept of clustering but not always by the concept of balance. Some complications arise, however, if one realizes that a *coalition process* is often operative (cf. Gamson, 1964). Three antagonistic cliques (representing a perfect clustering) can segregate into a pair and an isolate—a structure which is both balanced (decomposed) and clustered. But if a three-clique split does not tend to remain as such, then three-clique structures (which are clustered) are unstable, hence violating the hypothesis that clustered structures are basically stable, but supporting a decomposition (balance) hypothesis.

The clustering hypothesis has received some empirical support, despite its relative newness. A re-analysis of Newcomb's (1961) sociometric data (cited in Abelson, 1967) showed a marked increase in the *degree* of clustering over a period of three months ("Coefficient A," defined below, was used as the index of degree of clustering). Likewise, Phillips' (1967) index, discussed in the foregoing section, ostensibly an index of clustering rather than of balance, predicted changes over time in cognitive structures better than indices of balance (Indices 1 and 4).

As pointed out earlier, Phillips' results can be interpreted as showing increases in clustering but no changes in balance, suggesting support of a clustering hypothesis over a balance hypothesis. DeSoto et al. (1968) find that clustered structures representing interpersonal networks are easier to learn than unclustered structures. Davis and Leinhardt's (1967) massive re-analysis of sociometric data on 60 groups taken from a pool of 427 groups studied by 162 investigators provides some evidence in favor of clustering, although the investigation was not directly oriented toward testing the clustering hypothesis. Finally, Davis (1968) notes the near-universal tendency for sub-groups to form on the basis of common socio-economic and demographic characteristics such as age, class, race, religion, proximity, etc. That such subgroups number three or more favors a clustering hypothesis rather than a balance (decomposition) hypothesis, if the focus is on "large" groups rather than small ones.

The insight that all balanced structures are clustered but that all clustered structures are not necessarily balanced has additional implications not mentioned above. The concept of clustering is defined so that it can explain all that the formal concept of balance can explain, and more. *No other extrabalance property can make this claim.* Some extrabalance concepts focus upon properties of structure other than (*but not including*) balance: transitivity, completeness, positivity, and type of relation. Other *non*-extrabalance concepts complement but cannot replace the balance concept, since they *presume* either a preference for or a tendency toward balance: least cost, plausibility, and differentiability. (Symmetry (reciprocity), agreement and lateral symmetry can be treated as deducible from the balance concept itself, and are thus sub-types of the balance concept.) Davis' formal definition of clustering dictates that balance is a sub-type of clustering. Whereas the other extrabalance properties, cognitive biases, etc., can *collectively* challenge the explanatory power of the balance concept, clustering can do it "singlehandedly." That certain cognitive and group processes are reducible to a balance explanation is itself a mildly encouraging realization; but that even more (certainly not all) group processes are reducible to a clustering explanation is an exciting insight, indeed.

6 • 2c Indices of Clustering

Just as the formal graph-theoretic concept of complete balance was introduced in the third chapter prior to an examination of indices of *degree* of balance, so at this time we may introduce the idea of *degree* of clustering. To say that a structure "is clustered" only if it is *completely* clustered places an extreme limitation on empirical studies of clustering. Consequently, one or more indices of degree of clustering seem desirable.

Davis notes that for a structure of any size, the degree of clustering can be reflected by examining only three-line cycles (triadic structures) in the total structure. In the clustering formulation, absent lines can appear either within or between clusters. Hence, in an index of clustering, absent lines are ignored. If each line is nondirected (hence symmetric), then only four triadic configurations are possible: those containing three, two, one or no positive lines. Each configuration is represented by the expressions N_3, N_2, N_1, and N_0, respectively. The cluster theorem requires that for any triad in the structure, $N_2 = 0$; namely, there can be no three-line cycles with two positive (hence one negative) lines. The degree of clustering, Davis' "Coefficient A," can then be expressed in terms of the presence of N_2 type triads in the total structure (cited in Abelson, 1967):

$$\text{Coefficient } A = \frac{3N_1N_3 - N_2^2}{3N_1N_3 + N_2^2}$$

$A = 1$ if the structure is completely clustered; $A = 0$ if it has no clustering, and A will be negative if there is any amount of "anticlustering" in the structure. The following structure is completely clustered:

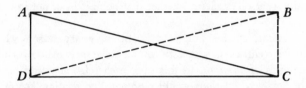

To compute Coefficient A, record the number of N_3 type triads (one), the number of N_2 type triads (none), and the number of N_1 type triads (three). Hence,

$$\text{Coefficient } A = \frac{3 \cdot 3 \cdot 1 - 0}{3 \cdot 3 \cdot 1 + 0} = \frac{9}{9} = +1,$$

indicating complete clustering.

"Anticlustering" is illustrated in the following structure:

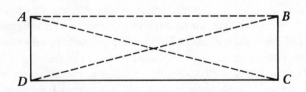

The value of $N_3 = 0$; $N_2 = 2$; and $N_1 = 2$. Thus:

$$\text{Coefficient } A = \frac{3 \cdot 2 \cdot 0 - 2^2}{3 \cdot 2 \cdot 0 + 2^2} = \frac{-4}{+4} = -1,$$

illustrating complete anticlustering.

If it is cumbersome to count and examine all three-line cycles in a large structure containing many points and many relations, then Coefficient A can be computed on a random sample of three-line cycles drawn from the total structure. If this is done, then the degree of clustering in the total structure will be inferred probabilistically.

As previously argued, Phillips' (1967) index of "balance" can instead be regarded as reflecting the degree of clustering. The use of factor analysis has important implications for the clustering concept. Relations between persons would become entries in an adjacency matrix. If a factor analysis of the adjacency matrix is undertaken, the following could be ascertained: (a) the number of clusters, as indicated by the number of factors; (b) the "strength" of each cluster, as indicated by the variance explained by a particular factor representing a particular cluster; (c) the *degree of clustering of the total structure,* as indicated by the sum of the variances explained by all factors (if an orthogonal factor solution is used, thus assuming independence between factors); (d) note that if a factor represents a particular cluster, then the factor "loading" for a particular point (person) reflects whether that point is in or not in the particular cluster.

There seems, at this point, to be no *necessary* reason why relations between persons (entries in the cells of an adjacency matrix) could not be expressed in terms of *strength*. In this case, each relation would have a ±1.00 limit; zero or near-zero relations would represent "no relation" (or a relation of zero strength). In this instance, a factor analysis of the matrix and a subsequent factor rotation seems straightforward; it is directly analogous to analyzing a correlation matrix, where the correlation coefficients are analogous to the relations, and each "variable" is analogous to a point (person or cognitive element). Due to the newness of this approach, and due to the lack of a complete understanding of the complex implications of such a procedure, this latter suggestion is highly tentative. Perplexing problems arise when the strengths of relations are considered. For example, whereas a correlation matrix is symmetric ($r_{ij} = r_{ji}$), the possibility of asymmetry in P-to-O and O-to-P relations—if strength is considered—is the rule rather than the exception. Even a relatively small difference (a PO relation of +.93, an OP relation of +.84) requires a matrix that is not symmetric. Furthermore, one would have to experiment with different values in the diagonal of the matrix, different factor solutions (orthogonal versus oblique), different rotational procedures, and different criteria for deciding when to stop extracting factors. Factor indices of either balance or clustering are as yet undeveloped. A number of exploratory studies will be necessary before any confidence can be placed in such indices.

6 • 3   THE PROBLEM OF CYCLE LENGTH AND NON-LOCAL CYCLES

Given a graph representing an interpersonal or cognitive structure containing four or more points, and letting the focal person be represented by one of these points (point *P*), then a *local cycle* is any cycle that passes through point *P*. A *non-local cycle* is any cycle that does not pass through point *P*. Note the following structure:

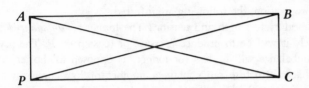

The *ABCA* cycle is a non-local cycle. Three 3-cycles are local (*PABP*, *PACP*, and *PBCP*). The only 4-cycle in the structure is a local cycle. The *length* of a cycle is the number of lines in it. Either a local or a non-local cycle may be characterized by its length.

6 • 3a   *The Effects of Local Cycle Length*

It stands to reason that the longer a local cycle, the less effect it will have on the focal person. It is much easier to perceive and "be aware of" the relations between one's self and only one other, or perhaps two others. But can one adequately perceive even a single cycle that contains four, five, six or more persons (and thus four, five, six or more relations)? It seems reasonable to speculate that the greater the length of a local cycle, the less the effect of its balance or unbalance (its algebraic sign) upon *P*.

There is some limited evidence in support of this speculation. Zajonc and Burnstein (1965b) find that errors made in learning a cycle are a function of cycle length; the longer the cycle, the harder its relations are to learn. This effect was found to be independent of the effects of the balance–unbalance of the cycle. From this we may deduce a "preference" for shorter cycles. Long cycles are outside the perceptual range of persons; they are harder to "absorb" and recall. From these findings, several implication (hypotheses) emerge:

1. Independent effects of local cycle length: Regardless of whether a local cycle is balanced or unbalanced, longer cycles are more difficult to perceive and harder to learn than shorter cycles. *Cycle length affects learning independently of its balance or unbalance.*

2. Local cycle length and preference: The greater the length of a local cycle, the less the effect of its balance or unbalance (its algebraic sign) upon *P*. Specifically, *the longer a local cycle, the less the degree to which P will prefer it to be balanced.*

3. Local cycle length and interdependence: The longer a local cycle, the less likely it is to form an *interdependent structure* of relations in *P*'s own mind.

The ability of P to meaningfully absorb the relations in a long local cycle is less than his ability to absorb the relations of a short local cycle. The longer the cycle, the more *irrelevant* the various relations in it are to one another; hence, the system-like (interdependent) quality of the relations will be less. *The longer a local cycle, the less likely its relations are to form an interdependent structure.* From this proposition, the following are inferred:

4. Local cycle length and tension: The longer an *unbalanced* local cycle, the less likely it will be to produce pressure or tension on P. The psychological impact of unbalance will be less for longer, as opposed to shorter, local cycles. Realizing that a structure can contain a number of local cycles, we can more precisely predict that the longer a given unbalanced local cycle, the less the extent to which P's tension is affected by *that* particular cycle. Generally, *the longer a local cycle, the less the effect of its balance or unbalance (its sign) upon P's tension.*

5. Local cycle length and balance tendency: Since balance tendency (change) is hypothesized to be a function of the tension aroused by unbalance, the next hypothesis follows from number 4 above: *The longer an unbalanced local cycle, the less likely P will be to alter or change one or more of its relations in the direction of balance.*

6. Local cycle length and indices of balance: *Indices of degree of balance should be weighted inversely according to the length of the local cycles contained in the total structure.* A short unbalanced local cycle will have a greater psychological impact upon P and hence less stability than will a long unbalanced local cycle. This suggestion has been made before in discussions of balance (e.g., McGuire, 1966), yet no theorist or researcher, formal or substantive, has yet seen fit to introduce such a weighted index of balance.

7. The most interesting implication arising from considerations of cycle length pertains to the rationale underlying graph-theoretic formalization. One does not necessarily need graph-theoretic formalization in order to describe the properties of small structures containing short local cycles. Formalization is more advantageous for large structures containing many long cycles. But if long cycles are outside of the focal person's scope of awareness, and if they do not affect P's tension, preference or change, then what good is formalization? Realizing this, we might suspect that while graph formalizations are perhaps appropriate for large *interpersonal* structures containing only objective relations (witness the Harary-Davis concept of clustering), they seem less appropriate for describing *cognitive* structures containing only perceived relations or both objective and perceived relations. But yet the mechanisms operative in the interpersonal balancing process are essentially cognitive; formalization would thus appear to have less applicability even to interpersonal structures, if long cycles are considered. In general, the limited empirical evidence suggests that balance dynamics, whether interpersonal or strictly cognitive, are less likely to operate for long local cycles. Therefore, there is less reason to employ graph theory in describing such

cycles in terms of balance properties. Clearly, much additional systematic research is necessary to establish the effects of cycle length. The ultimate value of formalization, to a great degree, seems to rest upon such investigations.

It should be noted that the above hypotheses, particularly numbers 1 through 5, are not stated as conditional propositions, in the manner that such propositions were stated in the previous chapter. This is because the evidence in favor of them is only very mildly suggestive. In keeping with our previously established practice of stating conditional propositions only when the data justify their statement, the above predictions are to be taken as hypotheses for further research.

6 • 3b *Non-Local Cycles*

The above discussion focused on the length of *local* cycles. What can be said about non-local cycles? Can cycles that do not pass through P actually affect P's preference for or tendency to balance these non-local cycles? Can balance or unbalance of non-local cycles affect P's tension? Certainly, one would expect local cycles (of short length) to affect P more than non-local cycles (of the same length).

Although it was not realized at the time, Morrissette's (1958) early study provides evidence in support of this latter statement. In his use of four-object structures which were presented to subjects for tension ratings, Morrissette computed two indices of balance (using Index 2, described in an earlier section above): Degree of *local balance* (considering only local cycles (of whatever length) passing through point P, the position with which the subject was asked to identify), and degree of *total balance* (considering all cycles, both local and non-local). It was found that only the local balance index predicted the subjects' tension ratings of the structures; the total balance index did not. Since the latter index incorporated both local and non-local cycles, whereas the former incorporated only local cycles, the inference is clear: The sign (i.e., the balance–unbalance) of a non-local cycle is less likely to affect P's tension than the sign of a local cycle.

At least one hypothesis follows from this re-interpretation of Morrissette's findings:

1. Local versus non-local cycles and P's tension: *The psychological impact of an unbalanced local cycle is greater than the psychological impact of an unbalanced non-local cycle.* Operationally, this means that the balance–unbalance (sign) of a local cycle is more likely to affect P's tension than the balance–unbalance of a non-local cycle. This would explain why Morrissette found "total" balance unrelated to tension; the total index included non-local cycles.

Additional hypotheses are suggested when one considers the possible range of effects of local versus non-local cycles of a given, or constant, length.

Since there have been no previous empirical investigations on the issue of local versus non-local cycles, nor has there been any prior detailed speculation on the matter, the following propositions can be taken as predictions for future test:

2. Independent effects of local versus non-local cycles: Non-local cycles are more likely to be outside P's scope of awareness than local cycles. Employing the learning framework of Zajonc and associates, one could speculate that *non-local cycles are harder to learn than (will be learned with more errors than) local cycles, regardless of whether the particular cycle is balance or unbalanced.*

3. Local versus non-local cycles and preference: *The focal person is more likely to exhibit a preference for balancing local cycles than he is to exhibit a preference for balancing non-local cycles.* In studies of the "complete this structure" variety, where the subject is asked to fill in the missing relations in the incomplete structure placed before him, this means that subject will tend to complete local cycles, rather than non-local cycles, in a balanced fashion.

4. Local versus non-local cycles and interdependence: *Non-local cycles are less likely to form an interdependent whole in the mind of the focal person than are local cycles.* The relations in a non-local cycle do not form a meaningful cognitive configuration; they will be irrelevant to each other. Thus, non-local cycles are less likely to reveal system-like qualities than are local cycles. From this one may infer that:

5. Local versus non-local cycles and balance tendency: *P will be more likely to alter or change the relations of an unbalanced local cycle toward balance than he will be to alter or change the relations of an unbalanced non-local cycle.* Under the condition that a change in a particular relation will balance *both* one or more local *and* at the same time one or more non-local cycles, then no distinction between local and non-local cycles need be made. But under the condition that balancing one type of cycle will unbalance the other one, then we would predict that P will balance the local cycle. Specifically, if balancing a local cycle would throw one or more non-local cycles out of balance, then P will balance the local cycle at the expense of balancing the non-local cycles. This latter condition, a type of "cross-pressure" situation (Davis, 1963), is illustrated by the following structure:

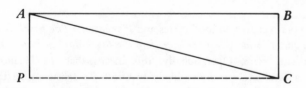

Assume that P can change *only* the AC relation (or his perception of it). If he leaves it as is, the non-local ABCA cycle is balanced, but the local PACP cycle is unbalanced. Changing the $+AC$ relation to (or in the direction of) $-AC$ balances the local three-line cycle, but unbalances the non-local three-line cycle. (Note that the four-line local cycle cannot be balanced by altering the AC relation.) In this respect, the structure constitutes a "cross-pressure" on P—a "damned if you do, damned if you don't" condition. If local cycles are hypothesized to have greater impact than non-local cycles, then one would predict the latter alternative (changing the $+AC$ relation to $-AC$ rather than leaving it positive).

6 • 3c   A Note on the Locality of a Cycle

There is no reason why the distinction between local and non-local cycles needs to be a dichotomy. A cycle can be described in terms of its "nearness" to P. For example, the $ABCA$ cycle in Figure 4A is a non-local cycle, but only one line or relation joins P with the cycle. In contrast, two lines join P with the $ABCA$ cycle in Figure 4B, and three lines join P with the cycle in Figure 4C.

A new concept, the *locality* of a cycle, can be introduced. Remembering that a *path* is one or more lines connecting any pair of points, the locality of a cycle can be defined as *the length of (the number of lines in) the shortest path from P to the nearest point in that cycle*. From this definition follows a *locality index, L*, the number of lines in the shortest path from P to the nearest point in the cycle. Index L describes P's "distance" from the cycle.

In Figure 4A, B and C, $L = 1$, $L = 2$, and $L = 3$, respectively. The meaning of the phrases "nearest point" and "shortest path" become clear upon examination of Figure 4D. There are three points in the $ABCA$ cycle. Each point may be reached by a number of paths from P: (a) Point A can be reached by three paths ($PFEA$; $PDBA$; and $PDBCA$). (b) Point B can be reached by three paths (PDB; $PFEAB$; and $PFEACB$). (c) Point C can be reached by *four* paths ($PDBC$; $PDBAC$; $PFEAC$; and $PFEABC$). The *shortest path* from P to any of the three points is that path containing the fewest number of lines. The shortest path to point A contains three lines ($PFEA$ or $PDBA$). The shortest path to point C contains three lines ($PDBC$). The shortest path to point B contains only *two* lines (PDB). Hence, point B is the "nearest point." Generally, the *nearest point* (to P) contained in a cycle is *that point in the cycle which is reachable by the shortest path*. Hence, the locality of the $ABCA$ cycle in Figure 4D is 2; i.e., $L = 2$.

Note that although the "nearest point" is that point which is reachable by the shortest path, there will generally be paths *other than* the shortest path that go to the nearest point. Hence, locality must be defined on the basis of both the nearest point and the shortest path to it.

Note that if a cycle is a local cycle, $L = 0$. There is no path to the cycle; P is contained in the cycle. If the cycle is a non-local cycle, then $L \geqq 1$. The distance from P to the nearest point in the cycle is given by the value of L. The

FIGURE 4   ILLUSTRATIONS OF CYCLE LOCALITY

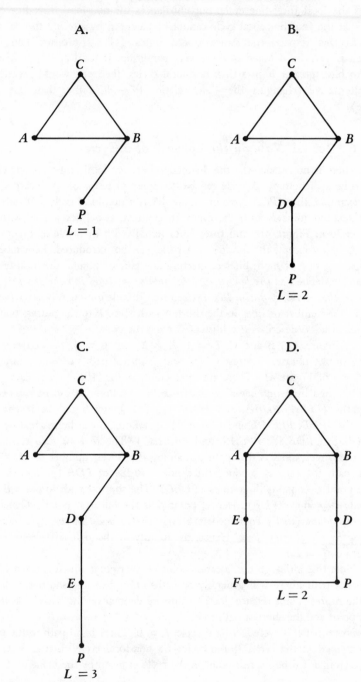

greater the L, the greater the length of the path from P to the nearest point in the cycle, and hence the *less* the locality of the cycle.

The general idea being conceptualized here is that the "farther away" P is from a cycle, the less the effect of the balance or unbalance of that cycle upon P. The concept of locality has intuitive appeal when we realize that one is affected more by the situation of a friend than by the situation of a friend-of-a-friend. Similarly, one is more concerned about and affected by the situation of a friend-of-a-friend than by the situation of a friend-of-a-friend-of-a-friend. We might be quite upset by an unbalanced structure of which we are directly part (a local cycle). We are perhaps less upset by the unbalance among a group of three persons, only one of whom is known to the self. Finally, we are not likely to be at all upset by the unbalance among three persons, one of whom is only remotely known to the self (cf. Figure 4C, where $L = 3$).

The issue to be raised, then, and the implication to be drawn is that the less the locality of a cycle in a total structure (i.e., the *greater* the size of L), the less the effect of the balance–unbalance of that cycle upon P's tension, his preference for balance of that cycle, and upon his tendency to alter or change the relations in the cycle toward balance. Consequently, is it not true that any index of balance of a total structure should be weighted according to the locality of all the cycles in the structure, particularly if one is interested in cognitive structures? If one is focusing upon interpersonal structures, the locality of cycles is of less importance, especially if one is dealing only with objective and not perceived relations. Nonetheless, some kind of correction for locality should at least be entertained. In addition, empirical studies on the effects of locality might prove interesting.

It is interesting to note that the value of L will vary considerably if the total structure is not completely connected, but if the structure is complete (all points are joined by one non-directed line), then L will always be either zero or one, but cannot be greater than one. This can be easily verified by drawing a completely connected graph of any number of points, picking any point as P, and noting that *all* non-local cycles, of whatever length, are joined to P by only one line. Hence, $L = 1$. It follows also that *any* point of any non-local cycle is the nearest point to P. For any local cycle, $L = 0$. This implies the statement of a "locality theorem": *If the structure is completely connected, the locality of any cycle of any length from any point is always one (if it is non-local) or zero (if it is local).*[4]

The substantive inference to be drawn from this theorem is that if a total structure is completely connected, the balance–unbalance of all non-local cycles will affect P equally (considering, of course, only non-local cycles that are of a given *length*). Regardless of what non-local cycle one picks, and regardless of what point is designated as point P, the effect of the cycle's balance–unbalance

---

4. This theorem does not hold if the structure is completely connected but contains two or more pairs of points which are connected by *directed* lines going *toward* P.

upon P's tension, preference and tendency to balance that cycle will be equal for all cycles chosen. If the structure contains a number of missing relations, then L can be greater than one. But if one posits a cognitive bias toward *completeness,* then at such time as the structure becomes completed in P's own mind, the effects of the balance–unbalance of all non-local cycles will be equal!

6 • 3d   Cycle Length and Cycle Locality

A concise summary of this section on cycle length and cycle locality would be the hypothesis that P's preference for or tendency to balance a particular cycle and the relationship between P's tension and the balance–unbalance of the particular cycle are a function of at least two variables: (1) the *length* of the particular cycle, and (2) whether the cycle is local or non-local (the *locality* of the cycle). Hypotheses employing both variables separately were stated above. If one considers both length and locality simultaneously, then clearly the kind of cycle having the greatest effect upon P is expected to be a short local cycle—a single two-line cycle between P and O, for example. A long cycle which is not local will have the minimum effect. But what about the *relative effects* of a short but non-local cycle versus the effects of a long but local cycle? In other words, which variable is more important in its effect upon P—length or locality? The evidence provides no leads. Should balance researchers see fit to systematically examine the effects of cycle length (which has been done only to a very limited extent), and should they see fit to examine the effects of cycle locality (which has not really been done at all), then possible answers regarding relative effects of each might be forthcoming.

6 • 4   A SIX-FOLD CONTROVERSY: PREDICTING THE STRENGTH OF AN UNKNOWN RELATION

Of interest to balance researchers is the matter of predicting the strength of an "unknown" attitudinal or interpersonal relation in a structure. This issue was introduced in the previous chapter in the review of the congruity model and the polarity corollary. The problem is essentially this: Assume that the sign and strength of two relations between three objects are known. For example, say that we know both the strength and the sign of P's liking for O, and the strength and sign of O's attitude toward X (or P's perception of it). P's attitude toward X is the "unknown" relation, the one we wish to empirically predict. The problem is to estimate both the sign *and strength* of that unknown relation. Predicting only the sign according to the Heider (balance), Newcomb (symmetry) and Osgood (congruity) models is not particularly difficult; it is simply the sign which would balance the structure—the product of the given (known) signs.

Predicting the *strength* of the unknown *PX* relation is quite another matter. This is where the controversy lies. No less than six procedures, each representing different theoretical positions, have appeared in the literature.

Before outlining the six procedures utilized, it is critical to point out that the sign and strength of the unknown relation is to be predicted on the basis of other relations *which are in the same cycle as the unknown relation*. Relations in cycles not containing the unknown relation are to be treated as irrelevant. Generally, the unknown relation will be part of a local cycle. Hence, relations in any non-local cycle are not used to predict the unknown relation. Furthermore, *local* cycles which do not contain the unknown relation are not used in predicting the strength of the unknown relation.

Examine the structure in Figure 5. The symbol R_o represents the unknown relation (in this case, P's attitude toward X), the strength of which we wish to predict. The relations R_1, R_2, R_3 and R_4 represent relations of which both the sign and strength are known. To predict the strength of R_o, only relations in cycles containing R_o are used. Hence, the cycle containing R_1, R_3 and R_4 is assumed to be irrelevant, even though it is a local cycle. The cycle containing R_o, R_1 and R_2, and the cycle containing R_o, R_2, and R_3 and R_4, are the cycles used in

FIGURE 5   A STRUCTURE CONTAINING ONE UNKNOWN RELATION, R_0

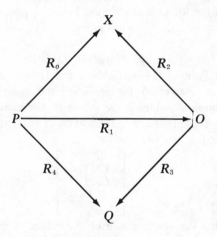

R_o = an unknown relation
R_1, R_2, R_3 and R_4 = relations for which both the sign
and strength are known

predicting the strength of R_o. Both cycles are local, and both contain the relation R_o.

For the sake of clarity of discussion, and to avoid the problem of cycle length, assume that we wish to predict the strength of R_o on the basis of the sign and strength of only R_1 and R_2. The expression K will be used to represent the number of *known* relations. In this case, since there are only two known relations, $K = 2$. Generally,

R_o = the predicted sign and strength of any *unknown* relation;

R_i = the sign and strength of any *known* (given) relation which is in the same local cycle as R_o; and

K = the number of known relation in the local cycle containing R_o.

To exemplify: Referring to Figure 5, let $R_1 = +1$ and let $R_2 = +3$. This means that both relations are positive, and the former has a strength of 1, the latter, of 3. The *sign* of R_o is expected to be positive. To predict the *strength,* one can use any number of procedures, one of which involves getting the average of R_1 and R_2; namely, $R_o = \Sigma R_i/K = (R_1 + R_2)/K = (+1) + (+3)/2 = 2$. Or, we may wish to get only the sum: $R_o = \Sigma R_i = R_1 + R_2 = (+1) + (+3) = 4$.

A description of six different procedures for getting R_o follows. For empirical studies employing one or more of these procedures, or some procedure analogous to one of the following six, the idea is to predict the value of R_o and then compare this *expected value* of R_o to *empirically obtained* values using actual subjects. Along with each description below, a note on the substantive theoretical assumptions underlying each is given.

1. *The Averaging (Osgood) Procedure.* According to Fishbein and associates (Triandis and Fishbein, 1963; Fishbein and Hunter, 1964), the Osgood formula (reviewed in Chapter 5) for predicting the strength of an unknown relation in a cycle implies averaging the values of the known relations in the cycle. The following formula is a direct extention of that used by Fishbein and Hunter (1964, p. 506):

$$(1) \qquad R_o = f\left[\frac{\displaystyle\sum_{i=1}^{K} |R_i|}{K}\right],$$

which demands taking the absolute sum of the values of the known relations (R_i's) and dividing by the number of relations (K). The symbol f is intended to mean "some function of," since R_o can conceivably be either a linear or non-linear function of the average. The absolute (rather than the algebraic) value of each R_i is taken, since the sign of R_o is expected to be the product of the signs of each R_i.

2. *The Summation (Fishbein) Procedure.* As discussed earlier, Fishbein and associates present evidence showing that the empirically obtained strength of

R_o more closely approximates the sum, rather than the average, of the strengths of the known relations. Furthermore, the values of different R_o's tend to approximate a linear function of the summation of each R_i in a particular structure. The results were interpreted as placing more weight on a "theory" of summation rather than on Osgood's model of congruity.[5] The substantive implication is that cognitive inconsistency is more a result of psychologically summing rather than averaging inconsistent cognitions; the impact of inconsistency upon the focal person is hypothesized to be so severe as to suggest a summation procedure. Less of an impact of inconsistency is reflected by an averaging procedure. The summation procedure is defined (by Fishbein and Hunter, 1964) as follows:

$$(2) \qquad R_o = f\left[\sum_{i=1}^{K} |R_i| \right],$$

stating that the expected strength of R_o is the sum of the absolute strengths of each R_i.

3. *The Discrepancy (Newcomb) Procedure.* One of Newcomb's basic hypotheses is that attraction between P and O will vary according to the degree of *discrepancy* between the PX and perceived OX relations. Discrepancy is a difference that is expressed in terms of strength, and is not to be confused with "agreement," which is a matter of similarity-dissimilarity in the *signs* of the PX and perceived OX relations. The inference from Newcomb (1953; 1959; 1961), according to Price et al. (1965) and Feather (1966; 1967) is that any R_o may be predicted on the basis of the discrepancy between two known relations (R_i's) in a structure. Taking the interpersonal PO relation as R_o, then discrepancy is defined precisely as follows: It is the *algebraic* (not absolute) difference between the PX and perceived OX relations. To understand how the discrepancy procedure works, assume that the PX and OX relations are of the *same* sign. In this case, the PO relation is expected to be *positive,* but its strength will *decrease* as the difference (discrepancy) between the PX and OX relations *increases* (i.e., it will approach zero; it will become "less positive"). However, if the PX and OX relations are of *opposite* sign, then PO is expected to be *negative,* but the *strength of PO will increase as the difference between the PX and OX relations increases* (it will move away from zero; it will become *"more negative"*). This is why the algebraic rather than the absolute difference between the PX and OX relations is taken. Note, however, that the sign of PO is still expected to be the product of the PX and OX signs. This interpretation is a straightforward inter-

5. The investigators (Triandis and Fishbein, 1963; Fishbein and Hunter, 1964) hold that their results question the applicability of *balance* theory. They err, however, in attributing the averaging procedure to "balance" theory per se. The balance (Heider) model predicts only the sign of R_o. The *congruity* (Osgood) model implies an averaging procedure to predict the strength of R_o. The investigators found that a summation procedure predicts R_o better than an averaging procedure. Hence, it is the congruity model, not the balance model, that is questioned by their data.

pretation of Newcomb, and agrees with the interpretation given in Feather (1967a, p. 107).

It is important to note that the averaging (Osgood) and summation (Fishbein) procedures, on the one hand, and the discrepancy (Newcomb) procedure, on the other hand, give differing predictions. Taking the PX and OX relations as known and the PO relation an unknown, as the average of the absolute strengths of PX and OX increases, the predicted strength of the PO relation will increase. Similarly, as the sum of the absolute strengths of PX and OX increases, the predicted strength of the PO relation will increase. *The discrepancy procedure predicts the opposite, if PX and OX are of the same sign:* As the PX/OX discrepancy increases, the strength of PO is expected to *decrease*.

We are assuming that the strength of the interpersonal PO relation is being predicted on the basis of the strengths of the attitudinal PX and OX relations. However, one might wish to predict PX on the basis of the strengths of PO and OX, or predict OX on the basis of the strengths of PO and PX. Thus, R_o can be treated as either the interpersonal PO or the attitudinal PX and OX relations.

The simplest way of expressing R_o as a function of the discrepancy between R_1 and R_2 is as follows:

$$(3) \qquad R_o = f(R_1 - R_2),$$

keeping in mind that R_o is an *inverse* function of the algebraic difference between R_1 and R_2 if both R_1 and R_2 are of the same sign. If R_1 and R_2 are of opposite sign, then R_o is a *direct* function of the algebraic difference between R_1 and R_2.

A formula for calculating "perceived discrepancy" has been suggested by Rapoport (cited in Price et al., 1965, p. 98) :[6]

$$(4) \qquad R_o = |R_1 - R_2| - \tfrac{1}{2}\left[1 - \left(\frac{R_1 R_2}{|R_1 R_2|}\right)\right]$$

If there are more than two known relations in the cycle containing R_o (if $K \geqq 3$), then expressing R_o as a function of discrepancy is complex. Since no procedures employing the discrepancy approach have yet been presented in the literature, some suggestions might be tentatively offered.

a. The algebraic difference for all *pairs* of relations can be obtained. If K is the number of known relations, then there will be $K(K-1)/2$ pairs of known relations. The resulting pair-differences could then be summed, treating all differences as though they were positive, thus giving an extension of formula 3 above:

$$(5) \qquad R_o = f \Sigma (R_i - R_j),$$

where

$R_i - R_j =$ the algebraic difference for a given pair of known relations.

---

6. The formula given in Price et al. (1965, p. 98) uses the symbol j in place of our R_1, and the symbol k in place of our R_2. Otherwise, the formulas are identical.

b. A second possibility would be to square each pair-difference, and sum the squares:

(6) $$R_o = f \, \Sigma (R_i - R_j)^2$$

c. Both formulas 5 and 6 could be divided by the number of pairs, $K(K-1)/2$, thus expressing R_o as a function of the average of the pair-differences:

(7) $$R_o = f \left[\frac{\Sigma (R_i - R_j)}{K(K-1)/2} \right] \, ;$$

(8) $$R_o = f \left[\frac{\Sigma (R_i - R_j)^2}{K(K-1)/2} \right]$$

d. Instead of focusing upon the pair-differences, R_o could be expressed as a function of the variance among the R_i's:

(9) $$R_o = f \left[\frac{\Sigma (R_i - \overline{R})^2}{K} \right]$$

where

$\overline{R}$ = the mean of the strengths of each known relation.

In each case, the sign of R_o becomes the sign of the product of the R_i's. If all R_i's are of the same sign (all positive or negative), then R_o is expected to decrease as either the pair-differences or the variance among the R_i's increases. This seems to represent a straightforward interpretation of the discrepancy procedure. However, if the R_i's are of differing signs (some positive and some negative), the interpretation is not simple. Formulas 5 through 8, or any analogous formulas, are at best only suggestive, and await further consideration.

4. *The Multiplication (Morrissette) Procedure.* An extension of the Cartwright-Harary (1956), Harary et al. (1965) and particularly the Morrissette (1958) definitions of balance would be to estimate R_o on the basis of the products of the strengths of each R_i. In order to be in balance with the R_i's in a cycle, both the sign and the strength of R_o is given by:

(10) $$R_o = f(R_1 \cdot R_2 \cdot \ldots \cdot R_K).$$

Note that the algebraic value of each R_i is used; hence, both the sign and the expected strength of R_o is given by this formula. The substantive assumption underlying this procedure is that the impact of inconsistency is far more severe than would be implied in an averaging, summation or discrepancy procedure. Psychologically multiplying the strengths of inconsistent cognitive relations would clearly imply a greater impact than would the other three procedures. To say that R_o is a multiplicative function of the R_i's suggests that the focal person "goes to extremes" in attempting to resolve inconsistencies among relations.

5. *Procedures Based on the Strength of an Interpersonal Relation in the Cycle (Feather).* Results presented by Feather (1966; 1967a; 1967b) suggest that if a cycle contains at least one known interpersonal (*PO*) relation, the strength of R_o—whether it is attitudinal or interpersonal—can be predicted on

the basis of the strength of the known interpersonal relation. For example, if the PO and perceived OX relations are known, the strength of the PX attitudinal relation is hypothesized to be a function of the strength of the PO relation. (The sign of PX is still expected to be the product of the signs of PO and OX.) The assumption underlying this procedure involves the "interpersonal" cognitive bias: It has been demonstrated that interpersonal relations tend to be used as "anchors," "cues" or "mnemonic devices" when P makes a judgment about some property of a structure (cf. Zajonc and Burnstein, 1965b, discussed in the previous chapter). Hence,

$$(11) \qquad R_o = f \mid R_{int} \mid$$

where

R_{int} = the strength of a known interpersonal relation in the cycle containing R_o.

6. *Procedures Based on the Strength of the Maximum Relation in a Cycle (Cartwright)*. Cartwright (cited in Morrissette and Jahnke, 1967, p. 195) has suggested that the impact of unbalance can be gauged on the basis of the strongest relation in a structure. The source of the tension aroused by inconsistency or unbalance is assumed to be the relation of maximal strength. This suggests that in order to minimize this impact, P will form the R_o relation on the basis of the R_i of greatest strength, rather than on the basis of other R_i's. Hence,

$$(12) \qquad R_o = f \mid R_{max} \mid$$

where

R_{max} = the strength of the strongest known relation in the cycle containing R_o.

After having reviewed the six procedures[7] for estimating the empirical

7. Phillips (1967) suggests a seventh procedure for predicting the strength of R_0 if $K \geqq 3$. In his study, subjects were asked to give their perceptions of the *signs* (not the strengths) of the relations between cognitive elements. The subject's *evaluation* of each element, E'_B, was then predicted on the basis of the eigenvalues describing the adjacency matrix of relations between elements. The subject's evaluation of an element (E'_B) was measured in terms of strength. (See pp. 192–198 for a description of Phillips' study).

The cognitive configurations examined by Phillips might be represented graphically as follows:

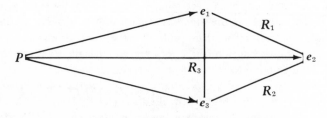

R_1, R_2 and R_3 are the "known" or "given" relations—the subject's (P's) perceptions of

value of R_o, our next question is simply: Which procedure generally best predicts empirically obtained values of R_o? Do certain procedures tend to work better than others? As previously discussed, Fishbein's results (Triandis and Fishbein, 1963; Fishbein and Hunter, 1964) favor a summation procedure (using formula 2) over an averaging procedure (using formula 1). The results of Byrne, Clore and Griffitt (1967), predicting the strength of the PO relation on the basis of the PX and perceived OX discrepancy, and using a procedure analogous (though not identical) to that given in formula 3, support a discrepancy procedure: Across several samples, the inverse correlation between discrepancy and attraction ranged from $-.23$ to $-.55$. Price et al. (1965) indirectly advocate a discrepancy procedure using formula 4. They first ranked structures according to an index which incorporated formula 4, and found that this rank-ordering correlated ($P < .01$) with "affect" (tension) ratings at the structures. Although the multiplication procedure is implied by Morrissette (1958), this procedure has not been directly applied to the problem of predicting the strength of R_o. The "maximum relation" procedure has been only suggested, but not yet tested—directly or indirectly. Finally, the interpersonal-relation procedure, researched most completely by Feather, has received considerable support. Furthermore, Feather's studies have contrasted four procedures against each other: averaging, summation, discrepancy, and interpersonal-relation. A description of Feather's research follows.

Feather's initial model (Feather, 1964) and study (Feather, 1965) of "communication effects" considered only the sign of the relations between four objects. The objects were: A source (S) of some bit of communication (C) about an issue (I); a second person (R) is the recipient of the communication. In general, Feather finds that balance forces operate quite strongly in determining the *sign* of the recipient's (R's) rating of the attraction of the source (S). More recent studies by Feather have evaluated the effects of the strengths of known

---

the relations among the elements, e_1, e_2 and e_3. Each directed line from P to e_i represents the *strength* of P's evaluation of element e_i. Phillips' formula for predicting this evaluation is:

$$E'_B = kR* E'_B$$

where

$E'_B =$ the transpose of the predicted (balanced) evaluation vector;
$R* =$ the adjacency matrix of relations between elements (expressed in terms of sign only—as positive, negative, or null); and
$k =$ the inverse of the eigenvalue corresponding to the dominant (largest) eigenvector of $R*$.

Phillips' formula was not discussed in the current section for three reasons. First, only the sign, and not the strength, of each R_i was measured, although R_o (the subject's evaluation of the element, e_i) was predicted in terms of strength. Second, his eigenvalue index, λ_1, is ostensibly an index of clustering, not of balance. Third, although factor (eigenvalue) indices could conceivably be used to describe the adjacency matrix ($R*$) even if the strengths of the relations among elements were known, the implications of such a procedure are exceedingly complex and for the most part not well understood.

relations upon the subject's judgment of a missing (unknown) relation (Feather, 1966; Feather, 1967a; Feather, 1967b). In these studies, abstract structures containing four objects (S, R, C and I) were presented to subjects. Some relations were given (the known relations, R_i), whereas others were omitted (the unknown relation, R_o). The subject was asked to give his own estimate of what he would want R_o to be.

A limitation of Feather's studies is that strength is measured only in terms of "strong" versus "weak." For this reason, it is difficult to express strength quantitatively. Thus, precise application of any of the six procedures is not possible. Nevertheless, his results tend to clarify a comparison between four procedures (averaging, summation, discrepancy and interpersonal-relation). The relevant conclusions to Feather's studies are:

1. Relations which are not in the cycle containing R_o are irrelevant for predicting the strength of R_o. This is true even if the cycle containing known R_i's is a local cycle.

2. A dominant influence is exerted by the strengths of interpersonal relations in the structures. An interpersonal relation tends to influence the strength of an attitudinal relation to a greater degree than an attitudinal relation influences the strength of another attitudinal or interpersonal relation. This confirms results obtained by students of cognitive bias, who suggest that interpersonal rather than attitudinal relations in a structure furnish the focal person with cues or anchors which are then used in making further perceptions and judgments about the structure.

3. Generally, the discrepancy procedure tends to work better than the summation procedure and the summation procedure tends to work better than the averaging procedure. Hence, the Newcomb (discrepancy) model is given somewhat more support than the Fishbein (summation) model, which in turn is given greater support than the Osgood (averaging) model. Remember, however, that strength was measured by Feather only in terms of "strong" versus "weak," whereas studies by Price et al. (1965), who focused upon the Newcomb model, and by Fishbein and associates and by Osgood and associates, all used quantitative measures of strength. We note in passing that these results are consistent with those of Fishbein, who contrasted the summation and averaging procedures, and found the summation procedure superior. But since Fishbein and associates did not employ a discrepancy procedure, one cannot say that the discrepancy procedure works better than the other two *if quantitative measures of strength* are used, although one would infer this from Feather's results. All things considered, it appears that both the discrepancy and summation procedures are highly workable, and that the averaging procedure has only limited applicability. Both the Fishbein studies and the Feather studies suggest that the averaging (Osgood) procedure is the least accurate of the three.

What is needed, of course, is a single study which contrasts all six procedures. Feather's research has come closest to this ideal, but quantitative strength and the multiplication and maximum-relation procedures were not considered. Such a study would seem critical, due to the differing theoretical assumptions underlying each procedure. What is needed is a study which would measure strength quantitatively and which would give six different values of R_0 according to the six procedures, and then simply ascertain which most closely approximated the obtained values of R_0. As noted before in this text, a severe limitation of past studies has been the lack of comparability due to greatly differing methodologies. In terms of the issue of predicting the strength of an unknown R_0, the relevant differences are: (a) quantitative versus qualitative measurement of strength of relations; (b) use of only non-person objects in the structure (Fishbein and associates) versus use of both person and non-person objects (Feather); (c) use of an interpersonal-concrete design (Price et al.) versus the use of interpersonal-hypothetical designs (Feather); and (d) differences with respect to the number of objects in the structure (three in the case of Price et al.; four in the case of Feather; from two to five in the case of Fishbein and associates). A single study contrasting the various procedures would have to hold these differences constant.

6 • 5 SUMMARY

It was the purpose of this chapter to review four sets of largely unresolved empirical issues involving graph-theoretic formalization of the theory of balance. The first set of issues concerned various *indices of balance* of a structure or graph. Five indices were described and contrasted. It was noted that one index (Index 5, Phillips' λ_1) appeared to measure *clustering* rather than balance. This led to a discussion of a second set of issues involving *extrabalance properties* of structures, the most intriguing of which was clustering. It was shown that all balanced structures are necessarily clustered, but that all clustered structures are not necessarily balanced. Hence, balance is a sub-type of clustering, which implies that the concept of clustering can explain that which is explainable by balance, and more. It was noted that no other extrabalance property could make this claim. The third set of issues concerned *cycle length* and *non-local cycles*. Limited empirical evidence suggests that (a) the longer a local cycle, the less its effect upon P; and (b) non-local cycles affect P less than local cycles. Several hypotheses on the effect of cycle length and local versus non-local cycles were presented. A new concept, the *locality* (L) of a cycle, was introduced. The locality of a cycle is the length of (the number of lines in) the shortest path from P to the nearest point in that cycle. It was hypothesized that the effect upon P of the balance–unbalance (sign) of a non-local cycle is a function of its locality. Implications concerning complete versus incomplete structures were discussed. The question of the relative effects of cycle length versus cycle locality was raised.

Finally, a controversy involving six procedures for estimating the strength of an unknown relation (R_o) in a structure was reviewed (the procedures involve averaging, summation, discrepancy, multiplication, the strength of an interpersonal relation, and the relation of maximum strength). Generally, the discrepancy (Newcomb), summation (Fishbein) and interpersonal-relation (Feather) procedures seem quite workable, the averaging (Osgood) procedure seems least workable, and the multiplication and maximum-relation procedures remain untested. It was pointed out that studies involved in this controversy are difficult to compare because of differing methodologies. It was advocated that a single study employing a quantitative measure of strength be conducted in order to contrast the six procedures against each other.

7. ● ● ● ● ● ●

Balance, Tension, Tension Release
and Antagonism in the Dyad

This chapter reports the results of a study conducted by the author.[1] Portions of the findings have been reported in previous papers (Taylor, 1966, 1967 and 1968), but this chapter includes additional data and interpretations which do not appear in these papers. The purposes of this chapter, and the contributions it attempts to make, are:

1. To re-define the problem of tension management in relation to balance forces, by focusing upon three types of variables, all treated as dependent: Tension, tension release behavior, and antagonism behavior displayed by the focal person as a member of a *POX* dyad.

2. To provide a test for both the Tension and Tension Reduction hypotheses. Longitudinal measurement of tension is employed, a technique not used in past studies. The Tension Hypothesis predicts that unbalance, at a given time, produces more tension at that time in the focal person than balance. The Tension Reduction hypothesis predicts that this tension can be reduced by molar changes in the direction of increased balance. The Tension hypothesis has been extensively researched in past studies, all reviewed earlier in this book (Jordan, 1953 and 1966b; Burdick and Burnes, 1958; Morrissette, 1958; Morrissette et al., 1966 and 1967; Schrader and Lewit, 1962; Sampson and Insko, 1964; Price et al., 1965 and 1966; and Rodrigues, 1965 and 1967). However, the Tension Reduction hypothesis has not been previously tested.

3. To examine the way in which tension release behavior (joking, laughing, and the like) varies as a function of balance–unbalance. Longitudinal measurement of tension release is employed, and it will be seen that the findings on tension release complement the findings on tension: While tension tends to fall

1. The author wishes to thank J. Zvi Namenwirth, Mark Abrahamson, Theodore Mills and Dorwin Cartwright for assistance and helpful comments offered during various stages of this research.

225

off or decrease as a result of changes toward balance, at the same time tension release tends to increase.

4. To examine the ways in which overt hostility, or antagonism, can be explained by the two parameter variables liking and agreement. A conceptual redefinition of states of balance and unbalance in terms of "counteropposing forces" will be presented, and a revision of the Heider balance model is suggested.

5. To critically evaluate Newcomb's (1968) recent three-category scheme of balance, nonbalance and unbalance. The results of the present study do not provide support for this scheme.

7 • 1   DESIGN AND HYPOTHESES

This investigation involved the study of forty dyads which were composed of one naive subject (P) and one role player (O). The subject and the role player discussed an issue (X) for thirty minutes. The design of the study was therefore *interpersonal-concrete:* P and O were in an actual interaction situation communicating with each other about X.

Four experimental conditions were created: (1) The subject (P) both likes and agrees with the role player (O) at the start of the thirty-minute discussion; (2) the subject dislikes and disagrees with the role player; (3) the subject likes and disagrees with the role player; and (4) the subject dislikes and agrees with the role player. Following Heider, the first two conditions constitute the *balance treatment condition;* the latter two constitute the *unbalance treatment condition.* Both conditions refer to the balance or unbalance that existed at the *start* of the discussion between P and O. Hence, the two conditions represent *initial* balance and *initial* unbalance, respectively. The exact procedures for obtaining the desired experimental induction will be described below.

The first two working hypotheses of the present investigation constitute deductions from the Tension and Tension Reduction hypotheses of balance theory. The Tension hypothesis predicts that unbalance at a given time produces more tension at that time in the focal person than does balance. It therefore follows that subjects who are under conditions of initial unbalance will reveal more tension during the initial portion of the discussion than will subjects who are under conditions of initial balance. Taking treatment condition as the independent variable and initial tension as the dependent variable, the first research hypothesis becomes:

H1   *(Tension): During the* initial portion of the discussion, *the subject's tension under the unbalance treatment condition will be significantly greater than the subject's tension under the balance treatment condition.*

As a result of the high initial tension under conditions of unbalance, molar changes (changes in attitude, liking, etc.) are expected to take place. This, in turn, is expected to produce a decrease or reduction in the focal person's tension. The dependent variable, tension reduction or decrease, can be expressed as a function of either (a) changes made in the direction of balance, or (b) initial balance–unbalance. The present study treats tension reduction as a function of initial balance–unbalance. The question of molar changes occurring in the forty dyads studied is explored in detail elsewhere (Taylor, 1967). Thus, it is being predicted that subjects under conditions of initial unbalance will start high in tension, but this initial tension will decrease rapidly. By contrast, subjects under conditions of initial balance will start low in tension, and there should be no relative decrease in tension.

However, past small-group studies by Bales and associates in areas besides balance have demonstrated quite conclusively that tension *in general* tends to decrease during conversations (Bales, 1953; Borgatta and Bales, 1953; Heinicke and Bales, 1953). For this reason, the second research hypothesis must be stated in terms of *differential rates* of tension decrease. Thus, although the subject's tension under both initially balanced and initially unbalanced conditions is expected to decrease, subjects under the unbalance condition are expected to reveal greater tension initially. As the conversation takes place, the subjects under the unbalance condition will decrease *more rapidly* in their tension than will subjects under the balance condition. The second research hypothesis, taking treatment condition as the independent variable and decrease in the subject's tension as the dependent variable, follows from these predictions:

H2 *(Tension Reduction):* During the course of the discussion, *the magnitude of decrease in the subject's tension under the unbalance treatment condition will be significantly greater than the magnitude of decrease in the subject's tension under the balance treatment condition.*

The present investigation attempts not only to explore how balance–unbalance is related to tension and tension reduction, but also how *tension release* is affected by conditions of balance and unbalance. Tension release is defined generally as any overt, observable behavior of the focal person which reflects relief, satisfaction, cheerfulness, buoyance, or pleasure. Behavior such as joking, sighing, laughing, "being silly" and "kidding around" are intended to indicate tension release (Bales, 1951, p. 179).

Past research in fields outside balance has shown that tension release behavior is extremely low at the outset of group discussions (Bales, 1953; Borgatta and Bales, 1953; Heinicke and Bales, 1953). Tension release is found to be particularly high during the latter portion of the discussion, however. Hence, tension release tends to increase during a conversation. One can therefore expect that subjects under the balance and unbalance conditions will not significantly differ in tension release during the initial portion of the discussion. However, taking into consideration the predictions made in the first two hypotheses, one would expect the rate of increase in tension release to differ between the two treatment conditions. Subjects under conditions of initial unbalance are expected to experience high tension initially, followed by a rapid reduction in this tension. Consequently, a rapid increase in tension release behavior would be expected. *Tension which was high under conditions of initial unbalance will have a chance to "drain off."* Increased tension release will accompany a reduction in tension. By contrast, under conditions of initial balance, tension is expected to be initially low, and decrease at a less rapid rate. It therefore follows that less of a drain off of tension—tension release—will occur during the conversation. The third and fourth research hypotheses, taking initial tension release and tension release increase as the respective dependent variables, become:

H3 *(Tension Release): During the* initial portion of the discussion, *the subject's tension release under the unbalance treatment condition* will not significantly differ *from the subject's tension release under the balance treatment condition.*

H4 *(Tension Release Increase):* During the course of the discussion, *the magnitude of increase in the subject's tension release under the unbalance treatment condition* will be significantly greater than *the magnitude of increase in the subject's tension release under the balance treatment condition.*

To summarize: The independent variable of the study is balance–unbalance at the outset of a conversation between a subject (P) and a role player (O). There are four dependent variables: Initial tension, change in tension, initial tension release, and change in tension release. Under the unbalance treatment condition, the subject's tension is expected to be initially high but decrease at a rapid rate, whereas tension under the balance treatment condition is expected to be initially low and decrease at a less rapid rate (hypotheses H1 and H2). Furthermore, the two treatment conditions are expected to reveal no differences in initial tension release, but the subjects under the unbalance treatment condition are expected to reveal a greater magnitude of *increase* in tension release than subjects under the balance treatment condition (hypotheses H3 and H4). This suggests a "drain-off effect"—that tensions which build up under conditions of initial unbalance tend to decrease, while at the same time tension release behavior, or tension drain-off, tends to increase.

7 • 2   METHOD: PROCEDURES AND INSTRUMENTS

7 • 2a   *Procedures*

The entire study took four months to complete. The first stage of the study consisted of a general survey taken under the guise of a "Survey of Topics of Interest and Association Patterns." The survey was done on a simple random sample of 425 male Sophomore students at Yale University. The purpose of this survey was to determine how the students would rate twenty-seven issues according to (a) degree of importance of the issue, and (b) whether they were for it or against it. Mail-back questionnaires were used to gather this information. Of the 425 questionnaires mailed out, 288 were returned complete, representing a 68 percent rate of return. The list of twenty-seven issues was obtained in part from previous investigations by Newcomb (1961), Osgood et al. (1957) and Byrne (1961). Students were asked to (a) rank all issues according to their importance to themselves, and (b) rate each issue on a seven-point scale, from "strongly in favor of" to "strongly against." Examples of issues are: "Capital punishment," "getting high grades," "premarital sex relations," "admission of women as undergraduates," and "Western movies."

Of all issues rated, the issue of admission versus non-admission of women to Yale University was selected for use in the actual experiment for two reasons. First, the per cent favoring the issue (49 percent) was almost equal to the per cent not favoring the issue (47 percent). Second, the issue was high in mean rank of importance (fourth out of twenty-seven).

Another purpose of the survey was to assess the respondent's degree of liking for two well-known Sophomore students, who were listed by name on the survey schedule. It is important to note that the 288 Sophomores sampled represented potential *subjects* (*P's*) for the experiment; the two well-known Sophomores were potential *role players* (*O's*). Well-known Sophomores were used in order to maximize the number of students who would indicate some degree of like or dislike for the role players. Each student rated each of the role players on a seven point scale, ranging from "like very much" to "dislike very much."

The second stage of the study involved the assignment of potential subjects to one of the two role players. Subjects who indicated like or dislike for either role player were randomly assigned to one of the two role players. Subjects who were neutral toward both role players were eliminated. In addition, the following subjects were eliminated from the study: (a) non-whites; (b) subjects who indicated a neutral response toward the issue of admission of women; (c) subjects whom the role player knew "quite well" or "extremely well;" and (d) subjects with whom the role player had previously discussed the issue.

The third stage of the study involved the random assignment of subjects to either the balance treatment condition or the unbalance treatment condition. Subjects who—on their survey schedule—indicated some degree of *liking* for their pre-assigned role player were randomly assigned to either the *like-agree* (balance) or the *like-disagree* (unbalance) condition. Subjects who indicated some degree of *dislike* for their role player were randomly assigned to the *dislike-disagree* (balance) condition or the *dislike-agree* (unbalance) condition. Through the use of this assignment procedure, two things are accomplished: (a) Randomization across the categories of the independent variable is preserved; and (b) no experimental manipulation of the like-dislike variable needs to be employed.

The fourth stage was the experiment itself. The subject and the role player—posing as another subject—met in a small groups laboratory. They were then told that they were participants in an experiment on communication, and that they would discuss the issue of admission of women to Yale. At this point, a questionnaire containing the instruments (described below) for measuring the following variables was administered: The subject's attitude toward the issue (the PX relation), and the subject's liking for the role player (the PO relation). As the subject filled out his form, the role player pretended to fill out an identical form. These forms were collected, whereupon the investigator left the room and noted the subject's response on a criterion attitude item constructed for rapid identification of the subject's attitude.

Induction of the proper treatment condition was accomplished in the following way: The investigator reappeared and announced the "attitudes" of both subject and role player. Actually, the true attitude response of the subject was announced, but the announcement of the role player's "attitude" (the OX relation) was simply a cue to the role player as to whether he would argue "for" or "against" the issue. This announcement depended upon to which of the four conditions the subject had been assigned. For example, if the subject had been previously assigned to the *like-agree* condition, then if the subject's criterion attitude item indicated that he was "for" the issue (+PX), the investigator announced that the "attitudes" of *both* the subject and the role player were "for" the issue, thus cluing the role player to argue "for" the issue during his discussion with the subject, and accomplishing the +PX, +OX or "agree" induction. If the subject's criterion attitude item indicated that he was "against" the issue (−PX), then the investigator announced that both were against (accomplishing the −PX, −OX "agree" induction). If the subject had been assigned to the *dislike-disagree* condition, then if the subject's criterion attitude item indicated a "for" response (+PX), the investigator announced that the subject was "for" the issue but that the role player was against, accomplishing the desired +PX, −OX "disagree" induction. If the subject was "against," the role player argued "for" (the −PX, +OX "disagree" induction). Similar procedures were followed in the like-disagree and dislike-agree conditions. Under all conditions, the subject and the role player were told to "air their views" on the issue of admission of women for thirty minutes, after which time the investigator would terminate the discussion.

7 • 2b Instruments: Measures of Attitude and Liking

Before discussing the issue with the role player, the subject indicated his general attitude toward the issue by means of a dichotomous criterion item:

> In general, I am in favor of admitting women to Yale University as under-graduates.
>
> In general, I am not in favor of admitting women to Yale University as undergraduates.

To validate responses on this dichotomous item, subjects rated the issue according to ten bipolar adjective scales drawn from Osgood's Semantic Differential (1957), and which were also used in studies by Brinton (1961) and by Fishbein and Raven (1962). These ten bipolar adjective scales, presented in seven-point scale format, were: good-bad, fair-unfair, valuable-worthless, tasteful-distasteful, clean-dirty, just-unjust, honest-dishonest, beneficial-harmful, wise-foolish and healthy-sick.[2]

2. A principal axis factor analysis reveals that two factors underlie the ten scales used. The good-bad item, the criterion among the ten items, correlated highest among all items on the first factor; the first factor may therefore be identified as the "attitude" factor (cf. Osgood et al. (1957), pp. 189–216). Six of the ten scales correlated more highly on the first factor than on the second factor. They are: Good-bad, just-unjust, beneficial-harmful, wise-foolish, valuable-worthless and fair-unfair. For detailed results of this factor analysis, see Taylor (1966 and 1969); cf. Taylor, 1967.
In order to externally validate the subject's responses, factor scores on the first (attitude) factor were related to the subject's response on the dichotomous criterion item. A factor score, F_j, is defined as

$$F_j = b_{1j}X_1 + b_{2j}X_2 + \cdots + b_{nj}X_n,$$

where

$j =$ the jth factor (the first factor);
$n =$ the number of items; $n = 1 \ldots 10$;
$X =$ the *standardized* score of the subject on item n;
$b =$ the regression of item n on factor j.

The relationship between the subject's response on the dichotomous item and sign of factor score is highly significant:

SUBJECT'S RESPONSE ON DICHOTOMOUS ITEM	SIGN OF FACTOR SCORE	
	POSITIVE ("FOR" THE ISSUE)	NEGATIVE ("AGAINST" THE ISSUE)
"For"	22	0
"Against"	2	16 $N = 40$ subjects
$X^2 = 32.60$, $P < .0005$, direction predicted		

It will be remembered that the subject's degree of liking for the role player was measured during the general survey. As a means of validating subjects' responses on this survey item, subjects were asked to indicate their feeling toward the role player, before discussion of the issue, by means of five seven-point scales in Semantic Differential format. The scales were: like-dislike, friendly-unfriendly, affectionate-hateful, warm-cool, and close-distant.[3]

7 • 2c Instruments: Measures of Tension and Tension Release

Bales (1951) scheme of Interaction Process Analysis (IPA) was employed in order to measure the subject's tension and tension release. This scheme allows any bit or "act" or verbal or nonverbal behavior to be classified into one of twelve categories. Category 11 ("shows tension") was used as the indicator of tension, and category 2 ("shows tension release") was used as the indicator of tension release. Acts of subjects falling into all twelve of the Bales categories were continuously scored as the discussion between the subject and the role player took place.

A complete description of the IPA categories is found in Bales (1951, pp. 177–195). However, an abbreviated description of the tension and tension release categories (two out of the twelve major categories) can be given here.

1. An act of the subject is scored as *showing tension* if any one or more of the following six sub-categories are revealed: (a) Diffuse tension: Includes manifestations of restlessness or nervousness, such as doodling, biting the nails, fiddling. (b) Diffuse anxiety: Any manifestation of alarmament or dismay, such as hesitation, speechlessness, fluster, blushing, stammering, or gulping, as examples. (c) Shame or guilt: Acts suggesting that the subject is embarrassed, sheepish, or crestfallen, such as moaning, or cringing, or covering the face with the hands. Also included are acts which appear to be self-critical, self-defacing, or self-condemning, as examples. (d) Frustration: Acts revealing dissatisfaction,

3. Factor analysis of these five items showed only three of them to be internally valid: like-dislike, friendly-unfriendly and affectionate-hateful. The subject's response on the survey item was then related to his liking score, as a means of externally validating his liking for the role player before discussion. The results were as follows:

SUBJECT'S RATING OF ROLE PLAYER ON SURVEY ITEM	SUBJECT'S RATING OF THE ROLE PLAYER, BEFORE DISCUSSION OF THE ISSUE	
	Like	*Dislike*
Like	20	0
Dislike	1	19 $N = 40$ subjects

$X^2 = 36.19$, $P < .0005$, direction predicted

disappointment, disheartenment, despair, as examples. (e) Asking for help: Appeals to the mercy of the other, asking for aid, advice, support, or cowering or currying favor, as examples. (f) Withdrawal "out of field": The subject appears unattentive or bored, reflected in slouching, yawning, letting the eyes wander, or talking to the self or mumbling.

2. An act of the subject is scored as *showing tension release* if any one or more of the following three sub-categories are revealed: (a) Spontaneous indications of relief: Any manifestation of cheerfulness, buoyance, contentment, relish, zest, enthusiasm, delight, or pleasure, as examples. (b) Joking: Making friendly jokes, attempts to amuse or entertain, attempts at sillyness and "kidding around," as examples. (c) Laughing: Includes smiling, grinning, giggling, chuckling, or outright laughter.

While analyzing the IPA data, each thirty-minute session was divided into two halves of fifteen minutes each, the first being designated as T1, the second as T2. T1 is referred to as the "initial portion" of the session, and T2 as the "final portion." Any tension or tension release occurring during the initial portion of the conversation could then be captured by comparing dyads at T1, as required by hypotheses H1 and H3. Magnitude of *change* in tension or tension release, for a given subject, could then be determined by comparing acts at T1 to acts at T2, as required by hypotheses H2 and H4.

The percentage of either tension or tension release acts for either half of the session was obtained in the following manner:

$$\text{Indicator of Tension at } T_i = 100 \left[\frac{\text{frequency of tension acts attributed to the subject at } T_i}{\text{total frequency of all acts attributed to the subject at } T_i} \right]$$

and

$$\text{Indicator of Tension Release at } T_i = 100 \left[\frac{\text{frequency of tension release acts attributed to the subjects at } T_i}{\text{total frequency of all acts attributed to the subject at } T_i} \right]$$

where

$$i = 1, 2.$$

Thus, the measure of tension is simply the per cent of all of the subject's acts which were indicative of tension at either T1 or T2. The measure of tension release is the per cent of all of the subject's acts which were indicative of tension release at T1 or T2. For each subject, the arc-sine square root of each per cent score was obtained. This transformation procedure unifies the variance of the distribution of scores, prepares the data for analysis of variance, and helps eliminate regression effect (Tukey, no date).

In order to evaluate the magnitude and direction of a particular subject's *change* in either tension or tension release, the transformed score at T1 was subtracted from the transformed score at T2. Thus, a negative difference would indicate a *decrease* in either tension or tension release, and a positive difference would indicate an *increase*. The magnitude of change in either direction is indicated by the magnitude of the difference.

7 • 3   FINDINGS AND DISCUSSION

7 • 3a   *The Effects of Balance-Unbalance on Tension and Tension Release: The "Drain-Off Effect"*

Table 1 presents the findings on the relationship between treatment condition (balance–unbalance) and the following three variables: tension at T1, tension at T2, and change in tension from T1 to T2. The data in this table test hypotheses H1 and H2. The one-way analysis of variance technique is employed in testing the relationships for significance. Although the arc-sine square root transformation mentioned earlier was used in the analysis of variance test, the actual per cents are given in the table for the sake of clarity.

As predicted in hypothesis H1, the subjects under the unbalance treatment condition revealed significantly more tension at T1 than did subjects under the balance treatment condition. Note that from the first row of the table, 30.96 percent of all acts emitted by subjects at T1 under the unbalance treatment condition were indicative of tension. In contrast, for subjects under the balance condition at T1, only 17.15 percent of their acts reflected tension. The amount of tension displayed by the unbalance subjects was almost two times as great as the amount of tension displayed by the balance subjects.

TABLE 1   TENSION AT T1, TENSION AT T2, AND CHANGE IN TENSION, BY TREATMENT CONDITION

DEPENDENT VARIABLE	TREATMENT CONDITION BALANCE ($n = 20$)	UNBALANCE ($n = 20$)	SOURCE OF VARIANCE	D.F.	ESTIMATE OF VARIANCE[a]	F[a]
Tension at T1	17.15%	30.96%	Treatment	1	.2756	45.85, $P < .0005$
			Error	38	.0060	
Tension at T2	14.63%	15.40%	Treatment	1	.0013	.35, N.S.
			Error	38	.0038	
Tension change	−2.52%	−15.56%	Treatment	1	.2560	48.37, $P < .0005$
			Error	38	.0053	

a. Using arc-sine square root transformation.

The third row of Table 1 shows that as predicted in hypothesis H2, the magnitude of decrease in tension for the unbalance subjects (−15.56 percent) was significantly greater than the magnitude of decrease in tension for the balance subjects (−2.52 percent).

The second row of the table shows that the subjects in the two conditions did *not significantly differ* in tension at T2. This finding, though not explicitly predicted, clearly complements the two previous findings: Although tension at T1 under unbalance is considerably greater than tension at T1 under balance, the subjects under the unbalance condition decreased so markedly in tension from T1 to T2 that no significant differences between the two conditions exist at T2. Taken collectively, these three findings provide support for both the Tension and Tension Reduction hypotheses.

Table 2 presents the findings on the relationship between treatment condition and *tension release*. Three dependent variables are represented: Tension release at T1, tension release at T2, and magnitude of change in tension release. It is seen that subjects under the two conditions do not significantly differ in tension release at T1, as predicted in hypothesis H3. However, as predicted in hypothesis H4, subjects under the unbalance condition revealed a greater increase in tension release (+3.82 percent) than did the subjects under the balance condition (+.21 percent), even though tension release increased under both conditions. Due to these differing increases, tension release at T2 under unbalance (6.09 percent) is significantly greater than tension release at T2 under balance (4.17 percent). Collectively, these findings support H3 and H4.

The findings on tension release provide an extension of the Tension and Tension Reduction hypotheses of balance theory: As tension begins high and decreases under conditions of initial unbalance, at the same time tension release

TABLE 2   TENSION RELEASE AT T1, TENSION RELEASE AT T2 AND
CHANGE IN TENSION RELEASE, BY TREATMENT CONDITION

DEPENDENT VARIABLE	TREATMENT CONDITION BALANCE ($n = 20$)	UNBALANCE ($n = 20$)	SOURCE OF VARIANCE	D.F.	ESTIMATE OF VARIANCE	F
Tension release at T1	3.96%	2.27%	Treatment Error	1 38	.0137 .0067	2.06, N.S.
Tension release at T2	4.17%	6.09%	Treatment Error	1 38	.0431 .0081	5.32, $P < .025$
Tension release change	+.21%	+3.82%	Treatment Error	1 38	.0893 .0078	11.38, $P < .005$

begins low and increases. This shows that in the unbalanced dyadic *POX* situation where *P* and *O* are conversing about an important *X*, the tensions which built up under conditions of unbalance at the outset of the conversation tend to be released or expelled in an overt way as the discussion progresses. This simultaneous reduction of tension and increase in tension release can be labeled the *drain-off effect:* Tensions present at the outset of the conversation are drained off or relieved as the discussion takes place. By contrast, under conditions of initial balance, much less of a drain-off effect is observed. Tension begins low, and the magnitude of decrease in tension during the conversation is very slight. Consequently, at the beginning of the conversation, there is not much tension *to be* drained off, and for this reason only a slight increase in tension release is observed.

In consideration of the possible biasing effects of liking and agreement, the question is raised, "Are the observed effects on tension and tension release due to balance–unbalance or to the parameter variables of liking and agreement?" Is the observed drain-off effect a result of these biases, or of independent effects of balance–unbalance? As will be seen in the following section, the effects of balance–unbalance on *both* tension and tension release are independent of the effects of liking and agreement. When each of these variables is held constant, the predicted effects remain. Yet, the variables of liking and agreement *also* exert independent effects—biasing effects—on both tension and tension release. The relevant results appear in the following section.

3 • 3b   *The Biasing Effects of Liking and Agreement*

In order to systematically determine whether the effects of treatment condition were independent of the effects of the parameter variables of liking and agreement, the following procedure was adopted: (a) Treatment condition (balance–unbalance) was related to tension at T1, tension at T2 and tension change, while in each instance liking (like-dislike) was held constant. The results appear in Tables 3 through 5. (b) Treatment condition was related to the same three dependent variables while agreement (agree-disagree) was held constant (Tables 6 through 8). (c) Treatment condition was related to tension

TABLE 3   TENSION AT T1, BY TREATMENT CONDITION AND LIKING

	THE SUBJECT'S LIKING FOR THE ROLE PLAYER	TREATMENT CONDITION	
		BALANCE	UNBALANCE
	Like	15.22%	31.00%
		(10)	(10)
	Dislike	19.08%	30.92%
		(10)	(10)

$F_{1,37}$ (Treatment Condition) $= 46.18, P < .0005$
$F_{1,37}$ (Liking) $=\ \ .97$, N.S.
$F_{1,37}$ (Interaction) $=\ 1.31$, N.S.

release at T1, T2, and change in tension release, while in each instance liking was held constant (Tables 9 through 11). (d) Treatment condition was related to the same three dependent variables while agreement was held constant (Tables 12 through 14). Two-way analyses of variance were employed to accomplish these ends.

Table 3 shows that even when liking is constant, balance–unbalance affects tension at T1 as predicted. Liking has no significant effect, nor is the interaction between balance–unbalance and like-dislike significant. Table 4 shows no effect of balance on tension at T2 (the same effect was obtained earlier in Table 1), nor is the effect of liking significant. However, balance and liking significantly interact, such that the highest tension at T2 is found under conditions of balance and liking—which is the *dislike—disagree* condition. In this instance, a biasing effect is quite evident. Table 5, however, shows that if tension *change* is taken into account, only the effects of balance are significant, and the effects of liking and interaction are not significant.

A similar (though not identical) pattern is revealed when agreement is held constant (Tables 6, 7 and 8). Table 6 shows a clear independent effect of balance upon tension at T1 (as predicted), but no independent effects of agreement or interaction. Yet, an independent effect of agreement is found when tension at T2 is analyzed (Table 7): Disagreement results in more tension at

TABLE 4 TENSION AT T2, BY TREATMENT CONDITION AND LIKING

THE SUBJECT'S LIKING FOR THE ROLE PLAYER	TREATMENT CONDITION BALANCE	UNBALANCE
Like	11.73% (10)	16.66% (10)
Dislike	17.53% (10)	14.13% (10)

$F_{1,36}$ (Treatment Condition) $=$ .46, N.S.
$F_{1,36}$ (Liking) $=$ 2.45, N.S.
$F_{1,36}$ (Interaction) $=$ 11.51, $P < .01$

TABLE 5 CHANGE IN TENSION BY TREATMENT CONDITION AND LIKING

THE SUBJECT'S LIKING FOR THE ROLE PLAYER	TREATMENT CONDITION BALANCE	UNBALANCE
Like	−3.49% (10)	−14.34% (10)
Dislike	−1.55% (10)	−16.79% (10)

$F_{1,37}$ (Treatment Condition) $=$ 47.41, $P < .0005$
$F_{1,37}$ (Liking) $=$ .11, N.S.
$F_{1,37}$ (Interaction) $=$ 2.34, N.S.

T2 than agreement. Neither balance nor interaction yield independent effects. Only the effect of balance is significant when changes in tension are analyzed (Table 8).

TABLE 6   TENSION AT T1, BY TREATMENT CONDITION AND AGREEMENT

AGREEMENT BETWEEN SUBJECT AND ROLE PLAYER	TREATMENT CONDITION	
	BALANCE	UNBALANCE
Agree	15.22%	30.92%
	(10)	(10)
Disagree	19.08%	31.00%
	(10)	(10)

$F_{1,37}$ (Treatment Condition)   = 46.18, $P < .0005$
$F_{1,37}$ (Agreement)   = 1.32, N.S.
$F_{1,37}$ (Interaction)   = .96, N.S.

TABLE 7   TENSION AT T2, BY TREATMENT CONDITION AND AGREEMENT

AGREEMENT BETWEEN SUBJECT AND ROLE PLAYER	TREATMENT CONDITION	
	BALANCE	UNBALANCE
Agree	11.73%	14.13%
	(10)	(10)
Disagree	17.53%	16.66%
	(10)	(10)

$F_{1,37}$ (Treatment Condition)   = .43, N.S.
$F_{1,37}$ (Agreement   = 11.03, $P < .01$
$F_{1,37}$ (Interaction)   = 2.44, N.S.

TABLE 8   CHANGE IN TENSION, BY TREATMENT CONDITION AND AGREEMENT

AGREEMENT BETWEEN SUBJECT AND ROLE PLAYER	TREATMENT CONDITION	
	BALANCE	UNBALANCE
Agree	−3.49%	−16.79%
	(10)	(10)
Disagree	−1.55%	−14.34%
	(10)	(10)

$F_{1,37}$ (Treatment Condition)   = 50.20, $P < .0005$
$F_{1,37}$ (Agreement   = 2.41, N.S.
$F_{1,37}$ (Interaction)   = .12, N.S.

Figure 1 clarifies these findings. This figure, in conjunction with the preceding tables, shows the following: (a) The effects of balance–unbalance upon tension at T1 and upon tension change are very marked, and they are independent of the effects of both liking and agreement. (b) Both unbalance conditions (the like-disagree and dislike-agree conditions) decreased in tension at practically the same rate. (c) Biasing effects of liking and agreement are *not* evident at T1. However, for tension at T2 (where the effect of balance is not significant), both liking (through interaction) and agreement exert effects on tension. Generally, disagreement results in higher tension at T2 than agreement, and dislike results in higher tension than liking. This explains why the *highest* tension at T2 exists under conditions of dislike and disagreement (see Figure 1). It also explains why tension at T2 is *lowest* under the like-agree condition.

FIGURE 1   TENSION MAGNITUDE BY CONDITION

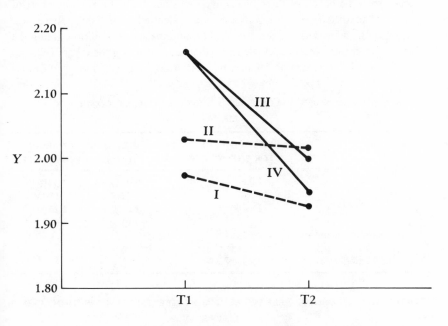

Y = Magnitude of Tension
(Arc Sine Square Root Transformation)
– – – – – = Balance Treatment Condition
———— = Unbalance Treatment Condition
I = Like-Agree Condition
II = Dislike-Disagree Condition
III = Like-Disagree Condition
IV = Dislike-Agree Condition

While the finding that tension is highest at T2 under the dislike-disagree condition (and lowest under the like-agree condition) does not severely challenge the balance principle, it clearly reveals that the effects of liking and agreement must be taken into account. It is interesting, also, to note from Figure 1 that the subjects under the dislike-disagree condition revealed the lowest rate of tension decrease from T1 to T2. Thus, so we might speculate, although this condition was initially balanced and hence revealed little change in tension, the combined biasing effects of dislike and disagreement produced almost no drop in tension, causing tension to be excessively high at the end of the conversation (at T2). As will be seen, the dislike-disagree condition reveals certain peculiarities in regard not only to tension, but also in regard to the overt antagonism displayed by subjects under this condition.

We come now to the analysis of *tension release.* Generally, the biasing effects of liking and agreement upon tension release are greater and more pronounced than the effects of these biases upon tension. Table 9 reveals no effect of balance (as predicted), but a significant independent effect of liking: Regardless of whether the subject is under a balanced or an unbalanced condition, liking the other results in more tension release at T1 than does disliking the other. Table 10 shows the predicted effects of balance, but also strong effects of liking and inter-

TABLE 9   TENSION RELEASE AT T1, BY TREATMENT CONDITION AND LIKING

THE SUBJECT'S LIKING FOR THE ROLE PLAYER	TREATMENT CONDITION BALANCE	UNBALANCE
Like	5.68% (10)	2.34% (10)
Dislike	2.00% (10)	2.23% (10)

$F_{1, 37}$ (Treatment Condition) $= 2.32$, N.S.
$F_{1, 37}$ (Liking) $= 5.51, P < .05$
$F_{1, 37}$ (Interaction) $= 3.29$, N.S.

TABLE 10   TENSION RELEASE AT T2, BY TREATMENT CONDITION AND LIKING

THE SUBJECT'S LIKING FOR THE ROLE PLAYER	TREATMENT CONDITION BALANCE	UNBALANCE
Like	7.12% (10)	6.24% (10)
Dislike	1.21% (10)	5.93% (10)

$F_{1, 36}$ (Treatment Condition) $= 6.77, P < .025$
$F_{1, 36}$ (Liking) $= 15.33, P < .001$
$F_{1, 36}$ (Interaction) $= 11.99, P < .01$

action. However, Table 11 shows no effects of liking or interaction upon change in tension release.

The effects of agreement (Tables 12, 13 and 14) reveal a similar pattern. Balance and agreement interact upon tension release at T1 (Table 12), such that the *highest* tension release appears under the agree-balance (i.e., the like-agree) condition, and is *lowest* under the disagree-balance (the dislike-disagree) condition. Table 13 shows that for tension release at T2, an independent effect of agreement is found (agreement results in more tension release than disagreement), and the interaction effect is significant: Again, tension release is highest under the like-agree condition, and lowest under the dislike-disagree condition. Despite these differences at T2, change in tension release (Table 14) is not explained by agreement. We noted that change in tension release was not accounted for by liking, either.

Figure 2 illustrates the foregoing findings. First, it is noted that tension release under the two *unbalance* conditions increased at practically the same rate. This is important to note, for it shows that changes in tension release are accounted for quite well by the variable balance–unbalance; it shows that the like-

TABLE 11   CHANGE IN TENSION RELEASE BY TREATMENT CONDITION AND LIKING

THE SUBJECT'S LIKING FOR THE ROLE PLAYER	TREATMENT CONDITION	
	BALANCE	UNBALANCE
Like	1.44%	3.90%
	(10)	(10)
Dislike	−.79%	3.70%
	(10)	(10)

$F_{1,37}$ (Treatment Condition) $= 11.45, P < .005$
$F_{1,37}$ (Liking) $= 1.04$, N.S.
$F_{1,37}$ (Interaction) $= 1.45$, N.S.

TABLE 12   TENSION RELEASE AT T1, BY TREATMENT CONDITION AND AGREEMENT

AGREEMENT BETWEEN SUBJECT AND ROLE PLAYER	TREATMENT CONDITION	
	BALANCE	UNBALANCE
Agree	5.68%	2.23%
	(10)	(10)
Disagree	2.00%	2.34%
	(10)	(10)

$F_{1,36}$ (Treatment Condition) $= 2.44$, N.S.
$F_{1,36}$ (Agreement) $= 3.29$, N.S.
$F_{1,36}$ (Interaction) $= 5.79, P < .05$

TABLE 13   TENSION RELEASE AT T2, BY TREATMENT CONDITION AND
            AGREEMENT

AGREEMENT BETWEEN SUBJECT AND ROLE PLAYER	TREATMENT CONDITION	
	BALANCE	UNBALANCE
Agree	7.12%	5.93%
	(10)	(10)
Disagree	1.21%	6.24%
	(10)	(10)

$F_{1, 36}$ (Treatment Condition) = 6.78, $P < .025$
$F_{1, 36}$ (Agreement) = 11.99, $P < .01$
$F_{1, 36}$ (Interaction) = 15.33, $P < .001$

TABLE 14   CHANGE IN TENSION RELEASE BY TREATMENT CONDITION AND
            AGREEMENT

AGREEMENT BETWEEN SUBJECT AND ROLE PLAYER	TREATMENT CONDITION	
	BALANCE	UNBALANCE
Agree	1.44%	3.70%
	(10)	(10)
Disagree	−.79%	3.90%
	(10)	(10)

$F_{1, 37}$ (Treatment Condition) = 11.53, $P < .005$
$F_{1, 37}$ (Agreement) = 1.44, N.S.
$F_{1, 37}$ (Interaction) = 1.04, N.S.

disagree and dislike-agree conditions are uniform or similar in the way in which they both explain changes in tension release. The second thing to note from the figure is that the dislike-disagree condition actually revealed a *decrease* in tension release, whereas no other condition did so. This clearly reflects the biasing effects of liking and agreement. If *P* both dislikes and disagrees with *O*, despite the fact that the condition is balanced, it is an unpleasant and uncomfortable state— so uncomfortable, in fact, that the minimal amount of tension release behavior displayed at T1 decreases. These findings directly complement the observation in Figure 1 that tension at T2 under this condition was excessively high.

This latter finding is further complemented by the fact that subjects under the *like-agree* condition revealed the greatest amount of tension release of all conditions at both T1 *and* T2. Overall, the like-agree condition revealed the highest tension release at both T1 and T2, and the dislike-disagree condition revealed the lowest.

FIGURE 2 TENSION RELEASE MAGNITUDE BY CONDITION

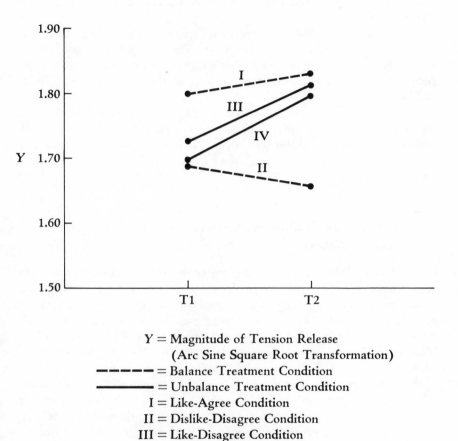

Y = Magnitude of Tension Release
(Arc Sine Square Root Transformation)
— — — — — = Balance Treatment Condition
——————— = Unbalance Treatment Condition
I = Like-Agree Condition
II = Dislike-Disagree Condition
III = Like-Disagree Condition
IV = Dislike-Agree Condition

In sum, the following clear patterns are revealed in the data:

1. Dislike tends to result in high tension and low tension release, whereas liking tends to result in relatively less tension and more tension release. Likewise, disagreement results in high tension and low tension release, whereas agreement results in relatively less tension and more tension release. The effects are generally independent of the effects of balance–unbalance. Note that both variables affect both tension and tension release in the same direction. The biasing effects of

liking and agreement are more pronounced at T2 than at T1, and the effects of these variables upon tension release are generally greater than their effects upon tension.

2. *At T2, the dislike-disagree condition reveals the highest tension and the lowest tension release of all conditions. The like-agree condition, at T2, reveals the lowest tension and the highest tension release of all conditions.* These complementary findings provide clear evidence of the *combined* biasing effects of liking and agreement.

3. Although independent effects of liking and agreement are observed, the variable balance–unbalance predicts both tension and tension release quite well. It is especially noted that for both unbalance conditions (like-disagree and dislike-agree), the *rate* of tension decrease from T1 to T2 is uniform, as is the *rate* of tension release increase.

7 • 3c *An Evaluation of Newcomb's Three-Category Scheme*

Recently, Newcomb (1968) has argued that tension data is better ordered on the basis of a three-fold scheme, defined as follows: *balance,* or liking and agreement; *unbalance,* or liking and disagreement; and *nonbalance,* or conditions of dislike-agree and dislike-disagree. He argues that the Heider two-category scheme of like-agree and dislike-disagree (balance) versus dislike-agree and like-disagree (unbalance) does not order data as well as the three-category distinction. Thus, any condition of dislike ($-PO$) is defined as somewhere between like-agree and like-disagree. For this reason, the lowest tension should appear under a like-agree condition, medium tension should appear under the two nonbalanced conditions, and the highest tension should appear under a like-disagree condition. Newcomb presents a detailed re-analysis of the results of studies by Jordan (1953), Price, Harburg and Newcomb (1966), and Rodrigues (1967). For the most part, the results of these studies do provide some support (though not crystal-clear support) for the Newcomb three-category scheme over the Heider two-category one.

Newcomb's theoretical argument is based on the concept of "engagement" (introduced by Price, Harburg and Newcomb, 1966). When engagement of P and O is low, the situation is characterized by indifference. When engagement is high, then there is less indifference; involvement is high. Newcomb speculates that under any condition of dislike ($-PO$), engagement is low; P is indifferent to the sum total of relations in the structure. Hence, it makes no difference to him whether he agrees or disagrees with O; it "doesn't really matter," since he does not like O anyway. For this reason, conditions of dislike (whether dislike-agree or dislike-disagree) should be uniform in tension. By contrast, conditions of liking are characterized by high engagement; P "cares" about the situation; there is low indifference. Thus, if P agrees with O, it is a pleasant and harmonious state, and tension is lowest. But if P disagrees with O, due to high engagement, it is a very upsetting and unpleasant experience; consequently, tension is expected to be highest.

In sum, if this scheme is correct, then tension data should be ordered as follows: The highest tension is expected to appear under a like-disagree condition, next highest under any dislike condition (dislike-agree or dislike-disagree), and lowest under a like-agree condition.

Although Newcomb's re-analysis (which also incorporates the re-analysis of studies which measure attitudinal and liking change) seem to lend support to his three-category scheme, there are two distinct problems connected with it: (1) The distinction between balance (like-agree) and unbalance (like-disagree) is actually a distinction only in terms of agreement. Thus, it is simply the "bias" of agree-disagree that is the explanatory variable, not "balance." (2) The data of the present study lend more support to the Heider two-category scheme than to the Newcomb three-category scheme. Let us take another look at the results reported above.

Table 15 summarizes the relevant results of the present study on six dependent variables: Tension at T1, at T2, and tension change, and tension release at T1, at T2, and tension release change. The four basic categories are labeled according to the Heider two-category and the Newcomb three-category schemes.

It is quite clear that the data for tension at T1 support the Heider distinction better than the Newcomb distinction: The dislike-agree and the like-disagree conditions yield nearly *identical* tension scores (30.92 percent and 31.00 percent, respectively). If the Newcomb scheme were correct, these two conditions would not be nearly as uniform. Furthermore, the difference in tension between the dislike-disagree and dislike-agree conditions is large (30.92 − 19.08 = 11.84), whereas these two conditions would be uniform if Newcomb's scheme were correct. In addition, the difference between the like-agree and dislike-disagree conditions is less than the former difference, thus supporting the Heider scheme.

Differences in Tension at T2 are not as marked, and yield no clear pattern. But when tension *change* is taken into account, the Heider two-category scheme again receives support: The dislike-agree and like-disagree conditions reveal nearly uniform rates of decrease (we noted this before), and the distinction between the dislike-disagree and dislike-agree conditions is great.

For tension release at T1 and T2, the results do not clearly support either scheme (note the relative effects of like-agree versus dislike-disagree, discussed above). But again, when change in tension release is considered, the two-category scheme is the better predictor: (1) The two Heider-unbalanced conditions reveal nearly identical and uniform rates of tension release increase; and (2) the difference between the dislike-disagree and dislike-agree conditions is great, thus

TABLE 15   A COMPARISON OF THE HEIDER TWO-CATEGORY AND NEWCOMB THREE-CATEGORY SCHEMES

COMBINATION OF LIKING AND AGREEMENT	HEIDER'S CATEGORIES	NEWCOMB'S CATEGORIES	TENSION AT T1	TENSION AT T2	TENSION CHANGE	TENSION RELEASE AT T1	TENSION RELEASE AT T2	TENSION RELEASE CHANGE
Like-Agree	Balance	Balance	15.22%	11.73%	− 3.49%	5.68%	7.12%	+1.44%
Dislike-Disagree	Balance	Nonbalance	19.08%	17.53%	− 1.55%	2.00%	1.21%	− .79%
Dislike-Agree	Unbalance	Nonbalance	30.92%	14.13%	−16.79%	2.23%	5.93%	+3.70%
Like-Disagree	Unbalance	Unbalance	31.00%	16.66%	−14.34%	2.34%	6.24%	+3.90%

not supporting Newcomb's hypothesis of uniformity between these two conditions.

The clearest observation to be made is that when *change* in *both* tension and tension release is considered, the Heider two-category scheme appears to order the data better than the Newcomb three-category scheme. The only point of agreement between the two schemes is that the like-agree condition consistently (at T1 and T2) reveals the *least* tension and the *most* tension release— showing that generally, it is by far the most "harmonious" or "psychologically balanced" condition of all.

The results suggest further that if any new distinctions are to be made, then the like-agree condition should be distinguished from the dislike-disagree condition: At T2, the former reveals the least tension and the greatest tension release; the latter reveals the greatest tension and the least tension release. It will be seen in the next section that when results on antagonism are taken into account, a major distinction between these two conditions is justified. In no way, however, do the results of the present study suggest combining the dislike-disagree and the dislike-agree conditions into one "nonbalance" category.

Since Newcomb's scheme was based upon the re-analysis of data from Jordan (1953), Price, Harburg and Newcomb (1966) and Rodriques (1967), it is worthwhile to suggest reasons why the results of the present study do not agree with the re-analysis of the results of these past studies. First, whereas all these past studies employed a self-rating tension measure, the present investigation employed behavioral measures (Bales' IPA). Second, a measurement of tension *release,* or some roughly comparable measure, was not employed in the other studies. Third, longitudinal measurement of both tension and tension release was used here, whereas the other studies measured tension on each subject only once—cross-sectionally. Finally, it should be noted that the three-category scheme does not order the tension data of these three studies in an unequivocal pattern; the re-analysis was suggestive, by Newcomb's own intent.

7 • 4 ANTAGONISM AND A "COUNTEROPPOSING BIASES" INTERPRETATION

It is quite apparent, at least from the results of this study, that the dislike-disagree condition reveals certain peculiarities anticipated neither by Heider's formulation nor by Newcomb's three-category scheme. This became even more evident to this investigation when *antagonism* behavior of the subject (*P*) toward the role player (*O*) was observed. Antagonism, reflected in category 12 of Bales' IPA, is indicated by any one or more of the following four sub-categories (Bales, 1951, pp. 193–195). The following behaviors are selected examples of acts scored as antagonism: (a) Diffuse aggression: acts of the subject involving rage, anger, belligerence, hostility, or quarrelsomeness. (b) Attempts at autonomy:

indications that the subject is harassing, badgering, belittling, perturbing or pestering the other, as examples. (c) Attempts to deflate the other's status: interrupting the other, making fun of the other's views, lampooning or satirizing the other, and acts of teasing, taunting, heckling, or mocking, as examples. (d) Asserting the self: the subject says something indicating that he has a "chip on his shoulder," such as over-reacting to a relatively harmless criticism.

When antagonism was taken as the dependent variable and related to liking and agreement, it was seen that antagonism at both T1 and T2 was extremely high under the dislike-disagree condition. The results of this analysis will be presented first (in Tables 16, 17 and 18, and in Figure 3) and then interpreted. No hypotheses were developed in regard to antagonism; the findings were strictly serendipitous and unanticipated. The theoretical position to be given after the presentation of the data is *ex post facto*.

Tables 16 and 17 reveal strong effects of the parameter variables liking and agreement upon antagonism at both T1 and T2: Dislike results in more antagonism than liking, and disagreement results in more antagonism than agreement. Of particular interest is the interaction of both variables upon antagonism:

TABLE 16   THE EFFECTS OF LIKING AND AGREEMENT UPON
ANTAGONISM AT T1

		LIKE	DISLIKE
	Agree	.89%	1.38%
		(10)	(10)
	Disagree	2.28%	11.15%
		(10)	(10)
$F_{1,36}$ (Liking)	= 23.39, $P < .001$		
$F_{1,36}$ (Agreement)	= 43.87, $P < .001$		
$F_{1,36}$ (Interaction)	= 17.98, $P < .001$		

TABLE 17   THE EFFECTS OF LIKING AND AGREEMENT UPON
ANTAGONISM AT T2

		LIKE	DISLIKE
	Agree	.85%	.83%
		(10)	(10)
	Disagree	1.51%	13.17%
		(10)	(10)
$F_{1,36}$ (Liking)	= 34.57, $P < .001$		
$F_{1,36}$ (Agreement)	= 49.26, $P < .001$		
$F_{1,36}$ (Interaction)	= 36.75, $P < .001$		

At both T1 and T2, antagonism is excessively pronounced under the dislike-disagree condition. Fully 11.15 percent of all of the subject's acts at T1, and 13.17 percent of them at T2, were indicative of antagonism toward the role player.

Figure 3 illustrates this marked interaction effect. While it would appear that the subjects under the dislike-disagree condition increased in antagonism from T1 to T2 while the other three conditions decreased, Table 18 shows that neither liking nor agreement, nor their interaction, significantly explain change in antagonism. Hence, it must be concluded that antagonism remained relatively constant in all conditions from T1 to T2.

FIGURE 3   ANTAGONISM BY CONDITION

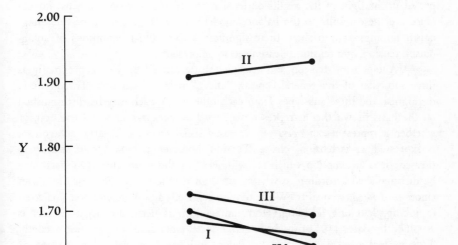

Y = Magnitude of Antagonism
(Arc Sine Square Root Transformation)
I = Like-Agree Condition
II = Dislike-Disagree Condition
III = Like-Disagree Condition
IV = Dislike-Agree Condition

TABLE 18   THE EFFECTS OF LIKING AND AGREEMENT UPON CHANGE
IN ANTAGONISM

		LIKE	DISLIKE
	Agree	−.04%	−.55%
		(10)	(10)
	Disagree	−.77%	+2.02%
		(10)	(10)
$F_{1, 36}$ (Liking)	= 1.14, N.S.		
$F_{1, 36}$ (Agreement)	= .02, N.S.		
$F_{1, 36}$ (Interaction)	= 2.98, N.S.		

How can these results be explained theoretically? How can they be interpreted in the light of the results on tension and tension release? Of what importance are these results to the balance model? In order to account of the antagonism findings and to show their significance, conceptual definitions of antagonism, tension, and tension release need to be presented.

Antagonism, tension and tension release can all be seen conceptually as three sub-types of the general concept "affect," or social emotion. Three criteria distinguish the three sub-types from each other: (1) Each may be distinguished on the basis of whether it represents a *covert or unexpressed* social emotion, or whether it represents an *overt or expressed* social emotion. Clearly, antagonism is expressed, as is tension release. Tension, however, is more covert and unexpressed: it is an emotion which is "withheld" by the personality. (2) Each may be distinguished according to whether it is an emotion of *positive* quality or an emotion of *negative* quality. While tension release is a positive emotion (reflected in joking, laughing, kidding, etc.), antagonism is decidedly negative, and is classified by Bales (1951) as the negative social emotion of the greatest strength. Tension is treated as negative by Bales, and has been defined as a type of "negative affect" by other researchers (e.g., Price et al., 1965). (3) Each may be distinguished according to whether it is *directed* at the other or *not directed* toward the other. Antagonism involves attempts to ridicule, deflate and harass the other—clear instances of the direction of emotion toward a specific other. Tension, on the other hand, is a non-directed, "autistic" emotion. Tension release can be directed or non-directed, though it should generally be regarded as directed. In an instance where the other tells a joke and the focal person laughs at it, to the degree that the laugh is "intended for" the other, to that degree tension release behavior is directed.

Generally, tension is defined as covert, unexpressed negative emotion which is not directed toward the other. In contrast, although antagonism is negative, it is an overt, expressed negative emotion which is directed at a specific other. Tension release is overt, expressed positive emotion which is generally directed toward the other.

To account for the findings on antagonism, and to integrate these findings with those on tension and tension release, three *postulates* need to be stated. The first two postulates are besed on past studies of the biasing effects of liking and agreement, and upon the results of the present study showing independent effects of antagonism (Tables 16 and 17).

Postulate 1: Liking bias: If *P* dislikes *O*, then there will be a tendency for *P* to express negative emotion (antagonism) toward *O*. If *P* likes *O*, then this tendency is less.

Postulate 2: Agreement bias: If *P* disagrees with *O*, then there will be a tendency for *P* to express negative emotion (antagonism) toward *O*. If *P* agrees with *O*, this tendency is less.

Postulate 3: The postulate of counteropposition of biases: It is expected that under conditions of like-disagree and dislike-agree, the two biases "counteroppose" each other, but under conditions of like-agree and dislike-disagree, they do not. Counteropposition is present under unbalanced conditions (as defined by Heider), and is not present under balanced conditions. When the variables liking and agreement are like-signed (like(+)/agree(+), or dislike(−)/disagree(−)), they do not counteroppose each other. When they are unlike in sign (like(+)/disagree(−), or dislike(−)/agree(+)), they do. Let us deal first with the like-disagree and dislike-agree (the "counteropposition") conditions.

The counteropposition postulate means that one bias can hold the other "in check," such that *the tendency for disagreement to result in antagonism is prevented by liking, and the tendency for dislike to result in antagonism is prevented by agreement.* Thus, under conditions of agreement and dislike, or disagreement and liking, the two biases constitute forces pulling in opposite directions; in this sense they counteroppose each other.

Under conditions of counteropposition of biases, the negative affect or emotion is withheld or restrained, and high tension will result. When one force (bias) results in a particular tendency (the tendency to be antagonistic) but another force prevents this, then discomfort, uneasiness and unpleasantness—tension—is expected to be produced. In short, the Heider-unbalanced conditions of like-disagree and dislike-agree are conditions of counteropposing biases; one bias prevents the other from operating, and high tension will develop.

In contrast to the counteropposition conditions of like-disagree and dislike-agree, the like-agree and dislike-disagree conditions do not involve the counteropposition of biases; neither holds the other "in check." Hence, tension is expected to be low. In order to clarify the meaning of the concept of counteropposition, each of the four conditions formed by the variables like-dislike and agree-disagree are examined in relation to antagonism, tension and tension release:

1. *The dislike-agree condition:* By Postulate 1 (the liking bias), there is a high tendency for *P* to be antagonistic toward *O*, due to his dislike for *O*. But

by Postulate 2 (the agreement bias), there is a low tendency for P to be antagonistic, since he agrees with O. Hence, by Postulate 3, P's tendency to express antagonism toward O, since he dislikes him, is held in check since he agrees with him. Since the tendency to express antagonism is prevented, high tension results. The findings on both tension and antagonism support this speculation: Tension at T1 is excessively high under the dislike-agree condition (Figure 1), and antagonism is moderate (Figure 3). Furthermore, these observations are complemented by the fact *tension release* at both T1 and T2 is intermediate in this condition, falling between the like-agree and the dislike-disagree conditions (Figure 2).

2. *The like-disagree condition:* As predicted by Postulates 1, 2 and 3 and by the Heider balance model, the dynamics of this condition are the same as those of the dislike-agree condition. By Postulate 2 (agreement bias), there is a high tendency for P to be antagonistic toward O, due to his disagreement with O. But by Postulate 1 (liking bias), this tendency is low, since P likes O. Thus, by Postulate 3, the biases counteroppose each other; the tendency to express antagonism is held in check, and high tension results. Again, the results are supportive: Tension at T1 is just as high under this condition as under the former (dislike-agree) condition (Figure 1). Antagonism is moderate (Figure 3). In addition, *tension release* at T1 and T2 is moderate, and nearly identical to the tension release at T1 and T2 under the dislike-agree condition (Figure 2).

3. *The like-agree condition:* By postulate 1 (liking bias), there is a low tendency for P to be antagonistic toward O, since he likes O. Similarly, by postulate 2 (agreement bias), there is a low tendency to be antagonistic, since P agrees with O. By postulate 3, neither bias counteropposes the other, and tension is low. From Figure 1, it is seen that in fact, tension at both T1 and T2 is lowest of all in this condition. This is complemented by the observation that tension release is *highest* under this condition (Figure 2). Furthermore, since both biases work in the same direction (liking combined with agreement—both are like-signed), antagonism is low (Figure 3).

4. *The dislike-disagree condition:* By Postulate 1, P will tend to be antagonistic toward O, since he dislikes him. And by Postulate 2, he will tend to be antagonistic toward O since he disagrees with him. *Thus, by Postulate 3, both variables are like-signed and neither bias counteropposes the other; neither holds the other in check. Both work in the same direction. Antagonism is excessively high; the negative social emotion is "released" in an overt way.* The marked interaction effect of liking and agreement upon antagonism at both T1 and T2 (Figure 3) lends strong support to this explanation. Since neither bias holds the other in check, tension should be low—an explanation which is upheld for tension at T1 (tension at T1 for this condition is lower than tension at T1 for the dislike-agree and like-disagree conditions), but not for tension at T2 (the dislike-disagree conditions revealed the highest tension of all for tension at T2). It is interesting to note that one explanation for the excessively low *tension release*

at T2 for this condition (see Figure 2) is that due to the combination of dislike and disagreement, the high tension (at T2) was "released" in the form of overt hostility or antagonism rather than in the form of tension release.

There is no doubt that the dislike-disagree condition constituted a most unwelcome situation for the subjects who participated in the experiment. In his earlier writings, Newcomb (1953) speculated that conditions of dislike and disagreement produce forces toward *dissolution*—that under such conditions, *P* and *O* will simply not want to have anything to do with one another. To the extent that the extremely high antagonism noted under this condition (coupled with the highest tension at T2 and the lowest tension release) indicates that *P* "wants out," then to that degree the results of his study support this hypothesis. As a matter of fact, during the experiment, two subjects under the dislike-disagree condition actually got up and left before the thirty-minute discussion was over—a clear occurrence of "dissolution"! This did not happen under any of the other three conditions.

It is evident that neither the Newcomb three-category scheme nor the Heider scheme accurately accounts for the findings on tension, tension release and antagonism. Should any scheme be suggested by the data gathered in this study, the following breakdown would account for the results:

1. *Balanced conditions:* Conditions involving liking and agreement between *P* and *O*. It is the most harmonious or "psychologically balanced" of all conditions, characterized by low tension, low antagonism, and high tension release.

2. *Counteropposed (unbalanced) conditions:* Conditions involving like-disagree and dislike-agree. Both of these conditions uniformly reveal high initial (T1) tension, suggesting that the liking and agreement biases counteroppose each other. A marked and uniform decrease in tension from T1 to T2 is noted under these two conditions. The hypothesized cause of this tension reduction is attitudinal and liking change in the direction of balance. Furthermore, there is a uniform *increase* in tension release from T1 to T2; namely, both conditions reveal a drain-off effect. Antagonism is low at both T1 and T2, due to the counteropposing biases.

3. *Dissociative conditions:* Conditions involving dislike and disagreement, where tension at T2 is high, tension release tends to be low, and antagonism at T1 and T2 is excessively high, since neither bias counteropposes the other. This suggests that forces toward dissolution are present; that *P* and *O* wish only to "go their separate ways," to have nothing to do with one another. The condition is, however, "stable" in Heider's sense, if no attitudinal or liking *changes* take place prior to dissolution. In fact, *the lack of such molar changes from this highly undesirable state can be hypothesized as the cause of dissolution.* Results from this same experiment reported in Taylor (1967) show that changes in

attitude, perceived attitude, and liking are not likely to occur under this condition; it is thus more "stable" by this criterion than the like-disagree and dislike-agree conditions, under which attitudinal and liking changes did take place.

It should be pointed out that the above distinctions integrate the concept of balance with the concept of cognitive bias (liking and agreement). The cognitive bias framework of Zajonc and associates can be seen as an alternative to the balance concept; this was the approach used in Chapter 5. However, in the balanced—counteropposed—dissociative scheme, the balance and bias approaches are combined. Note that the Newcomb three-fold scheme is not easily integrated with the concept of cognitive bias.

7 • 5 SUMMARY

Results of a study carried out by the author were reported in this chapter. The core findings and interpretations are:

1. Under conditions of initial unbalance between P and O with respect to an issue (X) they are discussing, tension starts high and decreases at a rapid rate, and tension release starts low and increases at a rapid rate. This simultaneous tension reduction and tension release increase, or *drain-off effect*, suggests that tensions which built up under conditions of initial unbalance tend to be expelled or relieved as the discussion progresses, and (by hypothesis) as molar changes in the direction of balance take place. No relative drain-off effect is observed under conditions of initial balance. (Results from this same study reported in Taylor [1967] show that in fact, molar changes toward balance under initially unbalanced conditions exceed molar changes toward balance under initially balanced conditions.)

2. Marked independent biasing effects of liking and agreement were noted, such that liking results in less tension and more tension release than dislike, and agreement results in less tension and more tension release than disagreement. Both variables affect tension and tension release in the same direction, and the effects are independent of balance–unbalance.

3. During the latter portion of the discussion (T2), the dislike-disagree condition reveals the highest tension and the lowest tension release, and the like-agree condition reveals the lowest tension and the highest tension release.

4. The data gathered in the present study lend more support to the original Heider two-category scheme of balance–unbalance than to Newcomb's (1968) recent three-category scheme of balance, nonbalance and unbalance. The primary reason for this was that Newcomb's scheme did not consider *changes* in tension (or tension release), whereas the present study employed change measures. In no way do the results on tension, tension release (and antagonism)

justify combining the dislike-agree and dislike-disagree conditions into one "non-balance" category.

Results on antagonism, where it was found that liking and agreement strongly interact or combine to produce excessively high antagonism of P toward O under the dislike-disagree condition, suggest that:

5. The biases of liking and agreement *counteroppose* each other under conditions of Heider-unbalance (like-disagree and dislike-agree) such that antagonism and tension release are low, but tension is high. In contrast, under balanced conditions, no counteropposition is present: With conditions of liking and agreement, tension and antagonism are low, and tension release is high. With dislike and disagreement, where there is no counteropposition, tension is "released" in the form of overt hostility or antagonism (rather than in the form of "tension release").

6. The combined results of this study suggest a theoretical revision of the Heider balance formulation into three categories: *Balanced:* Like-agree, a condition characterized by low tension and low antagonism at T1 and T2, and high tension release at T1 and T2. This is the most harmonious of all conditions. *Counteropposed (Unbalanced):* Conditions of like-disagree and dislike-agree, where the biases counteroppose and where tension at T1 is high but decreases uniformly, where antagonism is low, and where tension release at T1 is relatively low but increases uniformly from T1 to T2. *Dissociative:* The condition of dislike-disagree, where antagonism is excessive at both T1 and T2, and where tension (at T2) is high and tension release is low, suggesting that forces toward dissolution are operative. This latter three-fold scheme integrates the notion of cognitive bias (the liking and agreement biases) with the concept of balance.

8 • • • • • • • •

Current Issues and New Directions

The intent of this final chapter is to list and discuss what is for the most part unknown in balance research, and to give an overall critical evaluation of the literature. Whereas the preceding chapters organized and reviewed research evidence—what is "known"—this chapter focuses on what is not known and what remains to be done. Issues which were touched on before are summarized and pulled together. This chapter discusses the "state of the arts" in balance theory and research.

The chapter is divided into three major sections, the first (section 8.1) of which discusses conditions under which a balance principle is not likely to apply; i.e., conditions under which *un*balance rather than balance is likely to be preferred or tended toward. The second section (8.2) lists current unresolved issues in balance theory and research, from both conceptual and methodological points of view. The final section (8.3) attempts to integrate balance theory with three other small group theories: Asch's group pressure theory, the coalition model, and Homan's exchange theory.

One purpose of this chapter is to suggest hypotheses for future investigation. In certain places, hypotheses will be stated quite explicitly. In others, research hypotheses are only implied. In section 8.1, conditions under which tendencies toward unbalance may be found are listed. Along with each condition, a relatively specific hypothesis is given. In section 8.2, where "unresolved questions" are discussed, each unresolved question implies a number of hypotheses or studies which could be formulated to approach a settlement of the issue raised. In section 8.3, particularly in conjunction with the Asch and coalition models, highly specific hypotheses are stated.

8 • 1   TENDENCIES TOWARD UNBALANCE

In various places, we have often raised the question, "under what kinds of conditions does a consistency or balance principle not apply"; or more precisely, under what conditions is one likely to observe tendencies or preferences for *un*balance rather than balance. Evidence pertaining to this question was reviewed in Chapter 5, where a number of "strong" conditional propositions were stated, such as those on cognitive bias, self-evaluation, and cooperation–competition. However, the issue has not yet been approached conceptually. The task of assessing the "conceptual validity" of the theory remains. The current section focuses directly on this problem. Below, conditions are listed under which one is likely to find tendencies or preferences for unbalance. The conditions listed are based primarily upon speculation rather than on research evidence. For this reason, the following listings are to be taken as sources of hypotheses for further research.

1. *When unbalance or inconsistency is desirable or pleasurable.* All varieties of balance theory argue that any inconsistency (unbalance, asymmetry, incongruity, dissonance) results in high tension, and that cognitive preferences, alterations, shifts or changes are in such a direction so as to reduce this tension. But it can also be argued that certain unbalances and inconsistencies actually result in low tension; or, that there are certain instances where unbalance is desirable and pleasurable.

It is not difficult to think of instances of this kind. People go to a magician to witness inconsistency between perception (what the magician does) and "reality" (what the audience thinks "cannot be done"), and it is a pleasurable experience. Situations of humor often involve gross inconsistencies, and such situations induce pleasure. Visualize a fat person giving instruction on how to lose weight, or a bed-ridden lung cancer patient smoking five packages of cigarettes per day, or an income tax lawyer indicted for income tax evasion, or the Pope serving as consultant to a planned parenthood clinic. To the extent that any humorous situation derives its humor from the property of inconsistency, then to that extent inconsistency is pleasurable.

There is little doubt that certain unbalances and inconsistencies constitute a *creative* experience for many. Unbalances may be exciting and intriguing, suggesting that balances are dull. It is quite possible that if certain plays and novels involving interpersonal relations were graphed (as was done in the third chapter), then some of these plays and novels would no doubt end in unbalance rather than balance. The problem warrants some systematic investigation. It may just be that unbalanced, perplexing endings contribute to a work's greatness, and that plots ending in balance are unimaginative. If the works of Dostoyevsky, Pasternak and other Russian novelists were graph-theoretically analyzed, one might find grossly unbalanced endings. The immense emotional impact of such works as *Doctor Zhivago* may derive from an unbalance property. Many may feel that such works express deep truths. Indeed, in this context, one is led to wonder whether structural unbalance is the highest of all conceivable pleasures.

There is some limited anecdotal evidence that people prefer slight unbalances to complete balance. Recently, college students have engaged the services of computers in order to match them with an "ideal date." "Ideal," in this context, often (though not always) refers to being completely similar on a number of attitude-objects and personality traits. If such attitudes and traits become the X-objects in the Heiderian structure, and the two "matched" persons become P and O, then one deduction from the balance preference hypothesis applies—at least in theory: Mutual attraction will increase as degree of perceived similarity on X-objects increases. The greater the degree of similarity, the more successful the "match."

However, one recent account in a news magazine suggested that slight dissimilarities may produce maximal attraction. During an interview, one computer-matched couple claimed that they were so alike in so many ways that they literally ran out of things to talk about; that in fact, they found one another quite dull. Needless to say, the match was not a successful one. A slight amount of dissimilarity on X-objects may induce greater attraction than maximal similarity, simply because slight dissimilarity makes things more interesting. This suggests that the similarity-attraction relationship is not linear, as Byrne and associates have found (see section 4.2b, Chapter 4). It further suggests that slight unbalance (slight dissimilarity and maximal attraction) is more pleasurable than complete balance (maximal similarity and maximal attraction).

The examples involving humor, creativity, Russian novels and computer dating all seem to suggest the following generalization concerning tendencies toward and preferences for unbalance: *To the degree that unbalance produces relatively low tension (and/or pleasure), the focal person will tend toward or prefer unbalance rather than balance.*

2. *When high or optimal tension is desirable.* It was argued above that certain unbalances induce low tension and/or pleasure, and hence, the focal person will prefer such unbalances. But built into this argument is the assumption that, in fact, low tension is desirable over moderate or even high tension. The assumption that the focal person will seek low-tension states is part of all varieties of balance theory. What if the focal person, for one reason or another, actually prefers moderate or high tension? In such instances, it is reasonable to speculate that the person can prefer or tend toward unbalance *in order to* maintain a moderate or high tension state. Note that here, one must assume that unbalance produces more tension than balance—the reverse of what was argued directly above.

Despite the paucity of systematic balance research on this question, it is possible to cite instances where high "tension" is preferred. Eating sour candy, psychologically speaking, produces higher tension or "discomfort" than eating sweet candy. Yet people eat sour candy every day, and like it. Eating salted peanuts has the same effect. This suggests that persons will induce tension in order to prepare for some *later* ultimate tension reduction—such as drinking a cold beer after eating the salted peanuts. In a similar vein, we have all heard about the man who hits himself on the head with a hammer (tension) because it feels so good when he stops (tension reduction). Sexual foreplay is likewise tension-arousing (as indicated by common physiological indicators of tension such as GSR, pulse rate, etc.), and foreplay constitutes preparation for the anticipated tension-reduction of sexual climax.

If it can be argued that in interpersonal POX or POQ type situations, the focal person calculates that he can increase his tension by preferring unbalance, then it can be argued that he will prefer or tend toward unbalance—if he prefers high tension. Or maybe he desires low tension for himself but high tension for the *other*, in which case he might throw the structure into unbalance in order to hurt, harm or confuse the other. (Changing from $-PO$, $-PX$ and $+OX$ (balance) to $-PO$, $+PX$ and $+OX$ (unbalance) is one example: P changes to agreement with a disliked other in order to confuse the other because he dislikes him.) Generally, *if the focal person desires high tension for himself (or for the other), then the focal person is likely to prefer or tend toward unbalance as one means of achieving the high tension.* Entertaining the notion that high tension "now" is preparation for tension reduction "later," *to the degree that unbalance (and high tension) at time 1 makes balance (and low tension) at time 2 more pleasurable, the focal person will prefer or tend toward unbalance at time 1.*

3. *When balancing one system would unbalance another system of which P is part.* One of the difficulties of the balance literature is that P is considered to be a member of only one "system" (group, structure, experimental condition) at a particular point in time. The possibility of simultaneous membership in multiple systems is rarely considered, at least explicitly. At any given time, a person is a member of many groups, plays many roles, and has multiple commitments. It is therefore possible that balancing one particular system will at the same time unbalance another of which the person is part.

A concrete, convincing example of this condition is Davis' (1963) "cross-pressure" condition, involving one P, two O's and one X. In Figure 1A, the PO_1X structure or cycle constitutes one "system," and the PO_2X structure or cycle constitutes another. P is a member of both of these systems. O_1 may be a person that P is talking to at a given time, and O_2 may be a close friend with whom he is not interacting at the particular time. Clearly, making the PX relation negative balances the PO_1X system but unbalances the PO_2X system. And making the PX relation positive balances the PO_2X system but unbalances the PO_1X system. The focal person is thus in a "double bind"; he is "damned if he does, and damned if he doesn't." In this sense, P is under a cross-pressure from simultaneous membership in two systems.

The cross-pressure approach can be applied in a number of different contexts. Merton's (1957) "reference group theory" proposes that a person will structure his attitudes, beliefs and actions in accordance with his perception of the attitudes, beliefs and actions of a group toward which he is strongly attracted, his "reference group." Hence, one can graph P's relations to a reference group (RG), another person who is not a member of the reference group

(O), and an issue (X) (Figure 1B). In this instance, any members of the reference group are seen as unified in their attitudes toward X (and thus the representation of RG as one object in Figure 1B). If P is in a cross-pressure involving a friend and a reference group, then it would be reasonable to predict that P will balance the cycle containing the reference group at the expense of balancing the POX cycle. In making this prediction, one would have to assume that P's attraction (or liking or commitment) to the reference group is greater than P's attraction (or liking or commitment) to O.

Note that one may criticize experimental research which typically focuses upon only one system of which P is a member. This kind of focus tends to ignore other systems of which P may be part. Should an investigator obtain a tendency toward unbalance in a given structure (a "negative finding" or "deviant case"), this finding is potentially explainable by arguing that P balanced some other system rather than the system or structure being studied. A subject unbalancing

FIGURE 1   CROSS-PRESSURE CONDITIONS

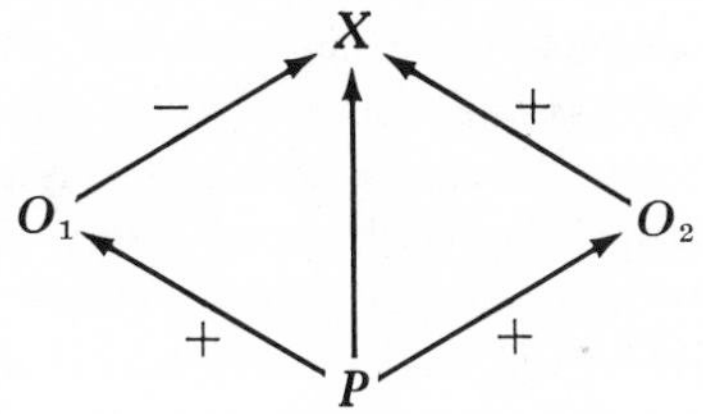

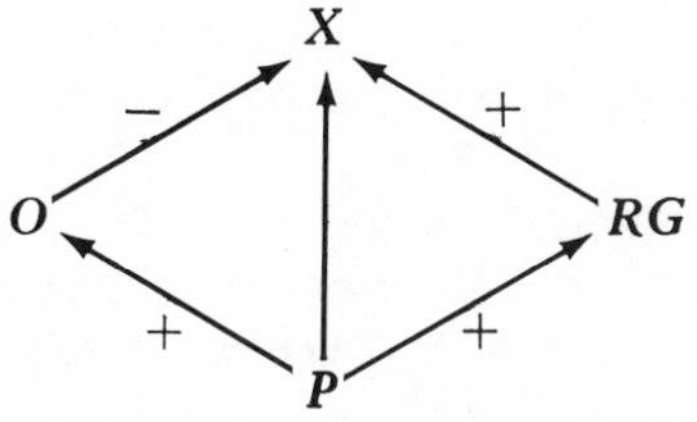

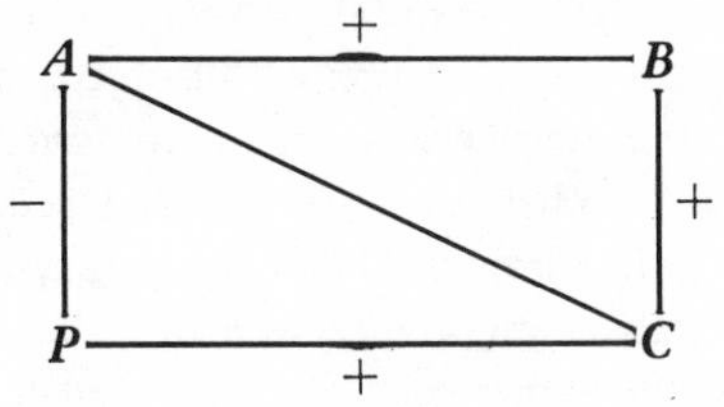

a structure containing himself and another (the dyad being studied) may only reflect his reluctance to be labeled a "hypocrite" by his college roommate who is not being considered in the particular study.

Another way to conceptualize the multiple-system problem, and hence the possibility of cross-pressures acting on P, is to visualize any single group where balancing a non-local cycle would unbalance a local cycle. Such a condition is graphed in Figure 1C. Assuming that P can change only his perception of the AC relation, then it is reasonable to expect a change toward or a preference for $-AC$ (which balances the local $PACP$ cycle but unbalances the non-local ABCA cycle) rather than for $+AC$. The idea that balance forces are greater for local cycles rather than non-local cycle was discussed earlier. The point is that tendencies toward unbalance in non-local cycles may be accounted for by assuming that P balances one or more local cycles instead.

Let us call a *focal system* any system upon which momentary theoretical or research interest is being focused. Then a *nonfocal system* is any system which is "not being considered" by a theorist or researcher. (Note that a local cycle can be part of a "nonfocal system"—see the PO_2X cycle in Figure 1A. This is a local cycle, but if such a cycle is being "ignored," it is a nonfocal system.) Generally, if balance forces in any nonfocal system exceed balance forces in a focal system, then P is likely to *un*balance the focal system and balance the nonfocal system instead. When are balance forces in nonfocal systems likely to be greater? The various corollaries to the theory offer certain leads. First, the *polarity* corollary would tell us that if the strengths of relations are greater in the nonfocal than in the focal system, then P will balance the nonfocal system at the expense of balancing the focal system. In Figure 1A, if the PO_2 and O_2X relations are strong, and the PO_1 and O_1X relations are relatively weak, then one would predict a greater tendency toward balancing the PO_2X cycle (the nonfocal system). Second, the corollary of *relative importance/commitment* would apply in Figure 1A if, say, P were relatively more committed to O_2 than to O_1, in which case one would expect P to balance the PO_2X cycle. Third, the corollaries on *cognitive bias* could be applied. In Figure 1A, positivity bias predicts a change toward $+PX$ rather than $-PX$, hence balancing PO_2X instead of PO_1X. Finally, due to the cross-pressure, P may elect to "neutralize" the PX relation, hence putting both cycles or systems into vacuous balance. This latter alternative might be expected if all relations in both systems are of equal strength, and/or if the relative importances of all objects are equal.

In sum: If the balance forces in one system are relatively greater than the balance forces in another, the P is expected to balance the former system. The sources of such differences in balance forces may lie in the principles of cognitive bias, polarity, relative importance, and the like. Generally, *if balancing a focal system will unbalance another (nonfocal) system of which P is part, then to the degree that balance forces in the nonfocal system exceed balance forces in the focal system, P will balance the nonfocal system and unbalance the focal system.*

4. *When internalized norms define an "unbalanced" condition as stable.* If any structure would be called "unbalanced" by the Heider (or Newcomb or Osgood) model, but if that same structure is defined as "stable" and/or "harmonious" *by the participants* in that structure, then certain unbalanced structures—as defined by the theory—are *more stable* than certain balanced structures. Consider two examples. First, assume that a man (*P*) and wife (*O*) love each other (+*PO*, +*OP*), that the woman very much enjoys cleaning house (+*OX*) and that the man dislikes housework (−*PX*). According to all balance models, this structure is sign-unbalanced, and hypothesized to be tense and unstable. Clearly, it is not. It is a symbiotic, stable, harmonious structure. Consider a second example, where the man and wife love each other, but both abhor housework, yet both like to live in a clean house. The model calls this sign-balance (hence stability and harmony). But what if the man and wife cannot afford to hire anyone to do the housework? After the rooms become filthy, the chances are the husband-wife relationship would deteriorate, suggesting neither stability nor harmony.

One may take the position that the norms internalized by the husband and wife result in their regarding certain structures as stable, and others as unstable. A *normative role* is any norm connected or associated with a status. Generally, in modern Western cultures, women are expected to enjoy doing housework (this is one normative role of women), whereas men are expected to neither enjoy nor do housework. These expectations (norms) are associated with the ascribed statuses of male and female. This is why such expectations are often referred to as "sex-roles." If both the husband and wife have internalized these mutual expectations and act in accordance with them (if their normative roles and "behavioral roles" coincide), then the condition where the wife likes housework and the husband doesn't is relatively stable. But according to balance theory, it would be "unbalanced." The condition of each intensely disliking housework (and not doing it) would be unstable for the man and wife, yet "balanced" according to the theory. In this latter case, if the wife *alters* her attitude toward housework and begins to like it and do it, then this represents an apparent change toward unbalance, yet toward greater stability of the structure. *To the degree that internalized norms define an unbalanced structure as "stable" to the participants in that structure, the participants will tend toward or prefer unbalance of that structure.*

5. *When P and O are competing for an object X which is in short supply.* Davis (1963) cites the "eternal triangle" of two men competing for the affections of one woman, or even two women competing for one man, as one kind of condition to which the hypotheses of balance preference and tendency do not apply. The sign-balanced condition of two male friends both in love with the same woman is neither very stable nor harmonious. Yet, the sign-balanced situation of both men disliking the same woman is stable. Thus, certain sign-balanced conditions can be treated as stable, whereas others cannot.

Similarly, using the same kind of example, certain sign-unbalanced conditions would be thought of as stable. Given two male friends, one of whom loves the woman and the other slightly dislikes the same woman, then we would be inclined to regard it as more stable than the all-positive structure. Still other sign-unbalanced conditions are relatively *un*stable: Even if two enemies passionately love the same woman, the (sign-unbalanced) condition is quite unstable, since both men cannot "have" the same woman.

The common property of these examples is that the woman (the "object" Q) is a short-supply object—only one person, either P or O but not both, can "have" or "love" this same object. If there are two or more loved objects (if each man loved a different woman), then the object is not in short supply. The same idea would apply to two brothers competing for their father's fortune—a sign-balanced but unstable structure. Hence, if P and O are competing for an object which is in short supply, then certain sign-balanced structures are unstable, and certain sign-unbalanced structures are relatively stable. Therefore, *under the condition that P and O are competing for a short-supply object, either P or O are likely to exhibit preferences or tendencies toward sign-unbalance rather than sign-balance.*

6. *If completeness is a stronger force than balance.* The cognitive bias of completeness was discussed in the fifth and sixth chapters. The postulated bias is that people prefer complete structures (all relations known) over incomplete structures (one or more relations unknown). But one may raise the question of whether cognitive forces toward completeness are relatively greater, or relatively less, than cognitive forces toward balance.

Conceptualize the following three kinds of structures: (a) Structures which are balanced and complete; (b) structures which are unbalanced and complete; and (c) structures which are incomplete. If a subject's relative preferences for each type of structure are measured (such as measuring the "ease of learning" for each type), or if the relative amounts of tension associated with each type are ascertained, then it would be possible to determine whether or not completeness forces were relatively stronger than balance forces: If the subject preferred type "c" (incomplete) over type "b" (unbalanced and complete), then one would infer that balance is a stronger force than completeness—unbalanced complete structures are *less* preferable than incomplete structures. But if subjects preferred type "b" over type "c," then a structure which is complete, even though it is unbalanced, is preferable over incomplete structures. Here, one would infer that completeness is a stronger force than balance.

If *in fact* completeness is stronger than balance, then a person will be more likely to prefer complete but unbalanced structures over incomplete ones. In this respect, a person would exhibit a preference for unbalance. *To the degree that preferences for or tendencies toward completeness exceed preferences for or tendencies toward balance, the focal person will prefer or tend toward complete yet unbalanced structures rather than incomplete structures.*

7. *If clustering is a stronger force than balance.* The reader will recall from Chapter 6 that while all balanced structures are necessarily (by definition) clustered, a structure can be completely clustered but unbalanced (the all-negative *POX* or *POQ* structure, for example). A structure can also be both unbalanced and unclustered. If clustering is a considerably stronger force than balance, then one might expect focal persons to exhibit preferences for clustered but unbalanced structures over balanced structures. One of the conditions under which this might occur is where very large structures are involved. Sociometric studies show that large groups tend to segregate into three or more cliques or clusters—suggesting that clustered but unbalanced structures are quite likely (since a large group with three complete clusters is unbalanced). It is also possible that generally, group structures may exhibit greater tendencies toward clustering rather than balance, whereas *cognitive structures* may exhibit the reverse—greater tendencies toward balance (rather than clustered but unbalanced configurations).

If one takes "size of the structure" (the number of objects) as a conditional variable, the following proposition is evident: *If the structure is small, then preferences for or tendencies toward balanced structures are very likely— possibly more likely than preferences for or tendencies toward clustered unbalanced structures. If, however, the structure is large, then clustering forces may exceed balance forces, such that preferences for, tendencies toward or occurrences of clustered but unbalanced structures are just as likely or even more likely than preferences for, tendencies toward or occurrences of balanced structures.*

8. *Other conditions under which unbalance preferences or tendencies may be observed.* Most studies on the similarity-attraction relationship find that attraction increases with increases in perceived similarity. Many investigations (such as those by Broxton, 1963; Byrne et al., 1967) find that increased similarity on personality "traits" (*X*'s) increases attraction. However, Winch (1952), among others, proposed the hypothesis that *complementarity* rather than similarity on certain personality traits results in high attraction. If one takes "sadomasochism" as the "trait" (hence the *X*-object in the *POX* structure), one sadist is more likely to get along with and like another who is a masochist, rather than also a sadist. A domineering person is more likely to get along with a submissive person than with another domineering person. Winch reports that this kind of complementarity is rather frequent among married couples. It is thus evident that the nature of the *X*-object in *POX* structures can determine whether "similarity" or "difference" results in high attraction.

Research seems to indicate that if some (not all) personality traits are taken as *X*-objects, then complementarity results in attraction, but if attitude-objects are taken as the *X*-objects, then similarity results in attraction. To the extent that one treats complementarity as "dissimilarity," then to that extent people prefer a type of unbalance (dissimilarity and high attraction). Note that the example cited earlier involving the wife who likes housework and the husband who doesn't could be considered a complementary (and stable) structure.

A second condition under which apparent unbalance may be preferred is any condition under which the P, O and X objects do not have *common relevance* (Newcomb, 1953, 1961; Pepitone, 1966). If you like to eat chicken, chickens like to eat chicken feed, but you do not have great fondness for eating chicken feed, the structure is unbalanced but you are not likely to be particularly bothered or tense. Note that even though the *relations* are the same ("like to eat" versus "not like to eat"), the *objects* are in different "cognitive spheres"; they do not have "common relevance." In Festinger's terms, the objects are "irrelevant" rather than consonant or dissonant. But the common relevance issue in balance research is a sticky and unresolved one, mainly because *balance theory provides no clear taxonomy or typology giving objects to which the theory is applicable and objects to which it is not applicable.* Heider initially seemed to assume that the X-object in his *POX* paradigm could be anything. This criticism is applicable to the above examples on complementarity: To what objects does a complementarity (rather than a similarity) hypothesis apply? By and large, the answer to this question is not known. Generally, with regard to certain objects (such as some personality traits; or, any objects which do not have "common relevance"— if common relevance can be defined), preferences for and tendencies toward apparent unbalance are quite likely.

8 • 2   UNRESOLVED ISSUES

The matter of unresolved issues and unsettled questions in balance theory and research has been brought up before. However, no listing of such issues, from both conceptual and methodological points of view, has yet been made. This section attempts to pull together some important issues that were only touched on earlier, plus some additional ones. The discussion is divided into two areas: important conceptual or theoretical issues, and primarily methodological issues. In the following discussion, one must assume, of course, that a balance principle is itself valid; specifically, that one is dealing with conditions under which balance does, rather than does not, apply.

8 • 2a   Conceptual Issues

1. *The definition and meaning of "balance" or "consistency."* Just what *is* unbalance? What combinations of objects and signs and strengths can be called truly "unbalanced" or "inconsistent," and which combinations can be called "balanced" or "consistent"? There are some very basic disagreements in both the theoretical and empirical literature on this obviously crucial question. The issue seems to involve four problems.

First, *there are fundamental disagreements on which sign/strength combinations are stable (and not tense) and which are unstable (and tense).* This issue was introduced in the second chapter, when the Heider, Newcomb and Osgood models were compared. An extension of that comparison will be made at this time. (It might be helpful to refer back to Figure 4, Chapter 2.) Table 1 below gives a comparison of the Heider, Newcomb and Osgood models according to the stability criterion. A given structure which is unstable (sign-unbalanced) according to Heider's model *is necessarily* unstable according to the Newcomb and Osgood models (first row of Table 1). A given structure which is stable according to Heider but unstable according to Newcomb *is necessarily* unstable according to Osgood (second row). A structure which is stable according to both Heider and Newcomb *can still be* unstable according to the Osgood model (row three). The fourth row of the table shows that a structure can be stable according to all three models, but more importantly, that a stable structure according to Osgood *is necessarily* stable according to Heider and Newcomb. Note also (from the third row) that a structure unstable according to Osgood but stable according to Newcomb is necessarily stable according to Heider.

These comparisons reflect two things: (1) that the models disagree on just what structures are stable and which are not; and (2) that the Osgood model is *more rigorous* than the Newcomb model, which is in turn more rigorous than Heider's. Hence, a source of the disagreement is the degree of rigor in the model. This is due to the Osgood principle of maximal simplicity of attitudes, and to Osgood's consideration of strength, both of which make his model more rigorous than Newcomb's and Heider's. Newcomb's consideration of strength (but elimination of the maximal simplicity principle) makes his model more rigorous than Heider's but less rigorous than Osgood's.

It seems obvious that one well designed study could resolve these disagreements. Where the Heider model would predict "no change in relations," the Newcomb model would predict change. And where the Newcomb model would predict no change, the Osgood model would predict change, and so on. Yet, no

TABLE 1   A COMPARISON OF THE HEIDER, NEWCOMB AND OSGOOD MODELS BY THE STABILITY CRITERION

	ACCORDING TO HEIDER'S MODEL	ACCORDING TO NEWCOMB'S MODEL	ACCORDING TO OSGOOD'S MODEL
A given structure is:	Unstable	Unstable	Unstable
A given structure is:	Stable	Unstable	Unstable
A given structure is:	Stable	Stable	Unstable
A given structure is:	Stable	Stable	Stable

>>>————————————→
Increasing rigor of the model

study or set of studies has carried out a convincing test of these basic, fundamental differences between the models. Thus, the disagreement on just what is "stable" and what is not still remains, although a soon to be published study by Truzzi[1] may approach a resolution to this problem.

A second disagreement involves the *six-fold controversy* discussed at length in the sixth chapter. Cognitive balance–unbalance is alternatively seen as a matter of psychologically averaging, summing, multiplying, or getting the difference (discrepancy) between inconsistent cognitions, or as a matter of gauging overall balance–unbalance of a structure on the basis of the relation of maximum strength, or on the basis of the strength of an interpersonal (rather than attitudinal) relation in a structure. The most vigorous controversy involves the averaging (Osgood), summation (Fishbein) and discrepancy (Newcomb) procedures. Each perspective defines consistency-inconsistency in a different way; the meaning of consistency-inconsistency is different in each case.

A third disagreement relevant to the broad issue (the broad issue being the definition and meaning of consistency-inconsistency, balance–unbalance, etc.) concerns *the case of the negative PO relation*. Newcomb (1968), following Price et al. (1966) and in part as a result of critiques by Jordan (1963, 1966a), claims that all structures containing −PO are "nonbalanced," hence less stable and more tense than strict "balanced" (like-agree) structures, but more stable and less tense than strict "unbalance" (like-disagree). The difficulties with this scheme were detailed in the previous chapter. This three-fold scheme modifies the original Heider model, but its implications for the Osgood model are grossly unclear, and it cannot be easily integrated with formalistic procedures. It appears that in certain respects, Newcomb's recent scheme tends to add to current confusion rather than alleviate it.

The confusion introduced by the Newcomb three-fold scheme is even further complicated by a fourth question involving *the case of the dislike-disagree condition*. Findings were presented in Chapter 7 which suggest that this condition can be combined neither with like-agree (as in Heider's model) nor with dislike-agree (as with Newcomb's scheme). One means of resolving this question (at least in part) was suggested earlier: Combining structures into balanced, counteropposed (unbalanced) and dissociative conditions. Although this scheme can be integrated with the concepts of cognitive bias (positivity and agreement), it cannot be easily integrated with the Osgood model, nor with current graph-theoretic (or matrix) procedures for defining balance.

2. *Different criteria for distinguishing states of consistency (balance) from states of inconsistency (unbalance)*. The previous issue arises to a great degree from this one: Balance theorists and researchers apply *different conceptual criteria* for determining which structures are to be called consistent or balanced, and which are to be called inconsistent or unbalanced. Three kinds of criteria

---

1. The study in question, M. Truzzi's doctoral dissertation (sociology, Cornell) is not available at the time of this writing.

can be seen in the literature: The logical, the operational, and the observational criteria.

The *logical* criterion seems to say "that which is logical is balanced, and that which is illogical is unbalanced." This criterion is evident, to a degree, in the Abelson-Rosenberg (1958) "symbolic psycho-logic" model, where syllogistic-like procedures are used as approximations of what is expected to be psychologically consistent and what is expected to be psychologically inconsistent in a person's mind. Festinger (1957) appeared to use the logical criterion in defining "dissonance" as involving the "obverse" of a cognition. The original Cartwright-Harary (1956) extension of Heider, a logical-mathematical criterion of defining balance–unbalance, has a syllogistic character: I like O (premise), I dislike Q (premise), therefore O must dislike Q (conclusion). The algebraic product of the first two signs (one positive, one negative) is negative. This algebraic procedure is a mathematical way of representing logical, syllogistic cognitive processes.[2]

A second criterion, the *operational* criterion, in many ways conflicts with the first. Two operational criteria for distinguishing balance from unbalance are employed in the theoretical and empirical literature. One is the stability criterion: "That which is stable (not likely to change) is balanced, and that which is

2. For those who are intrigued by the applicability of graph-theoretic procedures to logic, consider the following problem of theory building: Assuming one has three variables, X, Y and Z, then if X and Z are inversely ($-$) related, and Z and Y are positively ($+$) related, then the logical inference is that X and Y are inversely ($-$) related. As X increases Z decreases, and as Z decreases Y decreases. Hence, as X increases, Y decreases—and inverse ($-$) relationship. This reasoning is central to Zetterberg's "axiomatic" method of theory-building (Zetterberg, 1954). Note that for any set of given relationships (as, the given relationships between X and Z, and between Z and Y), the *sign* of the inferred or deduced relationship (the relationship between X and Y) is the algebraic product of the signs of the given relationships. Costner and Leik (1964) call this the "sign rule." The sign rule is true for any number of given relationships. For example, if A is inversely related to B, B is inversely related to C, C is positively related to D, and D is positively related to E, then the inferred relationship between A and E is positive. The product of the four signs is positive: ($-$) ($-$) ($+$) ($+$) = ($+$).

Now let a *variable* be represented by a *point* in any graph, and let any *relationship* between two variables (an "hypothesis" or "proposition") be represented by a *signed nondirected line*. Clearly, if the product of the lines in a given *cycle* is positive, then that cycle is "logical." If the product of the lines in a given cycle is negative, then the cycle is "illogical." Thus, if an entire graph represents a substantive *theory*, then the theory is "logical" and "internally consistent" only if all of the cycles in its graph are positive.

Note that: (a) A cycle is logical if it has an even number of negative lines. (b) The graph of a theory is logical if it satisfies the decomposition theorem. (c) A "logical" graph is a *balanced* graph, and an "illogical" graph is an *unbalanced* graph. (d) If the graph represents a theory, *then the theory is logical (internally consistent) only if its graph is completely balanced (if all of its cycles are positive)*.

It is evident that one may criticize a theory by graphing it and seeing if all cycles are balanced. If all cycles are balanced, then it is a consistent, logical theory (by this criterion). If one or more cycles are unbalanced, then it is not logical. The "degree" to which the theory is logical is simply an index of degree of balance of the theory's graph. Perhaps we should all concern ourselves more with *balanced theories,* and less with "balance theory"!

unstable (likely to change) is unbalanced." Another is the tension criterion: "That which is characterized by low tension is balanced, and that which is characterized by relatively high tension is unbalanced." The concept of "psychological balance" or "cognitive balance" (Jordan, 1953; 1963; 1966a) employs the tension criterion. Note that these two criteria can themselves conflict—a given structure can conceivably be characterized by low tension, yet be unstable (in any instance where the source or cause of the instability is something other than high tension).

In addition, the operational criteria can conflict with the logical criterion: A structure can be stable (and untense), yet be highly illogical. Recall Feather's (1964a) study, where high authoritarians chose an illogical conclusion to a syllogism because it was in agreement with ("balanced" with) a particular attitude of their own (and hence it was not likely to change—it was stable, in addition to being psychologically "comfortable" or untense). In other words, *balance dynamics can prevent logical thinking.* This is why—contrary to what some (e.g., Zajonc, 1960) have said—balance theory cannot be called a theory of human "rationality." Cognitive structures and thought processes which are comfortable and stable are often at the same time most illogical.

The third (*observational*) criterion, employed by Heider, Newcomb, and certain researchers (e.g., Kogan and Tagiuri, 1958) states "that which is frequently observed is balanced, and that which is infrequently observed is unbalanced." The idea is that if people are always preferring or tending toward that which *they* "define" as balance, then one will observe more balances than unbalances in everyday life. Hence, so the argument seems to run, we can infer that the "infrequently observed" must necessarily be defined as "unbalanced," both by observers (the theorists and researchers) and the observed. One of the interesting paradoxes in balance theory is that if people are, in fact, always seeking out balances and avoiding unbalances, then why is there so much unbalance around in the first place?

3. *Alternative modes of resolution of inconsistency or unbalance.* What does the focal person think or do when faced with unbalance? Throughout this book, the distinction has been made between *molar* alternatives to the resolution of unbalance, on the one hand and *microprocess* alternatives, on the other. Given unbalance in a POX structure, the focal person can change the sign and/or strength of one or more of the relations ("parameter variables") in the direction of increased balance. Any such change is a "molar" change. Which among several possible molar changes is most likely to occur? The various corollaries to the theory attempt to answer this. The Osgood polarity corollary predicts strong relations are more likely to change than weak relations. The Rokeach-Rothman corollary states that the likelihood of change in a relation (and its magnitude of change) is a function of the product of both the polarity of the relation and the relative importance of the object. The cognitive bias perspective predicts a number of things: Negative relations will tend to become positive, and positive

relations will tend to remain positive (positivity). The signs of the PX and OX (or PQ and OQ) relations will tend to change toward each other, independently of the sign of the PO relation (agreement and lateral symmetry). Interpersonal relations tend to become reciprocal or symmetric (the reciprocity bias), with changes toward positive reciprocal interpersonal relations being most likely (positive reciprocity). In general, interpersonal relations are more likely to change than attitudinal or unit relations (the bias toward interpersonal preference/change). The relations most likely to change are those which are the minimum changes necessary to achieve balance (least cost).

All these corollaries apply to changes in the sign or intensity of one or more parameter variables. But the focal person may do other things not directly involving manipulation of parameter variables. These are the microprocess alternatives to the resolution of unbalance, discussed in Chapter 2: Repressing or denying certain aspects of the structure (denial), splitting a cognitive object into two or more independent parts (differentiation or segregation), adding perceptions which minimize the impact of unbalance (bolstering), rejecting an object as "important" (decreasing the importance of an object), seeing the object "in a different light" (changing the cognitive status of the object), or simply bearing and "living with" the unbalance. Among microprocess sometimes cited in the literature is "cognitive dissociation"—perceiving that two objects are not related at all. For example, your friend telling you that he strongly disliked a novel you thought was brilliant is unbalance; you might convince yourself that he is not competent to evaluate the novel—you dissociate one object (your friend) from another (the novel). Note that this type of alternative is in effect putting the structure into vacuous balance: You "neutralize" the OX relation. It also may be seen as decreasing the *common relevance* of the two objects (cf. p. 266 above).

The literature on balance yields much evidence pertaining to the operation of molar alternatives to the resolution of unbalance or inconsistency (this literature was covered in Chapter 5), but yields no systematic evidence in regard to the operation of microprocess alternatives. The literature on microprocesses is only speculative. Consequently, important unresolved issues have arisen. Among them:

a. When, and under what kinds of conditions, does a microprocess resolution take place *instead* of a molar resolution? When, and under what kinds of conditions, can (and does) a microprocess alternative take place *prior to* a molar change? In other words, is a microprocess alternative itself an "alternative" to a molar process, or does the focal person often evoke a microprocess antecedent to making some molar change? Considering the tension variable, one hypothesis may be offered, suggesting that microprocess alternatives are evoked *instead* of molar alternatives. Assuming that unbalance produces more tension in the focal person than balance, *if any molar changes toward increased balance are prevented, then one or more microprocesses will be evoked by the focal person as one means of reducing the tension produced by unbalance.* Under what conditions is a molar change toward balance "prevented"? The literature provides certain leads—among them: (a) when all relations in the structure are of high polarity (when they are all "strong"); (b) when all objects are of equal relative importance to the focal person, or when all objects are of high importance, or when the focal person is highly committed to other persons in the structure; or (c) when changing a relation toward balance would violate a cognitive bias (such as having to change a relation toward the negative in order to achieve balance; or having to change many (as opposed to few) relations toward balance).

b. Is a microprocess resolution a temporary state, or is it a relatively "permanent" resolution of unbalance? Are the molar alternatives more permanent resolutions than the microprocess resolutions?

c. Considering the molar alternatives alone, under what conditions is one molar alternative violated in favor of another? Will the focal person change a *strong* relation toward balance, if it is initially negative (hence violating polarity but satisfying positivity)? Will the focal person change two weak relations toward balance instead of changing one strong one toward balance (hence violating least cost but satisfying polarity)? Evidence reviewed in Chapter 5, particularly the results of Burnstein (1967), allowed us to suggest that a hierarchy of biases (or a hierarchy of molar alternatives) is operative, and that the likelihood of the focal person evoking an alternative is in direct proportion to its hierarchical position. But this hypothesis leaves unanswered such questions as: What are the relative hierarchical positions of the molar alternatives? To what degree does the hierarchical position of an alternative depend upon personality predisposition? To what extent does it depend upon social-structural conditions, such as the size of the structure?

d. Under what conditions is "autistic" balance preferred over "realistic" balance? Newcomb (1961; 1963) finds that persons high in authoritarianism are more likely to elect autistic balance, where perceived (subjective) similarity with a liked other on some X exceeds actual (objective) similarity. What other personality conditions, besides authoritarianism, make autistic balance more likely? Are there any structural conditions which make autistic alternatives more likely? Does the likelihood of autistic balance vary with the strength of relations in the structure, or with the number of objects, or in accordance with any of the cognitive biases? Additional research is needed to help in answering such questions.

4. *"Surface" sentiments versus "depth" feelings.* Few would argue that "liking" is the same thing as "loving," and that "disliking" is the same as "hating." Heider's theory was meant to apply to surface sentiments (likings, attractions, etc.) rather than to "deeper" feelings of love, hate, sexual attraction, and so on. But balance theory has not been tested on such variables. One reason appears to be that while measuring instruments have been developed and refined for measuring likes and dislikes, depth feelings and emotions are less easily measured and quantified. Nonetheless, modern psychiatry must, and to a great

degree does, gauge such feelings. Even certain attempts at precise quantification are made every now and then. It might be of interest to see whether or not the balance principle applies to depth feelings and emotions. Some research on this question might prove instructive.

5. *Is the balance process a conscious process?* Do people consciously balance cognitive cycles or structures, or is the focal person unaware of the balance dynamics that supposedly go on inside his head? Do people *really* go around with little triangles in their heads, thinking: "If I like O and Q, then O and Q must like each other"? Heider[3] takes the position that the focal person is not able to describe the balancing process. If this is true, then the balance process is not wholly conscious, at least not until someone (like a balance theorist) tells the focal person he is balancing something with something else. Yet, the balance process lacks the properties of "unconscious" processes such as the ego-defense mechanisms of repression, fixation, regression, and the like, even though tendencies toward balance can be viewed as tension-reducing mechanisms, as can the mechanisms of ego defense.

One is struck by the similarity between the postulated microprocess alternatives to the resolution of unbalance (denial, segregation, etc.) and the Freudian mechanisms of ego defense. One difference, however, is that while an ego defense mechanism is presumably evoked when an unconscious fear or drive threatens to "pierce" the level of consciousness, the microprocess alternatives would probably operate differently. Discovering that a structure is unbalanced (and then "denying" it) cannot be thought of as analogous to an unconscious fear piercing the level of consciousness (and as a result repressing it).

It seems clear that the *objects* (*P*'s, *Q*'s, etc.) of a cognitive structure are wholly conscious. Likewise, so are the *relations* between these objects (likes and dislikes, favorable and unfavorable attitudes). But while the objects and relations of cognitive structures are conscious, the *balancing process itself,* which involves these objects and relations, is probably not. If the notion of *levels* of consciousness is entertained, then the objects and relations are at a fairly high level, but the process itself is at a relatively lower level—it is *relatively* less conscious.

6. *The reducibility issue.* Can a balance principle, and the cognitive bias principles, all be reduced to some other more general explanation or principle? Stated in another way, can the concepts of balance and cognitive bias *be deduced from* more general socialpsychological principles? The notion that certain biases (reciprocity, positivity, agreement, etc.) result from internalized norms was mentioned in Chapter 5. Another possibility is that the principles of balance and cognitive bias are reducible to a *frustration* principle: Liking the other and finding that you disagree with him is frustrating. Hence, unbalance can be seen as a type of frustration. Disagreeing with another, regardless of whether you like him or not, is frustrating in itself (the agreement cognitive bias). Changing only a

3. Via personal communication to the author.

few relations toward balance is less frustrating than having to change many relations toward balance (hence the least cost bias can be seen as avoidance of frustration). Complete structures are less frustrating than incomplete ones (thus reducing the completeness bias to a frustration principle).

A third possibility is that the balance concept and certain biases may be reducible to a more general *reward-punishment* explanation. Certain examples in this regard were cited earlier. We like those who are attitudinally similar to us because perceived attitude similarity is rewarding, and we like those who reward us. We dislike those who are dissimilar because perceived dissimilarity is punishment, and we dislike those who punish us. The reward-punishment explanation is taken up in more detail later in this chapter, where balance theory is briefly contrasted with Homans' (1961) "exchange theory."

Finally, the balance principle and certain biases may only reflect a general tendency for people to *simplify* or *stereotype* structures. Balance is clearer and simpler to understand and comprehend than unbalance. Reciprocity (a type of balance) is thus simpler than non-reciprocity. Changing the fewest relations toward balance is simpler than changing more than the fewest possible. Agreeing with the other is simpler than disagreeing with him, if only because the necessity of arguing with him is eliminated. Perhaps even complete structures are somehow simpler to absorb and perceive than incomplete structures.

The reducibility issue in balance theory is an important one. It has bearing on the matter of the "place" of balance theory among other theories in social psychology, sociology, psychology. Should balance theory be treated as a "theory" in its own right, or must it be treated as a set of specific deductions from other more general theories? In this respect, the problem of reducibility is a true "issue."

7. *Other conceptual issues.* Three additional issues are in need of clarification. First, there is the matter of *intervening variables,* discussed in Chapter 4. Is tension the only variable which intervenes between the perception of unbalance and changes toward balance, or can other variables or processes intervene (other possibilities were mentioned in Chapter 4)? Second, there is the question of *size* of the structure or group (the number of objects in it), particularly distinctions involving dyads and triads. The relative stabilities of dyads versus triads, and the amounts of tension in each generated by unbalance, was treated earlier.

A third issue concerns differences in balance tendency or preference *among different types of local cycles.* Recall Newcomb's delineation of four relations or variables as part of the focal person's "individual system" (cognitive structure): Liking ($P \rightarrow O$), perceived liking (P's perception of $P \leftarrow O$), attitude ($P \rightarrow X$), and perceived attitude (P's perception of $O \rightarrow X$). There are two three-line cycles in this structure, one formed by liking, attitude and perceived attitude, the other formed by perceived liking, attitude and perceived attitude. One cycle contains liking, the other contains perceived liking. Taylor (1967) finds that the cycle containing liking is more likely to tend toward balance than the cycle containing perceived liking. Since both cycles are local cycles, the principle that local cycles are more subject to balancing forces does not apply. In addition, the "interpersonal change" cognitive bias, which states that interpersonal (liking) relations are more likely to change than attitudinal relations, does not apply, since both liking and perceived liking are interpersonal relations. Furthermore, the positivity bias did not account for the differences in balance tendency between the two cycles, nor did any of the other biases. Note that the reciprocity bias was actually violated: Balance among liking, attitude and perceived attitude coupled with unbalance among perceived liking, attitude and perceived attitude necessarily violates reciprocity (the PO and perceived OP relations are of opposite sign). The only conclusion was that the cycle containing liking was more subject to balance forces than the cycle containing perceived liking. One possible explanation is that *objective relations* which are part of a local cycle are more subject to balance pressures than *perceived relations* which are also part of a local cycle. Namely, the focal person is more concerned with balancing the cycle containing liking, attitude and perceived attitude than with balancing the cycle containing perceived liking, attitude and perceived attitude.

8 • 2b *Methodological Issues*

1. *The definition and measurement of tension.* Just how tension is to be conceptualized, defined and measured is as much a "conceptual" issue as it is a "methodological" one. The tension variable has been defined in at least three ways. First, a "tension" has been defined as a "motive" or "drive," such that the tension aroused by unbalance motivates the focal person to achieve balance (or deny or repress the unbalance), in somewhat the same way that one gratifies the hunger drive by eating, or the sex drive by coitus or masturbation. The drive/ motive conceptualization is important to the Festinger model, and references to the "drive state" of unbalance are seen in the works of Newcomb.

A second conceptualization has been that tension is an "internal" state (like a drive), but that it is a matter of "discomfort" or "uneasiness" or "unpleasantness," and does not have the properties of a true drive—it is *not as strong* a force as a drive. This would result in a taxonomic classification of unbalance (and resulting tension) as "something other than" a true drive. The concept of "psychological balance" cited earlier incorporates this second conceptualization of the tension variable.

A third conceptualization involves the "external field" or "stimulus field" of the focal person; the tension is not within the personality, but is somehow "outside" it, a *pressure* that acts on the focal person. Heider takes this position. This distinction bears resemblance to the distinction between a *stress,* on one hand, and a *strain,* on the other. A stress is some external force acting on the focal person, whereas a strain is some internal state. (If you stand on top of a box, you are the "stress," and you put the box "in strain.") Hence, whereas the first two conceptualizations define tension as a strain (an internal state), the third Heiderian one defines tension as a stress (an external force or pressure).

This lack of agreement in the theoretical literature on how to conceptually define tension has been (in part) responsible for a number of divergent procedures for *measuring* tension in experiments and studies. "Tension" has been variously measured by self-rating scales involving "unpleasantness" (Jordan, 1953; Runkel, 1956; Rodrigues, 1967), "discomfort" (Festinger and Hutte, 1954; Morrissette, 1958; Shrader and Lewit, 1962; Rodrigues, 1965; Morrissette et al., 1966; Morrissette et al., 1967), "nervousness" (Sampson and Insko, 1964), and "negative affect" (Price et al., 1965). Other studies have elected to use behavioral measures (rather than self-rating measures) of tension: GSR deflections (Burdick and Burnes, 1958), and "tension behavior" (Taylor, 1968; Chapter 7, above). Even though all these studies tend to give identical results (it is always shown that liking is less tense than dislike, agreement is less tense than disagreement, balance is less tense than unbalance), the potential danger in these diverse measures is that if and when a study *does* get results that conflict with other studies, the explanation that the results conflict because of different tension measures cannot be rejected.

This latter problem was encountered in our interpretation of Jordan's (1966b) re-analysis of the Price et al. (1965) data, reviewed in Chapter 5. Jordan found that the strength of the *PO* relation is not related to tension ("affect") when discrepancy is constant, and that discrepancy is not related to tension when the strength of *PO* is constant. This finding tends to conflict with other studies, particularly if "discrepancy" is seen as analogous to "agreement." Is it because the Price et al. study used a peculiar measure of tension? It is difficult to say. The question of the relationship between discrepancy and tension (and strength of *PO* and tension) is only confused because of the nature of the tension measure used.

It would appear that balance researchers think of themselves as somehow immune from assessing the *validity* of their tension measures. The Price et al. study uses questionable techniques for measuring "affect." First of all, the concept of "tension" is probably not equivalent with the concept of "negative affect" (affect is usually taken to mean "emotion"). Second, the subjects in the study placed a checkmark on one scale, with the adjective "uneasy" appearing at one end and the adjective "pleasant" appearing at the other. But "pleasant" may not be the same thing as "easy," and "unpleasant" may not be the same thing as "uneasy." The distinction between "pleasant-unpleasant" may be one continuum or concept, and the distinction between "easy-uneasy" may be another. It would have been advantageous for Price et al. to have used *two* scales (one being "pleasant-unpleasant," the other being "easy-uneasy"). It then would have been possible to *correlate* the two scales with each other, under the assumption that if they correlate highly, the idea that they measure the *same* concept (rather than two different concepts) *could not be rejected.* (This is the logic which underlies factor analysis as a procedure for validating scales.) One has yet to see a balance study which presents data on the validity of its tension measures, whether that procedure involves "internal" validation (inter-correlating two or more presumed measures of tension), "external" or "criterion" validation (correlating one type of measure with another type—e.g., correlating a self-rating measure with some behavioral measure), or any other validation procedure.

2. *Designs and analysis techniques biased toward getting supportive results.* When one performs an experiment or study of one kind or another, he must be careful so as not to "stack the deck" in favor of his hypotheses. Certain balance studies in effect do just that; the procedures used are often biased toward getting supportive results. The Sampson-Insko (1964) study reviewed earlier (Chapter 4) was a "biased design" in this respect: The investigators measured change in the PX and perceived OX relations, but did not measure change in the PO relation. Hence, they interpreted a change from, say, $-PX$, $+OX$, $+PO$ toward $+PX$, $+OX$, $+PO$ as a change toward balance. But it is possible that some subjects at the same time may have changed from $+PO$ in the direction of $-PO$, a change interpretable as a change toward an unbalanced structure. If such changes did in fact occur, then certain changes interpreted as changes in the direction of balance were actually in the direction of unbalance. Since the hypothesis of the study was that changes toward balance will exceed changes toward unbalance, the design did not fully permit the isolation of results which would tend to disconfirm a balance hypothesis. And in this way, it was "stacking the deck" in favor of a balance principle.

A good portion of research following the Osgood model can be subjected to this criticism. Studies on congruity typically measure the initial strength of the PC and PS attitudes, then link S with C by means of an assertion (designated in sign only rather than strength), then measure shifts or changes in the PC and PS attitudes. But in the meantime, the focal person's perception of the assertion could also have shifted or changed. Even studies which are otherwise exceptionally well designed (like the Rokeach-Rothman (1965) study reviewed in Chapter 5) have not measured possible shifts in the focal person's perception of the assertion. In studies such as these, whether they employ a balance or a congruity model, *to the extent that not measuring changes in certain relations did not allow the investigators to locate any changes toward unbalance, then to that extent the design did not permit disconfirmation of a balance (or congruity) hypothesis.* Such designs are biased toward obtaining supportive results.

The distinction between interpersonal-hypothetical and interpersonal-concrete designs ("real groups") was detailed earlier. It was pointed out that certain results in interpersonal-concrete situations (such as those obtained by Aronson and Worchel, 1966) tend to be less confirming of a balance principle than do results in interpersonal-hypothetical situations. This may mean that the balance principle is in fact more applicable to hypothetical than to "real group" conditions. But it may also mean that the bulk of balance research (particularly the Byrne research on the similarity-attraction relationship) is done with designs which lend themselves to supportive results; namely, that balance research reveals a tendency to *preselect* designs which are favorable to the balance principle.

Unfortunately, it can be argued that certain investigators have used *data-analysis* techniques which will give supportive results, and have ignored those which would have given unsupportive results. One example is the Price et al. (1965) study, which found strength of PO and discrepancy to be related to tension (affect). But recall that Jordan (1966b), using a different means of analyzing the Price et al. data (see pp. 139–140, Chapter 5), came out with a totally different conclusion: That neither strength of *PO* nor discrepancy was related to tension. Who knows what other balance studies would have given completely different results, if the data were reanalyzed using "better" or "more appropriate" analysis techniques?

The foregoing paragraphs must not, obviously, be interpreted to mean that a "biased" design or analysis technique was in any way the intention of a particular researcher. What is meant is that by not doing certain things (such as not measuring changes in some relations in a structure), some researchers have inadvertently biased their findings in such a way as to not completely allow for disconfirming results. It seems that there is a tendency or trend for some studies to lend themselves to this interpretation. Our criticism in no way applies to a particular study, but to the trend. The meaningful findings of important studies (like the Rokeach-Rothman findings on relative importance and polarity, to mention only one) are no less significant because of this apparent trend.

3. *Lack of comparability of studies.* Studies in balance which *should* be comparable on relevant criteria are generally not comparable. It would be helpful if studies measuring tension used the same instruments for measuring tension; if studies measuring "changes in relations" measured change in the same way, rather than have some measure "actual changes" and others measure "preferences for changing" a relation or relations; if all studies which have subjects "rate" structures in terms of preference, or "learn" structures, all included the subject as the "*P*" (the focal person) in the structure being rated or learned. Many studies, like the learning studies of Zajonc and associates, do not have the subject include himself in the structure. Studies differ on a number of other criteria, such as the number of objects in the structure, types of relations (sentiment only, attitude only, both), measurement of sign only versus measurement of sign and strength, and types of objects (persons, "X's", word concepts). Even when strength of relations are measured, differing means of measuring strength are employed: Five-point scales versus seven-point scales; decimal values (+.78, −.43, etc.) versus whole-number values (+3, +2, etc.); scoring the "number of strong relations in a structure" versus scoring the strength of *given* relations.

4. *Further notes on formalization.* Although issues involving graph-theoretic formalization have been already discussed in detail, a simple listing of unsettled issues is worthwhile. Many of the following issues can be taken as specific suggestions for further research.

a. No suitable procedure has been developed for measuring the direction of change of a given structure. Some indices will show a given structure as moving through time toward balance, others will show the very same structure as moving away from balance, and still others will reflect no change at all. This is one of the most critical current problems in balance research.

b. Differing indices of balance give different degrees of balance for the same structure at *one* point in time. Some indices consider only the signs of relations, others consider both sign and strength. Some indices (such as the Phillips index, discussed in the sixth chapter) appear to measure clustering rather than balance.

c. There is some limited evidence that non-local cycles have less of an effect upon P than local cycles. Hence, should cycles be weighted according to whether they are local or non-local? Since non-local cycles can vary in their "distance" from P, should non-local cycles be weighted according to their locality, L?

d. There is evidence that the longer a local cycle, the less its effect upon P. Hence, should local cycles be weighted according to their length?

e. What are the relative effects of length versus locality: Does a long but local cycle effect P more than a short but nonlocal cycle, or is the reverse more likely?

f. What is the relative explanatory power of such extrabalance properties as clustering and completeness? Is clustering more appropriate than balance for large structures, and balance more appropriate than clustering for small ones? Is clustering generally more appropriate for sociometric structures, and balance more appropriate for cognitive structures? Is an unbalanced but complete structure relatively more stable than an incomplete structure—suggesting that completeness is a stronger force than balance, and that the term "vacuous balance" is a misnomer?

g. How can the problem of ambivalent relations be treated in formalization?

h. How should strength be scored? Certain indices of balance use whole number scale values such as $+3$, $+2$, etc., whereas others use decimal values.

i. Should the signs and/or strengths of the lines in a structure be multiplied, or should they be added, or averaged, or perhaps even subtracted?

j. What matrix-algebraic or graph-theoretic procedures can be developed for determining the minimum changes (or deletions) in a structure that are necessary for complete balance? The computation of such a "least cost" index is at present much simpler for small structures than for large structures. It seems that persons skilled in matrix algebra could develop a procedure for obtaining the minimum changes/deletions necessary for balance of a large structure, but to the author's knowledge, no such procedure has yet been developed for large structures.

k. There seems little doubt that factor analysis *can* be used to construct indices of balance and of clustering. Yet, severe problems remain in regard to the compatibility of factor-analytic procedures and degree-of-balance indices based on graphs. This compatibility problem was treated in Chapter 6. Furthermore, questions arise involving what type of factor-extraction procedure to use, what type of factor rotation to use, what to put in the diagonal of the adjacency matrix, and how to treat asymmetric matrices (this is a sticky problem if strength is measured).

l. The apparent compatibility of matrix-algebraic and graph-theoretic procedures was briefly touched on in section 6.1, Chapter 6. The graph for a group or cognitive structure can be represented by an "adjacency matrix." But graph and matrix procedures are often not comparable; a matrix index of "balance" may not be the same as a graph index of balance (Phillips' index, treated in section 6.1, is a case in point). The Abelson-Rosenberg (1958) matrix treatment of "balance" does not appear to define balance in the same way as the original Cartwright-Harary (1956) procedure. The problem of equivalence between matrix and graph procedures must get *much* closer scrutiny than it has been given in the past.

m. Last but not least, there is the ultimate question of the usefulness of formal models. There is no doubt that formalistic procedures and indices are useful in some ways: They often result in certain conceptual clarifications (section 3.2, Chapter 3), suggest new and important hypotheses (for example, see sections 3.1c and 3.1d, where it was suggested that the person most likely to be scapegoated by the group is that person whose deletion would result in a balanced structure), and provide researchers with empirical indices of balance, clustering, completeness, positivity, and the like. But one cannot help but feel that under certain conditions, formalization is of little use and makes little sense. Does formalization make sense for describing large *cognitive* structures ("individual systems," in Newcomb's sense)? Formalization seems clearly more useful for large than for small cognitive structures. But then large structures may have no effect upon the focal person (this is the issue of cycle length and cycle locality), and formalization is not really *needed* as much for small structures. Considering both cognitive structures and group structures, the *size* variable seems critical; yet, size of structure has been given no systematic attention in the formal literature.

8 • 3　OVERLAPS BETWEEN THE BALANCE MODEL AND OTHER SMALL GROUP MODELS

In addition to citing "tendencies toward unbalance" (section 8.1) and "unresolved issues" (section 8.2) as a means of suggesting hypotheses for future investigation, a third means is to juxtapose balance theory against other models and theories of small group process. This is the task of the present section. It will be noted that certain models give predictions *opposite* to the predictions of balance theory, whereas other models give *supplementary* predictions. Below, Asch's group pressure model is seen as giving conflicting predictions. Specific hypotheses are suggested which integrate balance theory with the group pressure model, and a new "pressure-balance" principle is suggested. The coalition model is likewise seen as giving conflicting predictions. Homans' exchange theory is seen as giving supplementary predictions. It will be argued that balance theory is, to a degree, reducible to the concepts and propositions of exchange theory.

8 • 3a   *Group Pressure Theory*

The classic and much-cited experiments by Asch (1951) are often presented as evidence in favor of the extent to which a group can pressure an individual into doing (and even thinking) something which is against his better judgment. In Asch's words, such pressures can induce the individual to make perceptions which are "contrary to fact." In the original Asch experiments, a naive subject was asked to match the length of a given line with one of three unequal lines. On repeated trials, he publicly announced his judgments of line length to the group. This "group" consisted of confederates who were in alliance with the experimenter. These confederates purposely made incorrect judgments of the line length, their judgments being as much as 1¾ inches off. The confederates, on any one trial, would all voice the same unanimous opinion.

It was found that over repeated trials, the naive subject's announced judgment of the line length strayed farther and farther from the true length. In the face of the expressed opinions of a unanimous majority, the subject made judgments which were contrary to "fact"—contrary to his initial perception. The few subjects who did not shift in the direction of the majority revealed strong symptoms of tension. An additional finding which will interest us below was that the larger the majority (the greater the size of the group of confederates), the greater the number of judgment errors made by the subject. As the size of a unanimous majority increases, errors in judgment also increase. The relationship was not linear, however. The extent of error in judgment tended to level off when the size of the majority reached about four or more.

Let us assume that we are constructing a similar experiment, designating the naive subject as P. The group of confederates will be designated as "G." Any object about which P makes a judgment will be X; this may be the length of a line, or a political issue, or a discussion topic of some sort which P feels is important. In this PGX structure, the three relations are: (1) P's orientation to X; (2) G's unanimous orientation to X; and (3) P's orientation (liking, attraction, or commitment) to the group, G. The PX relation (P's orientation to X) is our dependent variable: We wish to predict P's change on it from its initial value. It would be measured before discussion with group G and afterward, the difference between the two measures indicating both direction and magnitude of change.

If the "group" (G) consists of only one person, then we have the standard POX dyad, and any effects of the GX relation alone upon the PX relation can be attributed to the "agreement" bias or principle. If P changes the PX relation in the direction of his perception of the GX relation regardless of (independently of) the sign of PG, then it is an "agreement effect." But if P changes the PX relation so that the direction of the change (toward the positive or toward the negative) is the algebraic product of the PG and GX relations, then we would of course call it a "balance effect." For example, given an initial structure of $-PG$, $+PX$ and $+GX$, then if P changed in the direction of $-PX$, and this was the only change, then the change is *toward balance* but *away from agreement*.

Now let us assume that G consists of two or more members. Any tendency for P to change toward the group's opinion (toward the sign of GX) independently of the sign of PG is clearly analogous to the agreement effect. But now it refers to the effect of a unanimous majority, so let's call it a "group pressure effect," to distinguish it from the agreement effect, where G is only one person. It is now evident that two kinds of forces will act on P: The pressure effect will "pull" his PX judgment or attitude toward the sign of GX, and the balance effect will pull it in such a direction as to be balanced with the GX and PG relations. Thus, given an initial structure of $-PG$, $+PX$ and $+GX$, the balance principle predicts that P will change on PX *away* from the opinion of the group (toward the negative). This is directly opposite to what the strict pressure principle would predict.[4]

This is not so much a criticism of "pressure theory" as it is a way of pointing out how the pressure principle and the balance principle give conflicting predictions. Refer to Figure 2. This figure suggests a design to test the pressure principle against the balance principle. In condition I, P is attracted toward the group, and his orientation toward X is the same as the group's. Since the PX and GX signs are the same, the pressure principle predicts little or no change in PX. Since both structures under condition I are balanced, the balance principle likewise predicts little or no change. In condition II, both principles predict change in PX, since the PX and GX signs are opposite (the pressure principle), and since the structures in condition II are unbalanced (the balance principle). Hence, in conditions I and II, both principles give the same predictions.

Consider the conditions under which P's attraction or liking for the group is negative (conditions III and IV). Here, the balance and pressure principles give conflicting predictions. Under condition III, the balance principle predicts change in PX (since the structures are initially unbalanced), but the pressure

---

4. Some of the Asch studies did consider the attraction of the subject toward the unanimous majority, finding that change in judgment toward the majority "is less" if attraction is low. Our juxtaposition of the strict Asch principle and the balance principle is simply to contrast the predictions of each; it is not being maintained here that Asch *ignored* the PG variable (attraction) in a number of his experiments. However, if the two principles are contrasted, the formulation of specific hypotheses not conceptualized by Asch is possible. The text following is devoted to these hypotheses.

FIGURE 2   A DESIGN TO EVALUATE THE RELATIVE EFFECTS OF BALANCE
VERSUS GROUP PRESSURE

The group's expressed opinion (the GX relation) is:

	The *same* as P's initial attitude (the PX relation):	*Opposite* to P's initial attitude (the PX relation):
P's liking, attraction or commitment to the group (the PG relation) is:		
Positive	**I.** 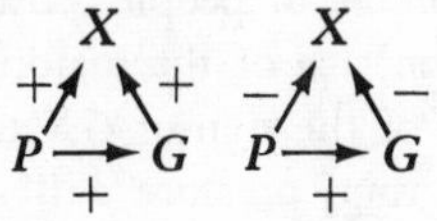 X X $+\nearrow\nwarrow+$ $-\nearrow\nwarrow-$ $P\xrightarrow{\ \ }G$ $P\xrightarrow{\ \ }G$ $+$ $+$ Balance principle: No change in PX is expected. Pressure principle: No change in PX is expected.	**II.** 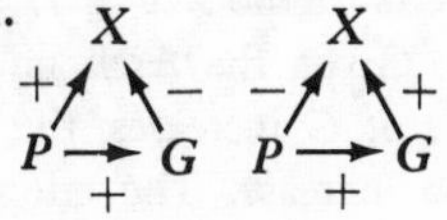 X X $+\nearrow\nwarrow-$ $-\nearrow\nwarrow+$ $P\xrightarrow{\ \ }G$ $P\xrightarrow{\ \ }G$ $+$ $+$ Balance principle: Change in PX is expected. Pressure principle: Change in PX is expected.
Negative	**III.** 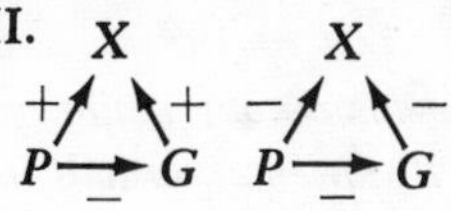 X X $+\nearrow\nwarrow+$ $-\nearrow\nwarrow-$ $P\xrightarrow{\ \ }G$ $P\xrightarrow{\ \ }G$ $-$ $-$ Balance principle: Change in PX is expected. Pressure principle: No change in PX is expected.	**IV.** 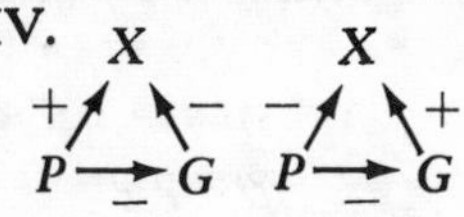 X X $+\nearrow\nwarrow-$ $-\nearrow\nwarrow+$ $P\xrightarrow{\ \ }G$ $P\xrightarrow{\ \ }G$ $-$ $-$ Balance principle: No change in PX is expected. Pressure principle: Change in PX is expected.

* The symbol *"G"* represents any group of persons (other than P) expressing a unanimous orientation to X.

principle predicts little or no change (since the PX and GX signs are initially the same). Under condition IV, the balance principle predicts no change, but the pressure principle predicts change. Generally, if P's liking for the group is negative, the balance and pressure principles give opposite predictions.

Note that to predict change in the PX relation, one has to assume that the PG relation and P's perception of the GX relation both remain constant. But to do so would render the design open to criticisms stated earlier. Hence, in the suggested design, and changes in PG or in P's perception of GX would be recorded.

The significance of this suggested design lies in a consideration of the effects of the *size* of G, the number of people constituting the unanimous majority. Given the Asch findings on size of the majority, one may infer that as the size of G increases, the effects of the sign of GX upon P's orientation to X will also increase. The effects of group pressure will increase as G increases. Asch found that a point of "diminishing returns" is reached when G consists of about four or more persons. Hence, as G increases, the effect of group pressure will increase "up to a point"—the effect will level off, or approach a constant value.

Now if the effect of group pressure upon P increases as G increases, then one would expect the *relative* effect of balance to decrease, when P's attraction to the group is negative (conditions III and IV, Figure 2). As the unanimous majority increases in size, P's orientation toward X will be pulled more and more in the direction of the sign of GX; hence, the relative extent to which balance forces determine P's orientation will be less. This suggests a specific hypothesis:

1. *As the size of the unanimous majority (G) increases, the effect of group pressure on P's orientation will increase, and the relative effect of balance will decrease.*

Should one employ an analysis of variance procedure to evaluate the relative effects of balance versus pressure, one would compare the "percent variance explained" (in PX change, the dependent variable) by balance versus the percent variance explained by group pressure. Note that one source of variance is the independent variable "balance–unbalance" (conditions I and IV (balance) versus conditions II and III (unbalance), Figure 2). The other source of variance is the independent variable "pressure-no pressure" (conditions II and IV are the "pressure" conditions, since the PX and GX signs are opposite; conditions I and III are the "no pressure" conditions). If seen in this way, then one need not confine his interest to only conditions III and IV. As G increases, the percent variance explained by balance is expected to decrease, and the percent variance explained by pressure is expected to increase.

Assume that one can quantify both the "balance effect" and the "pressure effect" by taking the ratio of the two. (One could obtain the ratio of the variances explained by each.) We will call this ratio the *pressure/balance ratio* if one obtains the ratio of the effect on PX due to pressure *to* the effect on PX due to balance. It is the *balance/pressure ratio* if one obtains the ratio of the balance effect to the pressure effect, although one would actually need only one of the two ratios.

2. *As the size of the unanimous majority (G) increases, the pressure/ balance ratio will increase. (Or, as G increases, the balance/pressure ratio will decrease.)*

If G consists of only one person, the PGX structure is reduced to a POX structure. Hence, the effect of balance will be at a maximum, and the effect of pressure will be at a minimum. Thus:

3. *When G consists of one person, the pressure/balance ratio is at its minimum. (Or, when G consists of one person, the balance/pressure ratio is at its maximum.)*

Considering the diminishing (nonlinear) effect of group size,

4. *As the size of the unanimous majority (G) increases, the increasing effect of group pressure will approach a constant value.*

If the effect of pressure tends to level off or approach a constant value as G increases, then it follows that the *relative* effect of balance will also level off; the effect of balance will decrease at a *lesser* rate as G increases:

5. *As the size of the unanimous majority (G) increases, the decreasing effect of balance will approach a constant value.*

Thus,

6. *As G increases, the pressure/balance ratio (and the balance/pressure ratio) will approach a constant value.*

These hypotheses serve to illustrate how the balance and the Asch (pressure) models may be combined to predict changes in P's orientation or judgment of X during an interchange or discussion between P and a group. The combination of these two small group models suggests a new principle which determines changes in PX orientations, namely, a *pressure-balance principle* which combines the effects of balance and group pressure into one set of hypotheses. The effect of pressure on PX is expected to increase with majority size, hence making the relative effect of balance decrease. When G consists of one person, the effect of pressure will be at its minimum; hence, the relative effect of balance is at its maximum. When G reaches about four or more, the increasing effect of pressure is expected to level off, as will the (decreasing) effect of balance.

Note that if P were to *publicly* report his orientation to X to the group, we might expect a greater change in this expressed opinion than in his *privately* indicated orientation. The effect of group pressure upon public reporting of opinions will generally be greater than the effects of group pressure upon private indications of opinion (Asch, 1951). But what about the effects of balance upon public versus private reporting? Evidence presented by Sampson and Insko (1964) suggests that the effect of balance is greater upon *private PX* orientations than upon public PX orientations. Hence, one can predict that the balance effect is relatively great when the dependent variable is P's private or covert orientation, but the pressure effect will be relatively great when the dependent variable is P's announced, overt position on X. From this, one may infer that:

7. *The pressure/balance ratio (whatever its value) will be greater for public expressions of PX than for private orientations of P to X. And the balance/pressure ratio (whatever its value) will be greater for private PX orientations than for public expressions of PX.*

This hypothesis, of course, assumes that G is constant: For a *given* size of G, the pressure/balance ratio will be greater for public expressions than for private orientations.

The above hypotheses leave open the question of whether the effect of pressure will exceed the effect of balance when G is small. When $G = 1$ person, the balance effect *may* exceed the pressure (agreement) effect. But what about the relative effects of balance and pressure when $G = 2$? At this point, does pressure exceed balance (giving a pressure/balance ratio of greater than 1), or equal the effect of balance (giving a ratio of 1), or remain less than balance (giving a ratio of less than 1)? Only empirical research can answer such questions. Figure 3 gives three possible outcomes (hypothetical).

In figure 3A, the effect of pressure (agreement) even when $G = 1$ exceeds the effect of balance. The effect of pressure increases as G increases (hypothesis 1, above), the effect of balance decreases (hypothesis 2), and both effects approach a constant value (hypothesis 4 and 5; cf. hypothesis 6). Note that the effect of pressure is expected to be minimal when $G = 1$, and the effect of balance is expected to be maximal (hypothesis 3). In Figure 3A, when $G = 1$, the pressure/balance ratio is greater than 1.00, and it will increase as G increases.

Consider Figure 3B. Here, the effect of balance will always exceed the effect of pressure, even though the former decreases and the latter increases. Consequently, the pressure/balance ratio is always *less* than 1.00, but it will approach 1.00 (or some constant less than 1.00) as G increases. The outcome plotted here seems to be the least likely, empirically.

Figure 3C suggests an interesting idea. Note that when $G = 1$, the bal-

FIGURE 3   THREE TYPES OF OUTCOMES IN A PRESSURE-BALANCE STUDY

A.

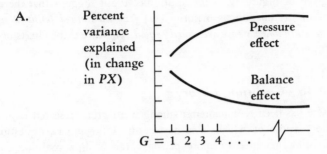

B.

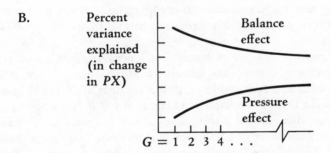

C.

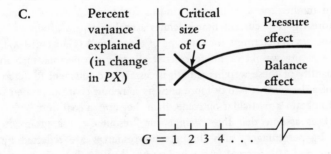

ance effect exceeds the pressure effect, but when $G = 2$ (this is only a hypothetical value), the effects "cross" so that when $G = 3$ or more, the effect of pressure will exceed the effect of balance. The pressure/balance ratio is less than 1.00 when $G = 1$. The ratio is exactly 1.00 when $G = 2$, and is greater than 1.00 when $G = 3$ or more. This outcome seems to be the most likely, empirically. (The reason is this: Remember that any effect of pressure when $G = 1$ is simply an effect of "agreement." In general, research on balance reviewed in earlier chapters suggests that the effects of balance upon PX changes are generally greater than the effects of agreement, although this inference is tentative.) The outcome given in Figure 3C is interesting because it suggests that there exists a *critical size* of the unanimous majority (G), *the theoretical point at which the effects of pressure and balance are exactly equal.* Thereafter, the effects of pressure will be greater.

8 • 3b   *Coalition Theory*

There has been recent interest among small group researchers in coalition theory, one purpose of which is to answer the following two questions for a group consisting of three or more persons: (a) Will a coalition form; and (b) if a coalition forms, who will coalesce against whom? In the text following, the three-person (ABC) condition is briefly discussed. The central concern will be instances in which coalition theory and balance theory will give conflicting predictions.

A *coalition structure* is defined in a general way by Gamson (1964) as any partitioning of a group into subparts on whatever basis. Hence, if A and B like each other and both dislike C, then a coalition of A and B against C is formed on the basis of sentiment or liking. If A and B "gang up" on C during an argument, then there is a coalition of A and B against C. If A and B are members of a committee of stockholders, and they both vote against C and obtain control of the stock, then there is a coalition of A and B against C. If two boys beat up a third, there is a coalition. Even a brother and sister playing together while their mother cooks dinner is a kind of coalition.

More rigorous current usage defines a coalition in a group as "the joint use of resources to determine the outcome of a decision" (Gamson, 1964, p. 82). A *resource* is any weight or influence controlled by the persons such that some critical quantity of these weights is both necessary and sufficient to determine the outcome of a decision. If two or more persons somehow coordinate their resources in order to obtain a particular outcome, then they are "a coalition."

Let us assume that the "weight" or "resource" of a group member is measured by percentages, such that greater resources are reflected by greater percentages, and 100 percent is the maximum. Assume that one is examining a group consisting of three candidates at a nominating convention. Each candidate controls a certain percentage of the delegate vote; this is the "resource" or "weight" of each. If any one candidate controls 51 percent or more of the votes, then a coalition of any sort is unlikely. But assume that candidate A controls 40 percent of the votes, B controls 35 percent, and C controls 25 percent. Who will form a coalition against whom?

Gamson outlines four separate theories which predict the outcome, only one of which will interest us here: "minimum resource" theory. First of all, the theory predicts that *any* coalition is more likely than *no* coalition in the above

40-35-25 situation. Second, note that in any three-person situation, three coalitions are possible: *A* and *B* versus *C*, *B* and *C* versus *A*, and *A* and *C* versus *B*. Minimum resource theory predicts the *BC* versus *A* coalition is most likely. The basic idea is that a coalition will form "in which the total resources are as small as possible while still being sufficient" to win (Gamson, 1964, p. 86). In the above convention example, a 40-35 combination (*AB* versus *C*) gives a total of 75 percent of the votes, a 40-25 combination (*AC* versus *B*) gives 65 percent, and a 35-25 combination (*BC* versus *A*) gives 60 percent. This latter coalition gives the minimum necessary to win the nomination; hence, it is the most likely. The crux of minimum resource theory is the apparent paradox, "strength is weakness." *A*'s strength of 40 percent is his weakness; he can lose the nomination even though he controls the most votes.

It can be shown that minimum resource coalition theory gives certain predictions which conflict with deductions from balance theory. Following Heider, a *unit relation* between two or more persons may be defined as common membership in a family, club, fraternity, clan, gang, or clique within a larger group, or even a racial or ethnic group. If two people are members of the same group, unit, race, etc., they are members of the same *set*. If they are members of different groups, they are members of different sets. Note that a single person can be a member of two or more sets (people always have multiple memberships in many groups of various kinds).

In any three-person situation, where any one person may be either in or not in the same set with either one or both (or neither) of the other two persons, there are eight possible configurations or conditions, diagrammed in Figure 4. In condition I, persons *A*, *B* and *C* are all members of different sets (groups or units). In condition IIA, persons *A* and *B* are members of the same set, and *C* is in a different set. Conditions IIB and IIC are isomorphic to condition IIA. Under condition IIIA (and conditions IIIB and IIIC), two persons are members of two different sets and the third is a *common member* of these two sets.

The concept of *set-balance* may now be introduced. If you are in a coalition with, say, your brother, and this coalition if formed *against* someone who is not in your family (not in your "set"), then this is "set-balance." But if you form a coalition *with* someone *not in* your family against your brother, then this is "set-unbalance." Generally, *set-balance* exists if one person is in a coalition with another who is in his set, or if one person is not in a coalition with another who is not in his set. *Set-unbalance* exists if one person is in a coalition *with* another who is *not in* his set, or if one person is not in a coalition with another who is in his set. Arguing generally that any kind of balance is more likely (preferred or tended toward) than any kind of unbalance:

1. *Set-balance is more likely than set-unbalance.*

To exemplify: You and your brother are in the same "set" (family). Hence, if you are both involved in a coalition against some third person who is

FIGURE 4   PREDICTED COALITIONS ON THE BASIS OF SET-BALANCE

	CONDITION	PREDICTIONS
I.		All three coalitions are equally likely.
IIA.		The *AB* versus *C* coalition is most likely.
IIB.		The *BC* versus *A* coalition is most likely.
IIC.		The *AC* versus *B* coalition is most likely.
IIIA.		The *AC* versus *B* or *BC* versus *A* coalitions are more likely than the *AB* versus *C* coalition. The *AC* versus *B* and *BC* versus *A* coalitions are equally likely.
IIIB.	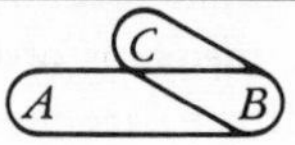	The *AB* versus *C* or *BC* versus *A* coalitions are more likely than the *AB* versus *C* coalition. The *AB* versus *C* and *BC* versus *A* coalitions are equally likely.
IIIC.	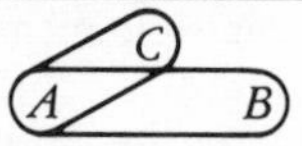	The *AB* versus *C* or *AC* versus *B* coalitions are more likely than the *BC* versus *A* coalition. The *AB* versus *C* and *AC* versus *B* coalitions are equally likely.
IV.	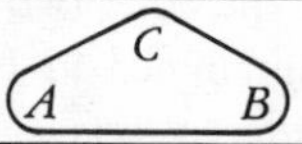	No coalitions are likely.

not in your family, then the structure is set-balanced. If, however, you form a coalition with someone *not in* your family against your brother, then this is a set-unbalanced structure. The maxim "blood is thicker than water" is the crux of the whole idea. When the "chips are down," you are more likely to do the former than the latter. It is being hypothesized that the same idea applies to fraternity membership, clique membership, peer group membership, departmental membership in an organization, to membership in a racial or ethnic group, and so on.

The concept of set-balance is highly similar to Mazur's (1968) concept of "identity consistency," used in his treatment of coalition likelihood among clan members in primitive societies. Note also the similarity between set-balance and the notion of balance–unbalance of any *two line cycle* in graph theory: If *A* and *B* are members of the same fraternity (a positive unit relation, often represented in graph theory with a bracket,

$$\overbrace{}^{+}$$

A   *B*), and if they coalesce against each other (*A* ———— *B*), the two-line cycle formed is unbalanced. The concept of set-balance is a deduction from the general balance concept, and is therefore not an "extrabalance property" (cf. Chapter 6, section 6.2).

The two following hypothesis are deductions from hypothesis 1 above. Hypothesis 2 applies to "with whom" a person will or will not opt or bargain for a coalition, and hypothesis 3 applies to "against whom" a person will or will not opt or bargain.

2. *A person is more likely to opt or bargain for a coalition with another who is in his set than with another who is not in his set.* (To do the latter would be set-unbalance.)

You are more likely to form a coalition with a brother (or fellow fraternity member, or clique member, etc.) than with a non-brother.

3. *A person is more likely to opt or bargain for a coalition against another who is not in his set than against another who is in his set.* (To do the latter would be set-unbalance.)

You are more likely to form a coalition against a non-brother than a brother.

Looking back at **Figure 4,** the principle of set-balance, and hence hypotheses 2 and 3, allows one to predict which of the three possible coalitions for any given triad is most likely—the three possible coalitions being *AB* versus *C*, *BC* versus *A*, and *AC* versus *B*. Under condition I, all three coalition possibilities are equally likely: Hypothesis 3 predicts that each person will opt for a coalition against either of the other two, since each is a member of a different set. (This prediction will become clearer after condition IV is discussed.) Under conditions IIA, IIB and IIC (all isomorphic), the predictions are straightforward, The two members of a set will coalesce with each other (hypothesis 2) against the one who is not in the set (hypothesis 3).

Under condition IIIA, person *A* will opt for a coalition *with C* (hypothesis 2) *against B* (hypothesis 3). And *B* will opt for a coalition with *C* (hypothesis 2) against *A* (hypothesis 3). Note that *C* is not likely to opt for any coalition. It makes intuitive sense to expect that he would not, due to his "dual loyalties" or joint membership in the two sets or groups. Interestingly, *C* will clearly "gain" in the sense that he will be a member of *either* coalition. In condition IIIA, then, the *AC* versus *B* and the *BC* versus *A* coalitions are equally likely; furthermore, either of these coalitions are more likely than the *AB* versus *C* coalition. Conditions IIIB and IIIC are isomorphic to condition IIIA; hence, so are the predictions.

In condition IV, no coalitions seem likely, since any one coalition would violate the principle of set-balance. Note carefully what is being assumed here:

A person is likely to form a coalition *with* another who is *not in* his set *against* *another who is also not in his set.* Hence, in condition I, it was predicted that each of the three coalitions are equally likely. This is a violation of the set-balance principle (coalescing with someone not in the set), but it is not as "severe" a violation as a person coalescing *against* another *who is in* his set. Coalescing with someone who is not in your family against someone who is in a *third* family is not as bad as (hence more likely than) coalescing against someone who *is* in your family. Therefore, it was predicted that no coalitions are likely in condition IV.

Returning to the convention example and the minimum resource theory of coalitions, one must ask: What if minimum resource theory predicts one coalition and the principle of set-balance predicts another? Consider the above case where candidate *A* controls 40 percent of the vote, *B* controls 35 percent, and *C* controls 25 percent. The minimum resource hypothesis predicts a *BC* versus *A* coalition.

But what if, say *A* and *B* are old fraternity buddies (condition IIA, Figure 8.4)? If this were so, *B* would not be likely to coalesce with *C* against *A*, his fraternity buddy. To do so would violate set-balance. What if *A* and *C* are fraternity buddies (condition IIC)? Hence, *C* is not likely to opt for a coalition against *A*. Again, this would be a violation of set-balance. For these two conditions, then, minimum resource theory and the set-balance model give conflicting predictions. Note that in condition IIB, both models give the same predictions: The *BC* versus *A* coalition satisfies both minimum resource theory and set-balance. Generally,

> 4.   *A coalition is not likely to form on the basis of minimum resources if such a coalition would violate set-balance.*

This means that any coalition which satisfies both principles is most likely to form, and a coalition which violates both is least likely to form. Hypothesis 4 implies that a coalition satisfying set-balance but violating minimum resource is more likely to form than one which satisfies minimum resource but violates set-balance. An empirical study, perhaps of the game-theoretic variety used by many coalition researchers, would lend some insights.

The major thrust of the above discussion seems to be this: In coalition research, many "nonrational" coalitions form which are unpredicted by such theories as minimum resource theory. Not coalescing against a "brother" only because he is a brother is "nonrational" to the extent that it prevents a person from "winning" a game of some sort. One "theory" reviewed by Gamson, called "anticompetitive theory," seems to incorporate the idea that people do not always coalesce "rationally." If coalition researchers were to systematically vary fraternity membership, race, etc. among the subjects in their experiments, and then apply the set-balance model (or some similar model) suggested above, it would be an aid in permitting systematic predictions of coalition likelihood. The major advantage of the suggested set-balance model is that a "set" is broadly defined.

8 • 3c   Exchange Theory

The balance model can be integrated with what has came to be known as "exchange theory." Homans' (1961) variety of exchange theory (cf. Thibaut and Kelley, 1959) views human interaction as a matter of investment and return on these investments. When people involve themselves in groups (one type of "investment"), these persons are expected to do certain things if they anticipate some return on the investment, and do other things if they anticipate little or no return on the investment. In this respect, the theory is one of human social "exchange." Based upon Skinnerian psychology and elementary economics, four of the basic concepts in the model are reward, punishment, cost, and profit.

A person is *rewarded* by the other if the other does something to or for that person which is pleasurable or pleasant to that person. For example, if O likes P, and P perceives this, then it is a reward for P. If P likes O, then it is a reward for O. If P and O like each other, then a condition of mutual reward exists.

A person is *punished* by the other if the other does something to that person which is unpleasant for that person. If O dislikes P, and if P perceives this, then it is relatively punishing for P. If P dislikes O, it is punishment for O. If they dislike each other, a condition of mutual punishment may be said to exist.

The *cost* to a person of an interaction situation, or any attribute thereof, is defined in three ways: (1) Cost is the amount of reward connected with some foregone or unchosen alternative. For example, having to "give up" an old girl friend in order to marry someone could be conceptualized as "cost." (2) Cost is the amount of punishment connected with the chosen alternative, or with some present state, whether chosen or not. An example would be putting up with the faults of one's chosen spouse after marriage; this is a type of "cost." (3) Cost is any form of investment of energy, such as "getting involved" with another person, or simply having to spend time talking or interacting with another. In the context of balance theory, having to *change* a relation from its initial value, in contrast to not having to change it, is a form of cost. This latter interpretation of "cost" is relevant to the least cost cognitive bias, to be discussed below.

Psychological profit (P) is defined as reward (R) minus cost (C):

$$P = R - C$$

Profit exists if reward exceeds cost, and does not exist if reward and cost are equal. A "loss" would exist if cost exceeded reward. Homans hypothesizes that a person will not emit an "action" unless he anticipates that the action will be profitable. Thus, the "likelihood of emitting a particular action" is a dependent variable in Homan's theory, with reward, punishment, cost, and profit constituting the independent variables. Homans is careful in saying that persons do not always maximize profit, but that an action is not likely to be emitted *unless* it is profitable. The action is not likely to take place unless the difference between reward and cost is a positive one (rather than zero or negative).

Where Homans takes "action" as his dependent variable, we will take the variables *preference* and *change* as the dependent variables, as we have done throughout this text. Thus "change" can mean "change in a relation toward balance," "change in a relation from positive to negative," and so on. Preference can be phrased in terms of balance (balance is preferred over unbalance), single relations (positive relations are preferred or chosen over negative ones), or learning (certain structures and/or relations are learned with fewer errors than others). The following hypothesis, deduced from exchange theory, will guide the discussion below. We will call it the "exchange hypothesis."

The focal person will exhibit preferences or make changes in such a way as to be rewarding and/or profitable to him. The focal person is less likely to exhibit preferences or make changes which are not rewarding and/or not profitable.

It is interesting to note that the balance principle itself plus five out of the seven cognitive biases can all be treated as deducible from this single hypothesis. Balance is rewarding to P, and unbalance is relatively punishing. There are several ways to explicate this, some of which have been referred to earlier. P's perception of similarity and/or agreement with O on X is more rewarding than perceived dissimilarity; hence, P will like O, since people like those who reward them. If balance produces less tension than unbalance, then balance is less punishing (less tense) than unbalance. According to the exchange hypothesis just stated, one may say that balance is changed toward, preferred and sought *because* it is more rewarding than unbalance.

The *agreement* bias is similarly deducible from the exchange hypothesis. Perceiving that the other agrees with the self is rewarding to the self. Perceiving that the other disagrees is less rewarding. The *positivity* bias states that liking is rewarding, and disliking is relatively punishing. Note that if P likes O, and O perceives this, it is a reward *for* O. But if people tend to like those who reward them, then O will tend to like P, since P has rewarded him (O) by liking him. If it is also true that people tend to punish those who punish them, then the *reciprocity bias* is deducible from the exchange hypothesis: Reciprocal relations, whether both are positive (rewarding) or whether both are negative (punishing) are more likely than relations which are not reciprocal. Clearly, the most likely form of reciprocity is *positive reciprocity*. Positive reciprocity is a condition of mutual reward. Each member of the dyad rewards the other; hence, this state is the one most likely to be preferred or tended toward.

If one can argue that complete structure are somehow more rewarding (and/or less punishing) than incomplete structures, then the *completeness* cognitive bias is deducible from the exchange hypothesis. An incomplete structure may be thought of as "punishing" to the extent that it is vague (if vagueness is more punishing than non-vagueness) and uncertain (if uncertainty is more punishing than certainty). The *interpersonal change* bias is not easily conceptualized in terms of exchange theory. Similarly, the *extremity* bias does not seem to lend itself to a definition in exchange terms.

The least cost bias can, however, be treated as deducible from the exchange perspective. Remembering that psychological profit is reward minus cost, if "cost" is defined as "having to change a relation," then the greater number of relations that the focal person has to change, the greater the cost. The less the number of relations he has to change, the less the cost. Hence, if reward is constant, the minimum cost (changing the fewest necessary relations) assures profit. Our restatement of the exchange hypothesis tells us that changes are not made unless they will be profitable. This would explain why the focal person will attempt to achieve balance by the fewest possible changes. He assures profit by minimizing cost—by changing the fewest relations. If he changes more than the minimum necessary relations, then his profit is less.

The exchange hypothesis has a wide range of applications to situations and empirical studies which would otherwise be seen from a strict balance perspective. Only one study will be briefly reinterpreted here. The study in question is Burnstein's (1967) excellent study of balance, positivity, reciprocity, and least cost, reviewed in Chapter 5. The results of this study lend some insight into the question of whether a person will *maximize reward* as a way of assuring profit, or whether he will *minimize cost* as a way of assuring profit. Recall that Burnstein found that for certain structures, the subject would satisfy balance and the positivity and reciprocity biases, but would violate the least cost bias. For example, given a structure containing $-PO$, $-OP$, $+PX$ and $+OX$, the subject would change the two interpersonal relations to $+PO$ and $+OP$. This violates the least cost bias, since the subject could have achieved balance by changing to $-PX$ or to $-OX$. Yet, changing the two interpersonal relations satisfies the positivity and reciprocity biases. We suggested in Chapter 5 that a "hierarchy of biases" may operate in balancing dynamics, with the least cost bias occupying a lower hierarchical position than positivity and reciprocity.

The significance of the Burnstein findings for the exchange hypothesis is this: Note that since profit is reward minus cost, a person may assure profit by increasing reward and/or decreasing (minimizing) cost. Which is he more likely to do in interpersonal POX structures? The Burnstein results suggest that the focal person will increase reward and not minimize cost. Note that we are considering a situation where he cannot do *both*—he cannot increase reward and at the same time minimize cost. This is precisely the case with a structure containing $-PO$, $-OP$, $+PX$ and $+OX$. If the focal person changes to $-PX$ *or* to $-OX$ (thus satisfying the least cost bias—minimizing cost), then he does not increase reward (he does not satisfy positivity and reciprocity). If he changes to $+PO$ *and* $+OP$, he increases reward, but does not minimize cost. Thus, in regard to POX-type structures, the following inference can be made: When the focal person faces a "dilemma" of either increasing reward and not minimizing cost versus not increasing reward and minimizing cost, then he will elect the former alternative (rather than the latter) as a means of making the preferences or changes profitable ones.

8 • 4 DOES BALANCE REALLY WORK?

In any treatment of balance theory, the ultimate question is really whether or not balance theory is useful. Does the balance concept and its derivatives explain "enough" of the human interaction process to be a "good" theory? One index of the utility and explanatory power of the theory is the number of kinds of empirical situations to which the theory is applicable. The reader is no doubt aware that while the major focus of this book was on small groups, the balance perspective has been applied in other areas of social psychology, sociology and psychology. Lane and Sears (1964) briefly discuss the applicability of the Osgood model to public opinion and attitude change. Where X is any public issue, P is a person and S is a source of information on the issue, the potential applicability of balance-like hypotheses is straightforward. The concept of balance has been integrated with the sociological concept of status consistency by Sampson (1963) and by Zelditch and Anderson (1966). One can speculate that a person incongruent on status dimensions (e.g., high in occupational rank and low in amount of education) is "inconsistent" (unbalanced), will undergo tension (cf. Jackson, 1962), and as a result make attempts to bring his status dimensions into congruence, such as becoming "mobile." The applicability of the balance concept to role theory—to problems of "role strain" and "role conflict"—is worth investigation. In the area of international relations, letting the "objects" be "nations" (or representatives or diplomats therefrom) and the "relations" be "friendly-hostile," "communist-noncommunist," etc., balance theory shows at least some promise. An integration of the balance and coalition models seems possible in the study of international relations.

Although one of the advantages of balance theory and its relatives is its potential applicability to such areas, one is struck by the increasing amount of speculation and research on conditions under which a balance principle does not apply. Clearly, *as the number of observed conditions under which balance is not applicable increases, the utility and generalizability of the theory is less.* The balance perspective is now undergoing this kind of metamorphosis. Empirical studies on balance are increasing rapidly; yet, at the same time, the discovery of conditions of non-applicability is also increasing. The theory is continually having qualifications, confounding conditions, "but's" and "however's" added to it. Of no less significance is the reducibility issue—whether or not the balance model is reducible to (hence deducible from) other concepts or theories, such as exchange theory, or a frustration principle, or even the concept of clustering.

While these qualifications and limitations place some clouds on the horizon for balance theory, other developments in social science contribute to its attractiveness, if not to its utility. At least three things seem responsible for current interest in balance theory: (1) The theory lends itself reasonably well to formalization and to quantification. Formal models are somewhat "in vogue"; those who are attracted by mathematical theory-building are attracted by balance. (2) The simplicity of the theory makes it attractive to some (and no doubt unattractive to others). The model is at a low level of abstraction. It is a "middle-range" theory. Those who find more affinity with such theories than with "grand theory" will find balance appealing. (3) The theory can be rather easily integrated with other theories in social psychology. Suggested lines of integration were discussed in this chapter. Recently, McGuire, in Abelson et al. (1968), contrasts balance theory with psychological theories not treated in the present text. In many instances, balance theory will explain what other theories cannot explain, if only because certain predictions from balance contradict predictions derivable from other models. This latter point seems to be a distinct advantage. Social science would indeed be dull if all theories gave the same predictions.

But one must conclude that the balance principle is a limited one. In the game of science, it is by no means likely to have the impact or the utility or the attractiveness of Freud's discovery of the unconscious (the comparison is humorous), or of the discovery of absolute zero, or of the discovery of quasars, or of the systematic listing of the effects of social class, or perhaps even the impact of Asch's "discovery" and codification of the effects of group pressure. The balance concept is not overwhelmingly exciting, and seems doomed to be more the province of academic men than the interest of participants at cocktail parties. One question that balance theory is never likely to answer is why there is, in fact, so much inconsistency and unbalance in everyday social life everywhere. The desirability, excitation and intrigue of unbalance is probably far more pleasurable for many.

REFERENCES

Abelson, R. P. Mathematical models in social psychology. In L. Berkowitz, ed., *Advances in Experimental Social Psychology,* vol. 3. New York: Academic Press, 1967.

——, E. Aronson, W. J. McGuire, T. M. Newcomb, M. J. Rosenberg, and P. H. Tannenbaum, eds. *Theories of Cognitive Consistency: A Sourcebook.* Chicago: Rand-McNally, 1968.

—— and M. J. Rosenberg. Symbolic psycho-logic: a model of attitudinal cognition. *Behavioral Science.* 3 (1958): 1–13.

Adorno, T. W. E., E. Frenkel-Brunswick, D. J. Levinson, and R. N. Sanford. *The Authoritarian Personality.* New York: Harper and Row, 1950.

Allport, G. W. *The Nature of Prejudice.* Boston: Beacon Press, 1954.

Aronson, E. and J. Mills. The effect of severity of initiation on liking for a group. *Journal of Abnormal and Social Psychology,* 59 (1959): 177–181.

—— and P. Worchel. Similarity versus liking as determinants of interpersonal attractiveness. *Psychonomic Science,* 5 (1966): 157–158.

Asch, S. E. Effects of group pressure upon the modification and distortion of judgments. In H. Guetzkow, ed., *Groups, Leadership, and Men.* Pittsburgh: Carnegie Press, 1951.

Bales, R. F. Adaptive and integrative changes as sources of strain in social systems. In A. P. Hare, E. F. Borgatta and R. F. Baes, eds., *Small Groups: Studies in Social Interaction.* New York: Alfred A. Knopf, 1955.

——. The equilibrium problem in small groups. In T. Parsons, R. F. Bales and E. A. Shils, *Working Papers in the Theory of Action.* Glencoe: Free Press, 1953, pp. 111–161.

——. *Interaction Process Analysis.* Cambridge: Addison-Wesley, 1951.

—— and F. Strodtbeck. Phases in group problem-solving. *Journal of Abnormal and Social Psychology,* 46 (1951): 485–495.

Berger, J., B. P. Cohen, J. L. Snell and M. Zelditch. *Types of Formalization in Small Group Research.* Boston: Houghton Mifflin, 1962.

Berkowitz, L., ed. *Advances in Experimental Social Psychology,* vol. 1. New York: Academic Press, 1964.

——, ed. *Advances in Experimental Social Psychology,* vol. 2. New York: Academic Press, 1965.

——, ed. *Advances in Experimental Social Psychology,* vol. 3. New York: Academic Press, 1967.

Bion, W. R. *Experiences in Groups.* New York: Basic Books, 1959.

Bonney, M. E. A sociometric study of the relationship of some factors to mutual friendships on the elementary, secondary, and college levels. *Sociometry,* 9 (1946): 21–47.

Borgatta, E. F. and R. F. Bales. Interaction of individuals in reconstituted groups. *Sociometry,* 16 (1953): 302–320. (1953a)

—— and R. F. Bales. The consistency of subject behavior and the reliability of scoring interaction process analysis. *American Sociological Review,* 18 (1953): 566–569. (1953b)

Brehm, J. Increasing cognitive dissonance by *fait accompli*. *Journal of Abnormal and Social Psychology*, 58 (1959): 379–382.

———— and A. R. Cohen. *Explorations in Cognitive Dissonance*. New York: John Wiley and Sons, 1962.

Brinton, J. E. Deriving an attitude scale from Semantic Differential data. *Public Opinion Quarterly*, 25 (1961): 289–295.

Brown, R., E. Galanter, E. Hess and G. Mandler. *New Directions in Psychology*. New York: Holt, Rinehart and Winston, 1962.

————. *Social Psychology*. New York: Free Press, 1965.

Broxton, J. A. A test of interpersonal attraction predictions derived from balance theory. *Journal of Abnormal and Social Psychology*, 66 (1963): 394–397.

Buckley, W. *Sociology and Modern Systems Theory*. Englewood Cliffs: Prentice-Hall, 1967.

Budner, S. Intolerance of ambiguity as a personality variable. *Journal of Personality*, 30 (1962): 29–50.

Burdick, H. A. and A. J. Burnes. A test of 'strain toward symmetry' theories. *Journal of Abnormal and Social Psychology*, 57 (1958): 367–369.

Burnstein, E. Sources of cognitive bias in the representation of simple structures: balance, minimal change, positivity, reciprocity, and the respondent's own attitude. *Journal or Personality and Social Psychology*, 7 (1967): 36–48.

Byrne, D. Authoritarianism and response to attitude similarity-dissimilarity. *Journal of Social Psychology*, 66 (1965): 251–256.

————. Interpersonal attraction and attitude similarity. *Journal of Abnormal and Social Psychology*, 62 (1961): 713–715. (1961a).

————. Interpersonal attraction as a function of affiliation need and attitude similarity. *Human Relations*, 14 (1961): 283–289. (1961b).

————. Response to attitude similarity-dissimilarity as a function of affiliation need. *Journal of Personality*, 30 (1962): 164–177.

———— and Blaylock. Similarity and assumed similarity of attitudes between husbands and wives. *Journal of Abnormal and Social Psychology*, 67 (1963): 636–640.

———— and G. L. Clore. Predicting interpersonal attraction toward strangers presented in three different stimulus modes. *Psychonomic Science*, 4 (1966): 239–240.

————, G. L. Clore, and W. Griffitt. Response discrepancy versus attitude similarity as determinants of attraction. *Psychonomic Science*, 7 (1967): 397–398.

————, G. L. Clore and P. Worchel. Effect of economic similarity-dissimilarity on interpersonal attraction. *Journal of Personality and Social Psychology*, 4 (1966): 220–224.

———— and W. Griffitt. A developmental investigation of the law of attraction. *Journal of Personality and Social Psychology*, 4 (1966): 699–702. (1966a).

———— and W. Griffitt. Similarity versus liking: a clarification. *Psychonomic Science*, 6 (1966): 295–296. (1966b).

————, W. Griffitt and C. Golightly. Prestige as a factor in determining the effect of attitude similarity-dissimilarity on attraction. *Journal of Personality*, 34 (1966): 434–444.

————, W. Griffitt, W. Hudgins, and K. Reeves. Attitude similarity-dissimilarity and attraction: generality beyond the college sophomore. *Journal of Social Psychology*, in press (1968).

————, William Griffitt, and D. Stefaniak. Attraction and similarity of personality characteristics. *Journal of Personality and Social Psychology*, 5 (1967): 82–90.

————, O. London and K. Reeves. The effects of physical attractiveness, sex, and attitude similarity on interpersonal attraction. *Journal of Personality*, 36 (1968): 259–271.

—— and C. McGraw. Interpersonal attraction toward Negroes. *Human Relations*, 17 (1964): 201–213.

—— and D. Nelson. Attraction as a function of attitude similarity-dissimilarity: the effect of topic importance. *Psychonomic Science*, 1 (1964): 93–94.

—— and D. Nelson. Attraction as a linear function of proportion of positive reinforcements. *Journal of Personality and Social Psychology*, 1 (1965): 659–663. (1965a).

—— and D. Nelson. The effect of topic importance and attitude similarity-dissimilarity on attraction in a multistranger design. *Psychonomic Science*, 3 (1965): 449–450. (1965b)

—— and R. Rhamey. Magnitude of positive and negative reinforcements as a determinant of attraction. *Journal of Personality and Social Psychology*, 2 (1965): 884–889.

—— and T. J. Wong. Racial prejudice, interpersonal attraction and assumed dissimilarity of attitudes. *Journal of Abnormal and Social Psychology*, 65 (1962): 246–253.

Cartwright, D. and F. Harary. Structural balance: a generalization of Heider's theory. *Psychological Review*, 63 (1956): 277–293.

Chapanis, N. P. and A. Chapanis. Cognitive dissonance: five years later. *Psychological Bulletin*, 61 (1964): 1–22.

Cohen, A. K. *Delinquent Boys*. Glencoe: Free Press, 1955.

Costner, H. L. and R. K. Leik. Deductions from 'axiomatic theory.' *American Sociological Review*, 29 (1964): 819–835.

Davis, J. A. Clustering and structural balance in graphs. *Human Relations*, 20 (1967): 181–187.

——. Social Structures and Cognitive Structures. In R. P. Abelson, E. Aronson, W. J. McGuire, T. M. Newcomb, M. J. Rosenberg, and P. H. Tannenbaum, eds., *Theories of Cognitive Consistency: A Sourcebook*. Chicago: Rand-McNally, 1968.

——. Structural balance, mechanical solidarity, and interpersonal relations. *American Journal of Sociology*, 68 (1963): 444–462.

—— and S. Leinhardt. The structure of positive interpersonal relations in small groups. Manuscript, August, 1967. Abbreviated version read at the American Sociological Association Convention, August, 1968.

Davol, S. H. An empirical test of structural balance in sociometric triads. *Journal of Abnormal and Social Psychology*, 59 (1959): 393–398.

DeSoto, C. B. Learning a social structure. *Journal of Abnormal and Social Psychology*, 60 (1960): 417–421.

——, N. M. Henley, and M. London. Balance and the grouping schema. *Journal of Personality and Social Psychology*, 8 (1968): 1–7.

Deutsch, M. The effects of cooperation and competition upon group process. *Human Relations*, 2 (1949): 129–152 and 199–231.

—— and L. Solomon. Reactions to evaluations by others as influenced by self-evaluation. *Sociometry*, 22 (1959): 93–112.

Feather, N. T. Acceptance and rejection of arguments in relation to attitude strength, critical ability, and intolerance of inconsistency. *Journal of Abnormal and Social Psychology*, 69 (1964): 127–136. (1964a).

——. Cognitive dissonance, sensitivity, and evaluation. *Journal of Abnormal and Social Psychology*, 66 (1963): 157–163.

———. Effects of institutional affiliation and attitude discrepancy on evaluation of communications and interpersonal attraction. *Human Relations*, 20 (1967): 101–120. (1967a).

———. The prediction of interpersonal attraction: the effects of sign and strength of relations in different structures. *Human Relations*, 19 (1966): 213–237.

———. Reactions to communications in relation to source responsibility and source coercion. *Australian Journal of Psychology*, 17 (1965): 179–194. (1965a).

———. A structural balance analysis of evaluative behavior. *Human Relations*, 18 (1965): 171–185. (1965b).

———. A structural balance approach to the analysis of communication effects. In L. Berkowitz, ed., *Advances in Experimental Social Psychology*, vol. 3. New York: Academic Press, 1967. (1967b).

———. A structural balance model of communication effects. *Psychological Review*, 71 (1964): 291–311. (1964b).

——— and D. G. Jeffries. Balancing and extremity effects in relations of receiver to source and content of communication. *Journal of Personality*, 35 (1967): 194–213.

Feldman, S. *Cognitive Consistency: Motivational Antecedents and Behavioral Consequences*. New York: Academic Press, 1966.

Festinger, L. *A Theory of Cognitive Dissonance*. Evanston: Row, Peterson and Co., 1957.

———, H. Riecken and S. Schachter. *When Prophecy Fails*. Minneapolis: University of Minnesota Press, 1956.

——— and E. Aronson. The arousal and reduction of dissonance in social contexts. In D. Cartwright and A. Zander, eds., *Group Dynamics: Research and Theory*. Evanston: Row, Peterson and Co., 1960.

——— and H. A. Hutte. An experimental investigation of the effect of unstable interpersonal relations in the group. *Journal of Abnormal and Social Psychology*, 49 (1954): 513–522.

Fishbein, M. and R. Hunter. Summation versus balance in attitude organization and change. *Journal of Abnormal and Social Psychology*, 69 (1964): 505–510.

——— and B. H. Raven. The AB Scales: an operational definition of belief and attitude. *Human Relations*, 15 (1962): 35–44.

Flament, C. *Applications of Graph Theory to Group Structure*. Englewood Cliffs: Prentice-Hall, 1963.

Frank, R. Gang and character. *Beihefte Zeitschrift für Angewandte Psychologie*, 58 (1931).

French, E. G. and I. Chadwick. Some characteristics of affiliation motivation. *Journal of Abnormal and Social Psychology*, 52 (1956): 296–300.

Friedman, E. P. Spatial proximity and social interaction in a home for the aged. *Journal of Gerontology*, 21 (1966): 566–570.

Gamson, W. A. Experimental studies in coalition formation. In L. Berkowitz, ed., *Advances in Experimental Social Psychology*, vol. 1. New York: Academic Press, 1964.

Gerard, H. B. The anchorage of opinions in face-to-face groups. *Human Relations*, 7 (1954): 313–325.

Guetzkow, H. and W. R. Dill. Factors in the organizational development of task-oriented groups. *Sociometry*, 20 (1957): 175–204.

Hagen, E. E. Analytical models in the study of social systems. *American Journal of Sociology*, 67 (1961): 144–151.

Harari, H. An experimental evaluation of Heider's balance theory with respect to situational and predispositional variables. *Journal of Social Psychology*, 73 (1967): 177–189.

Harary, F. 'Cosi fan Tutte': a structural study. *Psychological Reports,* 13 (1963): 466.

———. On the measurement of structural balance. *Behavioral Science,* 4 (1959): 316–323.

———. On the notion of balance of a signed graph. *Michigan State Mathematics Journal,* 2 (1953–54): 143–146.

———. Structural study of 'A Severed Head.' *Psychological Reports,* 19 (1966): 473–474.

———, R. Z. Norman, and D. Cartwright. *Structural Models: An Introduction to the Theory of Directed Graphs.* New York: John Wiley and Sons, 1965.

Hare, A. P. *Handbook of Small Group Research.* New York: Free Press, 1962.

Heider, F. Attitudes and cognitive organization. *Journal of Psychology,* 21 (1946): 107–112.

———. *The Psychology of Interpersonal Relations.* New York: John Wiley and Sons, 1958.

———. Social perception and phenomenal causality. *Psychological Review,* 51 (1944): 358–374.

Heinicke, C. M. and R. F. Bales. Developmental trends in the structure of small groups. *Sociometry,* 16 (1953): 7–38.

Hilgard, E. R. *Theories of Learning.* New York: Appleton-Century-Crofts, 1948.

Homans, G. C. *The Human Group.* New York: Harcourt, Brace and Co., 1950.

———. *Social Behavior: Its Elementary Forms.* New York: Harcourt, Brace, and World, 1961.

Horowitz, M. W., J. Lyons and H. V. Perlmutter. Induction of forces in discussion groups. *Human Relations,* 4 (1951): 57–76.

Insko, C. A. and J. Schopler. Triadic consistency: a statement of affective-cognitive-conative consistency. *Psychological Review,* 74 (1967): 361–376.

Jackson, E. F. Status consistency and symptoms of stress. *American Sociological Review,* 27 (1962): 469–480.

Jones, E. L. and H. B. Gerard. *Foundations of Social Psychology.* New York: John Wiley, 1967.

Jordan, N. Behavioral forces that are a function of attitudes and of cognitive organization. *Human Relations,* 6 (1953): 273–287.

———. Cognitive balance, cognitive organization and attitude change: a critique. *Public Opinion Quarterly,* 27 (1963): 123–132.

———. Experimenting with the POQ unit: complications in cognitive balance. *Journal of Psychology,* 64 (1966): 3–22. (1966a).

———. Perceived discrepancy in attitude intensity between the actors A and B in ABX situations and its effect upon affect, or, why don't experimenters utilize all their available data in testing hypotheses? *Journal of Psychology,* 63 (1966): 299–308. (1966b).

Kind, B. Attitude toward gifts as a reflection of balance pressures. Unpublished manuscript, University of Pennsylvania, 1965.

King, M. G. Structural balance, tension, and segregation in a university group. *Human Relations,* 17 (1964): 221–225.

Koenig, Dénes. *Theorie Der Endlichen und Unendlichen Graphen* (The Theory of Finite and Infinite Graphs). Leipzig: Akademische Verlagsgesellschaft, 1936. Reprinted in New York: Chelsea Publishing Co., 1950.

Kogan, N. and R. Tagiuri. Interpersonal preference and cognitive organization. *Journal of Abnormal and Social Psychology,* 56 (1958): 113–116.

Lane, R. O. and D. O. Sears. *Public Opinion.* Englewood Cliffs: Prentice-Hall, 1964.

Lansing, J. B. and R. W. Heynes. Need affiliation and frequency of four types of communication. *Journal of Abnormal and Social Psychology,* 58 (1959): 365–372.

Lerner, M. J., R. C. Dillehay and W. C. Sherer. Similarity and attraction in social contexts. *Journal of Personality and Social Psychology*, 5 (1967): 481–486.

Levinger, G. and J. Breedlove. Interpersonal attraction and agreement: a study of marriage partners. *Journal of Personality and Social Psychology*, 3 (1966): 367–372.

Lewin, K. Field Theory and experiment in social psychology: conceptual methods. *American Journal of Sociology*, 44 (1939): 868–896.

———. *Field Theory in Social Science*. New York: Harper and Row, 1951.

———. *Principles of Topological Psychology*. New York: McGraw-Hill, 1936.

Longmore, T. W. A matrix approach to the analysis of rank and status in a community in Pennsylvania. *Sociometry*, 11 (1943): 192–206.

Lundberg, G. A. and V. Beazley. 'Consciousness of kind' in a college population. *Sociometry*, 11 (1948): 59–74.

Mazur, A. Heider's balance theory and the Jewish mother-son relationship. Unpublished manuscript, 1967.

———. A nonrational approach to theories of conflict and coalitions. *Journal of Conflict Resolution*, 1968, in press.

McGuire, W. J. The current status of cognitive consistency theories. In S. Feldman, ed., *Cognitive Consistency: Motivational Antecedents and Behavioral Consequences*. New York: Academic Press, 1966.

McLeod, J. M., E. Harburg and K. O. Price. Socialization, liking and yielding of opinions in imbalanced situations. *Sociometry*, 29 (1966): 197–212.

McWhirter, R. M. and J. D. Jecker. Attitude similarity and inferred attraction. *Psychonomic Science*, 7 (1967): 225–226.

Merton, R. *Social Theory and Social Structure*. Glencoe: The Free Press, 1957.

Miller, L. K. and R. L. Hamblin. Interdependence, differential rewarding, and productivity. *American Sociological Review*, 28 (1963): 768–778.

Mills, T. M. Authority and group emotion. In W. G. Bennis, E. H. Schein, D. E. Berlew and F. I. Steele, eds., *Interpersonal Dynamics: Essays and Readings on Human Interaction*. Homewood: The Dorsey Press, 1964.

———. *Group Transformation*. Englewood Cliffs: Prentice-Hall, 1964. (1964b)

———. *The Sociology of Small Groups*. Englewood Cliffs: Prentice-Hall, 1967.

Moran, G. Dyadic attraction and orientational consensus. *Journal of Personality and Social Psychology*, 4 (1966): 94–99.

Morrissette, J. O. An experimental study of the theory of structural balance. *Human Relations*, 11 (1958): 239–254.

——— and J. C. Jahnke. No relations and relations of strength zero in the theory of structural balance. *Human Relations*, 20 (1967): 189–195.

———, J. C. Jahnke and K. Baker. Structural balance: a test of the completeness hypothesis. *Behavioral Science*, 11 (1966): 121–125.

———, J. C. Jahnke, K. Baker and M. Rohrman. Degree of structural balance and group effectiveness. *Organizational Behavior and Human Performance*, 2 (1967): 383–393.

Mosher, D. L. The learning of congruent and incongruent social structures. *Journal of Social Psychology*, 73 (1967): 285–290.

Newcomb, T. M. *The Acquaintance Process*. New York: Holt, Rinehart and Winston, 1961.

———. An approach to the study of communicative acts. *Psychological Review*, 60 (1953): 393–404.

———. Individual systems of orientation. In S. Koch, ed., *Psychology: A Study of a Science*, Study I, vol. 3. New York: McGraw-Hill, 1959.

———. Interpersonal balance. In R. P. Abelson, E. Aronson, W. J. McGuire, T. M.

Newcomb, M. J. Rosenberg, and P. H. Tannenbaum, eds., *Theories of Cognitive Consistency: A Sourcebook*. Chicago: Rand-McNally, 1968.

———. The prediction of interpersonal attraction. *American Psychologist,* 11 (1956): 575–586.

———. Stabilities underlying changes in interpersonal attraction. *Journal of Abnormal and Sociol Psychology,* 66 (1963): 376–386.

———. Varieties of interpersonal attraction. In D. Cartwright and A. Zander, eds., *Group Dynamics: Research and Theory*. Evanston: Row, Peterson and Co., 1960.

Olmstead, M. S. Orientation and role in the small group. *American Sociological Review,* 19 (1954): 741–751.

Osgood, C. E. Cognitive dynamics in the conduct of human affairs. *Public Opinion Quarterly,* 24 (1960): 341–365.

———, G. J. Suci and P. H. Tannenbaum. *The Measurement of Meaning*. Urbana: University of Illinois Press, 1957.

——— and P. H. Tannenbaum. The principle of congruity in the prediction of attitude change. *Psychological Review,* 62 (1955): 42–55.

Parsons, T. *The Social System*. Glencoe: The Free Press, 1951.

———, R. F. Bales and E. A. Shils. *Working Papers in the Theory of Action*. Glencoe: The Free Press, 1953.

——— and E. A. Shils, eds. *Toward A General Theory of Action*. Cambridge: Harvard University Press, 1951.

Penny, R. and L. Robertson. The Homans sentiment-interaction hypothesis. *Psychological Reports,* 11 (1962): 257–258.

Pepitone, A. Some conceptual and empirical problems of consistency models. In S. Feldman, *Cognitive Consistency: Motivational Antecedents and Behavioral Consequences*. New York: Academic Press, 1966.

Phillips, J. L. A model for cognitive balance. *Psychological Review,* 74 (1967): 481–495.

Pilisuk, M. Cognitive balance, primary groups and the therapist-patient relationship. In W. Bennis, E. H. Schein, D. E. Berlew and F. I. Steele, *Interpersonal Dynamics: Essays and Readings on Human Interaction*. Homewood: Dorsey Press, 1964.

Price, K. O., E. Harburg and J. M. McLeod. Positive and negative affect as a function of perceived discrepancy in ABX situations. *Human Relations,* 18 (1965): 87–100.

———, E. Harburg and T. Newcomb. Psychological balance in situations of negative interpersonal attitudes. *Journal of Personality and Social Psychology,* 3 (1966): 265–270.

Psathas, G. Phase movement and equilibrium tendencies in interaction process in therapy groups. *Sociometry,* 23 (1960): 177–194.

Riecken, H. W. and G. L. Homans. Psychological aspects of social structure. In G. Lindzey, ed., *Handbook of Social Psychology*. Cambridge: Harvard University Press, 1954.

Rodrigues, A. The biasing effect of agreement in balanced and imbalanced triads. *Journal of Personality,* 36 (1968): 138–153.

———. Effects of balance, positivity and agreement in triadic social relations. *Journal of Personality and Social Psychology,* 5 (1967): 472–476.

———. On the differential effects of some parameters of balance. *Journal of Psychology,* 61 (1965): 241–250.

Rokeach, M. *The Open and Closed Mind*. New York: Basic Books, 1960.

——— and G. Rothman. The principle of belief congruence and the congruity principle as models of cognitive interaction. *Psychological Review,* 72 (1965): 128–142.

Rosenberg, M. J. and R. P. Abelson. An analysis of cognitive balancing. In M. J. Rosenberg, C. I. Hovland, W. J. McGuire, R. P. Abelson and J. W. Brehm, *Attitude Organization and Change: An Analysis of Consistency Among Attitude Components*. New Haven: Yale University Press, 1960.

————, C. I. Hovland, W. J. McGuire, R. P. Abelson and J. W. Brehm. *Attitude Organization and Change: An Analysis of Consistency Among Attitude Components*. New Haven: Yale University Press, 1960.

Runkel, P. J. 'Equilibrium' and 'pleasantness' of interpersonal situations. *Human Relations*, 9 (1956): 375–382.

Sampson, E. E. Status congruence and cognitive consistency. *Sociometry*, 26 (1963): 146–162.

———— and C. I. Insko. Cognitive consistency and performance in the autokinetic situation. *Journal of Abnormal and Social Psychology*, 68 (1964): 184–192.

Scott, W. A. Cognitive complexity and cognitive balance. *Sociometry*, 26 (1963): 66–74.

Shaw, M. E. Communication networks. In L. Berkowitz, ed., *Advances in Experimental Social Psychology*, vol. 1. New York: Academic Press, 1964.

Sheffield, J. and D. Byrne. Attitude similarity-dissimilarity, authoritarianism, and interpersonal attraction. *Journal of Social Psychology*, 7 (1967): 117—123.

Shrader, E. G. and D. W. Lewit. Structural factors in cognitive balancing behavior. *Human Relations*, 15 (1962): 265–276.

Slater, P. E. Displacement in groups. In W. G. Bennis, K. D. Benne and R. Chin, *The Planning of Change*. New York: Holt, Rinehart and Winston, 1962.

Stanton, R. G. 'A Midsummer Night's Dream': a structural study. *Psychological Reports*, 20 (1967): 657–658.

Tannenbaum, P. H. Attitudes toward source and concept as factors in attitude change through communication. Unpublished Ph.D. dissertation, University of Illinois, Urbana, 1953.

————. The congruity principle revisited: Studies in the reduction, induction, and generalization in persuasion. In L. Berkowitz, ed., *Advances in Experimental Social Psychology*, vol. 3. New York: Academic Press, 1967.

———— and R. W. Gengel. Generalization of attitude change through congruity principle relationships. *Journal of Personality and Social Psychology*, 3 (1966): 299–304.

Taylor, H. F. Balance and change in the two-person group. *Sociometry*, 30 (1967): 262–279.

————. Balance, tension and tension release in the two-person group. *Human Relations*, 21 (1968): 59–74.

————. Balance and tension in the two-person group. Ph.D. dissertation (Yale University, New Haven). Ann Arbor: University Microfilms, 1966.

————. Semantic Differential factor scores as measures of attitude and perceived attitude. *Journal of Social Psychology*, 1969, in press.

Thibaut, J. W. and H. H. Kelley. *The Social Psychology of Groups*. New York: John Wiley and Sons, 1959.

Triandis, H. C. and M. Fishbein. Cognitive interaction in person perception. *Journal of Abnormal and Social Psychology*, 67 (1963): 446–453.

Tukey, J. W. Some idiosyncrasies in the use of statistical techniques and quantitative approaches. Unpublished manuscript, Harvard University, no date.

Von Bertalanffy, L. General system theory. In R. W. Taylor, ed., *Life, Language, Law*. Yellow Springs: Antioch Press, 1957.

————. An outline of general system theory. *British Journal of the Philosophy of Science*, 1 (1950): 134–165.

White, P. Eigenvalue and eigenvector computations of a matrix. *Journal of the Society for Industrial and Applied Mathematics*, 4 (1958): 393–437.

Winch, R. F. *The Modern Family*. New York: Holt, 1952.

Wolf, K. *The Sociology of George Simmel*.

Yinger, J. M. Contraculture and subculture. *American Sociological Review*, 25 (1960): 625–635.

Zajonc, R. B. Cognitive theories in social psychology. In G. Lindzey and E. Aronson, eds., *Handbook of Social Psychology* (second edition). Cambridge: Addison-Wesley, 1968.

———. The concepts of balance, congruity, and dissonance. *Public Opinion Quarterly*, 24 (1960): 280–296.

——— and E. Burnstein. The learning of balanced and unbalanced social structures. *Journal of Personality*, 33 (1965): 153–163. (1965a)

——— and E. Burnstein. Structural balance, reciprocity and positivity as sources of cognitive bias. *Journal of Personality*, 33 (1965): 570–583. (1965b).

——— and S. J. Sherman. Structural balance and the induction of relations. *Journal of Personality*, 35 (1967): 635–650.

Zelditch, M. A note on the analysis of equilibrium systems. In T. Parsons and R. F. Bales, eds., *Family, Socialization and Interaction Process*, Glencoe: Free Press, 1955.

——— and B. Anderson. On the balance of a set of ranks. In J. Berger, M. Zelditch and B. Anderson, eds., *Sociological Theories in Progress*. Boston: Houghton-Mifflin, 1966.

Zetterberg, H. *On Theory and Verification in Sociology*. (1954).

Name Index

Subject Index

Abelson-Rosenberg index of balance. *See* "Indices of degree of balance"

Abelson-Rosenberg model. *See* "Rosenberg-Abelson model"

Accuracy of perception 26

Additive (non-system model) 4–5, 9

Adjacency matrix. *See* "Graphs, adjacency matrix of"

Affiliation need 91, 106, 169–170, 184

Agreement; agree-disagree 21–22, 23, 34–37, 45–48, 95, 100, 103, 123, 132–133, 139–142, 199, 230, 236–244, 268. *See also* "Cognitive bias, agreement bias"; "Discrepancy"; "Similarity"

Agreement cognitive bias. *See* "Cognitive bias, agreement bias"

Alteration of relations. *See* "Relations, alteration of"

Ambivalence; ambivalence of relations. *See* "Relations, ambivalence of"

Antagonism 225, 226, 247–255

Asch's group pressure theory 257, 281–288

Assertion 33–34, 147–148, 156
  assertion constant 37n, 155–156
  constant assertion 34n, 148n, 155

Asymmetric causation 6

Asymmetric relations. *See* "Relations, symmetry of"

Asymmetry. *See* "Relations, symmetry of"; "Asymmetric causation"

Attitude
  concept attitude 33, 146–159
  defined 20, 231–232
  perceived attitude 20–21, 24–25, 183
  polarity of. *See* "Polarity"
  and Semantic Differential 149–150
  similarity of 15, 104–110, 175–177, 180, 184, 265
  sign of. *See* "Relations, sign of"

Attitude (continued)
  strength of. *See* "Relations, strength of"
  source attitude 33, 146–159
  See also "Discrepancy"; "Relations, attitude relations"; "Relations, symmetry of"; "Similarity"

Attraction
  as a cognitive bias 121. *See also* "Cognitive bias, positivity bias"
  and attitude similarity 104–110, 145–146, 168–169, 170, 175–177, 180, 184, 265
  defined 20
  in graph theory 53
  and perceived similarity. *See* "Attraction, and attitude similarity"; "Similarity"
  See also "Liking"; "Relations, sentiment relations"; "Similarity"

Authoritarianism 91, 105, 119, 159, 166–169, 184

Autistic balance; autistic alternative to balance maintenance 26, 41, 49, 167, 184, 272. *See also* "Subjective balance"

Autokinetic apparatus 95

Averaging procedure. *See* "Indices of degree of balance"

Balance
  Cartwright-Harary definition 57–60, 123
  comparison of definitions 34–37, 266–270
  of a graph 57–64
  Heider's definition 14–20
  "logical" criterion for defining 269
  measurement of changes in 73–75
  Newcomb's definition 20–27
  "observational" criterion for defining 270